LABOUR'S GRASS ROOTS

For Rachel and Alex

*In recognition of their invaluable
encouragement and friendship*

On the Leeds side streets that you slip down

Labour's Grass Roots

Essays on the Activities of Local Labour Parties
and Members, 1918–45

Edited by
MATTHEW WORLEY

ASHGATE

Published by
Ashgate Publishing Limited
Gower House
Croft Road
Aldershot
Hants GU11 3HR
England

Ashgate Publishing Company
Suite 420
101 Cherry Street
Burlington, VT 05401-4405
USA

Ashgate website: http://www.ashgate.com

British Library Cataloguing in Publication Data
Labour's grass roots : essays on the activities and experiences of local Labour
    parties and members, 1918–45.—(Studies in labour history)
1.Labour Party (Great Britain)—History 2.Political participation—Great Britain—
History—20th century
I.Worley, Matthew
324.2'4107'09041

Library of Congress Cataloging-in-Publication Data
Labour's grass roots : essays on the activities and experiences of local labour
parties and members, 1918–1945 / edited by Matthew Worley.
        p. cm.—(Studies in labour history)
    Includes index.
    ISBN 0–7546–4007–8 (alk. paper)
    1. Labour Party (Great Britain)—History—20th century. 2. Local government—
Great Britain—History—20th century. 3. Labor unions—Great Britain—Political
activity—History—20th century. 4. Working class—Great Britain—Political
activity—History—20th century. I. Worley, Matthew. II.
Series: Studies in labour history (Ashgate (Firm))

    JN1129.L32L276 2004
    324.24107'09'041—dc22
                                                    2004022203

ISBN 0 7546 4007 8

Printed in Great Britain by Antony Rowe Ltd, Chippenham, Wiltshire

Contents

Studies in Labour History
General Editor's Preface

Labour history has often been a fertile area of history. Since the Second World War its best practitioners – such as E.P. Thompson and E.J. Hobsbawm, both Presidents of the British Society for the Study of Labour History – have written works which have provoked fruitful and wide-ranging debates and further research, and which have influenced not only social history but history generally. These historians, and many others, have helped to widen labour history beyond the study of organised labour to labour generally, sometimes to industrial relations in particular, and most frequently to society and culture in national and comparative dimensions.

The assumptions and ideologies underpinning much of the older labour history have been challenged by feminist and later by postmodernist and anti-Marxist thinking. These challenges have often led to thoughtful reappraisals, perhaps intellectual equivalents of coming to terms with a new post-Cold War political landscape.

By the end of the twentieth century, labour history had emerged reinvigorated and positive from much introspection and external criticism. Very few would wish to confine its scope to the study of organised labour. Yet, equally, few would wish now to write the existence and influence of organised labour out of nations' histories, any more than they would wish to ignore working-class lives and focus only on the upper echelons.

This series of books provides reassessments of broad themes of labour history as well as some more detailed studies arising from recent research. Most books are single-authored but there are also volumes of essays centred on important themes or periods, some arising from major conferences organised by the Society for the Study of Labour History. The series also includes studies of labour organisations, including international ones, as many of these are much in need of a modern reassessment.

Chris Wrigley
British Society for the Study of Labour History
University of Nottingham

List of Contributors

Stuart Ball is a Reader in the School of Historical Studies at the University of Leicester. His previous books include *Baldwin and the Conservative Party* (1988), *The Conservative Party and British Politics 1902–51* (1995), *Winston Churchill* (2003), and (co-edited with Anthony Seldon) *Conservative Century: The Conservative Party since 1900* (1994) and *The Heath Government 1970–74* (1996).

Stefan Berger, Professor of Modern and Contemporary History and Director of the Centre for Border Studies at the University of Glamorgan, is currently chairing a five year programme of the European Science Foundation in Strasbourg entitled 'Representations of the Past: The Writing of National Histories in Europe'. He has published widely in the areas of comparative labour history, national identity studies and historiography.

Gidon Cohen is a Senior Lecturer in Politics at the University of Northumbria. His recent research focuses on the history of the British left. He is the joint author, with Kevin Morgan and Andrew Flinn, of *Communists in British Society, 1920–91* (2004).

Sam Davies is Professor of History at Liverpool John Moores University. He is the author of *Liverpool Labour: Social and Political Influences on the Development of the Labour Party in Liverpool, 1900–39*, (1996); co-author of *County Borough Elections in England and Wales, 1919–38: A Comparative Analysis*, (eight volumes, 1999 and following); and co-editor of *Dock Workers: International Explorations in Comparative Labour History, 1790–1970*, (two volumes, 2000).

Andrew Flinn teaches at University College London and the University of Westminster. He has written on the Labour and Communist parties in Manchester and elsewhere. At present, he is working on an ESRC funded project on Labour members and activists in post-war South London.

Karen Hunt is Senior Lecturer in History at Manchester Metropolitan University. She has published widely on the gendering of politics, most recently *Socialist Women: Britain, 1880s to 1920s* (2002) with June Hannam. She is currently writing a biography of a socialist woman, Dora Montefiore (1851–1933), and is about to begin a comparative study of the effect of women's enfranchisement on local political cultures in the 1920s.

Catriona Macdonald is Senior Lecturer in History in the School of Law and Social Sciences at Glasgow Caledonian University. Her major publications include *The Radical Thread: Political Change in Scotland, Paisley Politics 1885–1924* (2004), and (with E. W. Mcfarland) *Scotland and the Great War* (1998). She is currently completing work on her second monograph, *Whaur Extremes Meet: Scotland's Twentieth Century.*

Bob Morley is Senior Lecturer in History at Liverpool John Moores University. He is the co-author of *County Borough Elections in England and Wales, 1919–38: A Comparative Analysis*, (eight volumes, 1999 and following).

Nicole Robertson's doctoral research at Nottingham University was on the co-operative movement in the Midlands (1917–58), with a particular emphasis on co-operative politics. She is also working on comparative European co-operative history.

Duncan Tanner is Professor of History at the University of Wales Bangor, and Director of the Welsh Institute for Social and Cultural Affairs (WISCA). He writes on British and Welsh Labour Party history, and is currently running a collaborative and ESRC funded project on Wales and the history of devolution.

Andrew Thorpe is Professor of Modern British History at the University of Exeter. His publications include *The British General Election of 1931* (1991), *A History of the British Labour Party* (1997; second edition, 2001), and *The British Communist Party and Moscow, 1920–43* (2000). He is currently completing a monograph on political party organisation in Second World War Britain for Oxford University Press.

Daniel Weinbren works at the Open University. He has published material about mutuality and fraternity, the Labour Party, the armaments industries, and the Humanitarian League, 1891–1919. He is the chair of the Friendly Societies Research Group, http://www.open.ac.uk/socialsciences/fsrg.

Matthew Worley is a Lecturer in History at the University of Reading. He is the author of *Class Against Class: The Communist Party of Great Britain between the Wars* (2002), *Labour Inside the Gate: A History of the British Labour Party between the Wars* (2005), and the editor of *In Search of Revolution: International Communist Parties in the Third Period* (2004). He is currently undertaking research into Oswald Mosley's New Party.

Acknowledgements

Many thanks to everybody who has helped with this book, especially Andrew Thorpe, Stuart Ball, Chris Wrigley and Duncan Tanner for their expert advice over the course of the project. Thanks, too, to the contributors for providing a collection of insightful and valuable essays, and to all at Ashgate for their more technical help. Closer to home, Amelia has again been of great and loving support; putting up with labour history, Joy Division and Norwich City cannot make for an easy time. Thanks, also, to my parents, and to Jo and Chris for their continued encouragement, and to Rosa for being born in the midst of this project and helping to light up my life. As always, my appreciation goes to Chris, Pete, Emma, Sue, Stan, Ed, Eileen, Scott, Tess, Simon N., Tizzy, Terry and Bob, Jane N., Patrick and Eve, Rachel, Alex, Nick, Jamie and Earl Brutus, Pete C., Katie, Emily and Tommy, Mark B., Anne, Toby Wolfe, Rupe, Nim, Steph, Joel, Hannah and George, Ben, Katie, Melvin, Abi and Becks, Jon M., Cally, Richard and Joyce, Phil and Catherine, Andy, Dom W., Dom, Andrea, Pete B., Kath, Louise, John J., Mike, Stu and Mel, Tom, Keith, Dan, Simon W., Aileen, Mick, Thomas, Marty, B and Emma, Viki, Neil, Sarah, Lisa Li, Jo B, Daniel, Dunc, Steve the print, Stuart, Eric, and my friends and colleagues at Reading University. Finally, further gratitude must go to Roger and Vin, Dave and Sally Smith, and Alison and John Newland for their long-lasting support, with due mention to David Franklin, Colin Kay, Chris Husbands, Alan Spoors and Ann Carr, teachers at Heartsease Comprehensive who inspired me in earlier life. On the ball, City!

Chapter 1

Introduction:
Labour's Grass Roots

Matthew Worley

Sidney Webb's comment in 1930 that it was the 'fanatics and cranks and extremists' who dominated and maintained the Labour Party at constituency level was as condescending as it was unfair.[1] While trade union funds have traditionally and primarily financed the party, Labour has simultaneously depended on a core of loyal volunteers to sustain its organisation beyond the party headquarters, most of whom were driven by a deep-seated desire to change the world in which they lived. True, eccentric characters did join the party, and powerful political cliques did form within and around certain constituency organisations.[2] But it was more generally the selfless devotion, time and energy of ordinary party members and supporters – locally based men, women, trade unionists and socialists – that helped enable Labour to challenge and overturn the Conservative–Liberal hegemony of British politics existent prior to the Great War (1914–18).

Certainly, the need to establish an active and substantial party membership was recognised in the Labour Party constitution adopted in 1918. Its first stated national objective was to 'organise and maintain in parliament and in the country a Political Labour Party, and to ensure the establishment of a Local Labour Party in every county constituency and every parliamentary borough'.[3] As this suggests, the party was firmly committed to constitutional politics, seeking to achieve its aims through parliament and municipal government. Accordingly, the party needed a permanent, nationwide apparatus able to garner, mobilise and retain public support. In other words, Labour's progress was to a notable extent dependent on the healthy cultivation of its grass roots.

This book is designed to examine the activities and experiences of the Labour Party and its members in a number of towns, cities, counties and regions throughout Britain between 1918 and 1945. In so doing, it seeks to recognise the role played by party members and supporters in shaping Labour's wider social and political history. At the same time, it hopes to look 'inside' the Labour Party to reveal, explore and help understand the variegated nature of the party's organisation, political identity, and subsequent electoral fortunes.

Uncovering the Grass Roots

The activities and experiences of party members have too often been written out of interwar British political history. Not surprisingly, perhaps, the intrigues, debates and events of Westminster have tended to preoccupy the attention of historians, as have the lives of prominent party leaders and politicians. In this, the historiography of the Labour Party has generally conformed to type. The bulk of published work on Labour centres on the undulating fortunes of the parliamentary party and those who played a leading role within it.[4] Increasingly, however, the work of David Howell, Mike Savage, Duncan Tanner and others has done much to provoke an awareness of the 'dynamics' of local political development, its import in the wider (national) progress of the Labour Party, and the major regional variations in Labour's approach and appeal.[5] Consequently, the past 15 to 25 years have been marked by the appearance of a growing literature dedicated to the emergence and subsequent evolution of Labour within various British localities.[6] Many such studies have continued to concentrate on the 'classic' debate as to the reasons for Labour's usurpation of the Liberal Party as the principal alternative to the Conservatives in British politics. But they have also begun to delineate other areas of concern, not least the role played by Labour women in the building and sustaining of the party, and the different means by which local party members endeavoured to nurture and maintain Labour's identity across the country.

Such a focus on constituency-level politics is particularly relevant to the period after 1918. It was, after all, from here on that the 1918 Representation of the People Act provided Britain for the first time with a democratic base inclusive of the majority of the adult population, enfranchising all men over 21 and most women over 30.[7] In response, all three of Britain's principal parties accepted the need to develop an active, loyal and extensive membership base in the years following the Great War, and the histories of all three can be said to have been shaped or at least affected by the activities, attitudes and aspirations of their wider memberships. With regard to Labour, the party conference adopted a new constitution in 1918, transforming it from a party organised as a federation of affiliated trade unions and socialist societies to one based on constituency (divisional) organisations comprising individual members alongside the union and socialist affiliates. The local party was no longer regarded as a temporary electoral organisation, but a permanent feature of the party apparatus overseeing, distributing and initiating party activity, propaganda and membership. Although the trade unions continued to form the bulk of Labour membership and remained the dominant force at the party conference, the importance of divisional parties undoubtedly increased over the interwar period as a whole.

To a notable extent, the composition of the newly formed constituency parties continued to reflect Labour's basic federal structure. Given that Labour was largely founded on the trade union movement, those parties established in industrial areas tended to be dominated by the relevant trade union branches. This was particularly so in mining constituencies, but those party members affiliated via their trade union also made up the bulk of Labour's divisional organisation in most towns, cities and industrial localities. Of course, an affiliated member was not necessarily an active member. Nor was trade union domination necessarily conducive to Labour's electoral advance. The party's association with a particular trade union (or unions) could deter as well as attract potential support; inter-union rivalry was sometimes evident; and overt union influence could shape a party's priorities in a way that failed to complement the wider constituency. Elsewhere, in areas where the trade union presence was less concentrated or less well-established, as in Scotland, London, parts of Yorkshire and cities such as Norwich, the influence of the socialist Independent Labour Party (ILP) on Labour activity continued to be important during the 1920s. Yet, the very formation of divisional parties challenged the ILP's place within the wider Labour Party, allowing non-union members to join Labour directly and assume the propaganda and social activities previously associated with the ILP. Accordingly, the ILP suffered a steady decline in both membership and influence from the early 1920s, leading eventually to its disaffiliation in 1932. Generally, therefore, the Labour Party continued to be comprised primarily of associated trade unionists. Twenty years after Labour had adopted its new constitution, a party membership of 2,642,613 included 2,170,408 affiliated via their trade union.[8]

Significantly, however, Labour's reorganisation in 1918 necessitated that the party widen its appeal beyond the ranks of the organised labour movement. Divisional parties were to be established in agricultural and non-industrial localities, middle-class recruits were to be courted, and the newly enfranchised female electorate was to be welcomed into the Labour fold. As a result, the composition and breadth of the Labour Party extended over the 1920s and 1930s. This was not always welcomed in places where the party was already established, with many existing members fearing a dilution of union or socialist influence. Despite (or perhaps because of) this, some of the most active and sizeable divisional organisations emerged in and around the Home Counties and beyond Labour's industrial heartlands. In some areas, moreover, the women recruited into local women's sections began to outnumber their respective constituency party's individual male members, while the proportion of parliamentary candidates sponsored by divisional parties (as opposed to trade unions) steadily increased over the interwar period. In addition, Labour continued to forge a complex relationship with the co-operative movement from 1918, as Nicole Robertson demonstrates in her chapter on co-operative politics in the Midlands. To this effect, Labour's grass roots were subject to a range of influences, with party members assuming or reflecting a number of identities, and with party organisations developing in an array of different contexts.

In response to such an observation, it may be argued that a closer study of divisional party activity and experience is essential to our wider appreciation of Labour Party history. At a basic level, such research will rescue from obscurity those men and women who helped sustain the party in the twentieth century, the party activists who gave up much time and energy to spread Labour's message. Although the party became more centralised and disciplined over the interwar years, the divisional organisations retained a degree of autonomy with regard to selecting parliamentary candidates, fighting both municipal and general election campaigns, and instigating party activity in between election times. As we shall see in the essays collected in *Labour's Grass Roots*, similarities and differences with regard to such activity were evident across the party. Indeed, the importance of local and regional variation throughout Britain to our understanding of the Labour Party's development should not be underestimated, and becomes clear once area studies are compared and contrasted. Labour's ability to win and retain support fluctuated throughout Britain and even within specific regions and localities; respective divisional parties were informed by a range of economic, demographic and cultural factors, and party members sought to understand, articulate and focus Labour's appeal in a variety of ways, often adapting their message to suit, project or reflect a particular community. This, in turn, feeds into the on-going debate as to the relationship between politics, social position and experience.[9] If no inevitable or indivisible link can be established between the Labour Party and the broad but divergent ranks of the British working class, to what extent was the party a product of its environment, and to what extent did Labour shape the social-political priorities, loyalties and aspirations of its constituents? Whatever our conclusion, it is only by looking at the actions of local party activists in the context of their communities that we can adequately hope to answer such questions.

On a social and cultural level, meanwhile, local and regional research into the Labour Party helps shed light on the broader experiences of Labour members and supporters. In particular, Labour activists endeavoured to sustain, finance and extend the party through a range of activities, including socials, dances, teas, choirs, sports clubs and whist drives. The extent to which this influenced Labour's electoral fortunes may be debated, but such initiatives undoubtedly formed an integral part of many a member's own understanding of Labour Party life during the interwar period.[10] Moreover, the local level was obviously the domain in which Labour's members, voters and opponents lived, worked and functioned. Hence, as Savage has pointed out, the study of local Labour Party history is important in facilitating an awareness of the relationship between the practical politics of everyday life and formal politics 'based on struggles in and around the state'.[11] In such a way, the extent to which Labour was able to affect, articulate or demonstrate a link between the two can be seen as essential to the party's progress, or lack of it.

At present, the disparate nature of existing local Labour Party studies, in terms of their methodology and their focus, continues to raise problems with regard to our comprehending fully Labour's development across Britain as a whole. The need to forge a wider ranging and carefully comparative analysis utilising local and regional research is clear. Indeed, it may be argued that to fully appreciate the means by, and extent to which, the Labour Party progressed over the twentieth century we need to highlight and appreciate both differences and similarities in political approaches, experiences and contexts. To do this, the complexities of Labour's history have to be embraced, assimilated and assessed. By bringing together a collection of essays examining the Labour Party throughout distinct parts of the country, *Labour's Grass Roots* endeavours to act as a spur to such work.

Notes

1. Quoted in N. Riddell, *Labour in Crisis: The Second Labour Government, 1929–31* (Manchester, 1999), p. 17.

2. C. Howard. 'Expectations Born to Death: Local Labour Party Expansion in the 1920s', in J. Winter (ed.), *The Working Class in Modern British History: Essays in Honour of Henry Pelling* (Cambridge, 1983).

3. 'The Constitution of the Labour Party', *Report of the Annual Conference of the Labour Party, 1919* (London, 1919).

4. There is obviously not room here to provide a full bibliography of the Labour Party. So, for a few examples relating to the interwar period, see G.D.H. Cole, *A History of the Labour Party From 1914* (London, 1948); H. Pelling, *A Short History of the Labour Party* (London, 1961); R. Skidelsky, *Politicians and the Slump: The Labour Government of 1929–31* (London, 1967); R. Miliband, *Parliamentary Socialism: A Study in the Politics of Labour* (London, 1972); R. McKibbin, *The Evolution of the Labour Party, 1900–24* (Oxford, 1974); B. Pimlott, *Labour and the Left in the 1930s* (Cambridge, 1977); D. Howell, *British Social Democracy: A Study in Development and Decay* (London, 1980); K. Laybourn, *The Rise of Labour: The British Labour Party 1890–79* (London, 1988); G. Foote, *The Labour Party's Political Thought: A History* (Basingstoke, 1997, third edition); A. Thorpe, *A History of the British Labour Party* (Basingstoke, 1997); J. Swift, *Labour in Crisis: Clement Attlee and the Labour Party in Opposition, 1931–40* (Oxford, 2001); D. Howell, *MacDonald's Party: Labour Identities and Crisis, 1922–31* (Oxford, 2002); D. Marquand, *Ramsay MacDonald* (London, 1977); K. Harris, *Attlee* (London, 1985); B. Pimlott, *Hugh Dalton* (London, 1995 edition); J. Shepherd, *George Lansbury: At the Heart of Old Labour* (Oxford, 2002).

5. D. Howell, *British Workers and the Independent Labour Party, 1888–1906* (Manchester, 1983); M. Savage, *The Dynamics of Working-Class Politics: The Labour Movement in Preston, 1880–1940* (Cambridge, 1987); D. Tanner, *Political Change and the Labour Party, 1900–18* (Cambridge, 1990). Also, J. Lawrence and M. Taylor (eds), *Party, State and Society: Electoral Behaviour in Britain since 1829* (Aldershot, 1997).

6. For some examples, see J. Gillespie, 'Poplarism and Proletarianism: Unemployment and Labour Politics in London, 1918–34', and T. Jeffery, 'The Suburban Nation: Politics and Class in Lewisham', in D. Feldman and G. Stedman Jones (eds), *Metropolis–London: Histories and Representations since 1800* (London, 1989); A. Thorpe, 'J.H. Thomas and the Rise of Labour in Derby, 1880–1945', *Midland History*, 15 (1990); D. Clark, *We Do Not Want the Earth: The History of South Shields Labour Party* (Whitley Bay, 1992); A. Thorpe, 'The Consolidation of a Labour Stronghold, 1926–51', in C. Bindfield et al (eds), *The History of the City of Sheffield, 1843–1993* (Sheffield, 1993); H. Beynon and T. Austrin, *Masters and Servants: Class and Patronage in the Making of a Labour Organisation* (London, 1994)); C. Williams, *Democratic Rhondda: Politics and Society, 1885–1951* (Cardiff, 1996); S. Davies, *Liverpool Labour: Social and Political Influences on the Development of the Labour Party in Liverpool, 1900–39* (Keele, 1996); J. J. Smyth, *Labour in Glasgow, 1896–1936* (East Lothian, 2000); C. Macdonald, *The Radical Thread: Political Change in Scotland: Paisley Politics, 1885–1924* (East Lothian, 2000); D. Tanner, C. Williams and D. Hopkin (eds), *The Labour Party in Wales, 1900–2000* (Cardiff, 2000).

In addition, the *Manchester Region History Review*, 14 (2000) contained a series of essays on the Labour Party in the Manchester region. See also, C. Howard. 'Expectations Born to Death'; D. Tanner, 'Labour and its Membership', in D. Tanner, P. Thane and N. Tiratsoo (eds), *Labour's First Century* (Cambridge, 2000); D. Tanner, 'The Pattern of Labour Politics, 1918–39', in D. Tanner, C. Williams and D. Hopkin (eds), *The Labour Party in Wales*, pp. 113–39.

7. Male and female suffrage was equalised in 1928 with the passing of a further act giving the vote to all women aged 21 and over.

8. Labour Party, *Report of the Annual Conference of the Labour Party, 1939* (London, 1939), p. 92.

9. For various overviews of this debate, see C. Macdonald, *The Radical Thread*, pp. 13–21; D. Tanner, 'Class Voting and Radical Politics: The Liberal and Labour Party', in J. Lawrence and M. Taylor (eds), *Party, State and Society*; L. Black, 'Labour at 100', *Mitteilungsblatt des Instituts für soziale Bewegungen*, 27 (2002).

10. D. Weinbren, *Generating Socialism: Recollections of Life in the Labour Party* (Stroud, 1997).

11. M. Savage, 'The Rise of the Labour Party in Local Perspective', *The Journal of Regional and Local Studies*, 10, 1 (1990), pp. 1–15.

Chapter 2

Elections, Leaflets and Whist Drives: Constituency Party Members in Britain between the Wars

Stuart Ball, Andrew Thorpe and Matthew Worley

The social-political landscape of Britain changed dramatically in the wake of the Great War (1914–18). Alongside the experience of war itself, the relationship between the three principal mainland political parties shifted notably during and in the immediate aftermath of the conflict, with the formation of a coalition government, the split in the Liberal Party, and the emergence of a nationally organised Labour Party each helping to redraw pre-war configurations. The remit of the state, already expanding before 1914, had extended dramatically over the war years and, despite the best efforts of many, was not reduced back to its pre-war level thereafter. Industrial tensions were briefly exacerbated, and social relations were arguably changed irrevocably. Finally, of course, the 1918 Representation of the People Act conferred the franchise on all men over 21 and on most women over the age of 30, thereby facilitating what could for the first time be called a popular democratic system in Britain, a fact confirmed by the further granting of suffrage to women aged 21 and over in 1928.[1]

One obvious and important consequence of all this was the need for Britain's political parties to broaden their appeal and present a social and political vision that attracted and related to the widened electorate. To this effect, all three parties sought to interest, include and mobilise larger numbers of members from 1918, as (most) Conservative, Labour and Liberal organisations across the country endeavoured to 'open their doors' and offer a political home to those wishing to participate in the new age of popular politics. Membership campaigns, canvassing and social events designed to galvanise existing members and attract new ones became a constant part of many a local party or association's calendar; party organisation became more extensive and disciplined; the pressures and expectations applied to party officers became more intensive. Of course, the results and the extent of such change varied from place to place and from organisation to organisation. Yet, political parties and associations undoubtedly became a site of much activity during the interwar years, and they did so for a greater number of people than in any previous period of British history.

This article is based on a survey of local party archives in five British counties – Devon, Durham, Leicestershire, Midlothian-Peebles and Monmouthshire.[2] The five counties were chosen for their broadly representative character, with each comprising rural and urban constituencies, and to ensure that records relating to all three principal parties could be assessed. Although the party records consulted are not evenly dispersed, the five counties as a whole encompass solidly Conservative, Labour and (to a lesser extent) Liberal seats; safe-ish seats; as well as marginal constituencies. In terms of social background, the regions include divisions dominated by a single industry (coal mining), mixed industrial areas, farming communities, suburban and middle-class constituencies. The objective was to consider differences and similarities in party membership activity, and to record the experience of what it meant to be a party activist in the interwar period. As such, this is not an exercise in measuring regional variations or explaining the whys and wherefores of Britain's political development, though its findings may feed into such debate. Rather, it is an attempt to detail the context in which party members functioned and to document the activities in which those members took part.

Local party records have long been the Cinderella of modern British political archives. Public records, politicians' papers and the national-level archives of the main political parties have been, and continue to be, pored over by eager researchers; and yet those records which, in many ways, bring the political historian closer than any others to 'ordinary people' tend, for a variety of reasons, to be neglected. This is not to say that no use has been made of such sources: indeed, the last 25 years have seen much important work in this area.[3] Yet, for very good reasons, such work often remains at the level of the single party, or the single geographical area, or even the single party *in* the single geographical area.[4] This article attempts to help broaden the agenda by focussing on the three major parties in five separate counties.[5] Moreover, it aims to offer a broader comparison than has been generally available thus far, and, crucially, to offer a wider context within which the essays in this volume – which focus on *Labour's* grass roots – can be interpreted.

Structure and Composition

Before examining the activities of the party memberships, it is necessary first to outline briefly the structure and composition of local political organisation. To a certain extent, those divisional Conservative and Liberal associations established by the twentieth century had developed in tandem following the second reform act of 1867. During the interwar period they remained voluntary, self-financing organisations headed by committed activists organised in an executive committee or council. Within this, the position of president and, additionally for the Conservatives, chairman held the greatest status. The presidency was normally an honorific position within a Conservative Association, granted usually to a local dignitary or former parliamentary member for the constituency. So, for example, Lord Londonderry, Viscount Astor and Viscount Churchill each served respectively as presidents of the Stockton, Plymouth and Harborough Conservative associations during the interwar period.[6] The president of a Liberal Party was more akin to the position of Tory chairman, thereby serving as the party officer charged with running the association between election contests. Again, both the Liberal president and the Tory chairman tended to be of notable social standing, be they a professional, military man, businessman, local worthy or long-serving member of the association. In most instances, the Liberal and Conservative executives met irregularly, primarily at election times, on occasion to appoint a prospective parliamentary candidate, or to confirm arrangements for the annual general meeting. Quite often, therefore, the annual meeting merely ratified decisions and positions already decided within the association hierarchy. In addition, both parties appointed a number of vice-presidents, a position that was again associated with social status or the size of an individual's rate of subscription. The rest of the executive, aside from the treasurer, was allotted on a federal basis, comprising men and women from local branches and sections. As associations grew in size, moreover, so a series of sub-committees were appointed to oversee the management of the party, social events, education, finance and so on. These tended to meet more regularly so as to sustain party activity, raise funds and instigate propaganda. To this effect, much of the wider association work was undertaken by an 'autonomous periphery' of local branches, women's sections and, in the case of the Conservatives, the Junior Imperial League.[7] Finally, where finances allowed, Liberal and Conservative associations aspired to the appointment of a full-time party agent responsible for registration work and the administration of electoral affairs.

Given their contrasting political fortunes, the experience of the local Liberal and Conservative associations differed greatly over the interwar period, with the former seeing much of its organisation fall into disrepair while local Conservative associations continued in the main to function regularly and to expand. Across the five counties surveyed, records relating to the Liberal Party were both sparse and, where available, revealing of local associations struggling for survival. Between 1918 and 1922, disagreement over the party's relationship with the Conservatives, nationally and locally, caused splits within the Liberal organisation, as in Leicestershire and Edinburgh, while declining support and revenue over the period as a whole soon jeopardised the very existence of many a local association.[8] In Torquay, despite electoral success in 1923 and the lack of a substantial Labour challenge, the Liberal Association was reporting by late 1925 that its Liberal club could not be sustained with a membership of under 100. By the mid-1930s, the association was meeting evermore irregularly, with its already precarious financial position undermined further by the death of its patron and mainstay Sir Francis Layland-Barratt.[9] There were exceptions, such as the active and committedly independent Totnes Liberal Association, or the South Edinburgh Liberal Association with its evidently dynamic women's section that was able to report in 1930 that 'contrary to most constituencies throughout Scotland, South Edinburgh has not dropped its organisation, and has tried in this difficult period of Liberalism to keep going'.[10] Generally, however, where Conservative organisation continued to grow at a local and divisional level, so Liberal organisation became less widespread and often inactive, particularly by the 1930s. Although Lloyd George had helped finance a brief party revival in 1927–29, the failure to sustain such investment contributed to the precarious financial position of the Liberal organisation in the subsequent decade.[11]

Prior to 1918, the Labour Party was organised as a federation of affiliated trade unions and socialist societies with no provision for individual members. This changed with the adoption of the new party constitution in 1918, instigating the formation of constituency parties to which trade unions, socialist societies and individuals could each subscribe. Authority lay with the general committee, which appointed an executive to oversee the day-to-day business of the divisional party. This comprised a chairman, vice-chairman, treasurer, secretary and representatives of the local party branches, unions, women's sections and societies affiliated to the divisional party. Such a structure was then reproduced at a local (and county) level, with various sub-committees appointed to direct areas of particular interest such as socials and finance. Where possible, the party secretary doubled as secretary-agent, or organiser, working full or, more usually, part-time for the party to oversee its electoral administration and general organisation across the division. Trades councils often formed the basis for this arrangement, as in Edinburgh, where the Edinburgh and District Trades and Labour Council oversaw six constituency parties (including Leith) and a number of local party branches.

Elsewhere, divisional Labour parties were formed on the initiative of trade union branches or local Labour sympathisers, many of whom came to Labour via the Independent Labour Party (ILP). As this would suggest, affiliated trade union members often made up the bulk of the paper membership, and trade union officials tended to dominate the party leadership in many instances. A classic example of this was County Durham, where the Durham Miners' Association (DMA) overwhelmingly dominated the membership, leadership and political character of the divisional parties based in the coalfield. Thus, when the Durham Divisional Labour Party was inaugurated on 9 February 1918, the event was hosted by the DMA at the Miners' Hall. Leaders included men such as Jack Lawson, the MP for Chester-le-Street from 1919, whose position was connected to his holding a variety of offices within the community; Lawson's 'curriculum vitae' could list him as miner, checkweighman, county councillor, DMA executive officer, ILPer and chapel member. Will Whiteley, miners' agent and Methodist, was elected president, while other Methodist miners and checkweighmen such as Jack Swan and Joe Batey dominated the party executive and candidate list.[12] Certainly, the DMA did not always get its way – the Seaham Labour Party deliberately sought non-mining candidates, snubbing the DMA to win the services of Sidney Webb in 1922[13] – but the union and its representatives undoubtedly shaped the party's character and perspective throughout the region. In Monmouthshire, parties such as that in Ebbw Vale had a similar relationship with the South Wales Miners' Federation (SWMF). The strong ties between union lodges, party and community led the SWMF to nominate candidates, print badges, photos and posters, and employ agents such as John Panes in Bedwellty. By 1929, despite unemployment reducing the miners' political fund, the union was contributing £300 towards the election expenses of each constituency in the region.[14] Three of the seven parliamentary constituencies in Monmouthshire had miner-sponsored MPs throughout the interwar period: Abertillery, Bedwellty and Ebbw Vale.

Matters were less clear-cut in localities with a more 'mixed' or less industrial economy. In 'mixed' economic areas, such as Newport, Edinburgh and Leicester, tensions sometimes existed between the different trade unions, while the influence of the ILP and certain middle-class members could be more readily detected. Although the unions and their members formed the basis of all three of the aforementioned parties, many trade union branches remained aloof – in Newport, attempts formally to merge the party and trades council were not acceptable to many local union branches between the wars[15] – and the party's outlook was generally less determined by specifically industrial concerns. In such areas, too, women's sections – initiated by the party during its reorganisation in 1918 – were likely to become an integral part of Labour's organisation (see below). Though women's sections were formed in single-industry constituencies, as throughout Durham, female members in these areas tended to be less visible and wielded even less influence than in the more occupationally and socially diverse divisional parties.

Over the interwar period as a whole, Labour undoubtedly emerged as the most centralised and disciplined of the three parties. Not only did the national party centre develop widely effective and overreaching mechanisms of control, but the divisional party executives tended also to meet on a more regular basis, overseeing and directing their local branches and auxiliaries to a greater extent than either the Liberals or Conservatives. As such, a comparison of divisional Labour parties could give the impression of a relatively uniform political organisation; meetings followed very similar patterns of agenda (model standing orders were circulated though not invariably adopted), correspondence to and from Eccleston Square and, later, Transport House was consistent and extensive, and the booking of 'name' speakers from outside the locality was common. Most importantly, Labour's centrally appointed regional organisers made regular visits to the constituency parties and proved integral to the maintenance of the party organisation during the interwar period. Yet, to overstate such factors would in turn be misleading. The party centre's willingness to intervene decisively into local affairs was rare and usually consultative, while centre-periphery communication more commonly took the form of circulating party literature and information. Furthermore, the varied compositions of Labour's divisional parties and branches preclude any overly generalised assumptions. Divisional Labour parties saw themselves as a part of the national organisation, but they retained a degree of autonomy within a somewhat loosely defined political and organisational paradigm. By contrast, Liberal associations tended to zealously safeguard their 'independence', both political and organisational, though sometimes to the detriment of political consistency or coherency.

Conservative associations were linked to a central organisation which was better resourced and – especially in basic orientation – more united than the Liberals. However, possibly in part because of this, they were equally vigorous defenders of the principle of local autonomy. In practice, whilst the well-funded seats could go their own way with relative impunity, the marginal and weak constituencies inevitably were more dependent upon assistance from outside. Such needs encouraged co-operation and responsiveness to the national organisation, which in its turn maintained a tactful observance of the principle of autonomy, not only in form but also normally in substance.

In terms of membership numbers, the divisional organisations obviously varied in accord with the size of their respective constituencies and, initially at least, with respect to pre-existing social-political cultures and traditions. Taken generally, the Conservative associations boasted the largest and most active memberships, although the sparsity, fluidity and unreliability of membership figures, combined with the scope of the research sample, makes any detailed examination difficult. To take two admittedly arbitrary examples, the Harborough Conservative Association claimed an individual membership of over 3,000 for much of the interwar period, compared with a Labour Party that peaked at just over 1,000 in 1937. In Edinburgh, the North Edinburgh Unionist Association had 1,049 members by the end of 1933, compared with just 258 individual members in the Labour equivalent.[16] Conservative women's sections, too, could often attract memberships in their thousands, compared to tens and hundreds in the Labour Party. In many places, of course, Labour's core membership was bolstered by large numbers of trade union affiliates, something that could provide an electoral base if not an especially active party organisation. Indeed, any attempt to correlate membership and electoral performance is prone to misrepresentation; many of Labour's safest seats, such as Ebbw Vale or Bishop Auckland, had barely functioning party organisations, relying on the local miners' lodges to maintain support. Conversely, divisions such as Plymouth Devonport and Newport could build up memberships of over 1,500 and 3,000 respectively by the mid-1930s, yet still fail to overcome the respective constituencies' Liberal and Conservative hegemony. Not surprisingly, Liberal support often dissipated with the party's wider political presence, though strongholds continued to exist, at least over the 1920s, especially in parts of Devon (Plymouth Devonport) and Durham (South Shields). Generally, however, reference to apathy, inactivity and the need to recruit greater numbers of active party members formed a mantra heard across all three political organisations over the interwar period.

Throughout all the parties, men dominated the organisational and political hierarchy. Though each party and association sought, or claimed, to welcome and provide for the new female electorate, women consistently formed but a small minority of the party executive and generally remained detached from the main decision-making organs. As we shall see, this did not mean that women were necessarily without influence; nor should it suggest that women were somehow irrelevant to the party or associations' development and identity. Ironically, perhaps, many local and divisional women's sections proved to be among the most active sites for party members, with female membership sometimes outnumbering that of the men. We have already noted the South Edinburgh Liberal Women's Association, which provided the funds and organised the social activities that proved integral to the divisional association's survival. In Newport, the Labour Party women's section soon outnumbered its male counterpart, and thereby proved able to ensure party support and discussion of issues outside traditional male concerns, such as the benefits of linoleum for houses on the newly built Maesglas and Somerton estates.[17] In Harborough, meanwhile, where several of the smaller rural villages became mini-fiefdoms of the local Conservative Association over the 1920s, there existed Tory women's branches that counted over half of the local female electorate among their membership.[18]

In class terms, the Labour Party membership was, not surprisingly, overwhelmingly working class, with many party activists coming from the trade union movement. Equally, however, Labour officers were generally skilled workers, and not thereby representative of the majority of workers in their respective constituencies. By contrast, members of the middle and upper middle classes held the key positions and provided much of the membership of the Conservative and Liberal associations, with additional aristocratic flavour added in the form of wealthy patrons, presidents and, in some instances, the parliamentary candidate. Though there were working-class members, those who organised the socials or represented the party were overwhelmingly from the middle classes and generally catered for middle class tastes. Garden parties in manor houses and hotel teas for those specially invited were not the standard fare of most British people between the wars, despite talk of 'good work' being done to remove 'class distinction, prejudice and misunderstanding'.[19] Yet, Conservative associations (especially the women's sections) located in working-class areas did endeavour to court their working-class constituents. In Stockton, for example, Conservative women visited (and recruited) working-class women in their homes, arguably providing a sense of 'class' based on prestige, influence, superiority and taste rather than social position.[20] By 1929, the section boasted nearly 3,000 members and ran regular socials, teas and bazaars that were the envy of its male counterpart and, no doubt, its Labour equivalent.[21] Elsewhere, as in Harborough and Stockton, Conservative Labour Advisory Committees were established to organise and liaise with Tory trade unionists.[22]

Looked at generally, local parties and associations in the interwar period endeavoured to transform themselves from small groups of men supervising electoral work at particular times to larger and more continuous organisations of men and women with an array of campaigning, political and social functions. Nevertheless, parties and associations continued to rely on a committed core of activists to sustain political and associated activity between election times, the success and extent of which varied from place to place. Social and gender differences were apparent across all three parties, with distinct spheres of influence and political identities often being clearly marked. In such a way, the parties reflected the wider society of which they were part. Across all three parties, too, claims of local autonomy contested with national determinants: a problem with which the respective party organisations wrestled to varying degrees of success. That said, in a changed and changing political world, the improvement of party organisation and the extension of a party's appeal became a central objective that informed the mounting expectations demanded upon Labour, Liberal and Conservative party activists during the 1920s and 1930s. It is to the activities of the party members that we shall now turn.

Electioneering

Political organisations are formed to perform a specific function; that is, to elect representatives to positions of political power. Despite their usually very different political aims, the Conservative, Labour and Liberal parties were all committed to constitutional politics, with each seeking to achieve their objectives through parliament and municipal government. As such, the bulk of a local party member's politically active time was dedicated to preparing for and fighting elections, be they national or local. In particular, this involved the selection of party candidates, the registration of voters, the funding and carrying out of electoral campaigns and contests, and the propagation of a political programme relevant to the needs, fears and aspirations of their respective constituency.

The selection of parliamentary and municipal election candidates was perhaps the most important function of a local political organisation. In all three parties, the divisional associations retained a considerable degree of autonomy over this process. In the Conservative and Liberal parties, whilst the selection process might be influenced from outside, the final decision was taken entirely and exclusively by the constituency association, from which there was no appeal. The Labour Party's National Executive Committee (NEC) had the power to intervene in local party affairs if an unsuitable candidate was adopted (usually meaning a Communist), but this was relatively rare, and the NEC endorsed the vast majority of selected parliamentary nominees. There were circumstances in which local parties themselves invited an element of national involvement. The most obvious of these was when there was difficulty in finding a willing standard-bearer from within the constituency, and by default the party headquarters would be approached to publicise the vacancy or recommend names. Finding – and keeping – a candidate was a continual problem for seats where the chance of victory was remote, and assurances of financial support were often necessary to induce a candidate to stand. By definition, such seats could offer little from their own pockets, and subventions had to be looked for from the national party coffers. In some cases, divisions aroused by a particular local claimant – or rival claimants – could be avoided by seeking names from outside. Some of the safest Conservative seats regularly sought outside candidates because of their very attractiveness. Most frequently, the aim was to secure a wealthy candidate who would not only meet all of their own costs but also pay a substantial annual subscription to the association. Some such constituencies also considered themselves to merit a prestigious candidate, either a leading figure or a younger rising star.

As the fortunes of the Liberal Party waned during the interwar period, finding a willing candidate became increasingly difficult. In Torquay, for example, the divisional Liberal Association struggled consistently to find a 'suitable man' to represent the constituency following the general election of 1918. Although the Liberal chief whip and national headquarters were consulted in 1919, no progress was made until 1922, when Captain Piers Gilchrist Thompson was adopted. All seemed well, temporarily at least, with Thompson winning the seat in 1923, only to lose it in 1924 and resign his candidacy. Once again, the search to 'sound' a local man was undertaken and a list from headquarters procured. Over the course of

1926–27, however, a series of potential nominees were approached to no effect. Eventually, Richard Acland showed willing and was duly adopted in 1927, before he too resigned his candidature following defeat in 1929. The search then began once more, with Thompson declining to stand again and various other potential nominees being approached to no avail. Although the problem was alleviated somewhat by the association's willingness to support the Conservative candidate in 1931, it was to re-emerge soon after the election of the National government. This time, H. Samways agreed to be adopted just months before the 1935 general election in the event of another candidate not being found and despite warnings from his doctor that he should not stand.[23] Not dissimilarly, the South Edinburgh Liberal Association received regular rebuffs from those it approached to replace Dr. Laurie, the former candidate who was moving from the area in 1930.[24]

Clearly, different methods were applied across the parties with regard to how the candidate was selected. In the case of a parliamentary nominee, both Conservative and Liberal associations approached people deemed to be a suitable representative for the respective constituency.[25] So, when Sir Charles Yate retired as the Conservative MP for Melton in 1924, an association select committee contacted and met with W.L. Everard, landowner and chairman of the county's largest brewers, who was then recommended to become the prospective candidate at the subsequent general election. Following an appearance at some 79 socials and meetings, Everard was finally adopted officially at a 'special' meeting of Melton Conservatives in October and remained the constituency member throughout the rest of the interwar period.[26] In such a way, the choice of candidate was made by the inner caucus of leading association members, who then 'recommended' their nomination to a general meeting that unfailingly sanctioned the executive option. In coming to such a decision, a prospective Tory or Liberal member's credentials necessarily comprised a mixture of local or national prestige, social status, political belief and, often crucially, a sizeable bank balance. In Harborough, for instance, the defeated Liberal candidate at the 1918 election, Percy Harris, was deselected by the divisional association for not offering a large enough contribution to his election costs, despite promising £276 per annum to pay for an agent. His replacement, J.W. Black, was soon commended for his large contribution to the party finances.[27] In the same constituency, the Conservative MP for Harborough, Ronald Tree, was donating £500 per annum to his divisional association by 1936, a tidy sum considering an MP's annual salary stood at £400 per annum at this time.[28]

By contrast, potential Labour candidates tended to be nominated by affiliated bodies (trade union or ILP, for example) and selected at a 'special' or general committee party meeting, often within days of a preceding election. Accordingly, parties sometimes had a choice of candidate, with each one presenting the party members with details of their labour or socialist credentials. Thus, in Newport, three potential candidates put their case to the party in 1925. Reverend Lang, who stood as a socialist and a pacifist, claimed war to be 'fundamentally wrong', opposed the Sunday opening of public houses, and defined his socialism as 'an inherent right of equal opportunities [sic]'. Councillor James Walker then followed, underlining his twenty years' service to socialism and his experience as a leader of the steelworkers' union, before speaking 'strongly' on women's interests in the movement. Finally, P.C. Hoffman, an organiser in the shop assistants' union, spoke on unemployment, land, nationalisation and sugar beet. Not surprisingly, perhaps, 'Big Jimmy' Walker was duly selected, so beginning a prestigious parliamentary career.[29] Even so, the matter of financial support was often paramount in determining the eventual adoption of a Labour candidate, thereby allowing a dominant trade union to ensure representation, or paving the way for a wealthy aspirant promising to meet the agent's salary to gain nomination.

Labour also spent much time and effort on the selection of its municipal representatives. The Labour Party had led the way in politicising local government, and the divisional party executive and general committee took far greater interest in the adoption of local election candidates than either the Liberals or Conservatives. Although the latter two parties often co-operated at a local level as a bulwark against socialism, the selection of candidates or the definition of a specifically municipal programme were rarely if ever discussed within the association committees beyond ward level. Conversely, divisional Labour parties oversaw and helped appoint local candidates, drew up and co-ordinated political programmes and campaigns, and discussed both council policy and the performance of party representatives on the council. Local (ward) Labour parties, meanwhile, could often concentrate primarily on municipal issues, from candidate selection to poster campaigns to the drawing up of election addresses and party programmes.[30]

Looked at from a broader perspective, we can nevertheless pinpoint certain similarities between the parties. First, financial considerations were often integral to the adoption of a parliamentary candidate, whether the money came from the candidate him or herself or from a sponsoring organisation, such as a trade union. Second, the social position or status of a candidate was deemed important in all instances, although this was obviously interpreted differently across the parties. For the Conservative and Liberal associations, in particular, a sense of social hierarchy was overt in their choice of parliamentary representative. By contrast, for a Labour Party in a working-class or highly unionised area, the trade union, political, workplace and occasionally religious credentials of a candidate were deemed integral to a candidate's appeal and so highlighted. Even so, in more 'mixed' economic or middle-class areas, such as in Edinburgh, Labour would often appoint a professional as its prospective candidate, thereby focusing to some extent on social status to challenge the sitting Liberal or Conservative member. Third, parliamentary and municipal candidates were overwhelmingly, though not exclusively, male. Women were more likely to represent their political organisation at municipal level, but even then remained in the minority.[31] Finally, the candidate's location within the party's spectrum of acceptable political views was generally the least important consideration of all; only open rejection of its leaders or of central planks in its platform would rule out a potential nominee who scored highly in other respects. There were, of course, conventions to be followed, and most of the statements offered to selection committees and at public adoption meetings were bland and broadly orthodox.

Beyond the appointment of suitable parliamentary or municipal candidates, the maintenance of the electoral register and the canvassing of support became the next set of tasks for the party activist. The first of these was the responsibility of the secretary or agent, and although registration procedures were simplified from 1918, the updating of the electoral register retained an importance for party organisers, with most associations and parties aspiring to appoint a full-time paid party officer to undertake the necessary work. Of course, financial limitations could preclude this, especially for smaller parties and associations. For Labour, sponsoring trade unions could sometimes provide the funds and appointee, while wealthy candidates would often enable the party to make either a full-time, part-time or temporary appointment. Within both the Conservative and Liberal Party, fund-raising and donations from wealthy patrons provided the means for such an appointment. In the main, Labour agents had cut their political teeth in the trade union movement or ILP, while Conservative and Liberal agents tended to be upper-middle or middle-class members, often a former serviceman or professional.[32] Additionally, both the central Labour and Conservative Party sought to provide training for their agents, with the Tories arguably proving the more successful in this, certainly in terms of quantity.

Election work, meanwhile, meant a round of door-to-door canvassing, filling and sealing envelopes, organising and attending open-air and public meetings, and distributing party literature. In this, all three parties sought to mobilise as much of their party machine as possible, and it was in the immediate build-up to an election that parties were at their most active. Women's sections and children were rallied to help canvass the constituency and plans were drawn up to ensure the maximum success. In Edinburgh, Unionists were instructed to 'prepare well' before canvassing, to appoint approximately one party worker per 20 voters, and to always keep election expenses in mind.[33] Such instructions became ever more systematic over time, as the distribution of literature and personal appeals took priority over more traditional soapbox politics. Thus, by 1930, the Loughborough Borough Labour Party unanimously agreed 'that no useful purpose would be served' by open-air meetings; that it would be better to concentrate on 'canvassing and getting personal contact with the electors'.[34] Similarly, the Harborough Conservative Association's policy sub-committee concluded in 1927 that open-air meetings were of 'no particular value', while fetes and garden parties were 'very valuable', and indoor meetings were good if held with a social attraction. As for the 'indiscriminate distribution of literature', this was to be replaced by 'judicious selection and distribution'.[35] The Conservatives' mobile cinema vans were a particularly effective means of propaganda, especially in rural areas.[36]

But proficient canvassing did not ensure success; candidates had to present and personify a set of policies applicable to their varied constituents. There is not space here to examine the parties' effectiveness in this respect. Even so, it may be noted that each varied greatly in terms of political priorities. While Labour focused increasingly on social and welfare issues such as housing, social services (healthcare), unemployment and education, the Conservatives concentrated on broader issues of national interest, be they proactive (imperial preference) or negative (anti-socialism). So, to take two examples of Conservative Party election literature, Major Jack Herbert fought the Monmouth parliamentary by-election of 14 June 1934 under the slogan of 'British First', proclaiming the National government's achievement of turning 'the socialist party's defeat ... into credit' and restoring most economy cuts. Alongside 'practical assistance' to the 'agriculturalist, small holder and market gardener', Herbert stood for world peace, an increase in trade and commerce, better housing, the development of the empire's resources, and 'local needs'. In Tiverton, campaigning in the aftermath of the widespread industrial unrest that followed the war, Mr. H. Weston-Sparkes asked his constituents 'Electors, Which Will You Have?' – 'A parliament elected on the most representative and democratic basis, and which can be altered at any general election if it loses the confidence of the people', or 'A soviet with industrial conscription under socialist officials, which only a revolution can remove once they get into power'.[37]

Conversely, Labour election material often focused on the social circumstances of its constituents, particularly in those areas hit hardest by the economic uncertainties of the 1920s and 1930s. Will Lawther's electoral programme in South Shields in 1924 began with a commitment to peace, before listing his priorities as housing (low rents, slum clearance, separate dwellings for all), equal educational opportunities, schemes for the unemployed and better pensions.[38] Terms such as socialism were often used sparingly (if at all), though more regularly after 1931, with attention placed instead on the party's efficiency, morality and even-handedness. So, in Edinburgh South in 1929, Labour put forward the economics lecturer Arthur Woodburn with a 'constructive policy' centred on the abolition of war, solutions for unemployment, the prevention of disease, and care for public health. Details were vague, but support for the League of Nations and nationalisation with compensation were envisaged as the means by which to achieve peace and better 'efficiency in production and distribution'.[39] The Liberals, meanwhile, combined their traditional policies with a defensive anti-socialism. Thus, the Liberal appeal to the voters of Sunderland in 1924 led with a reaffirmation of 'Liberalism' and 'free trade', before praising Labour's foreign policy but criticising its plans 'at home'. The important associated questions, from a Liberal point of view, were unemployment, housing, land, and Ireland.[40] All parties, it should be noted, began to make direct appeals to the newly enfranchised women, some of the connotations of which will be discussed below.

At the risk of oversimplification, it may be concluded that Labour tended to appeal to the electorate from a moral perspective that endeavoured, simultaneously, to be relevant to the everyday concerns of its constituents. The Conservatives, meanwhile, regularly alluded to the 'nation' and the 'national interest'; a relatively flexible premise from which to develop policy. Though arriving at different conclusions and starting from a different set of premises, Labour and Conservative members often displayed opinions derived from general assumption, values or instinct rather than theoretical debate. This would change over the 1930s, as Labour began to articulate its socialism through the concept of economic 'planning'. Somewhat differently, the Liberals aimed, for the most part, to remain fixed on a set of 'traditional' policies deemed to have formed the basis for Britain's on-going social and economic progress. As noticeably, however, all three parties presented their opponents as an archetypal 'other', be they the officious revolutionary socialist, the representatives of 'vested interest', or the uncaring and greedy capitalist.

Maintaining the Party

As the interwar period progressed, party and association activity increasingly extended beyond purely electoral work. Attempts to recruit (and maintain) members began to concentrate the minds of the leading divisional activists, while educational schemes were sometimes programmed to foster a political consciousness amongst the wider membership. More popularly, social meetings and outings were arranged, with outdoor fetes or garden parties organised in the summer, often on the initiative of the local women's sections. In so doing, parties and associations hoped to integrate themselves within the wider community, so heightening their profile and raising necessary funds and support in the process. As importantly, they served to bolster party morale and sustain the party organisation between elections.

Most divisional parties and associations hoped to develop as large a membership base as possible. With the extension of the franchise, all three parties had necessarily to widen their electoral appeal, a fact to which they were acutely aware. Conservative leader Andrew Bonar Law, speaking in 1917, requested that his party adopt franchise reform and 'make the best of the situation that has arisen and to see that everything is done to make our party what Disraeli called it – and what, if it is to have any existence, it must be – a truly national party'.[41] Likewise, the Labour Party's reorganisation in 1918 was prompted, in part, by the extension of the franchise. In particular, the newly enfranchised female electorate was given much attention, with the formation of women's sections and specific appeals to women voters becoming an essential part of any election campaign. Thus, the Bedwellty Labour Party decided as early as September 1918 to send a 'personal invitation signed by the secretary of the women's group' to prospective members and voters.[42] In Seaham, Beatrice Webb sent regular letters to Labour women and 'the women electors' in the 1920s, while the national Labour Party issued pamphlets outlining 'why women should vote Labour'.[43] The Conservative and Liberal parties made similar appeals, endeavouring to ensure that the organisation of women was a task to be 'taken seriously in hand'.[44] Often, the wife of a prospective parliamentary candidate was brought into the spotlight to woo potential electors. Lieutenant Colonel Cuthbert Headlam's election campaigns in the 1930s were accompanied by a leaflet featuring him and his wife, with Beatrice Headlam appealing to local women to 'vote for my husband'. The Liberal candidate in Houghton-le-Spring, T.E. Spring, did the same, with Elizabeth Wing declaring that 'Like yourselves, I have to look after a house, and politics affects us even there'.[45] Of course, recruiting and accommodating women members was not the same as ensuring equal representation and influence within the party, something none of the three parties attempted seriously during the interwar period. More broadly, membership drives were organised intermittently and where necessary by divisional and local organisations. In between times, local parties and associations sought to organise the regular collection of subscriptions to maintain both numbers and finance.

The principal exceptions to such ambition were certain Labour parties in the mining villages of Durham and South Wales, where the influence of the miners' lodge effectively ensured Labour's domination. A classic example was the Bishop Auckland Labour Party, where its MP in 1929–31 and from 1935, Hugh Dalton, claimed that a 'healthy party is an inactive one'. 'Too many members might upset the applecart', he once said, 'and bring in militants'.[46] Here, the guaranteed vote of an overwhelmingly working-class mining community was assured by the DMA, while the rudimentary party organisation was overseen by Will Davies, the party secretary, and 'uncle' Bob Middlewood, the leader of Bishop Auckland council. In such a way, Labour retained its dominance in the constituency through networks of individuals whose position largely relied on the patronage of – and the support mobilised by – the DMA. In such circumstances, a constituency party was hardly deemed necessary. Indeed, Davies sometimes managed to allow a whole year to pass without a single executive meeting, claiming there was simply nothing for the party to discuss.[47] Similarly, the Ebbw Vale Labour Party regularly recorded the party minimum individual membership from 1928, yet it remained one of Labour's safest seats.[48]

Whatever the size of the party membership, the aim that all divisional and local organisations should be self-financing meant that fund raising was another key component of a party member's experience. An array of methods was devised, although Conservative, Liberal and Labour members all showed a particular penchant for the whist drive. Weekly, monthly, divisional, ward and regional drives were frequently organised by local associations and parties to raise money, despite the fact that whist was also played habitually at socials, dances, after meetings and sometimes instead of meetings all year round. In addition, bazaars, raffles, jumble sales, sweepstakes and dances became standard and often profitable points of party activity. Accordingly, most parties and associations had formed social committees by the 1920s. Yet, although these committees generally comprised men and women, it was more often than not the women's sections that organised, supplied and staffed such public events. As a result of all this, political and social activity began to coalesce across the three parties, as social gatherings doubled as fund-raising schemes that further included political speeches and dissemination of propaganda. Not only did such activity help attract members to the party, both for social and political reasons, but they also attracted publicity and gave the party or association a public profile that extended beyond its offices, clubs or rooms.

Of course, individuals and trade unions could also help solve financial worries. Conservative and Liberal associations, in particular, benefited from wealthy patrons willing to pay off overdrafts or finance party premises and activities. The Pease family regularly helped keep the financial wolf from the door of the Darlington Conservative Association, with Captain E.H. Pease donating £325 in March 1927 for the expressed purpose of clearing the association overdraft. The Conservatives particularly relied upon the candidate or MP to subsidise the local party, with sums equivalent to the entire parliamentary salary of

£400 per annum not unusual. The safer the seat, the larger the sum expected – and for this reason, being without a candidate was a double disadvantage. In Stockton, the generosity of Harold Macmillan regularly cut the overspending Conservative Association's overdraft and ensured that it was able to acquire permanent premises to act as a 'rallying place for our party'.[49] Whilst Macmillan remained, all was well, but the situation was much gloomier during the period after the 1929 defeat when he gave up the candidacy in search of a safer berth elsewhere, and only his return in 1931 restored the association to health and vigour. For Labour, the trade unions were the principal benefactors. In 1922, DMA-sponsored candidates filled six of Durham's eleven county seats, with the union financing both the election campaign and the political agents. The union's political fund for 1922–23 spread its services widely, spending £1,018/9s/4d on agents' salaries and contributing to the expenses of eight divisional parties.[50]

Beyond their financial raison d'être, the rounds of socials, outings and dances were held to maintain the party organisation and sustain morale. Popular among the divisional Conservatives and, to a dwindling but still notable extent, Liberal associations were garden parties, dinners and summer fetes. These were often held at the home of a local dignitary, and became regular features of both the association and the wider social calendar. For example, the Bosworth Conservative Association held its annual fete at the home of Lord Waring, while the countless social events organised by the Harborough Conservative Association, particularly its women's branch, included a Christmas fair in 1930 that comprised bridge, whist, various stalls, and a tea and buffet followed by a further round of whist and a dance.[51] Later, in 1938, the Darlington Conservative Association held a 'sunshine bazaar' (opened by the Marchioness of Zetland and Lady Bradford), a garden party, and organised outings to Holland, Glasgow, Blackpool and the Newcastle pantomime.[52] For the Labour Party, May Day processions (and the miners' gala in Durham) proved important rallying points for its members. Less dramatically, yearly day trips and children's picnics were often arranged.[53]

As suggested above, women's sections frequently took the lead in such activity. Indeed, the minutes of all three parties' women's section's show how the 'space' occupied by women was circumscribed by their male counterparts, but was nevertheless very active and not without some wider import. On the one hand, the party minute books suggest that women rarely featured in the executive meetings of the organisation, only occasionally intervening in debates on what could be called 'traditional' political matters.[54] This occasionally brought some protest, as in Stockton, where the Conservative women's section debated how women 'liked to manage their own affairs' but would like to be invited to discuss matters occasionally with the men; or in Harborough where simmering tensions between the men's and the (larger) women's association caused an almighty row in 1935.[55] Yet, the adoption of separate men's and women's sections was largely accepted, with the Tiverton Liberal Association reporting typically that 'women do not seem to take as much interest in a combined one [section] as they do when they have a separate association of their own'.[56] On the other hand, functioning women's sections often combined social activity with political discussion that, while not decisive in terms of becoming official party policy, was often wide ranging and more inclusive than debate within the party hierarchy. The aforementioned Stockton Conservative women's section regularly invited speakers on an array of topics to address its members. It also organised frequent and well-attended whist drives, dances and bazaars, and put on a number of association day trips, such as one to Norwich to visit the Colman family's mustard business. By 1929, it boasted nearly 3,000 members.[57] Similarly, though with a far smaller membership, the Loughborough Labour Party women's section's activities for 1934–35 included the regular round of whist drives combined with weekly or fortnightly meetings, jumble sales, socials, talks by party members on proposals for maternity homes, 'the milk question', the importance of female municipal candidates and the possibility of military sanctions over Abyssinia (with a vote of three for and ten against), and trips to Sheffield, Stratford and Derby laundry.[58] In this, women's meetings could sometimes (but by no means always) contrast with the dry and mostly administrative duties of the male-dominated executives and sub-committees. Although women were typically marginalised within their party or association, the activities – social and electoral – carried out by female members suggest that they could be crucial to the sustenance and construction of the public identity of their respective party.

Finally, all the parties sought to encourage political awareness among their members, with speakers' classes, lectures, and education and literature committees becoming standard components of local organisational life. These were not always the most popular of party activities, although the Durham Women's Advisory Council provided scholarships for several enthusiastic Labour members to attend its summer school at Barrow House in the 1920s and 1930s.[59] Certainly, social evenings, dances and teas tended to outnumber the more cerebral distractions. Elsewhere, ambitious members could take courses at centrally organised educational facilities, such as the Bonar Law Memorial College, established by the Conservatives at Ashridge in 1930. Closer to home, youth sections tended to concentrate on a mixture of social and education activities. As well as organising dances and socials, Labour Leagues of Youth or the Tory Junior Imperial Leagues (the Imps) took part in speaking competitions and staged debates on topics such as, 'do business girls make good wives'.[60]

Overall, the experience of a party member in the interwar period could be a broad and wide-ranging one. Local and divisional organisations sought to cultivate a political home for people that was both social and political, initiating events and activities beyond the simply electoral. Of course, the extent and success of this varied from place to place. Moreover, the extent to which individuals chose to integrate themselves into such a life varied from person to person. Material circumstances – geographical, sexual and occupational – could also inform the extent of person's political activity. Loosely speaking, however, we can denote three types of party member in the interwar period: the passive, the supportive, and the active. The first of these paid their subscriptions when asked, voted accordingly at election time, but generally remained detached from the party organisation. The supportive member similarly subscribed to and voted for their respective party, attending perhaps the odd social and annual meeting, but only really lending their assistance at election time. Finally, the active members were those men and women who sustained the party organisation throughout the year, attending a constant round of meetings, helping at the party office, and organising events associated with their respective party or association. Across the parties, the Conservatives arguably succeeded in creating an environment in which the social and political became indistinguishable. Attendance at a Conservative Association dinner, fete, executive or women's meeting was as much a part of the social calendar as it was political; it represented a sense of status for those who wished to see the world in such a way. For Labour, its social activities were unable to compete with attractions beyond the party (sport, cinema, pub, union etc), although they remained an integral and enjoyable part of many an active member's experience. In terms of format, Liberal social activity to some extent mirrored that of the Conservatives, although the dwindling party organisation over the interwar years meant that it was less widespread and less well attended. Thus, fetes and garden parties proved particularly popular. To take one example, a Leicestershire Liberal Association garden party held in September 1919 featured various sports events (organised by men), various stalls and refreshments (organised by women), a band, and a 'short' public meeting addressed by the president, A.E. Sawday.[61] The extent to which such activity impinged on the electoral fortunes of each of the three parties is more debateable, though it is something that perhaps warrants further investigation.

Confronting Difficulties

The existence of political organisations of all persuasions was fraught with difficulties of a political and organisational nature. To a notable extent, the vast majority of party or association members gave their unequivocal support to their national party whether in or out of government, although instances of dissent were of course common, as in the Conservative Party in 1929–31, the Liberal Party in 1918–29, and the Labour Party during the 1930s with regard to the policies (and expulsion) of Sir Stafford Cripps. Even so, loyalty to 'the cause' was held in high esteem, and the bulk of resolutions passed by all sections of a divisional organisation tended to endorse the objectives and position of the central party. Inevitably, there are exceptions to this, but intra-party disagreements were rarely political and, where so, concerned a vociferous minority rather than a substantial challenge to prevailing policies and loyalties. Thus, the divisions that wracked the Jarrow Labour Party in the wake of the 'Jarrow crusade' centred on a handful of 'left' Labour councillors whose criticisms of Ellen Wilkinson were not held by the majority of party members. Nevertheless, their actions caused a furore and threatened Labour's council majority if not the party's dominant position as the political wing of the local labour movement.[62] As such, although political, financial, organisational and personal differences were sometimes likely to cause disruption, local associations and parties can best be described as sites of unified purpose and camaraderie beneath which stifled tensions could sometimes be discerned.

For the Conservatives, the local associations constructed and presented an identity of solidity, continuity, patriotism, unity and caution, with a loyalty to king and country being regularly reaffirmed. 'God Save the King' was frequently sung at the end of annual meetings and even some executive or women's committee meetings. The public AGMs saw little debate, with the unanimous passage of a customary resolution which in general terms supported the party's leadership and mission. Concerns were kept for the private forums of the executive committee, and even here expressed reluctantly and rarely. However, there were common themes – so much so as to be a form of orthodoxy in themselves. In the 1920s these were the reform of the House of Lords, tariffs and the less controversial 'safeguarding' policy, and pressure for economy in government spending (citing the burdens of local and national taxation). In the 1930s, India caused much discussion and some dissent, whilst appeasement almost none of either. As for the Liberals, the divisions of 1916–22 cut deep, with divisional associations demonstrating an array of responses to the party crisis. Some accepted the coalition arrangement after the war and again in 1931, some rejected both (Totnes), while the split damaged others irrevocably.[63] When the chairman of the Scottish Liberal Federation (SLF), Sir William Robertson, resigned his position in 1920, he described the Liberal Party as an organisation traditionally composed of 'men who held advanced views, moderate views, and what may be described as Conservative–Liberal views'.[64] In so doing, however, he left a federation that was nominally opposed to the coalition government but unable to retain a unity with which to confront it. By the time of the 1923 general election, the SLF proved incapable of nominating more than a handful of candidates, often facing difficulties in those constituencies where its representatives did manage to stand. Thus, in Edinburgh East, the Liberal candidate J.M. Hogge was opposed by a former vice-president of the local Liberal Association turned Tory, C.J.M. Mancor, who described his erstwhile friends as having 'a soul ... so dead that they prefer their Association before the interests of their country'.[65] Hogge held his seat, but the following year Labour contested the constituency for the first time and won, putting forward Dr T. Drummond Shiels on a progressive platform that made him an attractive heir to the progressive politics of pre-war Liberalism and the most viable alternative to Conservatism. But despite this, Liberal associations in many areas continued to retain men and women willing to 'reaffirm our belief in the ultimate triumph of the Liberal cause', and keen to believe that ['the] continued existence of an organised Liberal Party is of vital importance to the country'.[66]

Labour Party unity was associated with its trade union roots, although inter-union rivalry could sometimes find its way into a local party organisation, and the historically tense relations between trade unionists and socialists could prompt disagreement. Certainly, many trade unionists in Newport and Edinburgh remained suspicious of the 'socialist' Labour Party, while tensions between Labour and the ILP, the Communist Party, or the Socialist League intermittently challenged party solidarity. Again, however, the majority of Labour members supported the party centre: proscriptions against Communists were widely observed, most ILPers continued in the party once the former disaffiliated in 1932, and the Socialist

League remained at best a minor presence in the five counties under review. The minutes of the Gateshead branch, for example, reveal a loyal section of the Labour Party keen to settle down to the usual round of whist drives and discussion.[67] Even at the lowest point of Labour's interwar history, 1931, the vast majority of party activists (though not all party members or voters) remained committed to the Labour Party and, where appropriate, their parliamentary candidate – with Ramsay MacDonald's Seaham constituency proving an obvious exception to this.

Quite clearly, potential sites of tension did exist and occasionally came to the surface. Financial worries threatened the existence of many a political organisation, leading to intra-party accusations over the distribution of effort or funds. In Harborough, where a large, financially solvent and extremely active Conservative women's association contrasted with a dominant if somewhat lacklustre men's association, attempts to solve the division's monetary worries by sharing management and financial responsibilities were fiercely resisted by the self-sufficient women. Threats of resignation met the proposed new rules and accusations flew in both directions, before a settlement was finally, if tenuously reached.[68] But financial concerns were usually felt by the organisation as a whole and, in many ways, helped galvanise party activity towards fund-raising ends.

The relationship between the party or association and their respective MP or parliamentary candidate was also a potential source of tension. In the main, relations were cordial and even congratulatory, as candidates and members of parliament became the 'star turn' at party events such as annual meetings, socials and fetes. Once elected, many MPs regularly 'reported back' to their constituency and were repaid by bolstering resolutions and support. Thus, the Darlington Conservative Association resolved that its MP, Charles Peat, had 'proved himself a first class member having conscientiously attended to his parliamentary duties and kept in close personal contact with his constituency, despite the great amount of work involved by his business responsibilities'.[69] The member for Bedwellty, Charles Edwards, was appreciated in similar ways. As he represented the constituency for Labour throughout the interwar period (and beyond), he gave frequent talks and updates to the divisional party, working closely with the party chairman Lewis Lewis in between times. Come 1931, Edwards was congratulated on his parliamentary work and his refusal to follow MacDonald into the National government, as the division rallied behind him and the wider Labour Party.[70] Indeed, some local organisations retained support for those members who occasionally deviated or challenged official party policy. For instance, Torquay Conservatives and North Edinburgh Unionists backed their respective members' opposition to the National government's India Bill in the early 1930s.[71] As such, disputes were rare. True, powerful local leaders such as Francis Acland did demonstrate a willingness to overturn their association's choice of parliamentary candidate, bemoaning in 1934 that Captain King, the prospective candidate for the Tiverton Liberals, 'was liked enough off the platform, but he could not and never would create a favourable impression on the platform'.[72] King was duly replaced. Furthermore, the Seaham Labour Party executive refused to endorse Ramsay MacDonald in 1931, although many inside and affiliated to the party did retain a (brief) loyalty to the erstwhile Labour prime minister.[73] But such dramas were rare, with the prospective candidate or sitting parliamentary member acting as a recognisable and popular figurehead for most parties and associations.

Noticeably, however, divisional party minute books suggest that a degree of tension did exist between many Labour parties and the Labour 'groups' representing both the party and their constituents at a local government level. Disputes usually revolved around either a lack of contact between councillors and party, or as a result of decisions taken by councillors deemed antithetical to Labour's programme or ethos. Thus, two Labour councillors in Edinburgh (Paris and Rhind) had the 'whip withdrawn' in 1932 for refusing to leave office in protest against 'the lack of fair play on the part of the other side [the Tory dominated Moderate Party] in refusing to allow Labour at least two Bailieships'. Conversely, any sign that Labour's own representatives were somehow profiting from their position was frowned upon. In Newport, the general committee resolved in December 1920 'that this meeting strongly resents the action taken by certain Labour councillors and other members of the party in attending the Mayor's banquet ...'. Not only did the 'spending of public money on Mayoral banquets and similar functions' challenge Labour scruples, but it also raised questions as to Labour's identity. An amendment to the committee's resolution stating that party representatives' 'personal or social relationship towards elected representatives of other parties is entirely a matter for the decision of the Labour councillors themselves' was defeated by ten votes to seven. Even so, the problem re-emerged in 1935, this time in the context of the 'unemployment and distress' being experienced by many Labour voters. Consequently, in February 1936, the party discussed whether all municipal candidates should be able to prove they had given three years' service to the party – careerists were evidently not welcome.[74] On occasion, too, affiliated trade unions would protest against decisions or positions taken by Labour councillors.

Looked at generally, personal or organisational rivalries proved to be more common sources of tension than political dispute within most divisional parties and associations. In addition to what has been listed above, individual animosities no doubt existed but failed to find their way into the minute books. Conversely, generational differences, or misunderstandings, are evident in the often irregular attempts made by associations and parties to maintain functioning 'youth' sections. The exuberance of youth, along with fears (sometimes substantiated in the case of the Labour Party) that youth sections would harbour militant attitudes, meant that relations were sometimes tense to say the least. Complaints about the conduct of youth sections or reports of social clubs getting 'out of hand' were not uncommon.[75] Where potential differences did occur, however, a dedication to an agreed common 'cause' generally ensured that unity prevailed, particularly in the Labour parties and Conservative associations. Of course, the particular position of the Liberals in the immediate wake of the Great War ensured that political and, more commonly, strategical disagreements did contrive to split local and regional associations, yet a core of redoubtable activists generally remained to keep the Liberal flag flying in name if not in numbers.

Conclusion

Research focused on local and divisional political organisation can reveal much about the experiences and activities of party activists in Britain between the wars. Though not always dealing in the cut and thrust of 'high' political debate or action of parliament and central office, it does help us understand just how and to what extent the nationwide network of associations and parties maintained and constructed political identities at a local level. Obviously, the particular histories of each major political party and their respective constituency organisations all differ in a number of ways. At the same time, records of local political organisations reveal that the life of a party activist, be they Labour, Liberal or Conservative, followed similar patterns and comprised similar concerns (mainly financial) and objectives. From a cynical point of view, the often administrative nature of local party or association business may help us understand why the majority of people remained aloof from organised politics in the interwar period, despite the extension of franchise. On the other hand, the reorganised or newly formed parties, women's branches and youth sections did offer a sense of purpose and a range of activities and responsibilities to those who wished to participate. In particular, the tireless effort exerted by party activists deserves due recognition, particularly given the voluntary nature of a political organisation. Alongside the regular rounds of meetings and canvassing, the holding of socials, teas, fetes and bazaars contributed to the evolving social and cultural environment of interwar Britain. Ultimately, too, it was the members and activists of these political organisations who personified the notion of popular democracy advanced from 1918, suggesting that their stories remain an under-researched yet valuable part of Britain's political history.

Notes

1. For the 1918 Representation of the People Act, see M. Dawson, 'Money and the Real Impact of the Fourth Reform Act', *Historical Journal*, 35 (1993), pp. 369–82.

2. We wish to thank the Leverhulme Trust for funding the research upon which this article is based. This research forms part of a 'pilot project' locating and assessing the records of Britain's constituency level political parties in the interwar period.

3. Chief among the pioneering works in the area were J. Ramsden, *The Age of Balfour and Baldwin 1902–40* (London, 1978); D. Howell, *British Workers and the Independent Labour Party, 1888–1906* (Manchester, 1983); D. Tanner, *Political Change and the Labour Party, 1900–18* (Cambridge, 1990).

4. More recent works on the Conservatives which incorporate such material include S. Ball, *Baldwin and the Conservative Party: The Crisis of 1929–31* (New Haven and London, 1988); S. Ball, 'Local Conservatism and the Evolution of the Party Organisation', in A. Seldon and S. Ball (eds), *Conservative Century: The Conservative Party since 1900* (Oxford, 1994); J. Ramsden, *The Age of Churchill and Eden, 1940–57* (London, 1995); S. Ball, 'National Politics and Local History: The Regional and Local Archives of the Conservative Party 1867–1945', *Archives*, 94 (1996); N.J. Crowson, *Facing Fascism: The*

Conservative Party and the European Dictators 1935–40 (London, 1997); N. McCrillis, *The British Conservative Party in the Age of Universal Suffrage: Popular Conservatism 1918–29* (Ohio, 1998). On Labour, see C. Howard, 'Expectations Born to Death: Local Labour Party Expansion in the 1920s', in J.M. Winter (ed), *The Working Class in Modern British History: Essays in Honour of Henry Pelling* (Cambridge, 1983); J. Reynolds and K. Laybourn, *Labour Heartland: A History of the Labour Party in West Yorkshire During the Interwar Years, 1918–39* (Bradford, 1987); N. Riddell, *Labour in Crisis: The Second Labour Government, 1929–31* (Manchester, 1999); the articles in *Manchester Region History Review*, 14 (2000); D. Tanner, 'The Pattern of Labour Politics, 1918–39', in D. Tanner, C. Williams and D. Hopkin (eds), *The Labour Party in Wales, 1900–2000* (Cardiff, 2000); S. Fielding, 'Activists against "Affluence": Labour Party Culture during the "Golden Age"', circa 1950–70', *Journal of British Studies*, 40, 1 (2001); L. Black, *The Political Culture of the Left in Affluent Britain, 1951–64: Old Labour, New Britain?* (Basingstoke, 2003). There is much less for the Liberals, but see G. Tregidga, *The Liberal Party in South West Britain since 1918* (Exeter, 2000).

5. Previous work that has sought to look beyond a single party includes A. Thorpe, *The British General Election of 1931* (Oxford, 1991); D. Tanner, *Political Change and the Labour Party*.

6. Minutes of the Stockton and Thornaby Constitutional Organisation, 1919–40 (Durham Record Office); Minutes of the Plymouth Sutton Division Conservative and Unionist Association, 1938–71 (West Devon Record Office); Minutes of the Harborough Conservative Association, 1912–33 (Leicestershire Record Office). Dignitaries, such as Lord Londonderry, were sometimes president of a number of Conservative associations.

7. S. Ball, 'Local Conservatism', p. 272.

8. Minutes of the Leicestershire Liberal Association, 1903–23 (Leicestershire Record office); Minutes of the Scottish Liberal Federation, 1920–31 (National Library of Scotland).

9. Minutes of the Torquay Liberal Association Financial Committee, 1913–38 (Torbay Liberal Democrats Constituency Office).

10. Minutes of the Totnes Division Liberal Association, 1924–39 (Totnes Liberal Democrats Constituency Office); Minutes of the South Edinburgh Liberal Women's Association, 1924–58 (National Library of Scotland).

11. For examples of worsening Liberal finances, see Minutes of the Annual Meeting of the [Totnes Liberal Association] General Council, 16 February 1935 (Totnes Liberal Democrats Constituency Office); Minutes of the Leicester Liberal Committee, 26 November 1930 and 23 February 1931 (Leicestershire Record Office). On the latter date, the executive resolved to register all telephone calls in detail so as to keep an eye on association expenditure.

12. Minutes of Durham Miners' Association Meeting and Durham Divisional Labour Party Minutes, 1918–47 (Shotton Family papers, Durham Record Office).

13. Such a trend continued; Seaham was later won by Ramsay MacDonald in 1929 and Emanuel Shinwell in 1935. See M. Callcott, 'The Nature and Extent of Political Change in the Inter-War Years: The Example of County Durham', *Northern History*, 16 (1980).

14. Minutes of the Bedwellty Divisional Labour Party, 16, February, 27 April and 27 July 1929 (Gwent Record Office).

15. *Newport Trades Council Annual Report, 1923*, in 'The Origins and Development of the Labour Party in Britain at Local Level' series (LSE). When Newport trades council members were canvassed on the issue in 1923, only two affiliated branches replied favourably, with the 'large majority' preferring to retain the trades council's 'separate identity'.

16. Minutes of the Harborough Conservative Association, 1913–33 (Leicestershire Record Office); Minutes of the North Edinburgh Unionist Association, 23 January 1934 (Edinburgh City Archive); *Report of the Annual Conference of the Labour Party* (London, various years).

17. Minutes of the Newport Labour Party, 14 November 1930 (LSE); D. Tanner, 'The Pattern of Labour Politics', p. 139.

18. Minutes of the Harborough Conservative and Unionist Association Women's Branch (Leicestershire Record Office).

19. Minutes of the Bosworth Women's Unionist Association, 1918–25 (Leicestershire Record Office).

20. P. Lynn, 'The Influence of Class and Gender: Female Political Organisation in County Durham During the Interwar Years', *North East Labour History*, 31 (1997), p. 55.

21. Minutes of the Stockton and Thornaby Women's Unionist Section, 1923–38 (Durham Record Office).

22. Minutes of the Harborough Conservative Association Labour Advisory Committee, 1930–1939 (Leicestershire Record Office); Minutes of the Stockton and Thornaby Constitutional Organisation Unionist Labour Advisory Committee, 1925–34 (Durham Record Office).

23. Minutes of the Torquay Division Liberal Association, 1913–38 (Torbay Liberal Democrats Constituency Office).

24. Minutes of the South Edinburgh Liberal Association, 1930–56 (National Library of Scotland).

25. To quote the Darlington Conservative Association executive, the management committee was 'to approach likely gentlemen for consideration as prospective candidates'. See Minutes of the Darlington Conservative Association, 2 November 1939.

26. Minutes of the Melton Conservative and Unionist Association, 1923–46.

27. Minutes of the Harborough Divisional Liberal Association, 15 March 1919 and 22 May 1920. For Harris, who went to have a prestigious career and served as deputy party leader during the Second World War, see P. Harris, *Forty Years In and Out of Parliament* (undated).

28. Minutes of the Harborough Conservative Association, 23 May 1936 (Leicestershire Record Office). The salaries for members of parliament varied over the interwar period. Between 1911 and 1931, MPs earned £400 per annum, falling to £360 in 1931–34, before rising to £400 in 1934 and £600 in 1937.

29. Minutes of the Newport Labour Party, 20 November 1925 (LSE).

30. For an example, see Minutes of the Storer Local Labour Party, 1932–39 (Leicester Record Office).

31. For a wider discussion of this, see M. Pugh, *Women and the Women's Movement in Britain, 1914–59* (Basingstoke, 1992), pp. 154–208.

32. S. Ball, 'Local Conservatism', pp. 279–80.

33. Minutes of Edinburgh West Division Unionist Association, 30 October 1918 (Edinburgh City Archive).

34. Minutes of the Loughborough Labour Party, 28 March 1930 (Leicester Record Office).

35. Minutes of the Harborough Conservative Association, 22 January 1927 (Leicestershire Record Office).

36. J. Ramsden, *The Age of Balfour and Baldwin*; T.J. Hollins, 'The Conservative Party and Film Propaganda between the Wars', *English Historical Review*, 96 (1981).

37. *Major Jack Herbert, The National and Unionist Candidate*, Monmouth Parliamentary By-election, 14 June 1934 (Gwent Record Office); *Electors, Which Will You Have?*' Leaflet for Mr. H. Weston-Sparkes, Coalition and Unionist candidate general election 1922 (Devon Record Office, Exeter).

38. *South Shields Parliamentary Election, 29 October 1929*, leaflet for Will Lawther (Tyne and Wear Archive).

39. *Parliamentary General Election, 1929 – South Edinburgh Division*, leaflet for Arthur Woodburn (National Library of Scotland).

40. *The Liberal Candidates*, 1924 general election leaflet for Major L. Andrew Common and I. C. Hannah (Tyne and Wear Archive).

41. Quoted in J. Ramsden, *The Age of Balfour and Baldwin*, p. 119.

42. Minutes of the Bedwellty Divisional Labour Party, 29 September 1918 (Gwent Record Office).

43. 'Letter from Beatrice Webb to the Women Electors', undated (Durham Record Office); *Why Women Should Vote Labour* (London, undated).

44. Minutes of the Harborough Conservative Association, 29 March 1919 (Leicestershire Record Office).

45. *Vote for Headlam*, Leaflets for the 1931 and 1935 general elections (Durham Record Office); *To the Electors*, Leaflet for the 1929 general election (Durham Record Office).

46. B. Pimlott, *Hugh Dalton* (London, 1995 edition), p. 176–77.

47. H. Beynon and T. Austrin, *Masters and Servants: Class and Patronage in the Making of a Labour Organisation* (London, 1994), p. 311.

48. The Labour Party did not compile individual membership figures before 1928. Even so, affiliation fees to the party were worked out on the basis that each party division had 180 and, from 1930, 240 members.

49. Minutes of the Darlington Conservative Association, 29 March 1927; Minutes of the Stockton and Thornaby Constitutional Organisation, 1923–30 (Durham Record Office).

50. M. Callcott, 'The Nature and Extent of Political Change', p. 218.

51. Minutes of the Harborough Women's Conservative and Unionist Association, 1925–33 (Leicestershire Record Office)

52. Annual Report of the Darlington Conservative Association, 29 April 1938.

53. For just two examples, see Minutes of the Newport Labour Party, 26 August 1935 (LSE) and Minutes of the Darlington Labour Party, 31 May 1922 (Durham Record Office).

54. The entries of party and association minute books make this something of an assumption. It is based on the fact that women were consistently in the minority on a party or association's decision-making committee.

55. Minutes of the Harborough Conservative Association, 12 October 1935 (Leicestershire Record Office); Minutes of the Stockton and Thornaby Women's Unionist Association, 9 February 1923 (Durham Record Office).

56. Minutes of the Tiverton Liberal Association, 6 December 1929 (Devon Record Office).

57. Minutes of the Stockton and Thornaby Women's Unionist Association, 1923–38 (Durham Record Office).

58. Minutes of the Loughborough Labour Party Women's Section, 1934–40 (Leicestershire Record Office).

59. Minutes of the Durham Women's Advisory Council, 1920–37 (Durham Record Office).

60. Minutes of the Stockton Branch of the Junior Imperial League, 1937 (Durham Record Office).

61. Minutes of the Leicestershire Liberal Association, 23 July 1919 (Leicestershire Record Office).

62. M. Perry, 'The Jarrow Crusade's Return: The 'New Labour Party' of Jarrow and Ellen Wilkinson MP', *Northern History*, 39 (2002).

63. Minutes of the Totnes Division Liberal Association, 1924–39 (Totnes Liberal Democrats Constituency Office).

64. 'Letter from Sir William Robertson to Mr Anderson' 14 December 1920, in Minutes of the Scottish Liberal Federation (NLS).

65. *Edinburgh Evening News*, 20, 23 and 24 November 1923.

66. Minutes of the Leicester Liberal Committee, 19 December 1935 (Leicestershire Record Office).

67. Minutes of the Socialist League – Gateshead Branch, 1932–36 (Tyne and Wear Archive).

68. Minutes of the Harborough Conservative Association, 1933–56 (Leicestershire Record Office).

69. Annual Report of the Darlington Conservative Association, 8 April 1938.

70. Minutes of the Bedwellty Divisional Labour Party, 1918–54 (Gwent Record Office).

71. Minutes of the Torquay Conservative Association, 1932–39; Minutes of the North Edinburgh Unionist Association, 12 April 1933 (Edinburgh City Archive).

72. Minutes of the Tiverton Divisional Liberal Association, 16 November 1934 (Durham Record Office).

73. The best account remains D. Marquand, *Ramsay MacDonald* (London, 1977), pp. 651–53 and pp. 668–71. Relevant material is deposited in the Durham Record Office. We should, perhaps, also note the case of Evan Davies in Ebbw Vale, whose 'shameful neglect' of his duties in parliament and his constituency eventually led the divisional party to replace him with Aneurin Bevan in 1929. See J. Campbell, *Nye Bevan: A Biography* (London, 1994), pp. 28–29.

74. *Annual Report of the Edinburgh and District Trades and Labour Council for year ending 31 March 1933* (LSE); Minutes of the Newport Labour Party, 2 December 1920, 15 March 1935 and 10 February 1936 (LSE).

75. Minutes of the Newport Labour Party, 14 December 1926 (LSE); Minutes of the Stockton and Thornaby Constitutional Organisation, 23 February 1931 (Durham Record Office).

Chapter 3

Following the Procession: Scottish Labour, 1918–45

Catriona Macdonald

The orchestrated Labour ranks of the 1925 May Day procession in Edinburgh amassed in 'sections' depicting the themes 'Agitation', 'Education', and 'Demonstration', and were followed by a series of tableaux. One of these, representing the themes 'Disunity' and 'Unity' showed on one side, 'the organisations pulling against each other, and the capitalist amusing himself' while on the other, the workers were united, 'pulling the capitalist, with the result he was prostrate'.[1] Around 3,000 activists made up the procession that year which ended at a rally in the Meadows, but it was estimated that an equal number followed the procession on the pavement. A local Labour journal commented: 'Edinburgh's respectability has a long way to travel yet.'[2]

Edinburgh citizens were not alone in Scotland in their tendency to follow at one remove the evolution of the Labour presence in the public life of the Scottish nation. And disunity marked the real as much as the imagined world of the Labour Party north of the border. In many ways, one might suggest, Labour's experience in Scotland in these years was very similar to much that was happening in England and Wales, where many constituencies flirted with their new Labour suitors and the Labour message was regularly lost in the cacophony of competing voices from the left.[3] But similar experiences frequently have divergent causes and are regularly interpreted in quite different ways. The principal hallmark of *Scottish* Labour's experience in the interwar years is to be found in how it dealt with its past, and the past of the wider political community. We discover it in its response to Liberalism's long death; in the legacy of wartime militancy and the reputations made in the Red Clyde years; in the faltering success of Labour 'on the ground'; in the strength of the Independent Labour Party (ILP), and in Labour's contradictory relationship with Scottish nationalism.

The Strange Death of Liberal Scotland

Liberalism was a faith in Edwardian Scotland, and the Liberal Party a broad church – supported as readily by Irish Catholics as Presbyterian Scots – in which believers found communion and leadership. In the years before 1914, Labour had regularly attempted to storm this citadel, but had been convincingly repulsed. Scottish

Liberals, confident in their supremacy, had no need for pacts with the minority Labour interest, as was the case in England. Only two Labour MPs were returned in Scotland in 1906, and while Labour in Scotland drew consolation in a rising share of the poll at by-elections over the next four years (though it never rose above 30 per cent), it failed to win another seat. In January 1910 Labour fought 11 Scottish seats at the general election, winning only two (in England and Wales 67 were fought and 38 won), and 11 months later a mere five Scottish candidates stood at the second general election of that year and only three were returned (in England and Wales 51 candidates stood and 38 seats were retained).[4] Thereafter, in the five by-elections fought by Scottish Labour in the immediate pre-war years, its share of the poll seldom rose above 20 per cent.

War challenged the faith of many Scottish Liberals, but it would not be until the 1930s that Labour would finally eclipse the party of Gladstone as the main opposition to the triumphant Unionism that emerged in the interwar years. In Scotland, electoral pacts between Coalition Liberal and Unionist interests in some areas extended well beyond the official break-up of the Coalition in 1922, offering artificial sustenance to Liberalism. (In November 1922, the *Glasgow Herald* could affirm that 'Here in Scotland there is a firm and loyal understanding between Unionists and Liberals'.) In other areas, the re-unification of the Liberal Party in Scotland in 1924, after the fissures and fall-outs of the war years, turned the tide of Liberal decline, and breathed new life into local organisations across the country. Then again, in the 1930s, strategic co-operation with Unionists at election time to hold at bay the left wing 'menace' attracted votes, if not adherents, to the (National) Liberal cause. Put simply, it took longer for Liberalism to die in Scotland than might at first appear, and how Labour dealt with this state of affairs is telling.

In 1924, negotiations surrounding a pact between Unionists and Liberals nationwide, uniting the 'house of the Moderates' against a 'common enemy', rested on decisions taken in Paisley.[5] Here, Herbert Asquith was defending a seat held by Liberals since 1832, which in 1924 was at risk of returning the Labour convert, Rosslyn Mitchell. In the end, local Unionists agreed to leave the way open for a straight fight between Asquith and the Labour candidate, and thus ensured that in 28 seats across western Scotland (around 85 across the country) Labour would face a 'combined enemy'.[6]

In Paisley, the pact failed to ensure Asquith's victory: Mitchell turned a six per cent Liberal victory (in 1923) into a seven per cent Labour victory. Indeed, for local Liberals, it brought about an organic crisis in the constituency. Referring in their annual report to the pact as an 'unwanted child of doubtful parentage', Dr McKenna, the chairman of the Liberal Association in the burgh, attracted unanimous support from members when he proposed that 'never again, so far as the present generation was concerned, would anything in the nature of a "Pact" be entertained'.[7] The pact – or more particularly the ways in which Labour exploited the pact – had lost the seat for Liberalism. More significantly, it had also lost to the Liberals any claim they had had on the radical tradition of the burgh. The local press asked: 'did the old Radical traits of the constituency so far disapprove of Toryism as to refuse to have any co-operation with it at all?'[8]

The way in which Labour exploited the *meaning* of the pact in Paisley throws light on how Scottish Labour 'on the ground' came to overwhelm the Liberal faith by claiming its icons, speaking its language and 'owning' its past. Hugh Roberton, founder of the Glasgow Orpheus Choir, spoke at Mitchell's opening demonstration:

> The Labour Party was not a new party, and it carried on the old traditions of the Chartists, the Radicals and the Land Leaguers, and was the lineal descendant of the Paisley weavers of 100 years ago (Cheers). Radicalism kept Liberalism alive, the old passionate desire for progress, but Liberalism was not only dead today, but was going to be buried in the bowels of Conservatism.[9]

Beyond the bounds of Paisley, others drew a lesson from the pact. In a letter published by the Ayr Burghs Labour Party in support of their candidate, John Airlie, A. MacCallum Scott, the late MP for Bridgeton and Lloyd George Liberal Whip for Scotland, decried the lack of a Liberal lead ('In order to save his own seat in Paisley, Mr Asquith has entered into a compact with the Tories'), and instead the Labour alternative was acclaimed. ('The programme put forward by the Labour Party in this election is one which Liberals can support, and most Liberals would rather see in power a Labour Government ... than a reactionary Tory Government pledged to Protection'.)[10]

Generally, across Scotland, Labour victories were achieved not through the denial of the Liberal ethos, but through the appropriation of its vocabulary of popular collectivism and the moral economy in its local form. But, at times, the party's claims on a Liberal past could be disabling. In 1935, the Melrose and Newtown St Boswells Labour Party branches confirmed that they did not support contesting the general election in their constituency as the Liberal candidate was 'a progressive individual who would reflect the majority of their opinions in the House of Commons'. The chairman of the constituency party agreed.[11]

Red Clyde and Reputation

In December 1918,

> headed by a gigantic Red Flag, ten thousand Socialists in procession marched from St Andrews Halls to George Square ... [Amid] shouts of 'Fall in', the huge multitude soon stepped into line and Sauchiehall Street was taken by storm. They marched along the principal thoroughfare from Charing Cross to George Square, singing all the Socialist songs, interspersed with cheers for John MacLean and the social revolution ...[12]

The reluctant marchers of Edinburgh are replaced here with a red ribbon of (capitalised) Socialists in Glasgow. The contrast is stark, but is it appropriate?

The years of conflict and the immediate aftermath of the Great War gifted Scotland a generation of Labour leaders whose personalities dominate much of what we know about this period.[13] They also appeared to confirm the more militant nature of Scottish Labour politics, and became the starting point of historiographical debates regarding 'Red Clydeside'.[14] But how representative were these Labour leaders of the movement in general? How successful was Scottish Labour in these years? And to what extent did the Red Clyde colour Scotland as a whole?

James Maxton (1885–1946), John Wheatley (1869–1930), Tom Johnston (1881–1965), Patrick Dollan (1885–1963) and Davie Kirkwood (1872–1955): the personalities that people Labour's interwar story in Scotland are almost iconic. Together they are frequently taken to personify a wider militancy pervading Scottish Labour as a whole. After all, it was Maxton who most energetically sought a socialist revival in the Labour Party in the late 1920s, and it was Maxton who led the ILP out of the Labour Party in 1932.[15] Wheatley produced the only notable welfare legislation of the first Labour administration in the shape of effective central government grants for housing, and Johnston made an early reputation for himself as the passionate journalist and editor of *Forward* – the organ of Clydeside Labour.

But the interwar years were to be a significant turning point for many of these men, and for all their early successes, they failed to provide the Scottish movement with effective leadership. The animosities that built up around them held the movement back. Some maintained the uncompromising stance of their younger years and distanced themselves from their more conciliatory erstwhile Red Clyde comrades. For example, Dollan's decision to remain within the Labour Party after ILP disaffiliation in 1932 led to problems with Maxton, who claimed the moral high ground. Even in the midst of a Second World War, Dollan was 'ill at ease' sharing a platform with Maxton and other Scottish ILPers at the unveiling of a bust of Keir Hardie in Glasgow's Kelvingrove Gallery.[16] Others, like Tom Johnston and Emmanuel Shinwell, became increasingly moderate (or simply strategic) in their views in the 1930s, and seemed to leave behind them the passions (or at least the style) of Clydeside on arrival in London. Emrys Hughes, editor of *Forward* from 1924, reflected on Johnston's elevation to the position of secretary of state for Scotland in 1941:

> The wheel turned full circle. Tom Johnston had been the most bitter critic of the Lloyd George Coalition and the Labour Ministers in it. Now he was in the Churchill government and, in *Forward,* I was taking much the same line as he had taken in the First World War.[17]

The Clyde did not run 'red' for long, it seems.

Reputations linger, however, long after that which gave them substance fades. It did not take long for 'Clydeside' to become a by-word for militancy, and just a little longer before 'Scottish' was adopted as convenient shorthand to denote radical sensibilities. In Dumbarton, Davie Kirkwood – one-time treasurer of the wartime Clyde Workers' Committee (CWC) – polled the largest number of votes cast for a Labour candidate in Scotland in the 1918 general election; Shinwell – sentenced to five months' imprisonment for his role in the George Square riot of January 1919 – was elected as Linlithgow's first Labour MP in 1928; and in 1935

Willie Gallacher (1881–1965), the former chairman of the CWC, was elected Communist MP for West Fife. So, clearly, the rhetoric of Clydeside had a resonance furth of Glasgow long after 1918. Elsewhere in the wider labour movement, Scotland also appeared to take the lead in the politicisation of working-class issues. From as early as 1901, the chairman of the Scottish Co-operative Wholesale Society had commented that, 'Co-operators across the border are not as frightened as their English brethren of a new departure (into politics)'.[18] And, in 1920, James Lucas would reflect that Scottish Co-operators had been 'keen politicians ... and followed the polemics of politicians with the same fervour that their ancestors had followed the polemics of theologians'.[19] But how deep did such 'fervour' go?

While prominent Scots may have earned a militant reputation for themselves in the interwar years, labour organisations and the wider membership were more cautious. The Labour Party's Scottish Advisory Council was so determined in the 1920s to prohibit Communist infiltration into Scottish branches that basic organisation was neglected.[20] Even in the ILP following disaffiliation, while many branches co-operated with the Communist Party, the majority of Scottish branches voted in 1934 to limit co-operation in future to 'anti-war, unemployment, German relief, or other such specific issues as they arise'.[21] Among the Scottish Co-operators, disinterest in political affairs proved a problem: James Deans, the secretary of the Scottish Section of the Co-operative Union, noted in 1922,

> Our membership has grown far beyond its own knowledge of principles, and large numbers who buy in the co-operative stores know no more and care no more for the creation of a co-operative system of trade and employment than if the idea had never been proposed.[22]

And, in trades councils, there was frequently a marked reluctance to engage with militant tactics. The Edinburgh District Trades and Labour Council noted in 1921, that:

> Political revolutionary heroics do not readily accord with the temperament of the men and women who made up the great body of our people, and there is accumulating evidence that our Council and Party will continue from strength to strength in their real progress to permanent emancipation from wagery [sic] by leading the workers to Governmental power.[23]

In many ways, the powerful imagery of the events which together made up the Red Clyde years and the strident personalities that peopled these times have distorted the historiography of interwar Scottish Labour. Conventional readings of Scotland as somehow more radical or more militant than the rest of Britain stand in need of reassessment. The evidence is compelling if we look to the grass roots across a range of issues. In Edinburgh, the Central Socialist Sunday School recorded a limited and near static membership throughout the 1920s of less than 30 and, throughout the interwar years, Labour periodicals bemoaned the apathy of voters.[24] In 1919, no Labour education authority candidates got in on the first count in Glasgow, and all the Labour successes of that year (bar Maxton's) were as a result of the Catholic vote.[25] Six years later, Edinburgh's *Labour Standard* complained that the working class looked on education as of less importance than 'a street corner brawl'.[26] But, at times, the Labour Party itself could prove slow in appreciating the significance of the 'big questions'. In 1922, the unemployed in Paisley complained bitterly about the party's failure to 'organise the unemployed on a proper basis' and, at the parish council elections of that year, the party paid the price for its inattentiveness when independent 'Unemployed' candidates stood against its nominees for elected office.[27]

If we turn to Labour's performance in organisation and the parliamentary elections of the interwar years, it becomes clear that Scottish Labour had much to learn.

'Other Ways of Looking at Things ...': Labour on the Ground

In 1931, Joseph Duncan, of the Scottish Farm Servants Union offered some advice in the pages of *Forward*:

> There are times when it is well to remember that there are other rivers in Scotland than the Clyde, and that the folks who dwell in their Straths have other ways of looking at things ...[28]

Away from the central belt and beyond Scotland's major conurbations, the Labour Party did poorly in the 1920s and early 1930s. Only with the appointment of a special organiser in 1933 did things begin to change. Until then, numerous problems beset Labour activists seeking to broaden Labour's appeal, and even after this, the experience of Labour at the grass roots shows a party often battling to stay alive.

The experiences of the Roxburgh and Selkirk Divisional Labour Party illustrate many of Labour's predicaments, and are offered here as something of a case study of Labour's experiences beyond the Clyde Basin. Encompassing many of the textile and market towns of the Scottish Borders, and a dispersed farming community, Labour activists became increasingly alive to the challenges they faced when, in 1923, their candidate, George Dallas, came in third behind Conservative and Liberal opposition with only 6,811 votes.[29] Within months, moves were afoot to establish women's sections in the area and appoint an organiser. A women's section was established in Hawick in December 1923, and John Airlie (Labour's former parliamentary candidate for Ayr) was duly appointed to the organiser's post by the close of 1924 at significant cost to the individual branches making up the division. (The Hawick Labour Party, with only 126 members in January 1925, pledged £100 to the organiser's salary.[30])

The enthusiasm which greeted such initiatives, however, dissipated. The women's section in Hawick appeared to grow from strength to strength in its early years, with membership increasing from 94 in January 1924 to 137 four months later. But a lengthy break in its minute books from 1931 to 1949 is telling. Both in March 1949 and March 1952, attempts were made to re-form the now defunct women's section. In February 1953, the majority of members voted that the section be wound up 'owing to lack of enthusiasm'.[31]

The hopes engendered by the appointment of an organiser were also found to be illusory: by the end of 1925, Airlie's position had been terminated, and he left under a cloud of controversy having achieved little in the Borders. Two years later, George Dallas declined the division's invitation to stand again as the Labour parliamentary candidate. He noted in March 1927: 'the position (in the constituency) was most disappointing and ... he had hoped for much better results than were in evidence'.[32] A month later, he confirmed: 'I do not think the Divisional Party are doing justice to the Party, nor to the candidate in continuing the very inefficient methods of organising the constituency.'[33]

Attempts *had* been made at divisional level to offer direction: the local executive published a report in 1926 emphasising its policy of 'concentration, consolidation and development', and instructing established branches to distribute leaflets in adjacent areas and pay increased attention to the registration of Labour voters.[34] The region also boasted its own Labour journal at this time, the *Border Observer*. But fundamental problems dogged Labour in the Borders and, indeed, elsewhere in Scotland: there was often disunity among Labour ranks on the ground and – at times – an inclination to lose sight of political goals. Restricted finances could limit activities, as could a lack of suitable parliamentary and municipal candidates for office. Membership declined in many areas in the 1930s, and the social, religious and class profile of local voters frequently offered barriers to expansion that Labour was ill-equipped to address.[35]

Hawick branch members regularly felt neglected by a division dominated by members from Galashiels, and – suspicious of waste – frequently encouraged greater economy on the part of divisional representatives.[36] In the 1930s, Hawick also found itself out of step with the policy of the Parliamentary Labour Party. In August 1931, its members unanimously agreed that 'those members of the late cabinet who had resigned rather than reduce the benefit of the unemployed' were to be congratulated[37]: the Constituency Labour Party (CLP) reflected that 'the chances of Hawick sending delegates to the CLP for the coming year were very doubtful'.[38] Thereafter, in 1939, leaders of the local Hawick party defended their part in Popular Front activities at a time when the CLP blamed 'the Leadership of the party in Home and Foreign Affairs' for the 'non-activity' within the constituency.[39]

Elsewhere in Scotland, similar division is evident. The Dalkeith Labour Party in March 1939 'expressed dissatisfaction with the methods the divisional Labour Party had of conducting business' and the town's Labour councillor, Mr Smith, indicated that he would be leaving the divisional party on a related issue.[40] Then, in 1941 and 1942, further discord between branch and division was evident over the matter of fees, and a year later the divisional party refused to 'betray the principles which brought the Labour Party into being by voting Tory' at a local by-election, despite the national political truce agreed by all the major parties.[41]

Branches could also be regularly distracted by matters hardly pertinent to organisation and the higher points of socialist principle. In 1932, the Annual General Meeting of the Hawick Labour Party was dominated by a complaint about gambling in the party rooms; six years later, the future of Dalkeith's carpet bowls equipment excited controversy[42]; and during the first months of the Second World War, the South Ward Labour Party branch in Leith was aggrieved by the dancers at its regular 'Socials' tampering with the party's wireless.[43] As early as 1925, the secretary of the North Ayrshire Labour Party (A. W. Brady) complained to John Airlie that 'the good comrades we have here are far too much concerned about socials and whist drives and what not's [sic] that they haven't time for the practical affairs of the movement'.[44] Even new branches could prove easily distracted: in Edinburgh's Merchiston Ward Labour Party, established in 1944, the organisation of a fund-raising garden party dominated early discussions to the exclusion of much else. Mr Boyle's difficulties in securing a piper for the Highland dancing display, his success in hiring a fortune teller, Lola Chand ('Mystic of the East'), and the services of Bimbo the clown are finely detailed in the minutes of this middle-class branch.[45]

Economic dislocation caused by the worldwide depression brought serious financial worries for Labour that could not be easily solved by 'socials'. In Hawick, the local party's credit balance had dropped to £41 by 1930.[46] At the general election in 1929, the local Labour candidate, Robert Gibson, contributed at least £170 to his own election expenses and, in 1932, the costs to the Roxburgh and Selkirk division for the repair of its typewriter (£2/15s) amounted to more than a fifth of its total monies.[47] A year after they tampered with the wireless, Leith's Labour dancers were in want of a venue as the local Labour branch ended its weekly socials 'to save the Ward useless expenditure'.[48] Lack of suitable candidates for party and elected offices was also often problematic. In 1926, the Hawick Labour Party failed to come up with any candidates for the municipal elections and, in Leith, it was anticipated in 1945 that the party would have difficulty in getting candidates for the November municipal contests, 'as so many members of the working class cannot afford to lose wages for time lost'.[49]

Both financial and candidature problems were either exacerbated by or founded on membership difficulties. In 1926, Hawick Labour Party boasted 124 members (excluding the women's section). A year later, however, it was found that only 88 had actually paid their annual subscriptions to the local branch.[50] For other branches, declining numbers were the cause of difficulties. Hawick and Galashiels for the most part held on to their members in the early 1930s, but Newtown St Boswells had only 20 members by 1935, Jedburgh had 16, and in Selkirk – with just nine members – it was noted that the local branch had 'great difficulty in maintaining interest'.[51] By 1938, the Galashiels branch was reported to be 'very inactive', while the Selkirk, Melrose, Kelso and Newtown branches were no longer affiliated to the constituency party. Thereafter, an attempt to reactivate the Kelso branch in 1939 foundered and, by 1940, the Selkirk, Melrose and Newtown branches had disbanded. Whist drives and socials sustained most Labour Party branches throughout the war years, as the regularity of branch meetings declined, but such activities did little to address the complex social and cultural challenges that Labour had been facing across Scotland since 1918, if not before.

As the example of Merchiston shows, the Labour Party was slow in establishing its presence in middle-class constituencies. Elsewhere, it faced the challenge of the influence of the landed elite: in rural areas, Joseph Duncan emphasised in 1931 that the 'farmers and small-holders vote with the lairds and their satellites'.[52] And in Lanarkshire and Ayrshire – home to the largest concentration of Irish immigrants in Scotland – Labour faced the sectarian divide. Labour's success in attracting the Catholic vote, following its support of the Education (Scotland) Act of 1918 that facilitated municipal funding for Catholic schools, and the establishment of the Irish Republic in 1922, did much to challenge the Presbyterian dominance (if not the rhetoric) that had characterised the early Labour Party in Scotland. But there was a price to be paid: many grew suspicious of Catholic influence in the Labour leadership, and working-class Unionists came to fear the implications of Labour victory for the unity of the Kingdom. In Ayrshire, for example, Ms Francombe was expelled from the Star of the West Ladies' Orange Lodge in 1924, 'owing to [her] having voted Socialist Labour' at the recent election.[53] By 1939, Labour may have come to terms with difficulties such as these across Scotland, but it had not fully addressed them, nor successfully dealt with their most pernicious influences.

Labour's electoral performance in the interwar years confirms the reality of a party whose managerialist rhetoric belied a patchy and inconsistent organisation on the ground.[54] Relative to the party south of the border, Scottish Labour performed well in the 1920s, but the debacle of 1931 dealt Scottish Labour a blow from which it failed to fully recover even by the eve of war. Nevertheless, growth was incremental if slow. Labour's share of the vote[55] increased from 32.6 per cent to 41.8 per cent between 1931 and 1935, and Labour built well on earlier success. But what delivered a Labour victory in interwar Scotland?

In 1929, George Mathers' election agent in West Edinburgh described how the local party had secured this new seat for Labour: 'It was the triumph of the living organism over the inanimate machinery of both our political opponents', he noted.

> The reaping of the harvest had not been left to the last hectic weeks of electioneering before the polling day. It had meant grinding away for months at the hard, thankless task of creating machinery when the crucial test arrived ... The MacDonald letter, distributed to every working class home, put the stamp of efficiency on our candidate's credentials. It epitomized Labour's fitness to govern. The rail ticket, too, was appropriate and spectacular. *First Class to Westminster* was the motto blazoned on one side. On the other, our message read:
> 1923 – Third
> 1924 – Second
> 1929 – First
> *You* can do it.
> Few would deny ... that the public were profoundly impressed by our advertisements in press, in house windows and hoardings.[56]

The model here of a party cultivating an almost 'organic' relationship with its locality appears compelling. But if we look to Labour's performance in interwar by-elections, we quickly discover it was far from typical. Indeed, Labour lost Edinburgh West in 1931.[57]

Labour gained only four *new* seats at by-elections in Scotland during the interwar years: Bothwell (July 1919), Kirkcaldy Burghs (March 1921), Dumbartonshire (March 1936) and Greenock (November 1936). At one remove from the passions, personalities and national questions which typically dominate general elections, these contests are a useful 'measure' of the local determinants of Labour's fortunes. In each case, we discover that the strategies of the local Labour machine were rarely the telling factor in delivering success, and at times Labour won despite itself.

The industrial character of the constituency and contemporary economic conditions had a significant impact on the outcome of all the by-elections. Bothwell was overwhelmingly a mining constituency, on the brink of facing new economic realities at the end of the Great War. At the 1919 by-election, the 'well kent' Labour candidate, John Robertson of the Scottish Miners' Union, faced as his sole opponent the Liberal Coalitionist, Provost James Moffat – the commercial manager of the Wemyss Coal Company. The choice for the constituency could not have been more stark at a time when 6s per ton had been added to the price of coal, and fortunes seemed bleak.[58] Not surprisingly, class issues (notably housing), and the question of nationalisation loomed large in the election.[59] Similarly, in Kirkcaldy, the Labour candidate, Thomas Kennedy, a political organiser, faced Sir Robert Lockhart – a former Provost of the burgh and a senior partner in a linen manufacturing enterprise. At the time of the election, short-time was being worked in local factories, and a three-day week had begun in the mines in the north east of the constituency.[60]

Religion also played a part. It was estimated that while Bothwell's Provost Moffat had secured the 4,000-strong Orange vote, Robertson benefited greatly from his 'understanding' with the Irish League.[61] In Kirkcaldy, Kennedy – aided by the support of T.P. O'Connor – absorbed the 2,000 or so 'Irish votes'.[62] Equally, a poor choice of anti-Labour candidate and the disunity of Labour's opponents worked in the party's favour. As industrialists, Labour could easily lampoon Moffat and Lockhart in their rhetoric and electioneering. And, in Greenock, the choice of an Englishman unknown to the burgh as the National Liberal candidate in 1936 was hardly a sensitive one. Even the president of the local Liberal Association admitted that many Liberal voters had not supported V.E. Cornelius on polling day.[63] In Dumbartonshire, the votes given to a Scottish Nationalist candidate in 1936 effectively delivered the seat to Labour. (The Nationalist, Robert Gray, attracted 2,599 votes, and Thomas Cassells' Labour majority was a mere 984 votes.)

Voter apathy also worked in Labour's favour: in Kirkcaldy and Dumbartonshire small polls were recorded. The Scotsman commented in 1921 that, 'At first blush it might be imagined that the Kirkcaldy electors are incapable of enthusiasm'.[64] Similarly, at the Dumbartonshire by-election, where the National government lost its first seat since the general election of 1935, it was noted that: 'Few elections in recent years have been attended by such marked apathy on the part of the constituency'.[65] In each of the four by-elections, suspicions were roused that many of Labour's opponents had simply stayed home on polling day.

Labour fortunes owed much to the peculiarities of local circumstance, as did the strength and character of its organisation. Across Scotland, contrasting and frequently conflicting experiences 'on the ground' made up the Labour story in the interwar years – a story that resists neat generalisations, challenges established reputations, and questions the inevitability of Labour's rise to power.

'Small and Intimate': The ILP in Scotland

For most of its early history, the ILP *was* the Labour Party in Scotland. John Wheatley, James Maxton, Patrick Dollan and Ramsay MacDonald amongst many others all entered the Labour Party via the ILP. And even in the 1920s, its profile in Scotland was higher than it was elsewhere in Britain. By 1925, the ILP in Scotland boasted 297 branches and, in the 1929 general election, 67 out of Labour's 68 candidates in Scotland were ILP members.[66]

The influence of the ILP on Labour policy, strategy and organisation in Scotland is a distinctive feature of the interwar years. The ILP presence in Labour's ranks and its influence on outlook up to 1932 meant that Scottish Labour appeared more in tune with native sensitivities when, nationally, generic forms of organisation and policy from the centre were asserting an increasingly strong influence. But the power of this quasi-autonomous body could also prove problematic.

In 1918, Willie Stewart credited the ILP with sustaining Labour in the dark days of war. He noted: 'it was the ILP that held the pass for Labour during all these four years. And in the years to come Labour will derive its inspiration from the ILP.'[67] By the 1920s, while Labour recorded significant advances at the ballot box, its constituency associations remained rudimentary, riven by factionalism, and frequently non-existent. In 1927, the Scottish membership of the party stood at 11,000, out of a UK total of 300,000.[68] In contrast, ILP branches regularly fulfilled the role of 'keeping the Labour interest alive' via a wide range of social and political activities.[69] Indeed, senior Labour activists regularly acknowledged the merits of the ILP approach. Arthur Woodburn, secretary of the Scottish Council of the Labour Party between 1932 and 1939, noted:

> [ILP] branches were enthusiastic individuals who worked together as a team, socially friendly, and with their interests centred in their branch. The Labour Party is a federal party and when a Constituency Party meets it is a group of delegates from branches of trades unions, local labour parties and ward committees. The power of the Labour Party is therefore exercised by delegates who have only a periodic association. The ILP was small and intimate. The Labour Party by its very size could not have this advantage.[70]

In the 1920s, the ILP was to the fore in politicising domestic issues relevant to women voters across Scotland, organising women's groups to complement their established branches. The Guild of Youth was also established in 1924. And

Scotland benefited from grants from the national party: in 1921 alone, Scotland received £190 in grants from the National Administrative Council (NAC).

But even in the 1920s there were portends of future difficulties. In 1923, the ILP undertook a survey of its Scottish operations. It discovered that the Highland Federation was made up principally of branches within easy reach of Inverness, and no presence was recorded in Orkney, Shetland, most of Caithness, Sutherland or Ross and Cromarty. Aberdeen dominated the Northern Federation, and only faltering steps were being taken towards establishing branches in the coastal towns and port communities. Things looked better in the six federations in the central counties, but in Perthshire propaganda was intermittent and chiefly characterised by summer activities; in Fife, Communist and Social Democratic Federation (SDF) influence was causing difficulty; in Stirlingshire, the full-time organiser had recently been dispensed with due to declining funds; and, in Dumbartonshire, the north of the county was almost entirely neglected. Even in its industrial heartland, problems for the ILP were evident: branches in Ayrshire were suffering due to the difficulties and disputes in the mining industry, in Renfrewshire the federation was not coming up to expectations, in Lanarkshire religious differences were affecting Labour's progress, and in Edinburgh the report indicated that 'there is not the proper spirit amongst the Federation Officials'.[71] Clearly, organisational difficulties were not confined to the Labour Party.

Long before its final departure from the Labour Party, the ILP was not the positive asset many have suggested. In 1920, Francis Johnson wrote to Willie Stewart, the ILP's Scottish secretary, of his reluctance to finance an ILP candidature and propaganda in Argyll when a tangible return was doubtful.[72] Three years later, complaints were heard at a national level of the high grants awarded to the Scottish Division, when affiliation fees from north of the border were less than those received from other divisions.[73] In 1924, an appeal from the Scottish Divisional Council (SDC) for £150 to undertake a campaign in the Highlands was rejected, despite Patrick Dollan's persistent efforts to push Scotland's case.[74] In the end, a National Bazaar, held in Glasgow's McLellan Galleries in April 1927, aimed to raise £1,000 to fund 'propaganda and organisational work in rural, agricultural areas', but little real progress was made north of the 'Highland Line'.[75] The Reverend William Macfarlane would describe Aberfeldy as 'one of the Darkest Districts of one of the Darkest Constituencies' for the ILP in 1929.[76]

Even in Glasgow, progress was frequently faltering. In 1925, the Glasgow Federation complained of the inadequate grants given to candidates for election expenses, and the Reformers' Bookstall was losing money on a weekly basis.[77] Success at the Glasgow municipal elections of 1926 gave way to disappointment in 1927 when the majority of the Moderates on the council rose to an 'effectively insurmountable' level.[78] The ILP Scouts in Scotland showed little progress, with an annual turnover of less than £30 during the 1920s, and an active membership restricted to Dundee, Edinburgh, Paisley, Govan and a few other Scottish towns.[79] In Fife, the Kirkcaldy ILP branch were struggling in the late 1920s with debts of between £30 and £40, and the Newcraighall branch – amongst many others – felt unable to contribute to central funds in 1929, and complained that 'Socials and Dances have ... been a drain on our funds rather than a help'.[80]

Increasingly it was also becoming apparent that many ILP members were growing frustrated with the policies of the Labour Party leadership. The Reverend Richard Lee wrote to Henry Brailsford in 1924, describing a recent visit to Glasgow by Ramsay MacDonald:

> The PM comes to Glasgow and makes uplifting speeches with not a word of Socialism and not a word to satisfy reasonable enquiry ... At his arrival, there were not two hundred people who came to greet him. The rest were the usual promiscuous crowd who gather up to see a dog fight or such like ... My daughter says that any Tory could have made Mac's speech.[81]

Maxton's chairmanship of the ILP from 1925 set the national party on an increasingly leftward course, but he did not necessarily reflect more moderate Scottish sentiments. The Cook–Maxton Manifesto was unveiled in Glasgow in 1928, but the Scottish Divisional Council rejected it – the only division to do so.[82]

Nevertheless, the disaffiliation of the ILP from the Labour fold in 1932 was of critical importance for Scottish Labour in the 1930s. Scottish Labour lost some of its most famous 'names' and many elected officials (seven ILP councillors in Glasgow left the Labour Party). More significantly, ILP members who remained within the party – organised under Patrick Dollan as the Scottish Socialist Party (SSP) – were a persistent obstacle for Labour Party organisers.[83] As Woodburn noted, 'the existence of the SSP meant that Labour Party workers were divided and that the work was duplicated in many towns and villages'.[84]

The ILP presence in Scotland continued throughout the 1930s, but never matched its earlier influence. Disputes between the Glasgow Federation and the SDC distracted the party from the more important business of propaganda in 1937. Rooted in petty personality clashes, such discord reflected persistent differences within the party 'between those who take a consciously revolutionary view and those who concentrate on the immediate grievances of the working class'.[85] These were never resolved. Active branches like Shettleston persisted in their activities, hosting economics classes, Burns suppers and seaside outings. But here too there were problems. In August 1937, Shettleston demanded 'closer contact' with the SDC – a body that seemed increasingly distant, and announced that it was 'in acute need of funds' by December of that year.[86] As early as April 1939, Shettleston ILP supported re-affiliation to the Labour Party.[87]

The Second World War exacerbated the ILP's problems in the north. Between 1939 and 1940, the income of the SDC fell from £1,714 to £909, and its anti-war message had lost it support and brought it into conflict with its erstwhile sympathisers. The Communist, Willie Gallacher, who had been involved in the early stages of drafting of the Cook–Maxton Manifesto, reflected:

> [The ILP] has no policy. It is a bankrupt political rump, living on its past, incapable of assisting the workers, but capable of assisting reaction by deceiving, confusing and disrupting the working class movement.[88]

Even with another Scot at its helm (John McGovern, MP for Shettleston, became ILP chairman in 1941), problems persisted amongst ILP bodies in

Scotland. There was controversy in Edinburgh in 1941, and problems in the Glasgow Federation came to the fore again in 1942. In August 1945, Dan Carradice, the Scottish organiser for the party, resigned 'due to the impossible housing conditions under which he and his family had been compelled to live'.[89]

By the end of the Second World War, the ILP in Scotland was a beleaguered force whose leaders were leaving its ranks, and whose rhetoric and sniping from the sidelines achieved little.[90] The torch of socialism was now in other hands. Regrets and recriminations dogged the party: Jim Taylor – an active ILP member in Glasgow – wrote to Francis Johnson in November 1946,

> There are so few of us left now who travelled the road with Hardie and know the brand of Socialism for which he gave his life ... How is it possible for the Labour Party to take the road of international socialism and the co-operative commonwealth dominated and financed by a body that has hardly a nodding acquaintance with socialism of any kind? That's as I've seen the position for many years now.[91]

With the war won, a majority Labour government in power and the promise of a new Britain an alluring possibility, no one seemed to be listening. The ILP, by 1945, had lost its power to injure the Labour Party. Clearly, 1932 had been a turning point for Scottish Labour. ILP disaffiliation arguably separated the Labour Party from its historic constituency, but it also freed it from its most regressive tendencies. After that the ILP was condemned to live in the shadow of its past.

Pledges and Plans: Dealing with the Scottish Question

The opening lines of the Scottish Labour Party's *Plan for Post-War Scotland* (1941) recorded: 'We recognise the first broad principle that ... Scotland is a nation with its own traditions, customs and law and with problems not encountered or understood outside its borders'.

From its early beginnings, the Scottish Labour Party had supported Home Rule for Scotland; in 1918, James Maxton had co-founded the Scottish Home Rule Association.[92] But during the first half of the twentieth century, Labour's position on the 'Scottish Question' often appeared contradictory. Indeed, in only one official Labour Party general election manifesto during the period was devolution mentioned: in 1929, the manifesto recorded Labour's intention to 'support the creation of separate legislative assemblies in Scotland, Wales and England, with autonomous powers in matters of local concern'.[93] Evidence from the early interwar period would suggest that at times, and in certain circumstances, Scottish nationalism was important to the Labour Party, but by the 1930s Scotland's future was perceived as merely part of a wider plan for British economic and social renewal.

In 1924 and 1927, Labour MPs (to varying degrees) showed support for two very different Home Rule Bills, neither of which was successful. But at no time during the 1920s was devolution given high priority by Labour either in power or in opposition. Instead, Scottish Home Rule was accepted as part of the traditions of the Labour Party in the north, worthy of preservation but little more. Attention to Scottish matters rarely went beyond the re-phrasing of campaign literature to take account of Scottish sensitivities.[94]

For Scottish ILPers like Roland Muirhead (a director of *Forward* since 1906 and, having left the ILP in 1927, the first chairman of the National Party of Scotland – a forerunner of the Scottish National Party (est. 1934) – in 1928), this was not enough. He wrote to Ramsay MacDonald in 1925:

> I must candidly admit that the failure of your Government to make any serious attempt to pass a Scottish Home Rule Bill caused your stock as a Scotsman to fall heavily in my estimation ... Scotland is still wallowing in the glaur of slumdom – how long is it to remain there?[95]

While Muirhead abandoned Labour in 1927, others with nationalist sympathies remained in the movement and regularly drew the 'Scottish Question' to the attention of party leaders. In February 1928, George Mathers emphasised in a letter to Ben Shaw of the Labour Party's Scottish Council that 'there is a very great and growing urge for some freedom from purely Westminster government'.[96] His frustrations were evident in a letter penned later that month to Arthur Henderson that focused on the role of the party's Scottish administration:

> In the Annual Conferences of the Scottish Council of the Labour Party we have repeatedly passed resolutions in favour of Home Rule but there is no appearance of result ... more attention must be paid to Scottish opinion (regarding Scotland) by our National Party ... there should be room for Scotland as a separate country with a different outlook and sufficient national pride to sometimes resent being tacked on at the tail of England in respect of legislation and even in the pronouncements of our own Party.[97]

The Home Rule principle was important in its own right, but also threw into relief the Scottish party's inability to shape policy at a national level: there seemed to be a democratic deficit at the heart of the Labour Party.

Interest in devolution among Scotland's Labour rank-and-file at the time was evident, if not overwhelming. In 1924, countless co-operative societies (and the Scottish Co-operative Wholesale Society itself) pledged themselves to Home Rule in the north. The nationalist message even appeared in trade union publications: the Glasgow branch of the Union of Post Office Workers devoted the front page of its journal *St Mungo* to Scottish devolution in October 1936. But there was some ambivalence. In 1921, the Scottish Trades Union Congress, meeting in Aberdeen, overwhelmingly supported a resolution proposed by the Textile Workers (and seconded by the Scottish Union of Dock Labourers) in favour of Scottish Home Rule. But there were voices of discord: delegates from the Workers' Union and the Theatrical Employees Union considered Home Rule a distraction 'of no consequence to the working class'.[98]

In the 1930s, the solution to Scotland's ills was an integral part of Labour's love affair with planning. In the 1937 *Report of the Labour Party's Commission of*

Enquiry into the Distressed Areas (Central Scotland), the future was boldly addressed:

> We believe that prosperity can be brought to Central Scotland, but that it can only be done by thorough-going state action.
> Central Scotland must be considered as an economic unit, and its future must be planned.[99]

Extending into the managerial approach of Tom Johnston as Secretary of State for Scotland in Churchill's wartime cabinet, the Scottish Council of the Labour Party readily adopted corporatist rhetoric as a palliative – its bigger dreams of devolved government having been thwarted. In its *Plan for Post-War Scotland* (1941), the Scottish Council sought to guard against the scenario in which Scotland, 'left behind in post-war reconstruction [would be] ... treated as a 'region' of Britain – a kind of legislative after-thought for which ill-considered and hurriedly devised addenda are tacked to permissive Acts of Parliament.'[100] Similarly, when it came to the Highlands, Labour in 1945 suggested that 'only common sense, energy and large-scale *planned* development will save the Highlands in the post-war years. We must *plan* or perish.'[101]

If anything, however, interest in devolved government had been encouraged by the war. The Leith Divisional Labour Party was addressed on 'Scotland: Past and Present' in 1941, during one of its somewhat irregular wartime meetings.[102] And, in Merchiston, one of the first motions debated by this new branch in 1946 was 'That the survival of Scotland and her people depends on immediate self-government which is contrary to the policy of the Government'. This joint debate – in association with the local branch of the Scottish National Party (SNP) – was introduced by the SNP's Dr Robert McIntyre, the victor of the Motherwell by-election of the previous year.[103] Despite his failure to hold the seat at the 1945 general election, this Merchiston meeting recorded 'a clear majority' for the motion. It is unclear just how many new Labour converts sided with the SNP on this occasion.

In the party's *Notes for Labour and Co-operative Speakers in Scottish Constituencies* for the general election of 1945, Scottish Labour policy on self-government was made clear: 'A British Parliament for British Affairs and a Scottish Parliament for Scottish affairs'. And just in case there could be any confusion as to exactly what was meant, it added, 'Labour does not support Dominion status or complete autonomy'.[104] But, despite such clarification of policy, questions remained. Alex Anderson, the unsuccessful Labour candidate at the Motherwell by-election some months before scarcely mentioned devolved government during his campaign – despite facing a popular SNP opponent. Yet, Tom Johnston held constitutional reform to be a priority: in March 1945, he considered 'the worst form of government [to be] long-distance bureaucracy'.[105] Not surprisingly, when many of Scottish Labour held aloof from Scottish Covenant activities later in the decade, Johnston was to the fore. At the time, he complained, 'the divorcement between governors and governed becomes steadily worse ...

public ownership to me never meant a resting of ... [economic] control in some department or Board, 400 miles away'.[106]

The victory of Attlee's Labour Party in 1945 clearly promised to deliver much for which Scottish Labour activists had striven since 1918, but fears were real that something more than mere tradition was being lost.

Conclusion

Between 1918 and 1945, Scottish Labour sought to come to terms with its past and embrace its future. In doing so, different areas of Scotland responded differently to the circumstances of the times and generated local histories often quite at odds with the experience of Labour's National Executive Committee or the Parliamentary Labour Party. Discordant voices are to be heard across Scotland in this period, claiming Labour's inheritance and asserting its destiny. Put simply, there is no singular Scottish story of these years.

The Liberal legacy of the previous hundred years affected each area differently. But just as 'there is more to Welsh Labour than the politics of the coalfield', there is clearly more to Scottish Labour in these years than the politics of the Red Clyde.[107] Organisation on the ground could be patchy and inconsistent, and electoral victory did not always affirm the existence of a strong Labour presence on the ground. The ILP certainly gave Scottish Labour a distinct tenor in the 1920s and beyond, but even at the height of its powers, problems dogged the party in Scotland. Its disaffiliation in 1932 was significant, but in some ways merely confirmed what many had known for years: namely, that the Scottish Labour Party had moved on. Finally, in its contradictory relationship with Scottish nationalism, we are made aware of the important interface between local and national dynamics at the heart of the party, and of the pull of tradition even in a party intent on planning the future.

Taken together, in these areas experiences in Scotland were distinctive, if not exceptional. This is not to suggest that one can easily identify a singular Scottish perspective. Scottish Labour did not speak with one voice, nor were its protestations taken to reflect a tangible and singular *Scottish* position. Rather, Labour in Scotland was contested and contradictory, regionally diverse, and marked by doctrinal conflict. The Labour procession took many routes.

Notes

1. *Labour Standard*, 9 May 1925.

2. *Ibid.*

3. See, for example, P. Thompson, *Socialists, Liberals and Labour: The Struggle for London, 1885–1914* (London, 1967); P. F. Clarke, *Lancashire and the New Liberalism* (Cambridge, 1971); K.O. Morgan, 'The New Liberalism and the Challenge of Labour: The Welsh Experience, 1885–1929', *Welsh History Review,* 5 (1972), pp. 288–312; J. Hill,

'Manchester and Salford Politics and the Early Development of the Independent Labour Party', *International Review of Social History*, 26, (1981), pp. 171–201; A. W. Purdue, 'The Liberal and Labour Parties in North-East Politics, 1900–14: The Struggle for Supremacy', *International Review of Social History*, 26, (1981), pp. 1–24; K. Laybourn and J. Reynolds, *Liberalism and the Rise of Labour, 1890–1918* (London, 1984); J. Smith, 'Class, Skill and Sectarianism in Glasgow and Liverpool, 1880–1914', in R.J. Morris (ed.), *Class, Power and Social Structure in British Nineteenth Century* Towns (Leicester, 1986); M. Savage, *The Dynamics of Working-Class Politics: The Labour Movement in Preston, 1880–1940* (Cambridge, 1987).

4. I.G.C. Hutchison, *A Political History of Scotland, 1832–1924* (Edinburgh, 1986), pp. 256–7.

5. *Paisley Daily Express*, 14 October 1924.

6. G. Brown, 'The Labour Party and Political Change in Scotland, 1918–29', Edinburgh University PhD (1981), pp. 331–44. The pact seems to have applied to 35 seats across Scotland.

7. Paisley Liberal Association Minute Books, 20 November 1924; *Annual Report, 1924* (Paisley Central Library).

8. *Paisley and Renfrewshire Gazette*, 1 November 1924.

9. *Paisley Daily Express,* 17 October 1924.

10. Airlie MS, 'Advice to Liberals', 1924, (National Library of Scotland; NLS). Scott joined the ILP in 1924.

11. Minutes of the Roxburgh and Selkirk Divisional Labour Party, 17 February 1935 (NLS).

12. *Forward*, 14 December 1918.

13. See W.W. Knox, *Scottish Labour Leaders, 1918–39* (Edinburgh, 1984).

14. See, for example, I. McLean, *The Legend of Red Clydeside* (Edinburgh, 1983); I. Donnachie, C. Harvie and I.S. Wood (eds), *Forward! Labour Politics in Scotland, 1888–1988* (Edinburgh, 1989); A. McKinlay and R.J. Morris (eds), *The ILP on Clydeside, 1893–1932: From Foundation to Disintegration* (Manchester, 1991); J. Foster, 'Red Clyde, Red Scotland', in I. Donnachie and C. Whatley (eds), *The Manufacture of Scottish History* (Edinburgh, 1992).

15. D. Howell, *MacDonald's Party: Labour Identities and Crisis, 1922–31* (Oxford, 2002), p. 280.

16., Letter from J. Taylor to Francis Johnson, 29 October 1939 (Francis Johnson Collection, ILP Archive).

17. E. Hughes, 'Forward and Backward', *The Guardian*, 1 April 1960.

18. Minutes of the National Administrative Council [NAC], 30 January 1901 (ILP Archive).

19. J. Lucas, *Co-operation in Scotland* (Manchester, 1920), p. 72.

20. I.G.C. Hutchison, *Scottish Politics in the Twentieth Century* (Basingstoke, 2001), p. 62.

21. NAC Minutes, 10–11 February 1934 (ILP Archive).

22. J. Deans, *Co-operative Memories: Reminiscences of a Co-operative Propagandist* (Manchester, 1922), p. 55.

23. *Annual Report of the Edinburgh and District Trades and Labour Council, 1921* (Edinburgh, 1921), p. 5.

24. Minutes of the Edinburgh Central Socialist Sunday School, 1924–31 (NLS).

25. *Forward*, 12 April 1919.

26. *Labour Standard*, 21 March 1925.

27. Trades and Labour Council Minutes, 25 January 1922 (Paisley Central Library).

28. 'Winning Scotland for Socialism', *Forward*, 13 July 1931.

29. Labour contested the Roxburghshire and Selkirkshire seat for the first time in 1918, when its candidate secured only 30 per cent of the vote in an election that saw a meager 55 per cent turnout. Labour did not contest the seat again until 1923, when Dallas' votes amounted to 26 per cent of the poll. Dallas stood again for the party in 1924, increasing his earlier tally by a mere 455 votes. Robert Gibson, who stood in the Labour interest in 1929 fared little better, securing only 28 per cent of the poll in an election which saw the Liberals narrow the gap with the successful Conservative candidate, the Earl of Dalkeith. No Labour candidate contested the 1931 election in the constituency, and at the by-election in 1935 necessitated by the succession of Dalkeith to the peerage as Duke of Buccleuch, the Labour candidate, J.A.C. Thomson, polled less than Dallas in 1923, securing only 6,099 votes. When, in 1945, Labour nationally celebrated a resounding victory at the polls, the local Labour candidate, L.P. Thomas, amassed 10,107 votes – Labour's highest poll yet, but this still represented less than 30 per cent of the electorate who cast their votes.

30. Minutes of the Hawick Labour Party, 20 December 1923, 28 February 1924, 27 January 1925 (NLS).

31. Hawick Labour Party Women's Section Minutes, 28 January 1924, 19 May 1924, 12 March 1949, 19 February 1953 (NLS).

32. Minutes of the Roxburgh and Selkirk Divisional Labour Party, 26 March 1927 (NLS).

33. *Ibid.*, 27 April 1927.

34. *Ibid.*, 9 May 1926.

35. Labour Party membership in Scotland declined after 1932: in 1939, the party in the north had only 29,159 members. By then, it was the 'smallest regional Labour Party in Britain'. W.W. Knox, *Industrial Nation: Work, Culture and Society in Scotland, 1800–Present* (Edinburgh, 1999), p. 248.

36. Minutes of the Hawick Labour Party, 21 July 1924, 26 July 1924 (NLS).

37. *Ibid.*, 25 August 1931,

38. Minutes of the Roxburgh and Selkirk Divisional Labour Party, 25 December 1932 (NLS).

39. Minutes of the Hawick Labour Party, 21 May 1939; Minutes of the Roxburgh and Selkirk Divisional Labour Party, 11 December 1939 (NLS).

40. Minutes of the Dalkeith Labour Party, March 1939, 4 February 1943 (NLS)

41. *Ibid.*, 1941 and 1942 *passim.*

42. Minutes of the Hawick Labour Party, 2 February 1932; Minutes of the Dalkeith Labour Party, 12 September 1935 (NLS).

43. Minutes of the Leith Divisional Party: South Ward Committee, 27 November 1939 (NLS).

44. Airlie MS, A.W. Brady to J. Airlie, 1925 (NLS).

45. Minutes of the Merchiston Ward Labour Party, 22 June 1944, 29 June 1944 (NLS).

46. Minutes of the Hawick Labour Party, 28 January 1930 (NLS).

47. Minutes of the Roxburgh and Selkirk Divisional Labour Party, 28 May 1932 (NLS).

48. Minutes of the Leith Divisional Party: South Ward Committee, 27 May 1940 (NLS).

49. *Ibid.*, 25 March 1945.

50. Minutes of the Hawick Labour Party, 1 February 1926, 1 February 1927 (NLS).

51. Minutes of the Roxburgh and Selkirk Divisional Labour Party, 19 January 1935 (NLS).

52. *Forward*, 9 May 1931.

53. Airlie MS, M. Armstrong (Ardrossan) to Sister Francombe, 22 November 1924 (NLS).

54. During the interwar years, the Labour Party in Scotland never entirely became the 'bland, professional, electoral machine' suggested by Knox (W.W. Knox, *Industrial Nation*, p. 247). Nevertheless, as he has noted elsewhere, the Labour Party in Scotland came increasingly to emphasise the significance of organisation and the management of the party in these years. See W.W. Knox and A. McKinlay, 'The Re-making of Scottish Labour in the 1930s', *Twentieth Century British History,* 6 (1995).

55. Includes ILP votes.

56. *Labour Standard*, 8 June 1929.

57. Mathers' majority of 2,829 in the 'three-horse race' of 1929 was transformed into a 18,703 majority for the Conservative candidate (W.G. Normand) in 1931, when no Liberal candidate stood for office in Edinburgh West. Mathers himself went on to re-take Linlithgow for Labour in 1935 – a seat held by Emmanuel Shinwell between 1928 and 1931.

58. *Glasgow Herald*, 14 July 1919.

59. *Ibid.*, 30 July 1919.

60. *Scotsman*, 19 February 1921, 26 February 1921.

61. *Glasgow Herald*, 14 July 1919.

62. *Scotsman*, 25 February 1921, 2 March 1921.

63. *Glasgow Herald*, 27 November 1936.

64. *Scotsman*, 22 February 1921.

65. *Glasgow Herald*, 18 March 1936.

66. Anon., *The Independent Labour Party in Scotland* (Glasgow, 1925), p. 5; W.W. Knox, *Industrial Nation*, p. 239.

67. *Forward*, 21 December 1918.

68. J.J. Smyth, *Labour in Glasgow, 1896–1936: Socialism, Suffrage and Sectarianism* (East Linton, 2000), p. 117.

69. I.G.C. Hutchison, *A Political History of Scotland,* p. 296.

70. Woodburn MS, 'Recollections' (Draft Form), pp. 76–77 (NLS).

71. Organisation Committee Minutes, Special Report (Division One) 1923 (ILP Archive).

72. NAC Minutes, 24 February 1920 (ILP Archive).

73. *Ibid.*, 15–16 November 1923.

74. *Ibid.*, 23–24 February 1924.

75. Scottish ILP, *National Bazaar, Souvenir Programme*, 29–30 April 1927.

76. Rev. W.A. Macfarlane (Manse of Dull, Aberfeldy) to Francis Johnson, 16 January 1929 (Francis Johnson Correspondence, ILP Archive).

77. NAC Minutes, 31 January 1925, 26–28 September 1925 (ILP Archive).

78. J.J. Smyth, *Labour in Glasgow*, p. 109.

79. National ILP Scouts (Scottish Council Accounts), 1912–33 (NLS).

80. William Lyon (Kirkcaldy) to Francis Johnson, 3 February 1919; John Kinnaird (Newcraighall) to Francis Johnson, 28 February 1929 (Francis Johnson Correspondence, ILP Archive).

81. Rev. R. Lee (Ross Street Unitarian Church, Glasgow) to H. Brailsford, 26 June 1924 Francis Johnson Correspondence, ILP Archive).

82. D. Howell, *MacDonald's Party*, p. 280.

83. See W.W. Knox and A. McKinlay, 'The Re-making of Scottish Labour', pp. 174–93; I. G. C. Hutchison, *Scottish Politics in the Twentieth Century*, p. 65.

84. Woodburn MS, 'Recollections', p. 70 (NLS).

85. 'Report of Glasgow Party Enquiry Committee, 1937', NAC Minutes (ILP Archive).

86. ILP Branches, Shettleston Minutes, 5 August 1937, 16 December 1937 (ILP Archive).

87. *Ibid.*, 6 April 1939.

88. W. Gallacher, *The Dodgers: An Exposure and Criticism of the ILP* (undated), p. 20.

89. NAC Minutes, 12 August 1945 (ILP Archive).

90. McGovern left in 1946 to join the Labour Party as did Campbell Stephen, MP for Camlachie in 1947.

91. Jim Taylor to Francis Johnson, 20 November 1946 (Francis Johnson Correspondence, ILP Archive).

92. I.S. Wood, 'The ILP and the Scottish National Question', in D. James, T. Jowitt and K. Laybourn (eds), *The Centennial History of the Independent Labour Party: A Collection of Essays* (Halifax, 1992), p. 63.

93. See I. Dale (ed), *Labour Party General Election Manifestos, 1900–97* (London, 2000).

94. Duncan MS, W. Henderson to J.F. Duncan, 4 October 1924 (NLS). Here, Henderson asks for help in the drafting of leaflets for circulation in Scotland, and 'the best way in which to present [Labour's] case to the Scottish electors'.

95. Muirhead MS, R. Muirhead to R. MacDonald, 19 June 1925 (NLS).

96. Mathers MS, G. Mathers to B. Shaw, 27 February 1928 (NLS).

97. *Ibid.*, 29 February 1928.

98. STUC, *Annual Report*, 20–23 April 1921, pp. 64–65.

99. *Report of the Labour Party's Commission of Enquiry into the Distressed Areas: Central Scotland* (London, 1937), p. 14.

100. *Plan for Post-War Scotland* (Labour Party Scottish Council, 1941), p. 3.

101. A.M. Weir, *Highland Plan: An Outline of Labour Policy for the Highlands* (Glasgow, 1945), p. 1 (My emphasis).

102. Leith Divisional Party: South Ward Committee Minutes, 25 May 1941 (NLS).

103. Merchiston Ward Labour Party Minutes, 28 February 1946 (NLS).

104. *Notes for Labour and Co-operative Speakers in Scottish Constituencies* (1945).

105. *Sunday Times*, 25 March 1945.

106. Johnston MS, Typescript article, undated (NLS).

107. D. Tanner, 'The Pattern of Labour Politics, 1918–39', in D. Tanner, C. Williams and D. Hopkin (eds), *The Labour Party in Wales, 1900–2000* (Cardiff, 2000), p. 113.

Chapter 4

'Happy Hunting Ground of the Crank'? The Independent Labour Party and Local Labour Politics in Glasgow and Norwich, 1932–45

Gidon Cohen

'[It] was really in the roots of the people, very close to them indeed' one activist recalled of the Glasgow Independent Labour Party (ILP) in the mid-1930s.[1] In Norwich, membership of the ILP even in the late 1940s was nearly double that of 1932. In both cities, Labour focussed much attention on, and reached electoral agreement with, the smaller party as well as relying on the ILP for control of the council. Such images and emphases sit uneasily alongside the conventional view of the ILP after it split from the Labour Party in 1932, that 'the wilderness reduced the party to a shambles, a sectarian shadow of its former self' and made it 'the happy hunting ground of the crank and the CP [Communist Party]'.[2] This chapter will explore this tension between the relative local success of the ILP in Glasgow and Norwich and the national picture of decline.

In this discussion of the disaffiliated ILP in Glasgow and Norwich, the central aim is to examine the relationship between national and local politics. The chapter begins with a brief discussion of the increasing emphasis historians have placed on local politics in the examination of the early ILP. This framework provides the starting point for the analysis of the ILP first in Glasgow and then in Norwich. From this discussion, three themes taken from studies of the early ILP appear central. First, attention is drawn to the distinctiveness of local trajectories. Second, stress is placed on the ways in which the local could often shape national politics. Finally, attention is given to the ways in which national events and issues impacted on the local level. Whilst the use of the themes suggests continuities between the ILP at different times, the chapter concludes with some reflections on how emphases must be shifted, and analytical mechanisms reversed, in order to provide a more satisfactory understanding of the ILP in the 1930s.[3]

Locality and the ILP

Since the 1960s, an increasing stress has been placed on local politics in historical writing on the early ILP. This emphasis perhaps emanates from Edward Thompson's seminal essay, 'Homage to Tom Maguire'. In this piece, Thompson skilfully weaves together a nuanced understanding of local economic and social conditions with an enthralling account of the activities and political philosophy of particular local activists. Taken together, this produces an understanding of the early Yorkshire ILP that shifts the way in which we understand the growth of the ILP nationally, emphasising the central importance of 'the provinces'. In the context of a movement 'exceptionally responsive' to local social, industrial and economic context, Thompson draws our attention to the importance of local actors with 'the capital human virtue of conscious political action in a conscious historical role'.[4]

Despite the changing times and conditions, an apparently similar emphasis on the importance of local activists can be seen in contemporary observations of the ILP as it made the decision to disaffiliate from Labour in 1932. Most notably, these local activists were central to the ILP general secretary John Paton's strategy. The party's 'hundreds of members' in 'key positions ... in the localities' were loyal to the ILP and would remain so, he suggested, if disaffiliation did not require these local activists to make a definite choice between Labour and the smaller organisation.

Paton's suggested strategy was perhaps most obviously applicable to Glasgow. After Labour's electoral disaster in 1931, the ILP held more parliamentary seats in Glasgow than the Labour Party held in the whole of Scotland. The party's continuing significance was widely recognised and discussed by contemporaries. This, perhaps, explains the singular interest which historians have paid to the disaffiliated ILP in Glasgow. Although older accounts have treated the ILP after disaffiliation solely as the dying embers of 'Red' Clydeside, a number of general histories of Glasgow and the Scottish labour movement provide some commentary on the party after this disaffiliation.[5] Nevertheless, although there is an excellent collection of essays on the Clydeside ILP prior to disaffiliation, this chapter offers the first systematic investigation of the ILP in Glasgow after 1932.[6]

The principal way in which the Clydeside situation can be addressed is through comparison with trajectories of the ILP elsewhere. Material for such a comparison is rather thin on the ground. One recent contribution examines the ILP in Derby, where the party had influence on the trades council, and suggests the importance of networking in generating a dynamic ILP branch.[7] In a less systematic way, another recent article examines the ILP in Jarrow, where an ILP presence in the mid-1930s developed from an internal split in the Labour Party.[8] This chapter examines Glasgow alongside a further case – Norwich. Norwich has been selected as perhaps the clearest example of a large and dynamic ILP branch which, whilst building on a substantial ILP tradition, was relatively unaffected by disaffiliation.[9] Further, in electoral terms, the ILP in Norwich, as in Glasgow, and unlike in Derby or Jarrow, was able at a certain level to present a viable alternative to the local Labour Party. Thus, Norwich and Glasgow shared the existence of an ILP tradition and sustained ILP influence after disaffiliation. It will be argued that these similarities were significant in shaping activist behaviours, generating in some cases overlapping problems and solutions. Of course, the direction of this argument is not meant to downplay the rather obvious differences between the two cities. The population of Glasgow was about eight times that of Norwich. Norwich had its slums, many of which were cleared in the course of the 1930s, but partly because of the work of the ILP MPs, Glasgow's East End became synonymous with the horrors of slum life. Norwich's economy diversified in the nineteenth century, with particular growth in engineering, food and drink, and – especially important for the labour movement – the boot and shoe industry. However, such diversity does not enable direct comparison with the complexity of Glasgow, where although heavy industry, skilled engineering and shipbuilding provided the foundations, the city encompassed a huge variety of forms of employment. Interwar unemployment in Norwich was severe, peaking at 7.4 per cent in 1934, but real as the problems related to unemployment were, in Glasgow the peak rate was over 33 per cent. The point of the comparison then, is not to overlook such points, but rather to suggest that the political similarities are all the more illuminating precisely because of these differences.

The ILP on Clydeside – Beyond Disintegration?

As the ILP moved towards disaffiliation after the 1931 general election, it was perhaps in Glasgow where the issue was most acutely felt. The ILP was central to the Labour politics in the city, whilst the Labour Party held real hopes of obtaining a majority over the Moderates on the city council. Labour's leader on the council was Patrick Dollan, who was also the Scottish representative on the ILP National Administrative Council (NAC). Along with other notable supporters, such as Thomas Johnston, the editor of *Forward*, the weekly Scottish Labour newspaper, he led the majority of the Scottish division in opposing the moves to disaffiliation. Indeed, Dollan, frustrated at the impediment of the disputes to his local political ambitions, could scarcely conceal his contempt for those calling for the ILP to make a 'revolutionary' break from the Labour Party.

If the calls for disaffiliation had been restricted to the 'revolutionary' minority within the ILP then no doubt affiliation would have been maintained, but Dollan faced much more formidable, although somewhat reluctant, support for disaffiliation centred on Glasgow and led by the charismatic figure of James Maxton, MP for Bridgeton. There was considerable personal animosity between Dollan and Maxton dating from the 1928 Cook–Maxton manifesto, which had moved ahead without proper consultation of ILP colleagues. However, of greater immediate significance, Maxton was the leader of the dissident ILP group in parliament. The group's regular conflict with the Labour leadership and anticipation of further disputes led to the revision of the standing orders of the Parliamentary Labour Party in January 1929. The parliamentary group's continued desire to remain free to criticise the 1929–31 Labour government led to ongoing arguments, and the failure to resolve these disputes meant that the Labour Party had refused to endorse ILP candidates first in by-elections and then again in the 1931 general election.[10]

After the decimation of the Parliamentary Labour Party in the 1931 election, the ILP parliamentary group, although reduced to five, contained four Clydeside MPs: James Maxton, John McGovern, George Buchanan and David Kirkwood. Of that group, only David Kirkwood regarded disaffiliation as a step too far. Whilst Buchanan, with a substantial majority in his Gorbals constituency, followed the lead of Maxton in supporting disaffiliation, McGovern had additional motivations. He had been selected as candidate for the Shettleston seat after the death of ILP leader John Wheatley in May 1930 just as relations between the Labour Party and the ILP were deteriorating. After McGovern had been chosen as prospective parliamentary candidate, local opponents made allegations of malpractice in his selection, although they accepted that no difference had been made to the end result. There was little indication that McGovern and his supporters had done anything outside of the customary practices in Glasgow politics. Nevertheless, his election caused a serious deterioration in relations between the two organisations. With the heightened tensions inside the labour movement, and given McGovern's chequered past in the anarchist and far left socialist movement, his actions were brought to the attention of the Glasgow Borough Labour Party (BLP) and from there to the Labour Party's National Executive Committee (NEC).[11] McGovern was declared unfit to be a Labour MP and was expelled, as were the three branches of the Shettleston ILP who later supported him when an official Labour Party candidate opposed him in 1931.[12] The situation in Shettleston meant that an important section of the ILP, and one of its MPs, already stood irretrievably outside the Labour Party during the disaffiliation debates.

After protracted negotiation with the Labour Party, a special conference of the national ILP decided on disaffiliation in July 1932. This split had an enormous effect on the organisation of the labour movement across much of Scotland and in Glasgow in particular. Indeed, the decision of the 'vast majority' of the Glasgow ILP was for the break, leaving Glasgow as Labour's 'weakest link in Scotland' according to *Forward*. The disaffiliation of ILP branches in the West of Scotland, including those in Shettleston, Govanhill, Carluke and Lanark, deprived constituency Labour parties of their whole organisational structure, whilst in Bridgeton and Hutchesontown it was not just the active membership but also all the officials who disaffiliated with the ILP.[13] In response to the disaffiliation decision, Dollan launched a short-lived campaign which sought to work within the ILP to prevent its implementation.[14] As a result of the campaign, two weeks after disaffiliation he and other leading advocates of affiliation, including Kirkwood and Johnston, were expelled from the ILP.[15] Expulsions of other significant figures within Glasgow continued over the ensuing weeks and months.[16] The Scottish Division of the ILP lost 128 of its 250 branches, but expulsion and final separation did not end the dispute over the legacy of the ILP in Glasgow.[17]

Dollan argued that the expelled affiliationists continued to be the real ILP.[18] The weight of Dollan's feeling about ILP identity, scepticism about the middle-class nature of the English affiliationist organisation the Socialist League, together with powerful feelings of Scottish independence, led him into forming the new Scottish Socialist Party (SSP). The SSP's claim to the ILP identity was made explicit in disputes over the rights to ILP property.[19] The SSP attempted to follow in its perception of this tradition, loyal to the Labour Party but with a distinctive socialist message, its own press, and with much work focused on the promotion of MPs.[20] However, the position of the SSP was somewhat precarious from the outset. Not all of those who joined were convinced of its value, there were worries about the potential for new rivalries with the Labour Party to develop, and there was significant tension between the SSP and the Scottish Labour Party under its new secretary Arthur Woodburn. The SSP never gained the widespread support needed to replace the position that the ILP had held in Scottish Labour politics prior to disaffiliation.

Following disaffiliation, the principal way in which the ILP nationally attempted to distinguish itself from the Labour Party was in terms of policy. The smaller party developed a 'new revolutionary policy' which in itself entailed considerable factional divisions between those inclined to see continuities with the past and those, led by the Revolutionary Policy Committee (RPC), who wanted a completely new approach. These factional divisions, so important in explaining the trajectory of the ILP nationally, had a limited impact on the ILP in Glasgow. The Scottish Division firmly opposed the RPC. Indeed none of the rival factions attained a significant following anywhere in Scotland.[21] The 'new revolutionary policy' was ignored to the extent that the NAC had to establish special meetings in Glasgow to encourage some implementation.[22]

Part of the reason for this lack of interest was that the ILP in Glasgow had more sustained confidence in an identity independent of the Labour Party, irrespective of policy. Although relations with the Labour Party were frequently discussed, even as the ILP nationally moved towards a desire for re-affiliation in 1938–39, the Glasgow party remained determined to retain independence. This feeling of confidence in a position outside the larger organisation was related to the strength of the ILP. This confidence is perhaps revealed by a discussion of formal politics at parliamentary and local level. In 1931, the unendorsed ILP had won four seats in Glasgow compared to the two endorsed Labour victories in the general election. Of its MPs, only David Kirkwood left the ILP in 1932. The 1935 general election was the first major test of the resilience of this support at parliamentary level, with the ILP fielding six candidates in Glasgow, including its three sitting MPs, Maxton in Bridgeton, Buchanan in Gorbals, and McGovern in Shettleston. Campbell Stephen, who had been a United Free Church Minister then a barrister, stood in Camlachie where he had previously been the MP from 1922–31.[23] In Govan, Tom Taylor, later Lord Taylor of Gryffe and, in 1935, the youngest member on Glasgow city council, contested the seat for the ILP. In Tradeston, another ILP councillor, James Carmichael, later ILP then Labour MP for Bridgeton, contested the seat.

The emphasis of the ILP campaign nationally was on the opposition to war in the wake of the Abyssinian crisis, and Taylor and Carmichael followed this lead.[24] However, the more established Glasgow candidates ignored the ILP's national campaign and chose a rather different focus, stressing unemployment, pensions, national health insurance, rents and the school leaving age.[25] The Labour Party gave no ground to the ILP, the Scottish executive poured extra funding into 'ILP areas' to promote the fight and attempts by local unions to mediate between Labour and the ILP were condemned in the strongest terms by both the Scottish executive and the NEC. The Labour Party went to considerable efforts to find the strongest possible candidates to oppose the ILP, and when the national agent (George Shepherd) toured Scotland in 1935, he stressed the need to concentrate campaigning and speakers on ILP areas.[26] Tom Taylor's opponent in Govan, Neil MacLean, was one of only two non-ILP Labour candidates who had won Glasgow seats in the 1931 election, whilst Carmichael faced Tom Henderson, who had held the seat prior to 1931.[27] In Camlachie, the Labour Party candidate was Ballie William Reid, a 'popular Sandyhill's man who by 1935 had represented Mile-end on the council for many years'.[28] However, despite their best efforts and the aims of Shepherd, in ILP heartlands the Labour Party had great difficulty both in finding suitable candidates or mounting substantial campaigns. In Gorbals, the Labour Party candidate, Alexander Burnett, was a man with no connection with the constituency. He entered the campaign late, and his attempt to displace Buchanan was described by the *Glasgow Herald* as 'extremely lack-lustre'.[29] In Shettleston, the Labour Party candidate, George Beggs, a Glaswegian native and Labour College lecturer, was faced with a Labour Party machine which had been effectively destroyed by a consistent ILP campaign dating back to the Shettleston ILP's expulsion from Labour in 1931. In Bridgeton, Maxton's Labour opponent, Samuel McLaren, chairman of Greenock Trades and Labour Council, had great difficulty in generating any enthusiasm for his campaign.[30]

The ILP saw four candidates elected in Glasgow in 1935. Its three sitting MPs were returned along with Campbell Stephen in Camlachie. In all four cases the Labour Party candidate lost his deposit. The election of the sitting MPs was perhaps no surprise, but the size of their majorities provoked substantial comment. Buchanan, for example, polled 75 per cent of the vote with a majority of over 17,000. Of perhaps even greater significance was the election of Campbell Stephen. He had faced more serious and more concerted Labour Party opposition and was a relatively uncharismatic figure who had done little to distinguish himself politically from his Labour opponent.[31] Stephen's election indicates the possibility of continued identification of a seat with the ILP rather than the Labour alternative. However, this was scarcely a basis for expansion. Even in Glasgow, apart from the four seats that the ILP won, the Labour Party was able to claim 'legitimacy' with the smaller party, although retaining its deposit, coming bottom of the poll.

The ILP's support at parliamentary level was maintained alongside and supported by local electoral politics. In elections for the city council, the ILP was in some wards able to take on and defeat the Labour Party for the majority of the working-class vote.[32] The ILP group on the council grew from the seven who disaffiliated in 1932 to a peak of 14 following a by-election in 1936. By the middle of the decade, the ILP was dominant in local politics in some areas of Glasgow. The six local seats in McGovern's Shettleston constituency were all held by ILPers, as were four of the six in Maxton's Bridgeton constituency. In the period 1932–33, these gains were made against Labour Party opposition. After 1933, when the Labour Party controlled the council with the support of the ILP, and in the wake of an electoral pact between the Moderates and the Protestant League, the two parties reached an electoral agreement. The ILP–Labour pact only covered seats which were already held by one of the two parties, and elsewhere the two working-class parties still found themselves in opposition, frequently denying each other victory.[33] Nevertheless, in the period to 1936, the ILP was able to make progress in new seats, often out-polling the Labour Party and successfully challenging the Moderates.[34]

On Glasgow council, in an initial period, the ILP and the Labour Party had a perhaps surprisingly close relationship. After the 1933 municipal elections, Labour and the ILP combined were able to command a majority on the council; indeed, the larger party relied on ILP support for its majority until the Second World War. On occasion, the ILP did succeed in getting the support of the Labour leadership for its proposals. Thus, the Labour leadership and hence the council voted for a municipal bread supply, to reassess the role of Palacerigg work colony, for the recognition of the National Unemployed Workers' Movement (NUWM), for the occasional free use of public baths, for the building of a new hospital, and for detaching Officer Training and Cadet Corps from High Schools.[35] However, after the Labour Party came to power, a feeling of opposition between Labour and ILP became clear. Mirroring the earlier disputes in parliament during the second Labour government, the ILP group accused Labour of deviating from 'socialist principles' with disputes emerging over a range of issues including the treatment of the unemployed at work camps, unemployment relief scales, council workers wages, the failure to use co-operative workers for council projects, the coronation, and the appropriate attitude towards the League of Nations.[36] Often, the ILP's strategy was restricted to the use of procedural points, although at the cost of finding themselves labelled 'obstructionists', 'ace talkers' and the 'go slow group' in the press.[37] However, there was considerable support even amongst Labour councillors for ILP complaints about Labour leader Patrick Dollan's use of authority. ILP opposition to Dollan's 'dictatorial methods' resulted in the infamous 'unholy alliance' between the ILP and the Moderates, when they combined to remove him from his post as treasurer in 1937.[38] ILP hostility only increased after Dollan was appointed the first Catholic Lord Provost of Glasgow in 1938. The smaller party argued that he suffered from 'a temperamental weakness of exhibitionism which shows itself in a desire to appear before as many audiences as possible and display himself in the regalia of pomp and influence'. Indeed, the ILP group suggested that Dollan's running of the Glasgow council could largely be explained as the actions of a frustrated megalomaniac.[39] These complaints over the nature of Dollan's leadership and over procedure may have been justified. However, these issues as an increasing focus of the Glasgow ILP did little to increase the party's appeal to a broader constituency.

With its continuing influence, however restricted, the vast majority of the literature on the post-1932 ILP in Glasgow centred on its role in the formal politics of Glasgow. However, as has been stressed in the analysis of the ILP on Clydeside prior to disaffiliation, much of the party's strength lay in informal networks.[40] The ILP made strenuous attempts to link its formal political role with work in trade unions and associational politics. To some extent, this saw the ILP maintaining and developing links with the unions, although this focus was seriously hampered by the concerted efforts of Labour Party and trade union leadership. Such disputes flared up particularly when any unions suggested giving financial support to the ILP.

This was most obviously the case within the small craft union, the United Patternmakers' Association (UPA), where ILP MP George Buchanan was the president. In the UPA, there had been serious tensions with the Labour Party at the time of disaffiliation. In addition to Buchanan, ILPers occupied important positions within the union, and one Glasgow branch had withdrawn affiliation from the Labour Party.[41] Subsequently, branches of the Patternmakers had been at the forefront of calls for anti-fascist action and for extensive support for the hunger marchers, and conflict with the Glasgow trades council developed after the Clyde district committee of the union organised public political meetings addressed by Buchanan. Buchanan's position as president of the union was emphatically reaffirmed in 1934, but as he was not a Labour Party member, his union sponsorship was withdrawn in 1935. However, members of the union anxious to continue supporting him balloted on raising a voluntary electoral fund despite the protestation of the Gorbals DLP and the declaration of the Labour Party NEC that even considering the question was an action inconsistent with the position of an affiliated organisation.[42]

Not only financial support, but any kind of support for the ILP, brought a reaction from the established labour movement. For example, the ILP had significant support within the National Union of Clerks (NUC); an ILPer mounted a substantial challenge for the post of general secretary in 1935, and the party had two executive members by 1937. In 1934, the largest Scottish branch of the union, the Glasgow food branch, passed a resolution urging the support of all trade unionists for the ILP candidate at the 1934 Pollockshaws by-election in Glasgow. That decision aroused considerable opposition from the Glasgow BLP, who referred it to the Scottish NUC general council. However, such pressures could, at least in the short term, be ignored, and the latter body, despite the appeal of the Scottish TUC general secretary, refused to disassociate itself from the actions of the branch.[43] Given the difficulties of work within the formal structures of the trade unions, the Glasgow ILP was also an important focus throughout the period for trade unionists in dispute with the official labour movement. For example, the Glasgow corporation bus workers involved in unofficial disputes were supported by the ILP in December 1936, and the Beardmore Parkhead Forge workers relied heavily on the ILP for support in unofficial disputes in the period from 1937 to the outbreak of war and beyond.[44]

. Despite sporadic influence and consistent intentions, the party was more successful outside of union politics. Throughout the 1930s, the Glasgow ILP focussed considerable attention on the organisation of demonstrations and rallies which were not exclusively ILP events. In the early part of the decade, these organised protests focussed on unemployment, with leading ILPers particularly active in the organisation of the 1934 hunger march in Glasgow. ILPers John McGovern and John Heenan were amongst the leaders, whilst others, such as ILP councillors Taylor and Gibson, put a considerable amount of effort into the organisation of the march, with Gibson acting as joint treasurer of the Campaign Committee.[45] The party was also active across Glasgow and the west of Scotland in the organisation of other unemployed activities such as setting up united action and agitation against cuts in unemployment relief.[46] Later in the decade, the focus of much of the ILP's associational activity moved to international events, with a particularly combative focus on the Spanish Civil War.

This activity was supported by a thriving social side, which played a significant part in both the ILP's aspirations and self-perception. The surviving cashbook of the Bridgeton branch gives a flavour of the range of events organised, including regular socials and parties, usually accompanied by food and a band, a dancing class, plays for the membership, and more usual activities such as jumble sales and election victory meetings. One real strength of the party lay in its ability to make imaginative use of resources available to make a substantial difference to the lives of its working-class members who would otherwise rarely have been able to escape the hardships of everyday life in the East End of Glasgow. Particularly important were the ILP's attempts to organise day trips. Occasionally, this was a day out sailing on Loch Lomand, but more typical were the 'sludge boat outings'. The 'sludge boat' went down from Glasgow to the Broomielaw to empty sewage; the ILP took advantage of this and organised regular outings for as many as 150 members at a time, and all the 'old women from Brigton Cross would go and have their day out down the river on the boat'.[47]

It was one of the ILP's enduring strengths that it was often able to make an explicit connection between the social and political aspects of its activity. Thus, the political aspects of the party's activity often had a substantial social focus. For example, ILP meetings in Glasgow, particularly when addressed by Maxton, could be attended by as many as 3,500 supporters and, according to contemporary reports, had a feeling much like a revivalist rally.[48] The ILP was also heavily involved in organising rallies and flag days.[49] Central to attempts to link the political and social were the annual May Day celebrations. During the early part of the decade, the ILP, together with the Communist Party, attempted to organise separate 'Socialist May Day' celebrations. However, by 1937 the parties were co-operating in a joint May Day demonstration with all working-class organisations, which it was claimed was the 'largest in Glasgow since the war'.[50]

In a similar way, the social often had an explicitly political intent. For example, the ILP organised groups to travel round the Highlands visiting underprivileged or delinquent boys who had been put out to crofters by the town council. The purpose was to keep tabs on the councillors who were meant to ensure that the boys were not being exploited. In a similarly 'outdoor-whilst-still-political' vein, the Glasgow ILP ran a 'Cycling Corps' under the leadership of Jack Taylor (the 1937 Scottish amateur cycling champion), which cycled out every Saturday to sell the *New Leader* in the areas surrounding Glasgow. It also made strenuous attempts to organise cyclists in the defence of their rights on the road.[51] The overall effect was substantial. Even on departing the ILP for the Communist Party in 1935, John Lochore recalled the importance of its social aspects and the attempts to connect these to political understanding:

> There was a lot of socialising in the ILP. This was one of the great advantages of the ILP ... It was done from a socialist point of view. This was one of the things I advocated when I did eventually join the Communist Party ... We started working for setting up branches so that the Party could get in local people and make it more of a family, homely type of thing, like the ILP.[52]

Thus, following disaffiliation the ILP retained a substantial electoral and cultural presence. However, it is important to recognise that this influence diminished substantially, particularly in the second half of the 1930s. This waning influence was visible in electoral and associational terms. As *Forward* reported after the 1937 May Day rally, for the first time at a joint event in Glasgow, the Communist Party presence seemed stronger than the ILP's.[53] Similarly, in electoral terms, the ILP lost one municipal seat in 1936, a further two seats in 1937, and another one in the final Glasgow municipal elections before the Second World War. In crude terms, the ILP gains of the early 1930s were reversed whilst most Labour Party gains from the same period were consolidated. Behind these small electoral shifts lay substantial problems, and in some cases failings, which undermined the likelihood of a continued ILP presence in the City.

One notable factor was the changing attitude of Catholic elites in Glasgow. In the early 1930s, it appears that the introduction of religious sectarianism into Glasgow politics and, in particular, the rise of the Scottish Protestant League pushed Catholic fears of 'ultra-leftism' into the background. The small ILP group also contained two of the six Catholics on the 116-strong city council. In this situation, it has been suggested that the Catholic establishment was even more concerned with 'maximising the natural Labour vote than the rival left wing parties which were engaged in a bitter battle for supremacy'. Certainly, the Catholic *Glasgow Observer* did not take sides in the disputes between the ILP and the Labour Party after 1932, and the Catholic Union in some wards seemed if anything more favourable to the ILP.[54]

However, the outbreak of the Spanish Civil War in July 1936 led to a rapid change in the position of the Catholic leadership. On the outbreak of war, the *Glasgow Observer* pledged support for Franco's rebels leading to an attack on the Labour Party who had 'now joined the war against Christ'. Divisions within both the Labour Party and the church authorities on the appropriate line allowed a truce to be negotiated based on the Labour Party's official position of non-intervention in Spain and the Archbishop's focus on freedom of worship and freedom of education. However, the same accommodation could not be reached with the ILP, whose support for the Republican cause was unequivocal. Indeed, John McGovern was quite possibly the most combative left wing politician over Spain anywhere in Britain. In November 1936, he accompanied John McNair, the ILP's international representative, to Barcelona with the purpose of investigating the Catholic position in Spain. On his return, he addressed a string of public meetings in Glasgow and elsewhere, publishing his view in a pamphlet entitled *Why Bishops Back Franco* with a circulation of 28,000. He argued that Franco was using churches as fortresses, that the Spanish church had become a thoroughly Capitalist institution', and that the 'Fascist Movement [in Spain] had its birth in the Church'. His strident attacks on the Catholic Church continued through 1937; at a meeting of 2,500 people in a cinema in the Parkhead district of Glasgow, he gave 'perhaps the most anti-clerical speech ever given by a Glasgow Labour MP'.[55] In June, a debate between McGovern and Glasgow Catholic journalist and Nationalist supporter Douglas Jerrold, has been labelled as perhaps the 'high-point of the Spanish controversy in Glasgow'.[56] Although George Buchanan was notably silent on the issue, the rest of the Glasgow ILP vigorously supported the party's position on the Spanish Civil War. With the ILP's vocal support for the Republicans, Catholic elites withdrew their support from ILP candidates, with this being widely accepted as the explanation for the loss of John Heenan's previously safe ILP seat in Shettleston in November 1936.

However, perhaps as serious for the ILP's presentation of itself as a viable opposition to the Labour Party in Glasgow were the damaging effects of bitter factionalism between two parts of the ILP structure. One group led by Joseph Payne, held positions in the Glasgow Federation. The other, largely younger members, including Tom Taylor, held positions on the executive of the Scottish Divisional Council (SDC). The SDC was frustrated about the lack of concerted activity in Glasgow, launching in 1936 an investigation into the work of the federation. As James Carmichael, secretary of SDC, wrote to Tom Murry, the secretary of the federation management committee about their activity: 'while we are trying to build a Socialist Movement with a revolutionary purpose we tend to leave the impression that we are village pump parish scale protectors'.[57] The management committee did not take kindly to being investigated and systematically blocked the SDC attempts to gather information.[58]

This situation was exacerbated by the behaviour of one leading member of the management committee, Councillor Payne, who had become obsessed with the minutiae of the tramways system and launched frequent and vitriolic attacks on the conduct of the tramwaymen.[59] These attacks strained the relationship between the ILP and the transport unions, and in order to protect this connection another of the ILP councillors, Tom Taylor, launched a series of public attacks on Payne. By August 1936, the situation had become so strained, and the SDC investigation so bogged down, that John McGovern drew it to the attention of the NAC.[60] In 1937, the situation reached new heights when Payne decided to take Taylor to court. The national party was forced to launch its own investigation, finding that the dispute was mainly due to clashing personalities and declared that the situation required the federation to recognise the supervisory rights of the SDC. The NAC laid the main blame on the management committee, declaring that 'the federation has done useful routine work but during the past two years meetings held under its auspices have often been a hindrance rather than a help to the party'. It was decided that the Scottish ILP was in need of a wholesale reorganisation. The main positions in the SDC went to non-Glasgow figures, and the leading protagonists, including Payne and the promising figure of Taylor, were removed from official positions. Payne was even barred from holding public office for the party for a year. The federation was reorganised with differential voting for branches based on their size, whilst the corporation group rules were changed so that officers were elected on 'the principle of selecting the ablest man for the job ... irrespective of the term he has served'. At the SDC level, Annie Maxton and Lachlan M'Quarrie, both from Barrhead and uninvolved in the Glasgow dispute, were elected chairman and secretary respectively.[61]

ILP influence was on the retreat from this period. The range and vitality of the ILP's social activity fell away sharply in the early part of the war and never recovered. George Buchanan returned to the Labour Party in 1939. ILP approaches to re-affiliate to the Labour Party were rejected immediately after the Second World War. The remaining ILP councillors joined the Labour Party in the wake of this decision. James Maxton died in 1946, and Campbell Stephen and John McGovern then quickly rejoined Labour. James Carmichael, elected as MP after the death of Maxton, and leaving the ILP the following year, followed their trajectory. With the ending of its electoral presence in the city, it is in the late 1940s rather than the early 1930s that the ILP on Clydeside can really be said to have disintegrated.

Norwich

Glasgow dominates the popular image of the disaffiliated Independent Labour Party. However, aside from the obvious arena of electoral politics, it is perhaps not Glasgow but Norwich which provides the most obvious example of thriving branch life in the 1930s. In 1932, the branch had 450 members. In the early 1940s, the membership of the Norwich branch was approaching 1,000, almost 40 per cent of the national membership. Norwich was the largest ILP branch by far; by itself, it contained over twice the total membership of the 37 Scottish branches combined.[62]

As in Glasgow, the disaffiliation decision caused considerable enmity between the ILP and the Labour Party. There was a history of ILP parliamentary candidacies in the dual member seat of Norwich. In 1923, Dorothy Jewson, who came from a wealthy coal and timber merchant family, was elected as an ILP-sponsored member alongside her Labour colleague Walter Smith. Both were defeated in the 1924 election and both stood again in 1929, when Smith was elected but Jewson defeated. However, in 1931, relations between Jewson and Smith were strained by the national dispute between the ILP and the Labour Party.

Jewson, as an ILP candidate in the general election, was refused endorsement by the Labour Party. With Jewson unendorsed and Smith the sole official Labour candidate, the Norwich Labour Party initially offered 'moral support' to Jewson's campaign. Smith was horrified, and initially resigned as Labour's prospective parliamentary candidate until the local Labour Party withdrew any suggestion of support for Jewson.[63]

Both Jewson and Smith were soundly defeated in 1931, and it was clear that the lack of official support had no bearing on Jewson's failure to be elected. Nevertheless, the Labour Party's refusal to endorse Jewson and other ILP candidates nationally enraged parts of the East Anglian ILP. They were one of only three of the nine divisions offering support for disaffiliation in the early months of 1932, with the first of their cited reasons being Labour's attitude towards ILP candidates.[64] The movement towards disaffiliation nationally and particularly in London, was being led by the Revolutionary Policy Committee. However, distinct from the RPC's proposals, in Norwich there was no desire to arrange co-operation with the Communist Party or to affiliate to the Third International. Further, whilst the division did vote for a 'revolutionary' policy, this meant something quite different from the suggestions of the RPC, being based more on the 'ethical Marxism' of the influential Norwich ILPer and literary critic John Middleton Murry.[65]

Middleton Murry had only joined the ILP in July 1931, following his conversion to 'communism'. His vision for the ILP was that it should be 'very small – and consist of men sustained by an absolutely "religious" conviction of the necessity of complete self-sacrifice'.[66] With such a view, he was a leading advocate of disaffiliation, turning the literary journal *The Adelphi* into what was effectively an ILP journal, and quickly becoming a force within the ILP in Norwich and beyond.[67] His was a powerful voice which added to the call for a split with Labour.

Following disaffiliation, the Revolutionary Policy Committee quickly became a substantial force within the national ILP. Norwich, however, in alliance with much of the Lancashire ILP, became a centre of opposition to the RPC. In 1933, the ILP adopted a 'new revolutionary policy' heavily influenced by the RPC, based on the idea of workers' councils and the formation of a united revolutionary party with the Communist Party. The Norwich branch, in opposition to this, ceased co-operation with the Communist Party and began working on an alternative set of policies. Frustration reached a height in October 1933, when a special divisional meeting was called to discuss an alternative policy. Middleton Murry presented a manifesto calling for a return to constitutional methods, and was enthusiastically supported by the divisional chairman, Norwich's George Johnson. This, in turn, was controversial within the branch and even more so within the division, and the manifesto was eventually rejected. But the conference also rejected co-operation with the Communist Party, the 'new revolutionary policy', and an NAC report downplaying the role of parliament in the ILP's strategy.[68]

After 1934, when the ILP national conference refused demands to reverse crucial parts of the 'new revolutionary policy', the Lancashire based Unity Group stormed out of the ILP, taking Middleton Murry and a number of other Norwich ILPers with them into the newly formed Independent Socialist Party (ISP).[69] With Middleton Murry's departure in 1934 and the RPC's decision to join the Communist Party in the following year, the position within Norwich settled down to increasing support for the now revised and moderated national policy of the party. At each divisional conference from 1936 to 1938, George Johnson launched a strong defence of ILP policy. However, influenced by declining membership by 1939, the Norwich branch led by Johnson had shifted its attitude and was amongst the areas supporting moves to re-affiliate to the Labour Party.[70]

Despite the unease of the Norwich ILP with the direction of the ILP nationally in the early 1930s, enthusiastic support for disaffiliation had further soured the already strained relations between the ILP and the Labour Party in the city. Following the split, the two parties opposed each other in four wards in the 1932 municipal elections, with the intervention letting in the Liberals in Catton ward.[71] Both parties appeared unrepentant. Herbert Frazer, president of the Norwich Labour Party, declared that the 'time was coming when the Norwich Labour Party must make up its mind that this faction must be broken'.[72] Alf Nicholls, the defeated ILP candidate in that ward, argued that:

> He was pleased he had been the instrument by which the Labour candidate was kept out in the Catton ward ... [as] he preferred to see a successful Anti-Socialist who in a straightforward fashion declared his position ... rather than the underhand tactics of the Labour Party locally and nationally.[73]

However, behind the scenes it seems that there was recognition on both sides of the damage caused by the hostility. By the following year, the parties had agreed a working arrangement to avoid conflicting candidatures. The results were good; in 1933, the 'best possible working arrangement' led to two ILP victories in the local council election: Dorothy Jewson, who had first been elected in 1929, and George Johnson, in Catton ward. The Labour Party had 32 seats on the council and, until 1936, relied on the ILPers for its majority. The larger organisation quickly sought to formalise co-operation and moved a resolution to establish a permanent joint committee between the two groups on the council, although the idea was eventually crushed on the advice of the Labour Party NEC.[74] In the following two years, first Alf Nicholls, a NUGMW activist, and then Arthur South, aged 21 and Britain's youngest councillor – he was later Labour leader of the city council and chairman of Norwich City Football Club – won further seats for the ILP in Catton ward. Following her marriage to R. Tanner Smith, Dorothy Jewson moved from Norwich in 1937.[75] In the resulting council by-election, the ILP candidate, Miss Utting, was given a free run by the Labour Party but was still beaten by a majority of 88. This surprising result, the ILP noted, was on a 29 per cent poll, blamed on a combination of Yarmouth races, a football match and a Co-op outing, leading to considerable frustration – 'when are the workers going to put their real interests before "circuses"?'[76] ILP strength on the council was returned to four in March 1939, when George Johnson was elevated to the Aldermanic bench and the subsequent vacancy was filled, unopposed, by W. Channell. Thus, the ILP vote in Norwich, especially in the Catton Ward where by the end of the decade all three councillors were ILPers, was not dependent on personality, but instead it reflected the extensive local activity in the ward where the ILP had a considerable following and the Labour Party had no ward organisation at all.

The ILP was anxious to build on this work at local level and reach agreements with the Labour Party about parliamentary elections. Although unable to persuade Dorothy Jewson to stand again, the ILP considered that it had a chance of doing reasonably well in Norwich. One indication of their hopes for the seat was that Fenner Brockway, aside from Maxton probably the ILP's leading personality, was selected as the ILP candidate for the 1935 election. In 1935, the ILP tried strenuously to persuade the Labour Party to only put forward one candidate in the two member seat, and offered support to one of the Labour candidates on the condition that the other pulled out.[77] With the experience of a split vote in council elections behind it, the Norwich Labour Party appears to have taken the ILP's suggestion seriously. Certainly, they took the matter to the NEC, but whilst locally many within the Labour Party may have been sympathetic to the ILP, the same cannot be said nationally. Under pressure from the NEC, with the threat not to endorse any candidate running alongside the ILP, the Norwich Labour Party noted that the national dimension was crucial in understanding why it was important to have an all-Labour ticket.[78]

Brockway, the architect of the ILP's national electoral focus on Abyssinia, placed international issues at the forefront of his campaign. He spent much of his time arguing that war was a direct result of the operation of capitalism and the struggle between competing capitalist groups for markets and economic resources.[79] Only limited attention was given to the relationship with the Labour Party. The larger organisation also tried to ignore the split. The ILP remained unmentioned until the days immediately before polling when, probably as a response to the National government candidates' focus on the ILP–Labour split, the Labour Party suddenly issued a leaflet with a scathing personal attack on Brockway.[80] The result was a disappointment for the ILP. The National Liberal and Conservative candidates were elected; Brockway polled 6,737 votes, finishing bottom of the poll and forfeiting his deposit. The result was almost as disappointing for the Labour Party. Although the split vote was not an obvious cause of Labour's failure to win, some within the Labour Party were not convinced. One of the Norwich Labour candidates, Kelly, argued that 'the ILP intervention altered the result more seriously than it appeared on the surface'. He pointed out that the turnout was 11,000 lower than in 1931, and 2,266 electors had voted for Brockway alone without casting a second vote, far more than had voted for any other single candidate.[81]

Based partly on this reasoning, the local Labour Party's conviction that an alliance with the ILP would be of electoral benefit continued. ILP approaches to negotiate with the Labour Party for an agreement about parliamentary electoral nominations were supported within the Norwich Labour Party and the local trade unions. The Norwich Labour Party tried to bring the issue of shared nominations to the 1937 Labour Party conference, although the NEC blocked any discussion. Indeed, despite repeated approaches from the Norwich Labour Party and Norwich Trades Council to the national Labour Party, the NEC maintained a decision that both seats were to be fought by official Labour candidates, making clear that any agreement explicit or tacit with the ILP would mean that no candidate would be endorsed for the city.[82] The only concession was the artful selection of ex-ILP general secretary John Paton as one of the Labour parliamentary candidates for the division.

As in Glasgow, a crucial element of the ILP's appeal was that it did not restrict its activity to the electoral arena. Party activists played an important role in the co-operative and trade union movement, and made strenuous efforts to link this activity to a thriving social arena. In terms of co-operative activity, the party maintained two members on the Co-op Board and four members on the Co-op education committee.[83] In its union work, the party did not have great strength in terms of activists in prominent local positions. Indeed, probably its most prominent figure, Alf Nicholls, an employee at the Colman's mustard factory, was removed from official positions including acting as a representative on Norwich Trades Council, following the NUGMW's interpretation of the 1935 anti-communist 'black circular'.[84]

Instead, it was in support of workers, especially the busmen, in unofficial disputes where the Norwich ILP was most notably active. According to the busmen, a take over by the Eastern Counties company in the early 1930s had led to wage reductions, increased duties and 'irritating regulations'. Initial unofficial action was taken by the men in January 1936. The company, after taking advice from union leaders, attempted to break the strike by bringing in men from Northampton. Without the support of the official labour movement, the men turned to the ILP. The busmen set up headquarters at the ILP's Keir Hardie Hall, and the party launched a concerted campaign to support them. Accordingly, following the action by the ILP and the busmen, the Northampton men refused to break the strike once the situation was explained to them. What was described as intimidation from officials of the Transport and General Worker's Union finally led the men to call off the action. However, the unresolved causes of the dispute led to further action being taken by the busmen the following year.[85] The busmen again made extensive, although ultimately unsuccessful, use of both local and national ILP speakers in their cause, culminating with a meeting at the end of April in the market place in Norwich, where Brockway, the ILP councillors, and a number of the strike leaders addressed a crowd of 7,000.[86]

The position in Norwich electorally and in trade union activity hints at the vibrancy of the continuing ILP presence to which those in dispute with the official labour movement could turn. However, the real strength of the ILP in Norwich came from its attempts to link these obviously political concerns with a strong social presence. The membership of the Norwich branch did not conform to either alternatives of 'rapid demise' or 'slow death' suggested in one recent piece of research.[87] The Norwich ILP was certainly affected by disaffiliation, 'most of the public representatives will be lost and a few old members', the branch wrote into the *New Leader*, 'but all the young and active members are standing firm'.[88] The report to the divisional council that the party had lost a 'few book members' was even more upbeat.[89] What was exceptional about such reports was not their content; similar and even more optimistic accounts flooded in from branches crippled by disaffiliation. Rather, what was exceptional was that in Norwich's case the optimistic tone was borne out by the long-term trajectory of the branch. Membership remained consistently at around 450 from prior to disaffiliation into 1933; a small decline at the end of 1933 was made up in the early part of 1934. The party claimed further membership increases after the 1935 general election campaign, and a membership of 500 by February 1936. This held steady through 1936–37, although it had fallen back to about 400 by 1939. Membership then remained at around this level, if somewhat inactive, through the Second World War. The Norwich branch entered the second half of the 1940s stronger than ever; rapid expansion meant that at the beginning of 1947 the branch declared 930 members, although by 1950 this had fallen away somewhat to around 700.[90]

The primary reason for this success was the impact that the party's premises and social club had on the ILP. The ILP club had been assessed in a 1910 social survey as the only place in Norwich 'to which a man can take his wife and child and enjoy a sober glass of beer under respectable circumstances'.[91] The club and associated Keir Hardie Hall attracted a significant portion of the membership to the Norwich branch. The hall held 500 and had a large number of committee rooms used by trade unions, a club lounge, and a bookshop which the branch attempted to ensure was always open. The rooms provided a base from which the ILP could organise its activities. This included the writing and printing of a local supplement to the *New Leader*, which the branch saw as part of the reason for its rather good sales of the paper – in the somewhat tongue-in-cheek *New Leader* sales competitions reported on weekly from 1934–36, the Norwich branch consistently came third, selling an average of over 600 copies a week.[92] It also provided the location for the branch meetings, held on alternate Mondays, and provided a working class information bureau on Thursdays between 10 o'clock and midday.[93] The financial position of the Norwich branch was excellent. By the end of 1937, the ILP had wiped out the debt on their premises, and it was one of very few branches which were able to provide the ILP head offices with donations to support its activity rather than the other way round. The impact of the social club on Norwich ILP was undoubtedly substantial. In 1950, the social club split from the ILP, effectively ending the significant ILP presence in the city. Although the scale of decline certainly overstates the ILP's reliance on the club – there were political reasons for the split and many of the ILP's most active members left with the club – the numbers are nevertheless indicative. Overnight, ILP membership fell from over 700 to just nine.

Conclusion: Making and Losing Political Space

Just as accounts of the early ILP have stressed local variation at the party's birth, so analysis of the party after disaffiliation must be adjusted to accommodate significantly different local trajectories. Of course, as in some frequently cited locations – such as Leicester and Bermondsey – members departed en mass in 1932. Yet, more sophisticated accounts need to address local variation. Glasgow and Norwich, where membership held up well, provide examples to set against Leicester and Bermondsey. Further, it should be remembered that two-thirds of the ILP's members chose to disaffiliate with the smaller party. With such wide variations, the study of Glasgow and Norwich helps us to remember that, although these experiences may not have been universal, the cases of Leicester and Bermondsey were also far from typical.

These divergent paths are suggestive of further differences. Just as with Tom Maguire and the early ILP, local activists in the 1930s found different solutions because they worked in very different political environments and faced distinctive problems and opportunities. The concerns of the ILP in Glasgow and Norwich were very different from the party nationally. One particularly noticeable feature was the absence of support for the 'new revolutionary policy', with its stress on workers' councils, in either city. Whilst the party nationally concentrated substantial efforts on the creation of this policy, these developments were strongly opposed in Norwich and, in Glasgow, they were simply ignored. This perspective was related to the benefit which the party in both places received from association with an ILP tradition, with considerable stress placed on the importance of electoral politics – including an established and widely recognised role for the ILP within the labour movement. In both places, this tradition played an important part in structuring electoral politics. In Glasgow, the position of the ILP MPs appeared unassailable, whilst in local elections the ILP was in places able to take on and defeat both Moderate and Labour opponents. Despite considerable personal animus between Labour and ILP activists, the potential cost of a split vote created considerable pressure for compromise. Further, the ILP in Glasgow had to work in a context structured by the complexities of religious politics. With religious influences stronger than anywhere else in mainland Britain, Catholic support was central to the party's success. Assisted by the rise of militant Protestantism, the ILP maintained substantial elements of this support in the early 1930s. However, in the later part of the decade, with diverging responses to the Spanish Civil War, this support for the ILP was increasingly fragile. In Norwich, the religious dimension was absent, but local differences still structured the ILP's position. The ILP claim to one of the parliamentary nominations was a powerful force, not least because of its acceptance by a significant section of the Norwich Labour Party. This, combined with the weakness of Labour Party organisation in particular wards, gave ILP activists the opportunity to develop a council presence. Further, the legacy of the well-established Keir Hardie Hall provided a focus for a wider political and social support.

As with the early ILP, it was not just that local trajectories differed, but that these varying regional events and attitudes combined to alter the party at national level. In part, this reflected the weight given to regional opinion in the structure of the ILP. The ILP's regional divisions accounted for nine of the 16 places on the party's central body, the NAC. Regional divisional conferences were formally responsible for submitting material for national conferences and, as importantly, the discussion at these conferences was in an informal way responsible for setting the agenda and expected scope of debate at national conference. More specifically, the ILP's retreat from its 'new revolutionary policy' from 1934 was in no small part due to the pressure of activists in Norwich and the failure of the policy to influence activity in Glasgow. Moreover, the strategy of the party nationally was profoundly affected by the 1935 general electoral struggle. The ILP victories in Glasgow were significant, affecting widely held attitudes to the resilience of the ILP vote. The vote also reinforced the dominant image of the ILP as a party of 'the Clydesiders'. Internally, however, Brockway's performance in Norwich was as significant, or perhaps even more so. His abject failure in what was considered a promising location signalled the difficulties in developing a local presence into electoral support at the parliamentary level. In combination with other similar outcomes, such as Tom Stephenson's in Whitehaven, this signalled the beginning of a new wave of disillusionment with the strategy of the ILP and moves towards reversing the breach with the Labour Party.

Thus, local political trajectories were often distinctive and frequently such regional perspectives affected the party at national level. In these ways, the relationship between national and local in the 1930s appears to repeat aspects found in accounts of the early ILP. However, the perspective of the early ILP cannot be brought on board wholesale; apparent similarities conceal significant differences. Emphases identified in the study of the Victorian party must be shifted, and in some cases mechanisms reversed, to provide an appropriate account of the organisation following disaffiliation. Even in the examples provided at the outset of the chapter, the continuing stress on the local shows substantial change as well as continuity. In Edward Thompson's discussion of the growth of the ILP, it was the dynamic and inventive behaviour of ILP activists such as Tom Maguire which enabled the growth of the ILP. In John Paton's discussion, it was the potential *in*activity and *in*decision of local activists clinging to traditional solutions and loyalties which provided the hope for the party.

> Many hundreds of our members held key positions in the Labour Parties in the localities, hundreds more were Labour Members of local authorities, very many of them were local leaders in the real sense – men and women of long experience and high repute with powerful personal followings. If the ILP had left them alone to make their own decisions as to their local relations with the Labour Party there is no doubt that many of them, held by their ILP traditions and the force of old associations, would have been stricken with doubts and ended by sitting tight and waiting.[94]

These perspectives perhaps overemphasise differences between ILP activists in different periods. Certainly, the accounts presented here have identified local

ILP activists who made significant contributions to the party's success after disaffiliation; individuals such as George Johnson and Dorothy Jewson in Norwich, and Tom and Jack Taylor in Glasgow. However, the ILP was itself aware of the failure of many of its activists to engage a wider working-class audience. In particular, one besetting weakness of the disaffiliated ILP was the energy activists spent on internal arguments and factional wrangling. Nationally, these disputes concentrated on the RPC and, in Norwich, it was opposition to this body which provided the focus for internal dissent and disagreement. In Glasgow, however, where the RPC was almost entirely absent, the party found other fault lines, of similar disinterest to the wider working class, along which it was able to split.

Perhaps more significant change can be found in the impact which the national party had on local politics. Such an emphasis is evident in the study of the early ILP. David Howell, for example, notes that 'the traffic' was 'never uni-directional', with national and local levels influencing each other. In particular, he notes, some cohesion could eventually be lent to local initiatives by the existence of a national party organisation, whilst activists came to see themselves as members of a national party. However, the stress of his account is on the limitations of national control with uneven growth and differing strategies appropriate to varying local circumstances being more central to his analysis.[95]

Despite the prominence of diverse local experiences in this chapter, the importance of the national dimension has been a recurring theme. This can be seen in the decisions and strategies of ILP activists themselves. The disaffiliation decision, taken enthusiastically in Norwich and by many in Glasgow, was given different local emphases and expressions. However, standing orders and the endorsement of ILP parliamentary candidates, central points in both Glasgow and Norwich, were national issues relating to the Parliamentary Labour Party. Although through the 1930s there was inevitably a discussion of local issues in both cities, it was the national and international scale which predominated. Indeed, as George Johnson noted when advocating reaffiliation, he wanted to rejoin the Labour Party not because of the failings of the Norwich ILP locally, but because local achievement was not enough.[96] However, the greatest influence of the national on the local came from the way in which national politics structured the political spaces available to the ILP. It was the Labour Party's NEC, along with its Scottish executive, which provided the finances and required the opposition to the Glasgow ILP. It was the NEC which prevented the Norwich Labour Party's suggested electoral pacts with the ILP. Within the trade unions, a similar restriction of political space emerges. Where there were local disputes, particularly where the official union movement refused assistance, the ILP was on hand to provide support. In both Glasgow and Norwich, the unofficial disputes involving the busmen provide the clearest examples. However, with an established set of national trade unions, a strategy supporting breakaway unions appeared inappropriate in the 1930s ILP. At the same time, these national trade unions further restricted the ILP's room for manoeuvre. The NUGMW provides an extreme case, with its requirement that all ILPers be removed from official positions in local branches affecting activists in both Glasgow and Norwich.

However, Buchanan's increasingly precarious position within the Patternmakers indicates the potentially problematic position activists faced even within a relatively supportive union – largely because of the union's relationship with the Labour Party. These patterns need to be qualified; the power of national politics to influence the local was heavily dependent on the aims of the local ILP branches and on the historic influence of the Labour Party. Thus, in some areas such as Great Yarmouth near Norwich, or Barrhead near Glasgow, where neither the ILP nor the Labour Party had had much in the way of organisation or electoral success, the ILP was able to establish an influence which did not conform to these patterns. Nevertheless, in both Glasgow and Norwich, the ILP placed considerable emphasis on electoral success and its influence was in part a continuation of traditions established in connection with the Labour Party prior to disaffiliation. In this situation, the national level played a central role in influencing the trajectory of even these exceptional localities.

Thus, there are many similarities in the relationship between national and local levels in the early ILP and the ILP after disaffiliation. Certainly, just as at foundation, after disaffiliation there was no one national trajectory followed uniformly in every area; the 1930s could be a time of growth as well as decline for ILP branches. Further, as in the party's early years, local events were central in moving the ILP nationally in particular directions, towards and away from particular policies. Finally, in both time-periods, national events and decisions provided a framework within which local developments took place. However, behind these apparent similarities there were substantial changes in the political environment. In particular, this account of the ILP at local level in Norwich and Glasgow – despite the distinctiveness of local trajectories and local sentiments – indicates a fundamental shift in the importance of the power of the national institutions within the unions and particularly within the Labour Party in explaining configurations of working-class politics.

Notes

1. John Lochore, in I. MacDougall, *Voices From the Hunger Marches: Volume II* (Edinburgh, 1991), p. 316.

2. R. Dowse, *Left in the Centre: The Independent Labour Party, 1893–1940* (London, 1966), p. 193.

3. This chapter is based on research conducted for my DPhil 'The Independent Labour Party, 1932–39'. I am grateful to the AHRB for the funding provided for the project, and to David Howell for his supervision and comments.

4. E.P. Thompson, 'Homage to Tom Maguire', in A. Briggs and J. Saville (eds), *Essays in Labour History* (London, 1960).

5. R.K. Middlemass, *The Clydesiders: A Left Wing Struggle for Parliamentary Power* (London, 1965); J.J. Smyth, *Labour in Glasgow 1896–1936: Socialism, Suffrage, Sectarianism* (East Linton, 2000); T. Gallagher, *Glasgow: The Uneasy Peace* (Manchester,

1987); I. Donnachie, C. Harvie and I. Wood (eds), *Forward! Labour Politics in Scotland 1888–1988* (Edinburgh, 1989).

6. A. McKinlay and R.J. Morris (eds), *The ILP on Clydeside 1893–1932: From Foundation to Disintegration* (Manchester, 1991).

7. R. Stevens, '"Rapid Demise or Slow Death"? The Independent Labour Party in Derby, 1932–45', *Midland History*, 22 (1997), pp. 113–30.

8. M. Perry, 'The Jarrow Crusade's Return: The "New Labour Party" of Jarrow and Ellen Wilkinson MP', *Northern History*, 39 (2002), pp. 265–78.

9. A brief discussion of the ILP in Norwich can be found in P.J. Thawites, 'The Independent Labour Party, 1938–56', London School of Economics PhD thesis (1976).

10. For more detailed discussions of disaffiliation, see G. Cohen, 'The Independent Labour Party, Disaffiliation, Revolution and Standing Orders', *History*, 282, 66 (2001), pp. 200–21; D. Howell, *MacDonald's Party: Labour Identities and Crisis 1922–31* (Oxford, 2002).

11. *Forward*, 14 March 1930; Labour Party NEC report 3–4 October 1930.

12. Labour Party, 'NEC Report', 21 April and 23 June 1931; 'Labour Party Organisation Sub-Committee', 17 February 1932. Taken form Labour Party, National Executive Committee Minutes [NEC Minutes].

13. W.W. Knox and A. McKinlay, 'The Re-Making of Scottish Labour in the 1930s', *Twentieth Century British History*, 6, 2, (1995), p. 176.

14. NAC Minutes, 13–14 August 1932 (ILP Archive).

15. *Ibid.*

16. For example, at its meeting of 8–9 October 1932, the NAC acknowledged the expulsion of 25 members from the Cowdenbeath and Tranent Branches.

17. NAC Minutes, 17–18 December 1932 (ILP Archive).

18. B. Pimlott, *Labour and the Left in the 1930s* (Cambridge, 1977), p. 101.

19. See, for example, *Forward*, 14 January 1933.

20. The SSP 'shared' *Forward* with the Labour Party and, in 1933, briefly established its own monthly paper *The Scottish Free Press*. The same year, the SSP claimed four MPs: David Kirkwood, Duncan Graham, Neil Maclean and William Leonard.

21. J. Gaster, 'On Leadership', *Controversy*, June 1934; *New Leader*, January 1934.

22. Executive Committee Report, November 16–17 1934 (ILP Archive).

23. For further information, see W.W. Knox and J. Saville, 'Campbell Stephen' in W.W. Knox (ed.), *Scottish Labour Leaders 1918–39: A Biographical Dictionary* (Edinburgh, 1984), pp. 253–55.

24. *Govan Press*, 8 November 1935; *Glasgow Herald*, 12 November 1935.

25. *Glasgow Herald*, 8 and 9 November 1935.

26. NEC Minutes, 27 March and 22 October 1935; *New Leader*, 18 October 1935; Minutes of the Scottish Executive of the Labour Party, 20 March and 16 November 1933, 11 March and October 21 1935; Labour Party, 'National Agents Scottish Tour Report', 27 March 1935. The NEC approved a special grant of £420 to boost the election funds in ILP strongholds in Glasgow.

27. *Govan Press*, 8 November 1935.

28. *Glasgow Evening Standard*, 2 November 1935.

29. *Glasgow Herald*, 7 November 1935.

30. *Glasgow Evening Standard*, 2 November 1935; *Glasgow Herald*, 5 November and 12 November 1935.

31. *Glasgow Herald*, 16 November 1935.

32. For an extended, if not always accurate, summary of the local electoral fortunes of the ILP and Labour Party in Glasgow, see J.J. Smyth, *Labour in Glasgow*, pp. 190–207.

33. For example, in 1934, the combined ILP–Labour vote in both Partick East and Whitevale was greater than the victorious Moderate total.

34. For example, in 1934, the ILP gained Shettleston and Dalmarnock from Moderate and Protestant candidates respectively, despite the opposition of Labour Party candidates.

35. *New Leader*, 28 December 1934; *New Leader*, 19 October 1934; *Scots New Leader*, 3 and 17 January 1936; *New Leader*, 16 December 1938.

36. *Forward*, 13 January 1934; *New Leader*, 4 May, June 29 and 19 October 1934, 18 January and 5 July 1935, 4 September and 20 November 1936, 12 February 1937.

37. *New Leader*, 27 November 1936.

38. *Glasgow Evening News*, 5 November 1937.

39. *Glasgow Herald*, 14 February 1938; *New Leader*, 13 January 1939.

40. A. McKinlay and R.J. Morris (eds), *The ILP on Clydeside*, pp. 14–16.

41. For example, James Richmond of Clydebank ILP was the Scottish organising secretary of the UPA. *New Leader*, 8 January 1937; Glasgow Borough Labour Party Minutes, 13 December 1932; Glasgow Trades Council Minutes, August 1933, 19 December 1933, 23 October 1934 (Mitchell Library, Glasgow). On the UPA, see J.D.M. Bell, 'Trade Unions', in H.A. Clegg, *The System of Industrial Relations in Great Britain: Its History, Law and Institutions* (Oxford, 1953), p. 137.

42. Labour Party Organisation Committee Minutes, 14 February 1934; *New Leader*, 14 August 1934, 7 June and 18 October 1935; NEC Minutes, 27 March and 24 July 1935.

43. *New Leader*, 15 June 1934.

44. *Ibid.*, 4 December 1936, 23 March 1937; NAC Minutes, 2 August 1937 (ILP Archive); *New Leader*, 2, 9 and 16 April 1937; Shettleston ILP Minutes, 28 November 1939 (ILP Archive). On the context and consequences of this apprentices' strike, see R. Croucher, *Engineers at War* (London, 1982), pp. 47–53, pp. 98–99 and, on ILP involvement in the war time militant engineering movement, pp. 176–78.

45. H. McShane and J. Smith, *Harry McShane: No Mean Fighter* (London, 1978), p. 207; J. McGovern, *Neither Fear Nor Favour* (London, 1960), pp. 80–85; *New Leader*, 5 April 1935.

46. For example, the Glasgow ILP, and James Carmichael in particular, were also involved in organising a deputation of 20 young Scottish unemployed to cycle from Glasgow to London to present demands to the National government in mid-1935. NAC, 'Report to Conference, 1935' (ILP Archive); *New Leader*, 12 July 1935.

47. John Lochore, in I. MacDougall, *Voices from the Hunger Marches*, p. 316; Attendance on the Sludge boat trips varied during the 1930s. Normally, over 100 members went, with 151 going on 4 July 1938. Once, in 1937 however, ticket sales only reached 36. See, Bridgeton Branch Social Committee Cash Book (Mitchell Library, Glasgow).

48. See, for example, *New Leader*, 26 August 1932.

49. The flag days were not permitted by the magistrates in the mid-1930s, a decision which was reversed in September 1936. *Guardian*, 19 August 1936; *Scots New Leader*, 4 September 1936.

50. *New Leader*, 7 May 1937.

51. *Ibid.*, 25 June 1937 and 28 January 1938.

52. John Lochore, in I. MacDougall, *Voices from the Hunger Marches*, p. 316.

53. *Forward*, 27 February 1937.

54. One important example is the unanimous support for ILP councillor John Heenan in Shettleston from senior clergy, led by the Rector of the chief Catholic School in Glasgow, at the Catholic Union meeting in 1934. T. Gallagher, *Glasgow*, p. 202.

55. *Ibid.*, p. 211

56. J. McGovern, *Why Bishops Back Franco: Report of Visit of Investigation to Spain* (London, 1936); T. Gallagher, *Glasgow*, pp. 210–11; *Forward*, 12 June 1937.

57. Carmichael to Murry, 12 February 1936 (Maxton Papers, Mitchell Library, Glasgow); Shettleston ILP Minutes, 5 March and 16 April 1936 (ILP Archive).

58. Correspondence between James Carmichael and Thomas Murry, 12 February to 30 June 1936 (Maxton Papers).

59. Shettleston ILP Minutes, 25 June, 26 November 1936 and 4 February 1937 (ILP Archive).

60. NAC Minutes, 1 August 1936 (ILP Archive).

61. 'Report of Glasgow Party Enquiry Committee', submitted to NAC meeting, 11 December 1937; 'Executive Committee Report', 22 October 1937; NAC Minutes, 13 November 1937 (ILP Archive).

62. In 1947, the nationally declared membership of the East Anglian Division was 718. Presumably, as in every other year, the overwhelming majority of these were based in Norwich. Indeed, figures in the divisional minutes give a membership of 930 in 1947. The nationally declared membership for the Scottish Division was 336. P.J. Thwaits, 'The Independent Labour Party', p. 27; Division Five Minute Book, January 1947 (LSE Library).

63. *Norwich Mercury*, 17 October 1931.

64. Division Five Minute Book, 10 January 1932 (LSE Library).

65. Minutes of Special Conference, Division Five Minute Book, 15 October 1933; Division Five Minute Book, 10 January 1932 (LSE Library); J. Middleton Murry, *The Necessity of Communism* (London, 1932).

66. Middleton Murry to A.W. Votier 7 January 1932, cited in F.A. Lee, *The Life of John Middleton Murry* (London, 1959), pp. 196–7

67. Middleton Murry had started the magazine *The Adelhpi* in June 1923. When he joined the ILP in 1931, the magazine, although no longer edited by him, reflected this political slant. In October 1932, *The Adelphi* claimed that it was entering a new phase in its history. The price was reduced in order to attract a larger number of socialist readers and it declared that the magazine would carry at least one article each month on the subject of the Independent Labour Party. Most of these articles were written by Middleton Murry himself.

68. Division Five Council Meeting Minutes, 1 June 1933 and 3 February 3 1934 (LSE Library); *New Leader*, 5 May 1934; Executive Committee Report, August 11–12 1934.

69. G. Cohen, 'Independent Socialist Party', in K. Gildart, D. Howell and N. Kirk (eds), *Dictionary of Labour Biography, Volume X* (London, 2003), pp. 231–38.

70. *New Leader*, 7 February 1936; *New Leader*, 18 February 1938; Division Five Minute Book, 12 February 1939 (LSE Library).

71. P.A. Cunningham, 'Unemployment in Norwich in the 1930s', unpublished PhD thesis, University of East Anglia (1990), pp. 133–36.

72. *Ibid.*, pp. 238–39.

73. *Eastern Evening News*, 1 November 1933.

74. NEC Minutes, 15 November 1933.

75. A. Holt and J. Saville, 'Dorothy Jewson', in J. Saville and J.M. Bellamy (eds) *Dictionary of Labour Biography, Volume V* (London, 1979).

76. *New Leader*, 24 October 1937.

77. *Ibid.*

78. *Norwich Mercury*, 9 November 1935.

79. *Ibid.*, 2 November 1935.

80. *Ibid.*, and 9 November 1935.

81. *Ibid.*, 23 November 1935; NEC Organisation Sub-Committee, 22 December 1936; NEC Minutes, 25 May 1937. The full breakdown of the voting was as follows: Hall 207; Kelly 150; Shakespeare 790; Strauss 530; Brockway 2,266; Hall and Kelly 20,749; Shakespeare and Strauss 33,458; Brockway and Hall 2,835; Brockway and Kelly 843; Brockway and Strauss 105; Hall and Strauss 50; Kelly and Shakespeare 274; Kelly and Strauss 39; spoilt 27. P. A. Cunningham, 'Unemployment', pp. 238–39.

82. In 1937, when it was made clear that there would be no arrangement between the two parties, the ILP selected a second candidate to run alongside Brockway in the event of a general election. *New Leader*, 7 May 1937; Labour Party Organisation Sub-Committee Minutes, 22 December 1936; NEC Minutes, 25 May 1937.

83. Division Five Minute Book, 2 February 1936, 11 February 1936 and 20 June 1941 (LSE Library); *New Leader*, 10 January, 2 February and 20 March 1936, 15 October 1937.

84. *New Leader*, 12 July 1935.

85. *Ibid.*, 1 January 1936.

86. *Ibid.*, 30 April, 7 May and 21 May 1937.

87. R. Stevens, '"Rapid Demise or Slow Death"?', pp. 113–30.

88. *New Leader*, 26 August 1932.

89. Division Five Minute Book, 4 September 1932 (LSE Library).

90. Membership figures from Division Five Minute Book.

91. Cited in P.J. Thwaits, 'The Independent Labour Party', p. 220.

92. *New Leader*, 26 April 1935.

93. *Ibid.*

94. J. Paton, *Left Turn: The Autobiography of John Paton* (London, 1936), p. 396.

95. D. Howell, *British Workers*, pp. 6–7.

96. Division Five Conference, 12 February 1939 (LSE Library).

Chapter 5

Making Politics in Local Communities: Labour Women in Interwar Manchester

Karen Hunt

It was in their neighbourhoods and local communities that most people, particularly women, practised their politics. It is therefore in these spaces that the meaning of Labour Party membership to women and the varieties of ways in which they experienced political activity can be traced. Of course, when women only have a walk-on part in most histories of the Labour Party, it is all too easy to homogenise them as 'Labour women'. A local study presents an opportunity to explore whether such generalisations are justified. Moreover, the local is also an important aspect of the existing historiography on women and the interwar Labour Party. Those who have studied women's interaction with the party at a national level tend to view local politics as the space in which women were able to affect, and even to gender, the policy of their party. Pat Thane has argued that Labour women's greatest achievement in this period was putting welfare firmly on the party's agenda, although this success did not reflect organised women's power within the party.[1] The accepted view is, as Martin Francis puts it, that 'In the 1920s Labour women contested Labour men's preference for issues relating to paid labour, and promoted an agenda concerned with social deprivation and welfare' and, in so doing, did 'a great deal to broaden the party's appeal in the interwar years'.[2] Neil Evans and Dot Jones, in their account of women in the Labour Party in Wales, emphasise that women's sections 'helped humanise its public face'. 'Labour had to speak to the nation as well as to the class in order to win elections and women helped to give it that voice'.[3] In these accounts, women members were clearly useful to the Labour Party, but what of women's experience of the party?

Local studies such as Sam Davies's of Liverpool underline how complex and varied the relationship could be between Labour parties and their women members.[4] In interwar Liverpool, women's influence in the party was stronger in the 1920s than in the 1930s. Davies found that the Liverpool example confirmed what Jane Mark-Lawson and her colleagues had found for Lancaster, Preston and Nelson: women's relationship with the interwar Labour Party was marked by the nature and extent of women's participation in local labour markets as well as the gender relations involved in their work.[5] The experience of local women members of the party was also affected by the nature of the local party elite. In the case of Liverpool, this was a group of Catholic councillors who brought religion to the centre of Labour politics. This group marked Liverpool women's perception of the party but so too did the fact that in the 1930s only one woman made any impact on Liverpool municipal politics. This was Bessie Braddock and she avoided working with the party's women's sections. Although Braddock was by no means a party loyalist, Davies suggests that, like the national women leaders of the party, she practised a politics that put party and class before sex. In Manchester, similar questions can be asked about the way in which the local political culture, the party elite or influential individuals shaped the experience of grass roots activists.

Another recent local study of Labour women also raises questions for the Manchester example. Here the focus is on Coventry, particularly on the city's pioneer woman councillor Alice Arnold. It is suggested that women encountered significant prejudice from within local Labour parties, particularly when they resisted or refused to be limited by their presumed role as champions of women and children.[6] Arnold, an organiser for the Worker's Union, was first elected as a union candidate to the city council in 1919 and served throughout the interwar period. Yet Cathy Hunt shows how Arnold was marginalised in her union and in her municipal politics, not just because she was a woman but also because of her class, single status and radical politics. In painting a picture of a woman rooted in her community and in her experience as a worker, Hunt questions many of the easy assumptions of homogeneity which lurk behind the phrase 'Labour women'. For Arnold was as marginalised from local women's sections and from the Women's Co-operative Guild (WCG) as she was from the local male party leadership, yet she continued to be returned for her ward and took an active part in Coventry municipal politics. She was involved in welfare issues but she did not allow herself to be limited to this.[7] Hunt raises many questions for other local studies, not least the different ways in which women interacted with the opportunities that local politics presented. It seems that what it meant to be a woman member of the Labour Party in the interwar years varied from place to place. How was this apparent in Manchester?

Women and the Labour Movement in Manchester in the 1920s

The new membership-based Labour Party was relatively quick to establish itself across the city in the aftermath of the war. By 1919, a divisional Labour Party existed in every constituency in Manchester except Exchange, which soon followed in 1920. In the same year, Manchester Labour Party estimated its membership at 22,683. Alongside and within the new Labour Party branches, the ILP continued to be active. Indeed, it was the ILP that provided many of the key personnel to develop the new Labour Party branches across the city.[8] Declan McHugh's study of the Labour Party in Manchester in the 1920s shows that individual membership was greatest in those divisions of the local party where trade union influence was the strongest. For example, inner city Ardwick had 4,000 paying members in 1924, which made it one of the biggest membership sections in the country, while in the same year middle-class suburban Withington only had 43 members. It was not only the local social structure of a ward and the degree of penetration of unionisation into the local workforce which marked the differential growth of Labour Party membership across the city, much also depended on the energies of local activists, organisers and officials. Thus, the organising skills of E.J. Hookway, briefly local party secretary, was a crucial factor in the significant individual membership in the more middle-class Rusholme ward.[9] The new party working to establish itself as a membership-based organisation across the city and its ability to chime with local political cultures and traditions is part of the context for the activities of local Labour women in this period.

Before the war, Labour women were to be found in local branches of the Women's Labour League (WLL) and the WCG as well as in the local trade union movement, particularly the umbrella Manchester and Salford Women's Trade Council.[10] Those who were also socialists would in addition be active in their own parties or groups. This was aside from whatever form their suffrage activism, if any, might take. All these radical movements were closely connected in Manchester. After the war, the terrain looked much the same aside from the advent in 1920 of the Communist Party (CP) to the left of the Labour Party.[11] Within the Labour Party, the constitution of 1918 saw the dissolution of the WLL and the creation of a new structure based on optional women's sections within branches.

According to McHugh, Manchester in the 1920s did not see the kind of growth in individual female membership of the party or of Labour Party women's sections that Savage found in Preston in the same period.[12] The experience in Manchester was much more varied, largely because this was a far bigger and more diverse conurbation. By 1921, there were five women's sections in the city (Ardwick, Blackley, Clayton, Platting, Rusholme), but coverage was piecemeal. For example, Withington did not establish a section until 1924. In addition, some sections only had a limited lifetime. Early attempts to sustain organisation in Hulme failed only to later revive, so that in 1926 it was viewed as the city's most promising women's section. More generally, it seems that female members were most numerous in wards dominated by the skilled, organised, industrial working class. McHugh found that in Manchester in the 1920s, Labour membership was most attractive to women with some trade union connection, either through their own or their husband's union membership. Slum and middle-class districts shared the characteristic of a lower density of trade union membership and so in these areas both female and male membership of the Labour Party was lower.

Yet, the effort put into recruiting and organising women members could make a difference. Thus, Ardwick Divisional Labour Party did not form its first women's section until 1920 when a group of women organised in the Ardwick ward. This ward's membership grew rapidly and soon accounted for 57 per cent of the division, yet less than half the women members in the ward actually joined the women's section.[13] As Marion Phillips (national women's officer) commented in her report on women's work in the party for 1921–22, the areas where progress in organising women was slowest included some urban areas 'where there is a feeling that to have a women's section with its own officers is to divide the sexes and create sex war'.[14] This was to be an anxiety throughout the interwar period. Phillips emphasised that one of the best ways to achieve an active women membership was through the formation of women's sections which in that year numbered 802. Yet, when the Manchester Labour Women's Advisory Council (MLWAC) reported in

1932 on the state of women's organisation in the district, it was noted that there were still three or four divisions that did not have women's sections.[15] The relations between local parties and their women's sections could also be difficult, such as that in St George's ward, Hulme, which necessitated the intervention of the regional women's organiser, Mary Anderson.[16]

Equally important to understanding women's experience of Manchester's labour movement, particularly in the 1920s, was the continuing influence of the ILP. It should be noted that all ILPers were members of their local Labour Party but could, in addition, join the Labour Party as an individual member. The Manchester branches of the ILP formed part of the Manchester and Salford Federation, which in turn was organised in the No. 9 Division. Although never officers of the federation, women were to be found on its executive and as branch officers as well as speakers and as elected members of the council or board of guardians. They were certainly not half of the party but their presence was definitely apparent. Obituaries show that many women members of the party, particularly those who had joined before the war, were married to other ILPers. For example, it was said of Mrs Quinn of North Manchester ILP, 'though she was not as well known as her husband, she did yeoman service for the movement. A staunch socialist and one of our ablest women members, her homely presence will be sadly missed by us all'.[17]

Before the 1920s, the ILP prided itself on being particularly woman friendly and not needing separate sections for its women members. After the war, concern over falling membership, particularly amongst women, led the ILP to reassess its attitudes to women's self-organisation. In the 1920s, the Manchester branches were as varied as their sister branches across the country in the arrangements they made for women to meet and to organise separately. By 1926, the division had 22 women's groups and plans were being made in Manchester and Salford to get the groups together for co-operative work.[18] The Divisional Council enabled women's groups within their region to set up their own democratic structure with an elected Women's Council which was a sub-committee of the Divisional Council. ILP women also elected one representative to sit on the MLWAC. Although women's groups were never part of every ILP branch in Manchester, some groups were remarkably tenacious and the division as a whole seems to have been supportive of a dynamic and democratic women's organisation within the party. ILP women's groups do not appear to have been as contentious in Manchester as they were in the party as a whole in the 1920s.[19]

Labour Women Activists at the Grass Roots

If we are to reach the experience of women in the interwar Labour Party, we have to recognise that membership was multi-layered. There was a spectrum of activism from those who merely held a party card to those who were elected to public office on the local council or the board of guardians. This was not a phenomenon peculiar to women, although the possible roles and presumptions about potential for activism and spheres of interest were often gendered. The most active women were the most visible, yet even among this group their presence and achievements barely appear in the historical record. Retrieving the names of other women who laboured at the grass roots of the party is more difficult still.

Studies of the Labour Party in Manchester in the 1920s do not ring with the names of women activists, whether as councillors, local officers or party officials, which suggests that women were not particularly well integrated into the local elite. Yet, Manchester City Council had a number of pioneering Labour women councillors in the interwar years. Of these Annie Lee gave the longest service in the Gorton South ward, which she represented from 1919 to 1936 when she became the first Labour woman alderman in the city. In 1931, she was profiled in the *Manchester & Salford Woman Citizen*. After over a decade of service she was the senior woman councillor and the only woman on the watch committee, as well as being a member of the education and town planning committees. In addition, she had been a long-serving guardian and was now a member of the public assistance committee, as well as sitting on the Lancashire Asylums Board.[20] Certainly, she was an extraordinarily active woman and clearly an activist.

John Marriott, commenting on Labour activists in interwar West Ham, felt that given prevailing attitudes amongst the local community and amongst Labour men, it was not surprising that the few women who were active in this period were either unmarried, middle class and educated, or powerful enough to assert their independence.[21] Annie Lee was not from the first category, but a pen portrait of her in 1929 suggests that she was certainly a feisty woman:

> Perhaps the outstanding quality in Miss Lee's character is fearlessness in the face of all opposition, and a passion for helping those she considers downtrodden – generally those of the female species, as Miss Lee evidently feels that the male members of the community are well provided with spokesmen! One is apt to feel sometimes in the meetings of the Council that she lays herself open to criticism by her somewhat truculent belabouring of the woman's point of view, but it was very largely due to her persistence that two important civic posts have been filled by women – that of the Assistant Police Surgeon ... and the new Deputy Chief Inspector of Schools ... Miss Lee's kindly manner and unfailing good temper make her popular with all her colleagues, though they may not agree with the policy she advocates.[22]

Listed as a trade union secretary when she stood for election, balancing all these different tasks and managing an uncertain income cannot have been easy. Indeed, in 1930, her local women's section resolved to send her £2/10s at once because she was experiencing adverse circumstances due to unemployment.[23] Although not officially commemorated in Manchester today, a contemporary remembered her as 'legend and tales about her were legion'.[24] Annie Lee's sustained activism was pioneering and determinedly focused on Manchester. But she was not alone.

So, what made the leading Labour women activists in Manchester in the 1920s?[25] Taking the women candidates who stood for the Labour Party for the city council, it is clear that many of them were already politically experienced. Mary Welch, councillor for Moston (1923–29), became an organiser for the National

Union of Distributive and Allied Workers (NUDAW) in 1917. Her pre-war suffragism and political engagement during the war led to her being described in 1923 as 'a woman of experience and ability'.[26] Welch's experiences were very similar to those of Ellen Wilkinson, councillor for Gorton (1923–26). She too was an organiser for the NUDAW, as were some of the other leading male Labour councillors such as Wright Robinson. Amongst the first generation of Labour women councillors, few defined their occupation as 'housewife', as was much more common amongst their Liberal and Conservative equivalents. Indeed, a surprising number were listed as trade union or Co-op officials and organisers.[27]

Those not directly employed in the labour movement often had training of some sort, for example as a teacher (Dora Taylor) or as a nurse, Swedish remedial gymnast, medical electrician and masseuse (L. Harrison). However, Ellen Wilkinson was unusual amongst this generation of Manchester Labour councillors in having received a university education, although Annot Robinson who had stood unsuccessfully in the Medlock Street ward in 1920 also had a degree. Although by no means a homogenous group, the Labour women candidates represented themselves as working women. A number were self-employed; for example, Mary Smith (councillor for Beswick, 1919–23) was a shopkeeper, while Edith Chorlton (councillor for Medlock Street, 1926–32) was an insurance agent. These were both forms of employment that earlier socialist activists, usually men, had adopted to overcome blacklisting at their trade or to forestall victimisation. The flexibility of self-employment was thought to combine well with political activism, but many found it hard to sustain a business alongside the demands of an activist's life.

Prior political experience was ubiquitous amongst Manchester's first generation of Labour women municipal candidates. A number of them had been or were guardians, such as Lee, Chorlton and Hannah Mitchell. Like many of the Manchester male activists, leading Labour women were members of the ILP (Annie Lee, Dora Taylor, Mary Welch). For some their ILP membership was much more important to them than their association with the Labour Party. When the ILP disaffiliated from Labour in 1932, Hannah Mitchell remained loyal to the party she had joined in the 1890s. Indeed, she was re-elected in 1932 to the council as an ILP candidate. In 1935, she retired from the council and left the ILP, which was now in disarray in Lancashire. She did not rejoin the Labour Party. Although ILP influence was strong among the Labour women candidates in Manchester in the 1920s, as important was the experience of being part of the WCG. Emily Beavan, Mary Earnshaw, Dora Taylor and Hannah Mitchell were all active members. Indeed, Beavan was elected national president of the Guild in 1932. Thus, when women managed to get nominated by the Labour Party to stand for the city council they often combined a broad range of political experiences. To take one example, when Dora Taylor stood in the Miles Platting ward in 1925, she was a longstanding member and propagandist for the ILP. She had been a district secretary of the Labour Party and of the WCG, a member of the Coal Control Board, the first national women's organiser for the Co-operative Party, and a co-opted member of the education committee.[28]

This first generation of Labour women candidates also had strong familial associations with the labour movement. For some there was a clear parental influence, such as Josephine Shaw, whose father was an active member of the old Radical Party and whose mother quietly supported the suffrage movement. Family political discussions had been a feature of her childhood.[29] Amongst the Labour activists of the 1920s, it was the choice of a politically concerned spouse which was most apparent. This feature was not limited to Manchester. In Newcastle and Gateshead, all but one of the women councillors were Labour and most were the wives of Labour councillors.[30] In Manchester, when female delegates were selected to attend the Labour Party conference in the 1920s, they were often the wives of local MPs: Mrs C. Compton (1922, 1923) and Mrs M.G. Davies (1921–23, 1927–28).[31] This was not just an exercise in saving money, as their husbands would be attending the conference anyway, for these were women who were active in their own right. Mrs Davies was secretary of Withington Divisional Labour Party from 1921 to 1924. There were certainly a number of married couples amongst Manchester's Labour activist population in the 1920s, such as the Comptons, the Coxs, the Davies, the Greens and the Hamnetts. This had been a trend amongst pre-war socialist activists, although often the male partner was more dominant and the wife's activity curtailed with children. Amongst the membership as a whole, equally active partners in a married couple remained unusual. Stella Davies, recalling the labour movement in Manchester in the 1920s of which she was a part, commented, 'The politically minded woman, though present in the period, was not usual and many wives found themselves unable to enter into their husband's interests'.[32] Political partnerships were not just important in sustaining and supporting the work of another activist, they could help to maintain the peculiar life that activism demanded and the toll that it almost invariably took on health and family finances.

Balancing the domestic requirements to sustain daily life with the demands of political activism was a challenge for the first generation of Labour women municipal candidates. A number of the most active Labour women in Manchester were single, such as Annie Lee, or had a grown-up family, such as Hannah Mitchell and Edith Chorlton. This did not solve the problem, but it could ease it. In 1926, the *Woman Citizen* commented:

> The reconciliation of public and private responsibilities is made easy for Mrs Chorlton by the sympathetic interest her husband and two grown-up sons take in her work which they show in very practical ways, such as arranging to have their midday meal out four days out of seven.[33]

For others, it was not so clear how they would reconcile these responsibilities if elected. For example, Dora Taylor first stood for the council when her son was five-years-old, while Josephine Shaw's daughter was only one-year older at her first contest. Hannah Mitchell managed to make a political point over the whole issue:

In regard to the claims of home versus public work Mrs Mitchell believes that while a woman's first duty is to her home and family that is not her whole duty. She finds by adopting labour saving devices and being methodical it is possible to run her home and carry on her public work. Fortunately her husband is sufficiently sympathetic and public spirited to realise that it is possible to eat a meal without his wife sitting by to sweeten his tea, and a friend is always ready to prepare a meal or help in other ways as her contribution to the general good. When there are young children it would be more difficult but still not impossible.[34]

Remaining a part of the neighbourhood had a practical as well as a political dimension for many of these women. It was from their neighbours that the necessary domestic support usually came to enable women to be activists and elected representatives. As Hannah Mitchell remembered gratefully, 'I could write a book on the good neighbours who have helped to make so much of my life'.[35]

Being rooted in a local community was also crucial to the way in which these women presented themselves to the voters. Edith Chorlton made the point to the electorate in Hulme that she knew the area well as she had begun to earn her living at ten delivering newspapers locally. 'Her strength of character, and ability to gain and hold the respect of the people who have known her from childhood is responsible for this attainment, while her intimate knowledge of the needs and the conditions of this congested area is invaluable in her work,' commented the *Woman Citizen*.[36] Such a local base was not unusual. In the same year, Josephine Shaw stood (unsuccessfully) for St Michael's ward where she had grown up. For others it was not just that they knew the neighbourhoods where they made their politics, but that they shared the experiences of those around them. So, when Mrs L. Harrison stood in the Cheetham ward, she emphasised that if she was elected she would vote solidly for direct labour.[37] She explained that this was because she had lived in a corporation house that had been badly built by contractors. She now lived in one with considerably superior workmanship that had been built by direct labour, and she wanted to ensure that others benefited from her experience.

Being rooted in local communities and sharing experiences with many of their electorate did not preclude women who were elected as councillors from being represented as different. A remark like, councillor Dora Taylor 'caused quite a stir in the council when she appeared in her Eton crop!', is given context by fellow councillor Hannah Mitchell's memory that 'One of the first things I sensed in public life was the undercurrent of anti-feminism which pervades public bodies. The Labour Party itself was only lukewarm on such matters'.[38] This, of course, was not peculiar to Manchester. In Coventry, for example, Labour councillor Ellen Hughes was accused by the mayor of being hysterical when she drew attention to the effects of inadequate housing on the lives of families.[39] Detailed studies of Manchester will reveal the social geography of ambivalence, even resistance, to women's public activity and its relationship to the presence of high-profile individual activist women and/or to organised Labour women, whether in women's sections or in ILP women's groups. It is quite likely that Mitchell's experience of repeated opposition from the leadership of her local Labour Party to her selection as a candidate to fight the Newton Heath ward was not that unusual. Her offence was her feminism and not being 'amenable to discipline'. In the end, the ILP's nomination of Mitchell was accepted when a candidate was needed to fight a by-election in the ward in 1924. She was selected because she was already well-known, and because the local ILP guaranteed to meet her electoral expenses.[40] Essentially the local Labour Party now needed her.

Whether the Manchester party as a whole felt it needed women to represent its public face is more debateable. If one looks at the statistics for interwar Manchester,[41] the picture is not as poor as Coventry, where Alice Arnold was the only woman on the council from 1922 to 1926.[42] In Manchester, there had been a woman on the council from 1908 (Margaret Ashton), with the first Labour women joining the by now two women Independents in 1919. From 1919 to 1929, seven Labour women were elected with a maximum of five councillors sitting at any one time. This meant Labour was the most successful party in electing women councillors in Manchester in the 1920s. In the 1930s, six Labour women were elected with a maximum of four Labour women sitting at any point. In the 1920s, there were ten failed Labour women candidatures, which rose to 18 in the 1930s. In effect, more women were having the opportunity to stand for the council but were becoming less likely to be elected. Many, like Annot Robinson, had been selected for 'impossible municipal wards'.[43] Yet, some women were remarkably persistent in their attempts to be elected. For example, Mary Knight stood twice in Rusholme ward (1935, 1936) and twice in Levenshulme (1936, 1937), before winning the New Cross ward in 1938.

These activities occupied the most committed and those who thought they would be able to cope with the demands of being a local councillor. Most of the Labour Party membership (female or male) would never stand for local office, but for the women amongst them they had to decide not only how much of their energies they could devote to politics, but also where they would channel those energies: the women's section or their local (mixed-sex) branch.

Separate Women's Organisation

In Manchester, there were a number of episodes where underlying tensions surfaced about separate women's organisation within the Labour Party. A leader in the provincial Labour paper, *Leeds Weekly Citizen*, set out the Labour position clearly. The purpose of women's sections from the party's point of view was 'to establish machinery which gives the women members complete freedom of expression as women, without isolating them as members. In the labour movement women are organised for political purposes, not separately but sectionally, and their sections ... are regimental units of the Labour army'.[44] But this was not always how rank-and-file women experienced the issue. Before the war, women's self-organisation within socialist parties had been problematic across the whole of the Second International as women struggled with their parent parties to gain a degree of autonomy as well as a place within decision-making structures.[45]

Manchester women soon made it clear that they were not satisfied with the accommodation arrived at by national leaders of Labour women and the party leadership. The bone of contention was the lack of powers granted to organised Labour women.[46] Late in 1921, the MLWAC circulated a resolution that recommended that Labour Party women ought to have their own National Council representing the women's sections, which would have direct representation on the National Executive Committee (NEC) of the party. The national party leadership moved to counteract this. At the annual Labour Party conference in 1921, Annot Robinson had put forward an amendment similar to the MLWAC resolution. But as the delegate of Blackley Labour Party, she was told that she could not move her amendment without the support of Manchester Borough Labour Party. This support was denied and the amendment fell. The following year, the Borough Labour Party representative, Tom Larrad, moved the resolution which was then defeated. In his speech, he stressed the esteem in which women were held by the Manchester party. Yet, there were few concrete signs of this.

It was not that all Labour women in Manchester would have agreed with one of their number who recalled of the women's sections: 'These I did not like. I believe in complete equality, and was not prepared to be a camp follower, or a member of what seemed to me a permanent social committee, or official cake-maker to the Labour Party'.[47] But this was the judgement of an ILPer (Hannah Mitchell) who remained unconvinced by what she saw as 'the domination of the party machine' over local activism in the 1920s. Mitchell may have chosen to eschew the women's sections, although she was part of her local ILP women's group, but many other female Labour Party members tried to make the sections work. Yet, in December 1929, Gorton women's section expressed its frustration when it sent a letter to the party executive 'protesting against the constant accusation that we want to be a separate entity'.[48] Party men could be just as ambivalent as many women about sections, although their worry was often that such a woman's space might be a breeding ground of feminist distractions rather than fundraising and social events. The fine balance could easily tip over into mutual suspicion. After a by-election in the Moss Side West ward, the MLWAC passed an angry resolution expressing the view that women candidates were not welcomed by party officials.[49] In 1932, the MLWAC attempted to renegotiate their constitution with the borough party in order to have 'more local autonomy'.[50] They were particularly concerned that their delegates to the executive were not allowed to vote. The reply from the party officials played on the longstanding fear of separatism, by suggesting that 'the advisory council is attempting to set up a Women's Labour Party and break away from the Borough Party'.[51]

The local context for this awkwardness was the long history of suffragism in the city, which had contributed to a determination that women should make effective use of their hard won citizenship. Some of this concern was expressed through the Manchester and Salford Women Citizen's Association (WCA), formed in 1913 as a non-party women's organisation to promote active citizenship. WCAs were formed across the country at the same time as the Labour Party inaugurated its women's sections. By 1925, there were 11 branches in Manchester, which had swelled to 19 in 1934. Fear of competition from organisations like the WCAs meant that in the immediate post-war period there had been considerable concern to ensure that members of women's sections were not distracted from their loyalty to the Labour Party. At the 1920 Labour women's conference, Marion Phillips moved the resolution which instructed members 'to avoid dissipating their energies in non-party political organisations'. A number of Labour women spoke up in favour of the WCAs as an *additional* space in which to make their politics. Manchester's Annot Robinson was one who drew on her own experience of socialist, suffrage and peace activism to argue 'women had for years been associated with other organisations, and had obtained special knowledge therefrom, which had been of immense value'.[52]

Despite hostility from the party's national women's officer, relationships between local Labour women and local WCAs varied considerably. In Manchester, although women affiliated to the Labour Party were never central to the group who led the local WCA, Labour women were involved. Hannah Mitchell wrote for the organisation's journal, *Manchester & Salford Woman Citizen*, and her fellow Labour councillor, Dora Taylor, was a member of Crumpsall WCA. Avice Trench who stood for Labour in the All Saints ward in 1931 was not only an active WCA member, but also a member of the *Woman Citizen*'s editorial board. Mary Stocks was similarly an active member of both the Labour Party and the WCA. Despite its non-party position, the *Woman Citizen* was also able to support Labour municipal candidates such as Ellen Wilkinson in 1923, as they were understood to be sympathetic to the aims of the WCA.[53] There was often considerable overlap between the programme of the Manchester and Salford WCA and Labour women candidates. Thus, the *Woman Citizen* could say, 'We are not in agreement with the full Labour Party programme set out in her election address but citizens of all parties will support her in her work ... to improve housing, to secure a pure food supply, more public wash-houses, and the abolition of smoke'.[54]

Although not without its problems, the relationship between local WCAs and Labour parties could be much more difficult and seemed to depend on the character of the local WCA. The experience of Manchester contrasts with that of Preston. Mike Savage reveals how the hostility of the local Labour Party to the feminism of the WCA drove the non-party organisation into the arms of the Conservatives in order to get support for local WCA municipal candidates. The Labour Party made no effort to put forward women candidates of its own. It was only in 1924 that Preston Labour Party formed its first women's section, and only later in that decade that Preston saw any 'loosening of the patriarchal stresses' of the party largely under the influence of that women's section.[55] Clearly, the relationships between women members of the Labour Party, both those involved in women's sections and those who chose not to be, and local non-party women's organisations have to be plotted carefully. This involves not only recognising the ways in which both groups changed across the interwar period, but also the ways in which this affected their interrelationship. Local political culture and traditions had their effect, as did the increasing pressure from national women officers to distance party women from anything that might be termed 'feminist' and thus divisive.

Yet, women could act together across these boundaries. In 1934, Manchester city council revisited the question of whether there should be a marriage bar for women teachers. The marriage bar had been rejected after much debate in 1928. In 1934, Hannah Mitchell and the Tory Miss Kingsmill Jones (both members of the

WCA) joined forces to speak against the marriage bar, although it was male councillors who moved and seconded the resolution.[56] Moreover, certain issues and organisations could find support from the WCA and the women's sections. Thus, the Women's International League (WIL) and its campaign to promote peace seems to have been generally well received. There were adverts in the *Woman Citizen* and women's sections were represented at WIL meetings.[57] Nevertheless, women's sections could be wary of non-Labour women and organisations. For example, Beswick women's section protested against the MLWAC's invitation to councillor Shena Simon to address a meeting because Simon was a Liberal.[58] She was also a key figure in the local WCA. Policing the boundaries of Labour women's organisations remained a feature of local women's politics throughout the interwar period and affected how individual Labour women practised their politics.

Labour Women's Organisations at the Grass Roots

When the leadership of the ILP called for women's groups to be formed from women members of local branches, their understanding of the difference between these groups and Labour women's sections was made clear. Women's sections of the Labour Party 'make an appeal for membership directly for the section, and are almost wholly concerned in their activities with electoral considerations'. In contrast, ILP women's groups were 'internal organisations within ILP branches; they do not appeal for members for the Group, but for members for the ILP; their main functions are to conduct educational work among ILP women, and to act as an auxiliary in the educational propaganda of the branch among the general body of women'.[59] Were these groups actually very different from one another in their activities and the role they adopted in relation to the parent party? The survival of primary sources allows some comparison in Manchester: of Gorton Labour Party women's section and Newton Heath ILP women's group.

With only one surviving set of minutes for a women's section in interwar Manchester, there is a danger of reading too much from one example. Nevertheless, the minutes of Gorton women's section from 1929 to 1934 are evocative, showing as they do a group of local women attempting to juggle various ideas about their function – their own, the local party's, and that of national women officialdom. The minutes reflect this in the curious mixture of topics discussed by the section. There are detailed discussions of the amounts required and the sourcing of Madeira cake or strawberries and cream for the many social events the section organised, together with the careful recording of responses to correspondence, reports back from their delegates to conferences or to other local bodies such as the trades council, as well as the selection and reporting of visiting speakers. Social evenings got a report just like the business meetings – 'the pianist very ably and willingly met the demands made upon them [sic]'[60] – and the relative success of the evening would then be discussed. But when they debated the merits of organising a potato pie supper versus afternoon teas in their own homes, they reminded themselves that such social events 'are held as a means of keeping contact with members of the section, rather than for the purpose of making money'.[61]

This section did not view itself as merely an auxiliary to the party proper. They had a somewhat abrasive relationship with the executive of their local party. In May 1930, they protested 'against working or being expected to work for any effort for the raising of funds whilst persons are being accepted unconditionally as members whom the party EC and we think are not entirely trustworthy'.[62] Nor were they happy about the powers of the Labour women's annual conference, where they felt resolutions never got any further than the conference hall.[63] Instead, they chose in 1931 to send resolutions through the local trades council to the party annual conference (on unemployment insurance and on pensions).[64] They were not shy of discussing contentious topics: family allowances (speakers for and against); whether public health authorities should give birth control advice; sterilisation of the unfit; finance and the crisis; and our ideals as a movement. This was in addition to regular reports from local councillors on their work.[65] These speakers were usually women. Even though they often could not afford to send their own delegate to the Labour women's annual conference, the section always welcomed a detailed report from a Manchester delegate.[66] These talks and discussions took place within what were usually weekly meetings and were scheduled after the section's business had been completed.

Late in 1931, the section resolved to take a new initiative: to start propaganda meetings addressed by speakers that would be advertised and open to all women. Each meeting would begin with a Labour song and close with the singing of the 'Red Flag'. Because this was something new, they agreed standing orders for the meetings, careful to protect the rights of existing members of the section. They did not want to blur the lines between public events and the section's own meetings, thus admittance to anything other than public meetings would be by membership card, and no-one would be eligible for nomination to official positions until they had been members of the section for at least 12 months. This new venture was not to be an excuse for any form of 'entryism', whether from Communists or non-party feminists.[67]

Gorton women's section agreed amongst themselves that whatever the expectations of others, their main object was not to raise money for the party but to educate women into Labour politics.[68] Much of their collective endeavour was directed inwards towards sustaining their own members through a range of social occasions and by informing themselves about key issues of the day. Many of these issues were 'women's issues', such as birth control, but they did not limit themselves to these nor were they afraid to engage with other contentious debates. Yet, at the same time, they continued organising social events and holding sewing meetings. They engaged with other women's sections, particularly through the local LWAC, and with other local groups such as the trades council. They made use of their rights of delegation where they could to make their case within the Labour Party. They saw themselves as socialists, for not only their public meetings but also their socials always ended with the singing of the 'Red Flag'.

In many ways, the women in Newton Heath who chose to organise together as a women's group in relation to the ILP were similar to their Gorton sisters. The crucial difference was the presence of Hannah Mitchell, even though Gorton too had a Labour woman councillor in this period – Annie Lee. Mitchell and her family[69] were central to their local ILP branch, whereas although Lee occasionally attended Gorton women's section, she does not seem to have been an integral member of it. As a councillor and guardian with many civic commitments, a local women's section may have been one meeting too many for Lee. However, there is no evidence that Lee shared Mitchell's antipathy to women's sections.

Newton Heath ILP, reformed in 1919, saw itself as facing a difficult task in a 'somewhat apathetic neighbourhood'. By 1925, it had an increased membership and felt it was doing useful work. Women speakers were seen as important in insuring the success of the branch, with Ellen Wilkinson singled out in particular, and an open meeting for women was held every month.[70] The branch saw itself as 'rich in capable women propagandists'.[71] Unlike Gorton women's section, ILP women in Newton Heath emphasised their indoor and outdoor propaganda work. The social side of the branch, which was not seen as being women's particular responsibility, was successful enough in 1925 to free the branch from financial worries. The women comrades within the branch made particular efforts to attract women to meetings, for example by holding end of street meetings preceded by canvassing to encourage women to attend. They were bringing the propaganda to the audience rather than the other way round. It was reported that the crowd 'enjoyed being addressed by their own sex, and are looking forward to more meetings of this type'.[72] Newton Heath ILP also organised a 'Lamp Day' (like a flag day) in aid of the locked out miners and their families. Unlike their male comrades, the women not only collected in the streets but also went round the public houses and the workshops too. In Newton Heath's reporting of these women's initiatives, members are praised. This contrasts with Longsight and Rusholme ILP, which complained that women comrades had done all of the collecting for the miners at the park gates and had sold literature. 'Unfortunately, our branch does not seem to recruit males who are prepared to assist in this very necessary work', they said.[73] The activities and attitude of the Newton Heath branch were clearly productive, as they raised about £50 for the relief of local miners during the lockout. As the municipal elections of 1926 approached, they campaigned for their candidate Hannah Mitchell, organising amongst other things an 'At Home' to which all women sympathisers were invited to hear the woman's point of view on municipal matters.[74]

In the branch's annual reports, considerable attention was always given to the women's group and its energetic activities; yet, the branch found it hard to sustain its optimism. Like the neighbouring Cheetham Hill ILP women's section and study circle, Newton Heath ILP women's group consisted of a 'small band of enthusiasts'.[75] Thus, in February 1927 they commented, 'We have all the elements which make for success, what we need is workers and still more workers if we are ever to see even a small instalment of "Socialism in Our Time". Surely one night a week is not too much to give towards such an ideal'.[76] Newton Heath ILP provides an example of a women's group which was integrated into the branch and which had a number of energetic activists. It also had the undoubted bonus of the presence of a remarkably committed long-term member of the ILP, Hannah

Mitchell, who in this period was a city councillor, JP, and speaker and writer for the cause. She clearly made a difference.

But individuals could only do so much. Despite its positive reputation, there was certainly some question of how open the ILP really was in its everyday politics to women and women's issues. This was raised locally when Jamie Widdup, a regular columnist in *Labour's Northern Voice*, wrote in 1926, 'the ILP has an honourable record in regard to women, but, taken as a whole, our working-class attitude is pronouncedly conservative, and miles off any basic conception of equality'.[77] Certainly, the regular 'Daisy Nook' column in the *Northern Voice* was premised on exposing the conservatism of the working-class male in order to remind ILPers of the work that still needed to be done on the journey to their long held ambition, equality of the sexes. Hannah Mitchell, who was 'Daisy Nook', also used these columns to underline her understanding of a politics inextricably linked to everyday life. It was here that she showed what she meant by her stated ambition as a Labour councillor, which was 'to make a bridge between the women in the home and the public authority, and to interpret one to the other'.[78]

A Bridge Between the Local Community and the Party?

Traditionally, women had been regarded by many in the labour and socialist movement as providing the social cement which held together a movement made up largely of male activists. This meant maintaining social networks and mutuality through the party. By the 1920s, some were beginning to worry that the social and collective activities which helped create a community among the membership were coming to substitute for political work itself, particularly when this was narrowly defined as a focus on electoral contests. W.A. Spofforth, secretary of Blackley Divisional Labour Party from 1919 to 1922, warned 'those who estimate their strength by the success of their dances might have a rude awakening when the time for fight arrives. It is not Labour's mission to fiddle whilst Europe is aflame'.[79] Yet, by 1925 he recognised that 'whether we like it or not members come to know and like each other and like the party, by creating a social spirit amongst them'.[80] This view fits with Christopher Howard's conclusion in his study of local Labour parties in the 1920s that the reconstruction programme of 1918 asked for a great deal of commitment from party members and that Labour organisers therefore made a conscious effort after the war to integrate each local party within the local community and 'mix politics with the social life of the people'.[81] The question is not only how successful was this strategy, but how did it impact on the female membership of the party?

Declan McHugh shows that for Manchester in the 1920s only a small minority of the membership was actively involved in the Labour Party and that many Labour activists' vision of the ideal community, with its emphasis on service and on education, proved unattractive even to most party members. He suggests that the most active element amongst Labour's members, upon whom the party's operation depended, were actually quite unlike the people they sought to represent.[82] Whether this was true, or remained the case, for its women activists is less clear. The working-class 'career politicians' who became more apparent in the interwar labour movement tended to be male, although there were exceptions, such as Ellen Wilkinson, who seems to have struck a number of her Manchester contemporaries as a careerist.[83] Apart from Wilkinson, Manchester's Labour women councillors and leading activists kept their focus on the local rather than the national stage during the interwar years.

Labour women municipal candidates not only emphasised their roots in the communities they sought to represent, but also tried to underline how they shared the everyday challenges of other working women. Thus, councillor Edith Chorlton, 'laughingly remarked that she doubted if any member of the [council's baths and washhouses] committee had served a better apprenticeship to the wash-tub than she had – certainly no member has shown a keener interest than Mrs Chorlton in getting the latest labour-saving devices installed in our public washhouses in order to lessen the labour of those who use them'.[84] Hannah Mitchell used her 'Daisy Nook' column not only to show that she understood that men and women had different priorities, but also to underline to the Labour hierarchy how important it was to take women voters' concerns seriously.[85] Mitchell made the case for drawing women closer to municipal politics by indicating how daily lives were affected by politics, for example by demonstrating the links between election day and washing day. She called for women to 'down washing tools and vote for more public washhouses'.[86] Mitchell was not alone among political women in stressing how important the municipal authority was to the housewife. She argued that 'no section of the community is more closely affected by the methods adopted by our local governing bodies than the woman in the home'. Indeed, the work of the city council could be seen as 'a sort of larger housekeeping'.[87] Others took this argument further, suggesting that women had a special responsibility for municipal politics. Lily Oldham argued that 'Local government should have a peculiar interest for women', emphasising health and housing (because it is women's workplace) while she saw education as 'a mother's concern'.[88] She urged women to be discontented and to vote Labour even if they had never done so before.

These kinds of arguments linked to the view that women also had a particular role to play *in* the movement. Mrs Bates, speaking at a Gorton ILP women's meeting, 'stressed the great need for the work which only the women can do in our movement, and whether it be high or low work it was all needed to bring about what socialists are aiming for, and that no progressive movement can carry on unless women have their work to do'.[89] Some local ILP women felt that this work should not consist of all the ancillary tasks associated with electoral contests. Instead, they looked back to an earlier form of socialist politics. For example, Clara Wilson said in 1926, 'We have got to remember that to be good socialists we must live outside the movement, and by that I mean not just to wear the cloak at our branch meetings and on our platforms, and then hang it up until such time as occasion demands that we wear it again, but to be constantly showing to the world that it is a pure religion with us, and an everyday one at that'.[90] This meant not only persuading the wider public of the general salience of socialist politics, but also to make a difference at a more practical and everyday level. Hence Hannah Mitchell's notion of local Labour councillors providing a bridge (with two way traffic) between the municipal authority and the local community – particularly the working-class woman in the home.

Another way in which women were identified with their neighbourhoods and through them to the local party was in the vexed area of organising social and fundraising events. Pamela Graves argues that Labour women regarded the domestic and social aspect of their work in women's sections with pride and accepted the gender division of labour within the party.[91] Certainly, before the interwar years, the accepted role for many women members of the labour and socialist movement was to be responsible for the social events and the fundraising so necessary to the more public interventions of their comrades. These expectations continued after the war but, as before it, not everyone was happy about the division of labour. 'Daisy Nook' made fun of these expectations in a column, 'Th' Kesmas Party', which described what happened when men, who assumed it would be easy, were left to organise the branch's festive party and made a complete mess of it. She made it clear that women organised social events because they were skilled at it. A local branch took Nook/Mitchell up on this and invited her to a party organised by the males for the female members, which went very well. She agreed to apologise for 'libelling the superior sex', but the women members thanked her for showing the men up and for revealing to them that if the men comrades were so good at domestic labour then they could begin to put this to use at home.[92]

Usually the social activities of the movement remained uninterrogated and in the background. The branch bulletins which appeared in *Labour's Northern Voice* described local campaigns and meetings, but were as likely to include references to whist drives, jumble sales and all sorts of fundraising schemes as well as treats such as 'chara' trips. Quite a lot of this was women's work. When Longsight and Rusholme ILP elected a social committee from its 50-strong membership, they were all women.[93] The next month one of their women members angrily suggested that ILPers should get it into their heads 'that those who perform the tasks that are not on view are quite as important and necessary to the well being of the movement as those who gallantly fight out our cause on the platforms'.[94] Yet, this was the same woman who had made the case the previous year for the importance of the social side of the movement. Social events should not just be seen as fundraisers, they were also an important way to make new members. Her experience was that 'the social atmosphere should, and does, lend itself ... to airing our views to others, either of different or indifferent politics'.[95] But usually social activities *were* tied to fundraising. This was particularly important for those branches which served a new community or had no trade union backing. Both these features were apparent in the Manchester suburb of Burnage, to which Stella Davies and her family moved in the late 1920s. She and her husband were both active in the Labour Party, joining a growing branch. As she remembered:

we financed elections by bazaars, jumble sales, raffles and such-like means of raising money as well as by subscriptions. I was actively engaged in all these activities. Encouraged by increased support during the thirties, the local Labour Party purchased a hall in which to hold its meetings, installed a billiard table and ran dances. Though without much hope of returning a Labour representative to parliament or council in the foreseeable future, our efforts enabled the Labour vote in the district to be registered and this seemed to us to be worth doing.[96]

1930s: Domesticity and Decline?

The 1930s have been represented as a decade which saw a decline in the vigour and assertiveness of the Labour women's movement, overwhelmed by the cult of domesticity. Martin Pugh argues that 'By 1933 women's questions, as distinct from social welfare policies, were slipping off the agenda, attendance at the women's conference dwindled and the organisation merely echoed the priorities of the party itself'.[97] Was this how the decade was experienced by Labour women at the grass roots in Manchester? Other local studies have noted a change in the 1930s. Savage has shown that in Preston women's activity in the Labour Party faded after reaching a peak in the late 1920s. By the 1930s, Preston women's section had begun to fight shy of political campaigns and became a support organisation for the party focusing on fundraising and social events.[98] Graves also argues that women's experience of, and relationship to, the Labour Party changed significantly in the 1930s. While at the national level no further claims were made by women for policy-making power in the party, at the local level there was a shift to greater sexual integration. Women members showed less enthusiasm for separate organisation which was reflected in the relative decline in women's sections despite a rise in individual female party membership. When it came to policy, any focus on gender disappeared to be replaced by an emphasis on class, while women-related campaigns were eschewed because they would be divisive.[99]

In Manchester, the picture is slightly different. What were thought of as women's issues were still able to galvanise Labour Party women, particularly maternal mortality. The issue had already been raised in the 1920s. Dora Taylor in her 1924 municipal candidacy stressed that becoming a mother had made this a more pressing issue for her. She felt that the maternal mortality rate in Manchester was far too high and that seven antenatal clinics were too few for a population of a quarter of a million people.[100] But, as an issue, it moved up the collective agenda in the 1930s. The borough party with the MLWAC organised a maternal mortality conference in January 1933, and this was followed by a further conference in April 1934. But it was the Molly Taylor case in May 1934 that made this a burning local issue. Mrs Taylor, a healthy nineteen-year-old, was turned away from St Mary's Hospital when she arrived already in labour. She gave birth on the steps of the hospital and then was taken on a difficult journey by ambulance across sett-paved streets to the former workhouse hospital at Crumpsall. Although the child survived, his young mother died the following day.[101] As *Labour Woman* said, 'It is a terrible story, which has roused thousands of women to the question of maternal mortality'.[102] The uproar in the city led eventually to a public inquiry in which the MLWAC took part, as well as the WCG and the Manchester and Salford WCA. This in turn led to a wider campaign for 'safe motherhood' in the city.

A key initiative in Manchester was the cross-party Maternal Mortality Committee (MMC). Most of the original energy for this came from WCG and CP women,[103] but it also involved delegates from women's sections and the MLWAC. The MMC was remembered by the secretary of the MLWAC, as 'not political. It was concerned with women irrespective of any kind of politics. We were concerned with the reduction of the death rate amongst pregnant women and babies'.[104] Yet, in 1939, this view was challenged. MLWAC delegates to the MMC were concerned that the committee was being politicised. Meetings were now being held in the headquarters of the Conservative Party and Conservatives dominated the committee. 'After discussion it was agreed that as the Mat. Mortality committee has become definitely identified with a Political Party its claim to be non-political ceases and we ask all Sections to withdraw their affiliation'.[105] The issue of who it was appropriate for Labour Party women to work with remained as troubling as it had been in the 1920s.

Other continuities are apparent; issues that had been important to the female membership, continued to be so. So, peace continued to preoccupy Labour women in Manchester, as in their attempt to get a 'Peace Day' established in the city's schools. Another issue was the provision and design of public housing for Manchester families, while in 1938 a vigorous cost-of-living campaign was launched.[106] Although often dismissed as evidence of the domestic overwhelming feminist concerns, these were all areas where it was possible to make gendered arguments and over which alliances could be forged with other political, if not always party, women in the city. These were also issues that touched women's daily lives.

Conclusion

Throughout the interwar years, there were tensions for women within the labour movement and one of the most important concerned the pull that women's issues and women's organisations could have for the female membership. The danger was always thought to be that women would primarily identify with other women and thus compromise class and party loyalties. Yet, in order to build a party in touch with the daily lives of ordinary people, particularly women, such women's issues as housing, washhouses and maternal and child welfare were bound to be stressed, and these issues carried within them the potential for alliances to be forged on single issues, such as maternal mortality, which brought together women across party and non-party groups such as the WCAs, and even from proscribed organisations like the CP. At the same time, women in the Manchester Labour Party were still struggling to establish a more satisfactory relationship with the local leadership of the party. The 1930s are usually assumed to be a more quiescent decade in the formal relations between the women's organisation of the party and the party hierarchy, yet despite the changing membership of the MLWAC there were still occasions when it was willing to challenge the male-dominated borough party leadership. For example, in 1935, MLWAC passed a resolution, 'That on matters of Party policy dealing with such questions as Education, Housing, and Maternity Services there shall be an immediate cessation of free voting on the part of the Labour Group in the City Council'.[107] This was an outright challenge to the political agenda of the local party as Labour women sought to make what were deemed 'women's issues' into political, indeed into *party* political, issues.

Individual women activists and local events (such as the Molly Taylor case) together with the local impact of national events, such as the disaffiliation of the ILP from the Labour Party, shaped Labour women's experiences in interwar Manchester. Locality was an important determinant of grass roots experience in this period, despite the growing 'nationalisation' of politics. It did make a difference where women experienced party membership. This was partly because the ambivalence about the function and even existence of women's sections in the interwar Labour Party was also emblematic of a wider uncertainty about how to harness the significant female membership. But neither activist women nor the broader female membership responded uniformly to the different pressures of the interwar period. 'Labour women' is not shorthand for a single experience or response to the possibilities and limitations that party membership presented. Nor can one city's grass roots experience be read as that of all provincial cities. There is still a great deal we do not know, but the pieces of the jigsaw that we have suggest we are now equipped to ask new questions about how women experienced party membership within and beyond the Labour Party. Only then will we understand what politics meant to people in their communities and the ways in which those experiences were gendered.

Notes

1. P. Thane, 'The Women of the British Labour Party and Feminism, 1906–45', in H. L. Smith (ed.), *British Feminism in the Twentieth Century* (Aldershot, 1990), p. 140. See also P. Thane, 'Women in the British Labour Party and the Construction of State Welfare, 1906–39', in S. Koven and S. Michel (eds), *Mothers of a New World: Maternalist Politics and the Origins of the Welfare State* (London, 1993).

2. M. Francis, 'Labour and Gender', in D. Tanner, P. Thane and N. Tiratsoo (eds), *Labour's First Century* (Cambridge, 2000), pp. 194–5.

3. N. Evans and D. Jones, '"To Help Forward the Great Work of Humanity": Women in the Labour Party in Wales' in D. Tanner, C. Williams and D. Hopkin (eds), *The Labour Party in Wales, 1900–2000* (Cardiff, 2000), p. 225.

4. S. Davies, *Liverpool Labour: Social and Political Influences on the Development of the Labour Party in Liverpool, 1900–39* (Keele, 1996), chapter seven.

5. J. Mark-Lawson et al, 'Gender and Local Politics: Struggles over Welfare Policies, 1918–39', in L. Murgatroyd et al (eds), *Localities, Class and Gender* (London, 1985).

6. C. Hunt, 'Alice Arnold of Coventry: Trade Unionism and Municipal Politics, 1919–39', Coventry University PhD (2004), p. 37.

7. *Ibid.*, pp. 304, 306–8.

8. See D. McHugh, 'A "Mass" Party Frustrated? The Development of the Labour Party in Manchester, 1918–31', University of Salford PhD (2001), p. 85.

9. *Ibid.*, pp. 97–101.

10. Manchester had six WLLs before the war, most of which were formed in and around 1910 when Annot Robinson was briefly employed as an organiser. C. Collette, *For Labour and For Women: The Women's Labour League, 1906–18* (Manchester, 1989), appendix two, p. 88.

11. R. and E. Frow, *The Communist Party in Manchester, 1920–26* (Manchester, undated c. 1979).

12. D. McHugh, 'A "Mass" Party Frustrated?', pp. 108–13. I am indebted to Declan McHugh for this account of Manchester Labour Party in the 1920s.

13. Although the foregoing relies heavily on McHugh's account, *Labour Woman* provides a slightly different perspective. The formation of Ardwick women's section is noted in *Labour Woman*, July 1920, although McHugh puts it a year later (p. 112). Such discrepancies have more to do with whether the source is from within the largely male bureaucratic structure of the party, distant from the female rank-and-file in particular, or from the smaller but increasingly bureaucratic women's organisation of the party. *Labour Woman* carried regular reports from the women's organisers employed by the party.

14. *Labour Woman*, June 1922.

15. Manchester Labour Women's Advisory Council (MLWAC) Minute Book, 4 April 1932 (Manchester Central Library (MCL), M449/1).

16. MLWAC Minute Book, 1 December 1930, 2 March 1931.

17. *Labour's Northern Voice*, 29 January 1926.

18. *Labour's Northern Voice*, 5 February 1926.

19. See J. Hannam and K. Hunt, *Socialist Women: Britain, 1880s to 1920s* (London, 2002), pp. 94–6.

20. *The Manchester & Salford Woman Citizen*, October 1931.

21. J. Marriott, *The Culture of Labourism: The East End Between the Wars* (Edinburgh, 1991), pp. 169–70.

22. *Woman Citizen*, November 1929.

23. Gorton Labour Party Women's Section Minute Book, 4 March 1930 (MCL, M450/1).

24. C.S. Davies, *North Country Bred: A Working-Class Family Chronicle* (London, 1963), p. 201.

25. The analysis of Labour women municipal candidates is based on the regular profiles of women candidates produced every October in the *Woman Citizen*.

26. *Woman Citizen*, October 1923.

27. See D. McHugh, 'A "Mass" Party Frustrated?', pp. 326–32.

28. *Woman Citizen*, October 1925.

29. *Woman Citizen*, October 1926.

30. M. Pugh, *Women and the Women's Movement in Britain, 1914–59* (London, 2000), p. 60.

31. D. McHugh, 'A "Mass" Party Frustrated?', p. 113.

32. C.S. Davies, *North Country Bred*, p. 196.

33. *Woman Citizen*, October 1926.

34. *Woman Citizen*, October 1926.

35. H. Mitchell, *The Hard Way Up* (London, 1977), p. 204.

36. *Woman Citizen*, April 1930.

37. *Woman Citizen*, October 1926.

38. *Labour's Northern Voice*, 11 March 1927; H. Mitchell, *The Hard Way Up*, p. 217.

39. *Midland Daily Telegraph*, 26 February 1929 quoted in C. Hunt, 'Alice Arnold', p. 204. See also P. Graves, *Labour Women: Women in British Working-Class Politics, 1918–39* (Cambridge, 1994), pp. 174–5.

40. H. Mitchell, *The Hard Way Up*, pp. 194–5.

41. The following figures are drawn from statistics compiled by Joanne Smith from the council's year books. My thanks are due to her.

42. C. Hunt, 'Alice Arnold', p. 253.

43. Obituary of Annot Robinson, *Labour's Northern Voice*, 11 December 1925.

44. *Leeds Weekly Citizen*, 29 May 1925.

45. See J. Hannam and K. Hunt, *Socialist Women*, chapter four.

46. See D. McHugh, "A 'Mass" Party Frustrated?', pp. 114–5.

47. H. Mitchell, *The Hard Way Up*, p.189.

48. Gorton WS Minute Book, 3 December 1929.

49. MLWAC Minute Book, 1 February 1932.

50. MLWAC Minute Book, 7 March 1932.

51. MLWAC Minute Book, 4 July 1932.

52. *Labour Woman*, May 1920.

53. *Woman Citizen*, October 1923.

54. *Woman Citizen*, June 1924.

55. M. Savage, *The Dynamics of Working-Class Politics: The Labour Movement in Preston 1880–1940* (Cambridge, 1987), pp. 171–3, 178.

56. *Woman Citizen*, March 1934.

57. *Woman Citizen*, October 1934; Gorton WS minute book, 5 November 1929.

58. MLWAC Minute Book, 2 March 1931.

59. ILP Women's Groups, typescript, undated (1926), in *Archives of the ILP: Organisations and Regional Records* (Harvester Microfilm).

60. Gorton WS Minute Book, 19 November 1929.

61. Gorton WS Minute Book, 4 March 1930. See also 3 March 1931.

62. Gorton WS Minute Book, 6 May 1930.

63. Gorton WS Minute Book, 1 July 1930.

64. Gorton WS Minute Book, 23 June 1931.

65. Gorton WS Minute Book, 23 September 1930, 6 May 1930, 22 July 1930, 4 November 1930, 8 December 1931, 14 March 1933.

66. For example, Gorton WS Minute Book, 5 July 1932.

67. Gorton WS Minute Book, 10 November 1931, 20 November 1931.

68. Gorton WS Minute Book, 3 March 1931.

69. In 1926, Hannah's husband, Gibbon, had completed four year's service as chairman of Newton Heath ILP, while her son, Frank, had been elected branch secretary (*Labour's Northern Voice*, 5 February 1926).

70. *Northern Voice*, 1 May 1925.

71. *Northern Voice*, 3 July 1925.

72. *Labour's Northern Voice*, 2 July 1926.

73. *Labour's Northern Voice*, 19 September 1926.

74. *Labour's Northern Voice*, 1 October 1926.

75. *Northern Voice*, 11 September 1925.

76. *Labour's Northern Voice*, 18 February 1927.

77. *Labour's Northern Voice*, 26 March 1926.

78. *Woman Citizen*, October 1926.

79. *Manchester Borough Labour Party Annual Report, 1919*, quoted in D. McHugh, 'A "Mass" Party Frustrated?', p. 132.

80. *Labour Organiser*, March 1925, quoted in D. McHugh, 'A "Mass" Party Frustrated?', p. 136.

81. *Labour Organiser*, September 1922, quoted in C. Howard, 'Expectations Born to Death: Local Labour Party Expansion in the 1920s', in J. Winter (ed.), *The Working Class in Modern British History: Essays in Honour of Henry Pelling* (Cambridge, 1983), p. 75.

82. D. McHugh, 'A "Mass" Party Frustrated?', pp. 142–3. See also chapter six.

83. See C.S. Davies, *North Country Bred*, p. 193.

84. *Woman Citizen*, April 1930.

85. *Northern Voice*, 30 October 1925.

86. *Labour's Northern Voice*, 21 October 1927.

87. *Labour's Northern Voice*, 22 October 1926.

88. *Labour's Northern Voice*, 29 October 1926.

89. *Labour's Northern Voice,* 26 March 1926.

90. *Labour's Northern Voice*, 9 April 1926.

91. P. Graves, *Labour Women*, p. 158.

92. *Northern Voice*, 24 December 1925, 5 February 1926.

93. *Northern Voice*, 5 March 1926.

94. *Northern Voice*, 9 April 1926.

95. *Northern Voice*, 27 November 1925.

96. C.S. Davies, *North Country Bred*, p. 235.

97. M. Pugh, *Women and the Women's Movement*, p. 139.

98. M. Savage, *The Dynamics of Working-Class Politics*, p. 181.

99. P. Graves, *Labour Women*, pp. 181–2.

100. *Woman Citizen*, October 1924.

101. For a contemporary account of the Molly Taylor case, see *Labour Woman*, January 1935. For the context, see J. Emmanuel, 'The Politics of Maternity in Manchester, 1919–39', Manchester University MSc (1982).

102. *Labour Woman*, October 1934.

103. J. Emmanuel, 'The Politics of Maternity', p. 45.

104. Interview with Lily Thomas, (Stalybridge Library, Manchester Studies Tape Collection 1072).

105. MLWAC Minute Book, 6 May 1939.

106. *Labour Woman*, June 1934, February 1938.

107. MLWAC Minute Book, 1 April 1935.

Chapter 6

Labour's Family: Local Labour Parties, Trade Unions and Trades Councils in Cotton Lancashire, 1931–39

Andrew Flinn

This chapter examines the politics of local Labour parties in the 1930s in the Manchester area, with particular reference to Lewis Minkin's 'contentious alliance' between the industrial and political sides of the labour movement. It will consider the view of the labour movement as a family, albeit a rather dysfunctional one – not only nationally but also locally.[1] The regional aspect of this study is conceived in the spirit of the recognition, by Mike Savage and Geoff Eley among others, that to properly understand labour movements and their relationship to the environments in which they exist and seek to prosper, it is necessary to examine the 'local contexts of militancy (not just geographically, but within particular subcultures of occupational, ethnic, gendered and other kinds of community, and in the sites and social spaces of everyday life)'.[2]

For a genuinely comprehensive understanding of Labour's grass roots politics, it is necessary to examine – amongst other things – occupancy, economic conditions, and the level and character of local industrial organisation. This recognises not only the role of the trade unions in establishing the party, but also their pivotal role in regaining control and sustaining the party during the depression and in the aftermath of the political disaster of 1931. The article will examine how this relationship functioned, how this control was exercised, and with what results and tensions. These are questions that have been studied in some detail nationally but with less attention at a local level.[3] The local context allows us to examine how the different politics, industrial concerns and histories of local unions were reflected in the arena of local labour politics. To put it another way, were local Labour parties located in predominately cotton areas different from parties in areas with a more mixed occupational base which included, for instance, engineers, miners or railway workers? If this is demonstrably the case, how much is the difference explicable in terms of the nature of local trade unionism? Among the factors which need to be examined in this framework are whether the union was active in local party organisation; if so, was it successful in ensuring its industrial agenda was adopted and promoted by the party; and did it actively work to exclude other possibly damaging (left-wing) views from the party? Electorally, did the unions provide the funding for campaigns; did they insist on their own candidates being selected for office; and were they successful in getting these candidates elected?

A related, but not marginal, aspect to this discussion relates to the organisational structure of local Labour parties. According to G.D.H. Cole, in many Lancashire towns it had been common for the trades council (the body which brought all the affiliated local trade unions together) and the divisional Labour organisation to be one and the same body, known as a joint Trades and Labour Council. However, with the development of the new party constitution in 1918 and the establishment of local constituency parties, there was a trend towards separating the party organisation from the local trade union centre. This trend was reinforced by the Conservative government's Trades Disputes Act in 1927, which sought to diminish union influence in political affairs. However, in 1930s cotton Lancashire, in towns such as Oldham and Stockport, these joint bodies continued the tradition of having the industrial and political sides of the movement acting in concert, functioning through one local structure. These joint organisations could make a difference to the character of the local labour movement. For instance, if the most active local union was the National Union of Railwaymen (NUR), described by Cole as having 'as a rule a high degree of political consciousness' and, as a result, being very active in trades councils and local Labour parties, and also referred to in a Labour Research Department survey as 'the life and soul of the trades council movement', then it was probable that the local movement would be more left-wing than one where more conservative unions determined the tone of local industrial and political policies.[4]

The condition of local industry and the depression had consequences for the unions' willingness and ability to participate in local political organisations. Some local unions financially impoverished by falling subscriptions and the costs of supporting benefits to unemployed members, withdrew from local Labour parties and political sides of Trades and Labour councils, leaving parties to their individual members and more politically committed local unions. Alan Clinton notes that in 1935, substantial numbers of the Amalgamated Engineering Union (AEU), NUR and Amalgamated Society of Woodworkers (ASW) branches were not affiliated to their local trades councils, and these were unions with reputations for being active participants in the trades council movement. In these circumstances, the arguments of those, often Conservative, members who sought to keep trade unions non-political and, invoking the Trades Disputes Act, only involved in industrial matters, tended to become louder and more persuasive.[5] Some have argued that a continued survival of syndicalist tendencies can be discerned in the anti-political organisation arguments of some trade union members and branches, but more often opposition to active involvement in the local labour movement came from a less radical, more narrowly industrial, outlook. From this perspective, it was argued that the mere fact of political affiliation undermined trade unionism by importing division into working-class organisation. For instance, opponents within the engineering union to more overtly and controversial political action, such as support for Republican Spain, asked 'what the AEU, formed for quite another purpose, has to do with it anyway'.[6] In Stockport, the majority of local textile and hatters' unions no longer actively participated in the Trades and Labour Council by the 1930s, while the AEU district organisation, dismissive of the political direction of the local party, also refused to be involved between 1934 and 1938.[7] In Oldham, many AEU branches disaffiliated from the party in the early 1930s on financial grounds. However, for those moderate or conservative minded unions, withdrawal often had the unintended effect of strengthening the influence of their political opponents within the local party or trades council. Those trade unions from either the left or the right, for whom political representation remained central to their industrial aims, tended to stay actively involved in the local movement.

This chapter focuses on those towns including and immediately surrounding Manchester described by Walton as 'cotton Lancashire'.[8] This area of south east Lancashire includes the urban centres of Manchester, Salford, Bolton, Bury, Oldham, Rochdale, Stockport, Ashton, Stretford, and Wigan.[9] Though popularly associated with textiles, and particularly with cotton spinning, industrially it was an extremely diverse area incorporating not only spinning but weaving as well, light and heavy engineering, coal mining and, in Manchester, a major commercial and distribution centre. Industrial diversity was matched by a further variety of ethnic, religious and political affiliations. Though trade unionism and socialist organisations had a strong association with certain parts of Lancashire, working-class Conservatism and, to a lesser extent, Liberalism remained popular in the 1930s. The Labour Party was not yet the dominant regional force that it would become later and, according to the most recent historian of the region, its progress towards that dominance was 'faltering and uneven'.[10] The region, Manchester especially, had substantial Jewish and Irish Catholic populations, and the general occupations and political affiliations of these groups further shaped the character of local labour movements. During the 1930s, local Labour parties and politics varied from a narrowly-defined labourism, to something resembling a form of ethnic or confessional politics, to a more radical yet perhaps more politically marginal socialism. These variations were the result of the interaction of a number of different factors, not least the impact of occupation and trade unionism on the local parties. Whilst it is accepted that the specifics of the local and regional context make it difficult to sustain generalised points, it is hoped that the evidence of the political influence of local trade unions in cotton Lancashire will illuminate similar relations elsewhere.[11]

One of the key regional differences and diversities to acknowledge from the start is the pre-eminence of Manchester as the political centre for the North West. When the Labour Party was considering how to extend its influence in the North West by establishing a Regional Council of Labour for Lancashire and Cheshire, the organisational sub-committee stressed the centrality of Manchester to the region's political life:

> [Manchester] is in fact the meeting place of all movements and interests in the North West. Lancashire and Cheshire folk when wishing to consult one another, think as readily of Manchester as the venue as the south does of London. Every city, town and village is within easy reach by train and bus, and no more time is expended in travelling to or from places like Bolton, Wigan, Oldham and many others than is expended in travelling to and from the City of London from the suburbs.[12]

All of which may not have accorded with the beliefs of those in Oldham or Bolton, let alone in Merseyside, but nonetheless is a clear indication of the contemporary political primacy of Manchester in the region. Its size and status as a regional economic and political capital contrast with the more orthodox, less varied political map of the cotton towns, or even Wigan and surrounding towns. Nevertheless, it would be a mistake to think of south east Lancashire towns as single industry mill or pits towns as found elsewhere in the country. Most towns and communities were multi-occupational. In Wigan, employment was split evenly between cotton and mining. Although Oldham and Bolton were pre-eminent spinning centres, they also had significant weaving and engineering industries. The importance of this area to the industrial revolution and the development of the broad labour movement has inspired an extensive literature on the industrial and political developments of Lancashire in the nineteenth and early twentieth centuries, including work focusing on the patterns of interwar working-class life and political allegiances.[13] This article seeks to expand on the interest in the region shown by these studies into the examination of grass roots labour politics in the 1930s.

Labour's Electoral Performance in Cotton Lancashire

The late 1920s and early 1930s were a disastrous period for the labour movement in Britain. After the 1926 General Strike and the onset of widespread economic and industrial depression, the employers held the upper hand and the unions, with falling memberships, concentrated on defence, often seeking co-operation with the bosses. For the Labour Party, the achievement of winning the 1929 election was overwhelmed by failures in government and the crisis in 1931, which led to the party splitting and losing office. A subsequent election defeat reduced the party to less than fifty seats. A limited recovery was made in the 1935 election, but the gains were nowhere near enough to bring the party back to government let alone anticipate the landslide of 1945.

The central concern of most members of local Labour parties and Trades and Labour councils in this period was to maximise the numbers of Labour representatives in parliament and on local councils. Nationally, after a brief hiatus, trade union leaders had responded to the MacDonald crisis and election defeat in 1931 by seeking to re-establish firm control over the party to ensure that it was not deflected from its purpose of representing the interests of organised labour. In the context of economic depression and mass unemployment, this was deemed especially pressing, nowhere more so than amongst the desperately badly affected coalfields and textile towns of Lancashire. Generally, those local unions that could afford to remain actively involved in the party were concerned to seek representation for their industrial concerns by maximising Labour electoral success, and by seeking, where possible, that specifically trade union candidates were selected for winnable seats. This could lead to a number of conflicts with local parties, both over the type of candidate selected for winnable wards and constituencies, and about the adoption of any left-wing or controversial policies which might alienate potential voters.

In Manchester and the towns that surrounded it, the Labour Party had made significant progress in parliamentary elections in the 1920s. However, the 1930s were a period of stagnation and reversal.[14] In the interwar years, Manchester was divided into ten seats: Ardwick, Blackley, Clayton, Exchange, Gorton, Hulme, Moss Side, Platting, Rusholme, and Withington. In the 1920s, Labour representation grew steadily beyond its traditional working-class bases in Ardwick, Gorton and Platting. In 1929, the party held half of the city's seats. Two years later, no Labour MPs were returned in the disastrous election of 1931. Progress was slim in 1935, with only the party's former strongholds in the industrial and highly unionised north and east side of the city – Ardwick, Clayton, Gorton and Platting – electing Labour MPs. In the southern half of the city, no Labour victories were scored at all in the interwar period in Exchange, Moss Side, Rusholme and Withington – only Hulme bucked the trend by returning a Labour MP in 1929. Stretford, including the expanding industrial Trafford Park area, did not vote Labour until 1945.

Elsewhere in cotton Lancashire, a similar story saw any progress which had been made in the 1920s reversed in the 1930s. In the overwhelmingly working-class constituencies of Salford, Labour won all three seats in 1923 and in 1929, but lost both elections in the 1930s.[15] In the spinning towns of Bolton and Oldham, both two-member seats, the party's high-water mark performances in the 1923 and 1929 elections contrasted with failure in the 1930s. In Stockport, the interwar anomaly of the party's victory in 1929 was not repeated even in 1945. In Bury, a town including weaving and spinning and a strong Conservative culture, the position was even worse, with Labour stubbornly polling around 35 per cent of the vote and losing every election.[16] The neighbouring Middleton and Prestwich party achieved similar levels of success.

The successful areas for Labour in the region were those associated more with mining than textiles. To the west of the region were those constituencies where Labour's interwar dominance was unchallenged. In Wigan, Ince and Westhoughton, the party did not lose an election between 1918 and 1945. In neighbouring Leigh, Labour only failed to win the 1918 election. Another predominantly mining seat, Farnworth, with the exception of 1931, also recorded a consistent set of victories. Only Ashton and Rochdale went against the grain of the trend of towns mainly associated with cotton rather than mining returning Labour MPs, only losing the 1931 election.

As with the national elections, in local and municipal contests the nadir of the party's performance came in the 1931 elections which immediately followed the general election. Subsequently, most borough parties experienced some recovery and even some – though typically short-lived – successes, but no great leap forward. For instance, good results in Bolton and Oldham in 1934, reversing the losses of 1931, were not sustained and the parties fell away again. In Oldham's case surrendering control of the local council after only one year. By 1937 in Oldham, Labour held only 15 seats whilst their opponents had 33; and in Bolton, Labour had 24 as opposed to 72 seats for the anti-Labour opposition. In Manchester after 1931, the party managed to stabilise its votes and council seats, not sustaining the losses experienced elsewhere in the region, but also not making any progress towards taking control of the city. For much of the 1930s, Labour representation on the city council stood at around 50 seats, with the other parties, as was common in interwar Lancashire forming anti-socialist alliances, holding over 90 seats. In Stockport, the local position was even less promising; 1929 marked a high point in the party's municipal and parliamentary interwar influence – with one MP and 19 out of the 72 seats. By 1938, however, that had fallen to just ten.[17] In towns like Bury, Ashton and Rochdale, the party barely got into double figures. The exception to this trend was once again Wigan, where the party had gained overall control of the local council in 1921 and subsequently extended its dominance. By 1937, Labour held 44 seats against its opponent's 12.[18]

It is the contention of this article that Labour's hostility to the left locally and nationally, both within and without of the party, was not only ideological but, particularly among some trade unions, based on coolly realistic electoral calculations that left-wing and controversial (for instance anti-religious) policies and campaigns would fatally alienate already unreliable supporters and members. Faced with the stagnation of the party's vote in the 1930s and the combination of local Conservatives and Liberals in anti-socialist blocs, many local trade unions sought to maintain the unity of the party membership and maximise its core support by insisting on a moderate, lower common denominator in policy terms. In cotton Lancashire, where the trade unions were active in their local Labour parties, they tended to use their influence to oppose left-wing or controversial initiatives from other party members. Those local parties which were more radical in this period tended to be those where the local unions were weak or disengaged from the party, or where the dominant union was more in tune with the radical initiatives of individual members. The mutual antipathy between trade unions and constituency party members, which resurfaces periodically throughout Labour's history, was evident in this period. This mistrust was most clearly exemplified on one side by the Transport and General Workers' (TGWU) leader Ernest Bevin's dismissal of middle-class intellectuals within the party as being temperamentally untrustworthy (MacDonald, Mosley) and, on the other side, by the emergence of a constituency party movement, the Constituency Labour Party Association, which campaigned for greater representation for local party members within the party and against the dominance of the party machine by trade unions.[19] However, it is not enough to characterise these divisions in political terms as being between middle-class radicals and right-wing working-class trade unionists. In fact, many trade unionists, whatever their politics, were wary of the motivations of constituency activists. Within the NUR, for instance, the future union president Jack Potts, although a local left-winger, was an active opponent of extending the constitutional independence of constituency parties. His union branch, Dukinfield, criticised the tendency among constituency parties to reject local trade unionists as parliamentary candidates in favour of middle-class 'frontbench' nominees. Attitudes regarding the political representation of industrial organisations within the party were often the product of age and class as of other political perspectives.[20]

Cotton Unionism and Labour Representation

Working-class support for the Labour Party in cotton Lancashire, and particularly in predominantly spinning towns like Oldham and Bolton, was far from assured in the interwar period. Despite the progress made in local and national elections in the 1920s, the party continued to compete with Conservatives for working-class votes and, in the 1930s, was often faced by anti-socialist alliances which united local Liberal and Conservative party machines. The unity of its opponents' supporters was a serious impediment to Labour's local progress. In response to the number of Conservatives ('Tories in clogs') amongst their members, and the fragile nature of the popular adherence to the Labour Party, those advocates for labour representation amongst the spinning and other cotton unions were primarily concerned with maximising the Labour vote and opposing developments that might alienate the electorate. In broad terms, the conception of the Spinning and Cardroom Amalgamations in Oldham and Bolton of the nature and purpose of labour representation had remained unchanged since the early 1900s – the unions sought, largely to the exclusion of socialism, to provide a platform for the purpose of raising the industrial interests and concerns of their organisations and members.[21]

Inevitably, some within the unions took it further. One Reddish Spinners' branch committee member argued that 'politics should not be tolerated in the Trade Union Movement' in any form. Not surprisingly, the branch often refused to affiliate to the political side of the Stockport Trades Council and Labour Party. Following the Trade Disputes Act and the financial difficulties faced by local organisations during the depression, the affiliation of members to the Labour Party by the cotton unions fell dramatically. The Spinners' Union, having by far the lowest figures, affiliated only a third of its members. Outside the major centres of Oldham and Bolton, the low levels of participation in the Labour Party indicated limited enthusiasm for the party amongst spinners and cardroom workers. Oldham had one of the largest memberships in the region, consistently affiliating between 3,000 and 4,000 members to the national party (with only 1932 showing a dramatic fall), whereas parties like Wigan, Stockport and Rochdale were all substantially smaller. In Leigh, the only textile candidate in the 1934 local elections was a Liberal. Even in Bolton, only one seat on the council was held by a cotton worker. Elsewhere, some Spinners' branches struggled to find delegates for the local party let alone candidates for elections.[22]

The political strategy of the cotton unions and their relationship to the Labour Party was handled by the United Textile Factory Workers' Association (UTFWA), the federation which brought the weavers, spinners and other cotton unions together. Attempting to reverse the lack of participation in the party, the UTFWA in 1933 launched a campaign to increase support for the Labour Party on the basis of a programme for the cotton industry. Local union branches were encouraged to actively assist in Labour's campaign and put forward officers for local elections. In 1936, the UTFWA conference rejected a proposal making it compulsory to affiliate local unions to the Labour Party as infringing on union autonomy, but also for being politically unworkable. Responding to the motion, one Ashton weaver drew attention to the number of Conservatives and Liberals in his association who made it simply impossible for his branch to affiliate to the local Labour Party.[23]

In contrast to towns like Stockport, where cotton unions had almost completely withdrawn from the political side of the movement, in Oldham and Bolton the cotton unions remained the dominant force in local labour politics. In both towns, spinning and cardroom unions (the Bolton and District Operative Spinners' Association, the Oldham Operative Spinners' Association, the Oldham Provincial Cardroom Operatives) provided the bulk of the affiliated membership of the local party and Trades and Labour councils. The composition of the executive committees of the trades councils reflected their pre-eminence. In Oldham, four of the 14 union members on the political executive were textile representatives. In Bolton, the executive included representatives of the main cotton unions, and they also provided many of the officers and trustees. Branches were actively encouraged to take part in local party affairs. The dominance of the union in Bolton was symbolised by its imposing headquarters, the Spinners' Hall, in which most other local labour movement organisations, including the trades council, held their meetings. However, the real power of the cotton unions came as a result of their financial support for local parties, particularly those which adopted textile candidates. Financial backing and subsequent executive positions meant the unions were well placed to direct local Labour parties. When left-wing initiatives came from the constituency activists and affiliated political organisations, they were invariably opposed and usually defeated by the trade union delegates and their supporters within the local party leadership.[24]

Generally, the cotton unions, in particular the Spinners' and the Cardroom unions rather than the Weavers', held a narrow view of the purpose of the Labour Party. The party was seen as the vehicle for the independent representation of labour rather than a socialist organisation. This had been the case when the unions affiliated to the party in the early 1900s and the cotton industry had been flourishing, and it remained true in the interwar period when the industry was beset not only by the problems of a world recession and widespread decline in international trade, but also by specific questions of competitiveness, over-production and industrial decline which affected the Lancashire cotton industry and pre-dated the depression.[25] Against this background, cotton trade unions viewed local and national labour representation by textile trade unionists as an important, perhaps crucial, mechanism for raising the problems of the industry, advocating the union's suggested solutions, and seeking direct government aid and assistance. Without such representatives, the unions felt that they were without a voice in parliament and government.

As a consequence, where cotton unions were actively involved in local labour politics, as in Bolton and Oldham, their activities reflected their instrumental rather than ideological commitment. They appealed to cotton workers to vote Labour not as a socialist party but as the political embodiment of the trade union movement. Mirroring national tendencies of the trade union movement to attempt to control the political agenda of the party ('the General Council's Party'), local cotton unions sought to exert a similar influence. In Oldham, for example, the unions insisted that the cotton industry was their responsibility alone, whilst at the same time feeling justified in resisting the political activities of local left-wing elements. In these circumstances, any political or 'left' ideology could be and was viewed as damaging, even when that policy was, like the nationalisation of the cotton industry, specifically designed to appeal to the interests and circumstances of cotton workers.[26] In the case of organising the unemployed, the unions were quite clear that this was not the responsibility of the political side of the movement. Cotton unions upheld the TUC's proscription of the communist National Unemployed Workers' Movement and repeatedly defeated attempts to establish trades council controlled Unemployed Associations. A broad based Unemployed Council was established in Bolton in 1933 and initially found some success, affiliating to the trades council, before falling victim to the sectarian politics of the Communist Party.[27]

However, despite this narrow approach, after the 1931 election, the cotton unions had no direct parliamentary representation until George Tomlinson was elected at the Farnworth by-election in 1938. As already shown, Labour performed poorly in Lancashire in the 1930s, and the unions' choice of candidates and constituencies were often inappropriate, with the result that the unions' ability to influence policy on cotton in the Labour Party and in parliament was minimal.[28] Attempting to ensure that trade union candidates were selected as candidates often led to tensions between local parties and the trade unions. Most local parties solicited trade union sponsored candidates as it usually entailed much needed financial support. However, many of these constituencies were, like Middleton and Prestwich, often very unpromising from an electoral point of view.[29] In safer seats, the unions often found themselves in conflict with the national and local party's promotion of prominent political individuals at the expense of trade union candidates. In Oldham, the textile unions mandated their delegates at a selection conference to back only textile and trade union candidates. In the Pennine seat of Elland, the UTFWA protested at the selection of a London lawyer rather than a weaver. That said, tensions between trade unionists and constituency activists were not confined to the cotton unions; resentment at the imposition of 'careerist' politicians over local 'able working men and women' was felt by the union movement generally. The selection of the Reverend Woods for the Rusholme by-election in 1933, and of Wedgwood Benn for the by-election in the traditionally solid trade union seat of Gorton in 1937, were both strongly criticised by local trade unions.[30]

At the 1935 general election, five UTFWA sponsored candidates contested the 'textile' constituencies of Blackburn, Bolton, Middleton and Prestwich, Oldham and Sowerby. The campaigns targeted cotton workers and the industry. In both Oldham and Bolton, senior local party officers identified cotton workers as being central to Labour's chances whilst acknowledging that their allegiance could not be depended upon:

> if for once we can rely upon the whole-hearted backing and support of the Textile Section in this town, the prospects will be more than good.

The *Cotton Factory Times* advised textile workers to vote for their class not their employers.[31] None of the UTFWA candidates were victorious. In fact, very few Labour candidates were elected at all in the textile areas. Only Ashton, Farnworth and Rochdale of the spinning towns around Manchester elected Labour MPs, the rest were won by the Conservatives on a programme which stressed the achievements of the National government for the cotton industry. The general secretary of the Cardroom

Amalgamation, Alfred Roberts, blamed the political apathy of the cotton union members:

> We may yet find that the solution is in our programme which ... is not and cannot be understood and endorsed by that majority which does not trouble to attend the meetings.

Others blamed a political conservatism still popular with cotton workers.[32]

For contemporaries there was a clear contrast between the apparent lack of purchase of Labour parties amongst the textile workers around Manchester and the party's success in the mining seats of Wigan, Ince and Leigh. One weaver from Wigan voiced the common perception that Lancashire miners returned Labour MPs 'because they were class conscious'. It was notable that the cotton unions' eventual success in getting a textile representative elected to parliament was in the mixed cotton–coal seat of Farnworth. In fact, much of the miners' support for Labour was as instrumental as cotton workers; they were seeking independent labour representation rather than demonstrating any deep adherence to socialism. It was true that the party's programme of nationalisation of the coal industry was more popular amongst Lancashire miners than the similar schemes for the cotton industry were amongst spinners, but it would be wrong to see the Lancashire coalfields as centres of political radicalism like Scotland or South Wales. Furthermore, Griffiths has argued that Labour's support in these areas was not as closely linked to occupation as might be expected. He believes that Labour's core vote, even in Wigan, was to be found among the religious and national identities of the Irish Catholic population.[33]

The defeats of 1935 did not alter textile union attitudes or tactics regarding Labour representation. If anything, they sought to redouble their control over local parties, attempting to secure representation for trade union candidates and combating what they viewed as political extremism. Particular attention was focussed on the activities of local Socialist League branches. Contemporaries and subsequent historians often characterised the League as a national organisation with well-known leaders like Stafford Cripps and William Mellor but little local organisation or grass roots support. The Labour Party's organiser in Lancashire, R.C. Willis, reported that the League had little branch support. In fact, it appears that there were a number of League branches in the area, often closely mirroring the pattern of pre-disaffiliation Independent Labour Party (ILP) branches. The League was active in Bolton, Oldham, Manchester and Stockport, and its organisation was a significant source of left-wing agitation within the local official labour movement.[34]

In 1934, a number of Socialist Leaguers and other left-wingers were among those elected as councillors in Oldham when Labour took control of the council. The new council was predictably portrayed by local Conservatives as extremist and unpatriotic. Much was made of Labour's decision to ban the territorial army from holding a 'militaristic' display to mark the King's Jubilee, and to overturn the Conservative ban on the sale of anti-war and political literature at the market. The attacks on the council were effective, not only did Labour fail to gain seats in cotton Lancashire at the 1935 general election, but the party also lost its overall majority on Oldham council. Across much of the region, the reverses in 1935 ushered in a period of electoral decline which lasted until the war and left-wingers found themselves particularly vulnerable. One prominent Oldham left-winger and trades council president, E.M. Hall, concluded that 'he had been defeated because he had been too strong a socialist'.[35]

Inquests in Bolton to discover the reasons for the repeated election defeats suffered by the party in local and national elections revealed a disorganised local movement, divided between trade union and party activists. Much of the blame was laid on the party secretary Harry Eastwood, and attempts to dismiss him split the party between 'the representatives from the trades unions and Labour clubs on the one hand, and the representatives of the League of Youth and some individual members on the other'.[36] Before the 1935 election, Eastwood had publicly welcomed the CPGB's support in the campaign and, later, the *Daily Worker* published his letter thanking the party for its assistance. Eastwood himself became increasingly wary of trade union influence within the Labour Party. In 1934, he had stressed the benefits of trade union members and branches becoming actively involved in the Labour Party; by the time of his dismissal, he was arguing for the end of the domination of the national and local parties by trade union block votes.[37] However, sacking Eastwood did not improve matters. The Bolton party was increasingly impoverished, and although the Spinners' assumed partial responsibility for the party's debt, the divisions in the party were deep-rooted:

> It appears to have become a recognised procedure of the delegates to turn down on principle anything the Executive Committee recommend.

By February 1938, it was reported that at the instigation of 'certain trade union leaders' the party was to be reorganised. Leading trade unionists were said to be angry, 'insulted' and 'fed-up' with their treatment by the local party. They insisted that the Labour Party 'should pledge themselves to the trade unions'. In reality, by this stage, while the unions claimed that the local party was failing to act in their interests, the organisation was barely functioning at all.[38] The Bolton party had, for this period, a relatively unique structure. Rather than a ward organisation in Bolton, the party continued to organise through local social clubs such as the Socialist Club and the Irish Labour Club. These institutions had only a very limited campaigning and educational function, their main purpose being cheap drinking clubs. Accounts of the atmosphere inside these clubs make clear that they were far from conducive to political organisation, and local commentators were in no doubt that the drinking club culture was one of the primary reasons for the failure of the local party to function as an effective political machine.[39] It is also likely that those from both sides were by now worn down and disillusioned by the constant splits, in-fighting, and decline within the local party.

Labour, Trade Unions and the Left: Sectarianism and Conformity

As just outlined, the over-riding interest of some trade unions in securing Labour representation meant that during the 1930s they were increasingly willing to use their influence (epitomised by the block vote), nationally and locally, to stifle dissent and curtail left-wing radicalism. Responding to a real and perceived threat from the left in the 1920s and 1930s, the party developed a disciplinary system more vigorous than anything that had previously existed. Dubbed 'Social Democratic centralism' by Eric Shaw, the new disciplinary code made association with Communists and other proscribed organisations, or even the advocacy of ideas perceived as being Communist-inspired, a potential reason for expulsion. The trade union imperatives of collective unity and loyalty, so essential in the industrial field, were imposed in the less structured milieu of political affiliation and belief. Inevitably, these disciplinary strictures were considered unjust and undemocratic by many, not just on the left, but in the constituency parties generally.[40]

In the early part of the decade, this dispute was at its clearest over the organisation of the unemployed, which cotton and other unions believed was a matter for them and not for political parties. Subsequently, most of the disputes nationally and locally were over the attitude to fascism, domestic and international, and whether the threat of fascism was such that it necessitated the uniting of all left-wing and, latterly, all progressive democratic forces in opposition. Many in the Labour leadership, and particularly in the trade unions, rejected this idea, arguing that any association with the Communists was more damaging to the party (electorally) than any benefits which might accrue from such alliances. A clear lead was given in this direction in 1936 by Ernest Bevin when, on advice from the TUC that it was a Communist-affiliated organisation, he refused to let his name be associated with the Northern Council Against Fascism, a Manchester-based initiative to try to co-ordinate all local anti-fascist opinion. When local Socialist Leaguers and others sought to support the United Front and Communist Party affiliation to the Labour Party, the cotton unions, especially the Spinners' and the Cardroom Amalgamations, were implacably hostile. The Oldham unions instructed their delegates to vote against Communist affiliation, and the Bolton union lectured its members on past disruptions.[41]

Attempts to bar Communists from positions within unions, and also from the wider labour movement, particularly from trade councils and the Labour Party, were generally pursued more actively by cotton unions than elsewhere in the region.[42] The TUC issued its 'Black Circulars' against Communist Party membership of trade unions and trades councils in October 1934 to a mixed reaction. While councils and unions in cotton Lancashire acted against local Communists or stated that they had no Communists to ban, in Manchester, the trades council took no action against its Communist members until the unity campaigns in 1937, when the likes of Mick Jenkins and Eddie Frow were excluded. Even then, the circular was not fully adopted or consistently implemented until the TUC was forced to intervene and reorganise the body at the time of the People's Convention campaigns in the winter of 1940.[43]

In truth, beyond Manchester, the Communist Party in south east Lancashire was weak, with very few members in the cotton towns, and even fewer actual cotton workers. Nevertheless, the politics of some local labour movements were strongly anti-communist, and attempts by left-wing party activists to campaign on issues associated with communism were actively opposed. In comparison not only with the much larger Manchester but also with Wigan and Stockport, the labour movement in the cotton towns was less active in the key left campaigns of the era, unemployment, anti-fascism and Spain. In the absence of real Communists, the Labour Party was often the target of 'red scares'; according to one Labour candidate in Bolton, local party activists were routinely described as 'Bolshies' and Conservative propaganda portrayed the party as being in the pocket of the USSR.[44] Here and elsewhere, the Conservatives were able to effectively exploit and mobilise popular patriotic feeling to Labour's distinct disadvantage.[45]

Generally, anti-communism within local labour movements was strongest in those areas where the union movement was well established but the allegiance of the working class to Labour was contested by a resilient working-class Conservatism. This was particularly the case in the cotton towns like Oldham and Bolton, where politically cautious and conservative local labour movements dominated by the local cotton unions sought to ensure the party was not damaged by the taint of Bolshevism. By contrast, under different circumstances in Wigan, Stockport and parts of Manchester, or even in the predominantly weaving towns of north east Lancashire like Nelson and Burnley, socialism had much deeper roots and the left within the local Labour parties was in a much stronger position, and thus the struggle between left and right was more evenly contested and prolonged.

At the end of 1936, the Labour left's association with Communists at public meetings and the party's support for Republican forces in Spain became an issue in the local elections in Oldham and Bolton. I have documented in detail elsewhere the splits within the party and the effect that these developments had on the Catholic vote in these towns,[46] but it is clear that the erosion of what was seen as Labour's core vote forced the party moderates led by the trade unions to act against left-wing rebels. Both Fielding and Griffiths have identified Irish Catholics as Labour's most 'consistent' supporters in Lancashire. Whilst the Irish population was not as numerous as in Wigan or in parts of Manchester and Salford, local party leaders in Oldham and Bolton were well aware of the significance of this group for their prospects for success. The Bolton Irish Labour Club was credited with ensuring that its wards regularly returned Labour candidates, and Oldham Conservatives were not the only people who asked 'how many seats would the Socialist Party hold in the Council if they had not the whole of the Irish vote?' Any threat to the electoral loyalty of this group, whether from association with Communism or Spanish Republicanism, or from advocating secularism or birth control, was inevitably opposed by those in the party who were primarily concerned with maximising the party's electoral support.[47]

When in January 1937 the Socialist League nationally associated itself with the ILP and the CPGB in the Unity Campaign, the opportunity arose to seek to marginalise the left and discipline its leaders. In Oldham, the Socialist League branch was disaffiliated from the Trades and Labour Council, and the council president E.M. Hall was censured for chairing local unity campaign meetings.[48] In Wigan, Labour's dominance of the local political environment was again built in large measure upon the support of the large Irish Catholic population. Rather than threaten to abandon the party, which after all controlled the town council and local education, Catholics allied themselves with trade unions such as the Wigan and District Weavers' Union to defeat the left and Communist sympathisers within the Labour Party and the trades council.[49]

Generally, the political character of the labour movement outside Manchester was moderate 'labourist' rather than socialist, but in Stockport the balance of forces was significantly different. Although there was not a strong Communist presence in the town (with exception of some engineering workers at Fairey Aviation), labour politics in Stockport in the 1930s had a distinctive leftist character. For instance, the Trades Council and Labour Party opposed the 'imperialist' League of Nations at the time of the Abyssinian crisis, supported the unity campaign, and opposed the national party's attack on the Socialist League. In a two-member seat, they selected a series of parliamentary candidates with radical, socialist reputations. The veteran ILP socialist and pacifist, James Hudson, was a candidate in 1935. He was succeeded by leading Socialist League member and advocate of the unity campaign, William Mellor, and, finally, the Aid to Spain activist and Communist Charlotte Haldane was only defeated by the narrowest of margins. In contrast, Jenny Adamson, Labour's national chairwoman, resigned as a candidate for Stockport only weeks before the 1935 election in protest about her fellow candidate and the local party's opposition to Labour policy on Abyssinia and the League of Nations.[50]

The battle in Stockport between left and right was keenly contested. Despite the shift to the left within the party, there remained a strong right-wing Labour loyalist opposition. The party only narrowly endorsed William Mellor's candidacy, and efforts were made by the National Executive Committee (NEC) and some in the local party to remove him on account of his role in the unity campaign. Some on the right laid the responsibility for a dramatic fall in local party membership from over 1,500 in 1935 to only 400 in 1937 on the leftist positions taken by the party, but this decline was subsequently reversed under a membership campaign led by Mellor.[51] Nevertheless, the main differences between the position in Stockport and the other Labour parties studied here were that in addition to there being a strong left-wing ILP tradition which formed the basis for an energetic Socialist League branch in the town, some of the branches of the most active union in the party, the NUR, were among the most prominent proponents of left-wing policies rather than their opponents.

As noted before, the NUR had been described as the 'life and soul of the trades council movement', and this certainly appeared to be the case in Stockport. Despite having nothing like the local membership of the cotton, engineering and hatters' unions, the NUR was a major force in the town's labour politics. While the local cotton and engineering branches did not consistently affiliate to the Labour Party in this period, and the Hatters restricted their participation to the industrial side of the trades council, all five of Stockport's NUR branches consistently affiliated to both the political and the industrial sides of the party. The local labour movement had a long tradition of close relationships with the railway unions and representation by railway union sponsored Labour candidates. George Wardle (editor of *Railway Review*) was elected in 1906 and 1910, and A. Townend, who was sponsored by the Railway Clerks' Association, won a by-election in 1925, and was returned again in 1929.[52]

Whilst not all the NUR branches were inclined to the left – indeed, the largest branch (Stockport No. 1) and its delegate A. Glynn were consistent opponents[53] – branches No. 2 and No. 3, and delegates like H. Roberts, were prominent advocates of positions critical of Labour Party policy and of seeking closer relations with the Communist Party. For instance, a report on a Socialist League anti-war conference in

Manchester in September by delegates including Roberts and Hudson was followed by the party adopting a resolution attacking the TUC's policy on Abyssinia and instructing the party's delegates to the Labour conference 'to oppose any and every proposal which will involve this country's participation in war'. The joint branches of the Stockport NUR then passed a very similar resolution, and the next year the council's delegate to the Lancashire and Cheshire Federation of Trades Councils was mandated to oppose any resolution supporting 'the League of Nations as a means of achieving peace'.[54]

Subsequently, Roberts and NUR No. 3 were key supporters of Communist Party affiliation, and promoted talismanic left issues such as support for a Popular Front, opposition to conscription and the NEC's decision to dismantle the League of Youth. Whilst support for Communist affiliation was defeated on a card vote of all (industrial and political) trades council affiliates by 2,306 to 1,871, and the party held a studied neutrality over Cripps' campaign for a Popular Front in 1939, Stockport Labour Party had moved decisively to the left in this period. As with Manchester and Salford Trades Council, this shift would only be reversed during the war and with the isolation and removal of those delegates who supported the People's Convention, including Roberts and other NUR No. 3 delegates.[55]

Internal Party Struggle: 'First Blood'

It is clear that the political battles over unemployment, fascism, anti-fascism, Spain and relations with the Communists, which transfixed the national movement, were just as important in some, if not all, local parties. As confirmed by the previous section, it is not possible to draw a simple correlation between, on one side, the left and individual members and, on the other, the right and the trade unions. However, in some circumstances it was true that local trade unions were often responsible for blocking the more leftist impulses of local parties. More generally, local party resentment over trade union control in the party provided the impetus for the formation of a constituency Labour parties movement which campaigned for democratisation of the party, with greater rights for individual party members and party organisations, and against the block vote and trade union dominance of the party machinery. Activists' frustrations over the direction of what was seen as trade union controlled party policy could spill over into the nature of the union-party relationship itself.

The political struggle at grass roots level was frequently bitter and extremely damaging. Attempts by the left to replace 'reactionary officials by those less reactionary' were, according to Stafford Cripps, 'a common element of constituency party life'. It is rare that we are able to document the raw human cost of such conflict, but in Manchester, the personal details and effects of just such a struggle are available.[56] William and Agnes Taylor were secretary and assistant secretary respectively of the Withington Labour Party, and members of the Manchester Borough Labour Party (BLP). They had worked devotedly for the party as ward secretaries, local candidates and propagandists for over ten years. However, by 1937, as related by Agnes Taylor and Ben Greene (of whose national

Constituency Party Association Taylor was a regional organiser), the constant fighting with the left and unity campaign supporters in the local party had pushed William to the point of a breakdown. At packed meetings, attempts were made to remove him from his positions in the Withington and the Borough parties. He was apparently replaced as delegate to the party conference by a Londoner who had only been in the party six months. In a letter to William Mellor, then a close associate of Cripps but not yet Stockport's candidate, Taylor's Communist opponents accused him of being a 'thoroughly unreliable political type' and guilty of 'political unscrupulousness of a very dangerous kind'. Echoes of events elsewhere in 1937 are hard to ignore.

For his part, Taylor seems to have tracked the comings and goings from Communist Party offices of leading Labour Party members, such as Manchester Borough Party chairman Eric Gower, and then passed his findings on to the BLP, which launched an investigation into Gower's activities and position. Gower, as secretary of the Exchange Divisional Labour Party, had been one of the leading local advocates of the United Front, and his election in place of councillor Larrad, 'a known right-winger', as BLP chairman was greeted by William Rust, then the Communist Party's organiser in Lancashire, as 'truly first-blood to Unity supporters'.[57] His supporters sought to 'circumvent any efforts to expel Gower and were hoping to turn the tables' by discrediting Taylor. Motivated in part by the desire to affirm his own socialist credentials and loyalty to the labour movement, which were under attack by those on the left, Taylor volunteered to fight in Spain. He only reached Paris where he had a nervous breakdown and, on his return to Manchester, went into a home for rest and treatment, a broken man.

Sectarianism and victimisation came from both sides. In Manchester, Gower – as chair of the BLP – was the public face of the Manchester Labour Unity Committee and, in Stockport, where the local party had chosen William Mellor as its parliamentary candidate, strenuous efforts were made to remove them from their positions. Such was the scale of the witch-hunt against local unity supporters that Stafford Cripps, citing the cases of Gower and Mellor in particular, refused to participate in Labour Party campaigns while the victimisation continued. While Mellor survived, Gower's activities in support of unity and association with Communists, presumably drawing on the evidence provided by Taylor, enabled his opponents to remove him as chairman of the BLP.[58]

The struggle extended into all parts of the local party organisation. In 1938, the Manchester BLP's support for the Popular Front was rejected by the local Women's Advisory Council in a bad tempered meeting. For one supporter of the BLP's position, Mrs Ireland, it was too much and she 'violently left the meeting slamming the door with the remark, "I have finished with the whole miserable lot of you"'.[59] Gower 'officially' joined the Communist Party in the summer of 1939 along with a number of other 'entryists'. Not many people were surprised, as there 'did not seem to be any reason why he should not have done so some time before he did'.[60] What became of William Taylor is not known.

Conclusion

In his work on the Labour Party and the left in the 1930s, Ben Pimlott argued that the Labour leadership and the trade unions necessarily defended the party against a 'noisy' unrepresentative extra-parliamentary left that acted against the party's philosophy and traditions.[61] This was an argument that would have found many adherents amongst local trade union leaders in cotton Lancashire. For those union branches which remained actively involved in their local parties in this part of Lancashire, they were mostly concerned with ensuring the election of their own representatives. The cotton unions most clearly, but other unions too, advocated labour representation rather than socialism as the guiding idea for the party. Partly, this was born out of electoral calculation: of the recognition of the need to maximise support in circumstances when the adherence of the working class of cotton Lancashire to the party could not be guaranteed, particularly given that the anti-Labour Conservative and Liberal vote was frequently united in the 1930s.[62] Of course, the conservative and cautious nature of much of the trade unionism in this period was not merely a product of electoral calculation; it was also deeply rooted in occupational and community identities, and in the experience of economic and industrial depression. Ultimately, union strategy with regard to the Labour Party was informed by the extent to which the membership held to any ideas of collective organisation, of socialism or labourism (notably state intervention or nationalisation), or whether they adhered to more individualistic, conservative ideologies. The correlation between some NUR or engineering union branches and more radical Labour politics reflects a longer and closer identification with socialist ideas. However, for the most part, Griffiths' contention that Labour's hold on working-class allegiance in this part of Lancashire at the end of the 1920s was at best partial and fractured was still largely true at the end of 1930s; in the main, the unions operated within this context.[63]

To return to the analogy of the labour movement as a family, many trade unionists viewed the relationship between the industrial movement and the political party as one of parent and child, with the child taking direction from its more experienced and mature parent. Jack Munro, secretary of the Manchester and Salford Trades Council and veteran of movement, asserted that the duty of the young within the labour movement was to 'be trained to understand that discipline was essential ... The movement will go in the right direction provided youth will be guided by the experience of elder persons'. In the eyes of many trade unionists, the duty of irresponsible elements within local parties was to take direction from the trade union movement.[64] For the most part, local parties welcomed trade union involvement in their affairs, not least because without their financial support many would have been unable to function. However, many in the constituency parties, and not just those on the left, also challenged and rebelled against the restrictions imposed by the 'parent'.

Notes

1. L. Minkin, *The Contentious Alliance: Trade Unions and the Labour Party* (Edinburgh, 1991), pp. 3–5.

2. M. Savage, 'The Rise of the Labour Party in Local Perspective', *Journal of Regional and Local Studies*, 10, 1 (1990) p. 1; G. Eley, 'From Cultures of Militancy to the Politics of Culture: Writing the History of British Communism', *Science and Society*, 61, 1 (1997) p. 127.

3. L. Minkin *The Contentious Alliance*, pp. 27–53; R. Shackleton, 'Trade Unions and the Slump', in B. Pimlott and C. Cook (eds), *Trade Unions in British Politics: The First 250 Years* (London, 1991), pp. 109–34; A. J. Reid, 'Labour and the Trade Unions', in D. Tanner, P. Thane, and N. Tiratsoo (eds), *Labour's First Century* (Cambridge, 2000), pp. 228–9.

4. G.D.H. Cole, *British Trade Unionism Today* (London, 1939), pp. 184, 295 and 306; S. and B. Webb, *The History of Trade Unionism*, quoted in A. Clinton, *The Trade Union Rank-and-File: Trade Councils in Britain, 1900–40*, (Manchester, 1977), pp. 98 and 169–71.

5. A. Clinton, *The Trade Union Rank-and-File*, pp. 141 and 169–70.

6. See, for instance, I. Richter, *Political Purpose in Trade Unions* (London, 1973), pp. 29–31 and 38–43; *AEU Monthly Journal*, November 1935, June 1936, March 1938 and April 1939.

7. Stockport and District AEU Minutes, September 1934 (DD/AEU/1/4 21, Stockport Central Library); Minutes of the Stockport Trades and Labour Council Executive Committee and AGM, 10 December 1936, 24 February and 21 April 1938 (B/MM/2/19, Stockport Central Library).

8. J. Walton, *Lancashire: A Social History, 1558–1939* (Manchester, 1987), p. 2.

9. Unfortunately, the records of the Manchester Labour Party and the Manchester and Salford Trades Council for this period did not survive the destruction of the party's offices by German bombs. It is possible to piece together something about the city's labour movement from other sources, but it can only be a partial picture in comparison to the other towns where fuller records are available.

10. T. Griffiths, *The Lancashire Working Classes, c.1880–1930* (Oxford, 2001), p. 272.

11. For a detailed discussion of working-class politics and organisation in the area in this period, see A. Flinn, 'Prospects for Socialism: The Character and Implantation of Working-Class Activism in the Manchester Area, 1933–41', University of Manchester PhD (1999).

12. Minutes of the Labour Party National Executive Committee (NEC) Organisation Sub-Committee, 16 May 1938 (Labour Party Archive, Manchester).

13. For instance, P. Joyce, *Work, Society and Politics: The Culture of the Factory in Late Victorian England* (Brighton, 1980), and *Visions of the People: Industrial England and the Question of Class, 1840–1914* (Cambridge, 1991); P.F. Clarke, *Lancashire and the New Liberalism* (Cambridge, 1971); J. White, *The Limits of Trade Union Militancy: The Lancashire Textile Workers, 1910–14* (Connecticut, 1978); A. Davies, *Leisure, Gender and Poverty: Working-Class Culture in Salford and Manchester, 1900–39* (Buckingham, 1992); S. Fielding, *Class and Ethnicity: Irish Catholics in England, 1880–1939* (Buckingham, 1993); A. Davies and S. Fielding (eds), *Workers' Worlds: Cultures and Communities in Manchester and Salford, 1880–1939* (Manchester, 1992); T. Griffiths, 'Work, Class and Community: Social Identities and Political Change in the Lancashire Coalfield, 1910–39', in A. Campbell, N. Fishman and D. Howell (eds), *Miners, Unions and Politics, 1910–47* (Aldershot, 1996); T. Griffiths, *The Lancashire Working Classes*.

14. See F.W.S. Craig, *British Parliamentary Election Results, 1918–49* (London, 1977). Useful information on Labour's electoral performance in Lancashire, including Bolton and Bury, can be found in S. Davies and B. Morley, 'The Politics of Place: A Comparative

Analysis of Electoral Politics in Four Lancashire Cotton Textile Towns, 1919–39', *Manchester Region History Review*, 14 (2000), pp. 63–78.

15. J. Henry, 'Salford Labour: A Party in Waiting, 1919–32', *Manchester Region History Review*, 14 (2000), pp. 47–62.

16. S. Davies and B. Morley, 'The Politics of Place', pp. 73–74.

17. For an overview of the Stockport party, see D. Howell, *The Records of Stockport Labour Party, 1896–51: An Introduction*, EP Microfilm (Wakefield, 1986).

18. T. Griffiths, *The Lancashire Working Classes*, p. 216; *Wigan Examiner*, 6 November 1936.

19. A. Bullock, *The Life and Times of Ernest Bevin: Volume One, 1881–40* (London, 1962), pp. 531–33; B. Pimlott, *Labour and the Left in the 1930s* (Cambridge, 1977), chapters 11–14.

20. Minutes of the Manchester NUR District Council, 7 and 9 May 1937 (Greater Manchester County Records Office); *NUR Reports and Proceedings*, June and September Executive Council Meetings and AGM, 1937.

21. P.F. Clarke, *Lancashire and the New Liberalism*, pp. 93–4; J. White, *The Limits of Trade Union Militancy*, pp. 152–66; J. McHugh and B. Ripley, 'The Spinners and the Rise of Labour', in A. Fowler and T. Wyke (eds), *The Barefoot Aristocrats: A History of the Amalgamated Association of Cotton Operative Spinners* (Littleborough, 1987), pp. 130–32.

22. Minutes of the Bolton Operative Spinners' Reddish Branch, 9 January and 14 March 1935; A. Fowler and T. Wyke (eds), *The Barefoot Aristocrats*, pp. 167–8; Minutes of the United Textile Factory Workers' Association (UTWFA) LC, 24 August 1933 and 25 June 1936; Amalgamated Spinners' Quarterly Reports, 1932–40 (details of branch/province membership and affiliation numbers); *Cotton Factory Times*, 12 October 1934; Minutes of the Bolton Operative Spinners' Manchester Branch, 1939–40.

23. Minutes of the UTFWA LC, 21 February, 20 March, 2 and 23 May 1933; UTFWA, *Annual Conference Proceedings, 1936*.

24. 'Draft Manuscript on Origins / History / Structure of Union' (13/A Worktown papers, Mass Observation Archive, University of Sussex); Stockport Trades Council and Labour Party, *Annual Reports*, 1932–40; Oldham Trades and Labour Council Register of Members, 1920–27 (Working Class Movement Library); Bolton and District United Trades Council, *Annual Report*, 1940.

25. A. Fowler and T. Wyke (eds), *The Barefoot Aristocrats*, pp. 167–8 and 177; L. G. Sandberg, *Lancashire in Decline* (Ohio 1974); J. Singleton, *Lancashire on the Scrapheap* (Oxford, 1991).

26. H. Pelling and A. Reid, *A Short History of the Labour Party* (Basingstoke, 1996), p. 65; R. Shackleton, 'Trade Unions and the Slump', p. 116; Minutes of the Oldham Trades and Labour Council Industrial Section, 21 March 1933 and 23 June 1936; Minutes of the Oldham Trades and Labour Council Political Section, 8 January 1935, 16 June and 7 July 1936; A. Fowler and T. Wyke (eds), *The Barefoot Aristocrats*, p. 177.

27. Minutes of the Oldham Trades and Labour Council Political Section, 16 January 1934, 8 Jan 1935, 16 June and 7 July 1936; and Industrial Section, 23 June 1936; *The Citizen*, January, March, June and November 1933.

28. A. Fowler, 'Lancashire to Westminster: A Study of Cotton Trade Union Officials and British Labour, 1910–39', *Labour History Review*, 64, 1 (1999), pp. 15–17.

29. Despite losing a series of elections between 1918 and 1935, Middleton and Prestwich sought a UTFWA sponsored candidate. See A. Fowler, 'Lancashire to Westminster', p. 15; Minutes of UTFWA LC, 28 September and 17 November 1936, 3 February and 30 July 1937.

30. Minutes of the UTFWA LC, 30 March 1936; *Cotton Factory Times*, 6 October 1933 and 10 July 1936; Minutes of the Oldham Operative Spinners' EC, 11 June 1937; Minutes of the Oldham Trades and Labour Council Political Section, 22 June 1937; *Labour's Northern Voice*, March 1937.

31. UTFWA General Correspondence, 22, 23 and 24 May 1935 (TU/3/3/17); Minutes of the UTFWA LC, 21 and 28 October 1935; Minutes of the Bolton Operative Spinners' Council, 23 October 1935; Minutes of the Oldham Provincial Cardroom Operatives, 22 June 1935; *Cotton Factory Times*, 1 and 8 November 1935.

32. For responses to the election defeats see, for instance, Minutes of the Bolton Operative Spinners' Council, 12 November 1935 and *Annual Report*, 1935; Oldham Provincial Cardroom Operatives Quarterly Report, 28 December 1935; *Cotton Factory Times*, 22 November 1935; cutting *Oldham Evening Chronicle* (undated) and Oldham Trades and Labour Council elections results scrapbook (Working Class Movement Library).

33. UTFWA, *Annual Conference Proceedings*, 1935; *Cotton Factory Times*, 15 and 22 November 1935; T. Griffiths, 'Work, Class and Community', pp. 212–17, and *The Lancashire Working Classes*, especially pp. 267–19; D. Tanner, 'The Labour Party and Electoral Politics in the Coalfields', in A. Campbell, N. Fishman and D. Howell (eds), *Miners, Unions and Politics*, pp. 76 and 82. The UTFWA sponsored candidate, G. Tomlinson, was elected at a by-election in Farnworth January 1938. See Minutes of the UTFWA LC, 29 November 1937 and 13 January 1938; *Daily Worker* 29 January 1938.

34. 'Reports of Organisers Respecting the Socialist League and the Unity Campaign', NEC Minutes, 24 March 1937; *Manchester Guardian*, 25 September 1933.

35. A. Bennett, *Oldham Trades and Labour Council Centenary Handbook, 1867–1967* (Oldham, 1967); Oldham Trades and Labour Council Election Records (Working Class Movement Library); *Oldham Evening Chronicle*, 6 May 1935; *Oldham Unionist*, May 1935; Oldham Trades and Labour Council Scrapbook, July and August 1935; *Manchester Guardian*, 28 May, 30 May, 31 May, 1 June, 3 June and 6 June 1935; *Daily Worker,* 3 August 1935; *Cotton Factory Times*, 8 November 1935.

36. Minutes of the UTFWA LC, 24 April, 18 May and 25 June 1936 and 25 April 1937; UTFWA General Correspondence, 23 May, 10 and 24 July 1936; Minutes of the Bolton Operative Spinners' Council, 14 July 1936.

37. *Daily Worker*, 31 October and 30 November 1935; *The Citizen*, September 1934; *The Labour Monthly*, July 1936.

38. Minutes of Reorganisation Committee, 29 November 1937; Labour Clubs, 13 July, Labour Party Post Mortem Discussions on Elections 4 June and 2 November 1937 (7/C, 7/H, 11/I, 13/D and 13/D, Worktown papers); Minutes of the Bolton Trades Council, 10 November 1937; Bolton Operative Spinners, *Annual Report*, 16 October 1936; *Cotton Factory Times*, 6 November 1936; *Daily Worker*, 3 November 1937; *The Citizen*, December 1936, August–December 1937 and February 1938.

39. Labour Party delegate meeting, 3 November 1937; Visits to Labour Clubs, 17 March, 11 and 17 April 1938; Labour and Left Wing Activists, Opinions on Labour Clubs (7/C, 7/H, 8/B, Worktown papers).

40. E. Shaw, *Discipline and Discord in the Labour Party* (Manchester, 1988), pp. 1–30; R. Shackleton, 'Trade Unions and the Slump'; L. Minkin, *The Contentious Alliance*.

41. TUC Archive, 17 and 24 June 1936 (MSS 292/743/4, Modern Records Centre); Minutes of the Oldham Trades and Labour Council Political Section, 14 and 21 January and 21 April 1936; Minutes of the Oldham Operative Spinners' EC, 27 January 1936; Bolton Operative Spinners' Council, *Annual Report*, 1936.

42. Bolton Oral History Project, No. 88.

43. For responses to TUC 'black circulars', including reorganisation of the Manchester and Salford Trades Council, see TUC Archive (MSS 292.777/1, 2, 3, 14, 18, 777.1/1–16); *Labour's Northern Voice*, January and February 1938, December 1940, January, February and March 1941.

44. Bolton Oral History Project, No. 14; Election meeting at Burtons, 26 January 1938 (12/G, Worktown papers).

45. Labour Party post mortem discussions on elections, 27 May and 4 June 1938 (11/1 Worktown papers); Bolton Oral History Project, Nos. 14 and 55.

46. A. Flinn, 'Prospects for Socialism', and 'Irish Catholics in South East Lancashire: A Conflict of Loyalties', *Manchester Region History Review*, 14 (2000). I am using 'Irish Catholics' as a shorthand, including not only those born in Ireland but also those born in England of Irish Catholic parentage.

47. S. Fielding, *Class and Ethnicity*, p. 105; T. Griffiths, *The Lancashire Working Classes*, p. 319; *The Citizen*, August and November 1933, and February 1935; *Oldham Unionist*, March 1935.

48. *Oldham Chronicle*, 16 and 30 October 1936; *Daily Worker*, 14 March, 2 October 1936 and 17 July 1937; *Oldham Labour Gazette*, February 1937; Minutes of the Oldham Trades and Labour Council Political Section, 9 February, 11 and 22 April, 17 and 20 July, and 14 December 1937.

49. *Wigan Examiner*, 24 October 1936; TUC correspondence with Wigan Trades Council, 10 April 1937 (MSS 292.777.1/17); Minutes of the Wigan and District Weavers' Union, 22 March, 3 May 1937, and 15 August 1938 (Wigan Archives Service).

50. Minutes of the Stockport Trades Council and Labour Party, 19 September, 28 November 1935, 14 May 1936, 15 April, 5 August, 30 September, 4 November 1937, 25 May and 29 June 1939.

51. *Ibid*, 5 and 26 August, 30 September, and 4 November 1937.

52. A. Clinton, *The Trade Union Rank-and-File*, p. 98; Stockport Trades Council and Labour Party, *Annual Accounts*, 1931–40; D. Howell, *The Records of Stockport Labour Party*, pp. 1–4 and 17–18.

53. Minutes of the Stockport Trades Council and Labour Party, 20 May and 26 August 1937; TUC Archive, 1 June 1937 (MSS 292.770.2/1).

54. Minutes of the Stockport Trades Council and Labour Party, 25 July, 12, 19 and 26 September 1935, and 14 May 1936; Minutes of the Stockport NUR Joint Branch Committee, 6 October 1936; *Labour's Northern Voice*, June 1936.

55. Minutes of the Stockport Trades Council and Labour Party, 9 January 1936, 30 July 1936, 16 December 1937, 3 November 1938, 9 February and 2 March 1939, 12 December 1940, and 23 January 1941.

56. For the following, see Letter from Ben Greene to Cripps, 30 July 1937; Letter from J.W. Collier to William Mellor, 18 July 1937; Letter from Agnes Taylor to Cripps, 19

August 1937 (files 505 and 514, Sir Stafford Cripps papers, Nuffield College). I am grateful to Kevin Morgan for originally drawing my attention to this material.

57. *Daily Worker*, 12 March 1937.

58. Letters of Cripps and Middleton and Gower, 5 September 1937, and from Gower to Cripps, 20 September 1937 (file 503, Cripps papers); *The Tribune*, 10 and 17 September 1937.

59. Minutes of the Manchester Labour Women's Advisory Council, 5 December 1938 (M449/1).

60. *Labour's Northern Voice*, December 1939. Gower stood as the Communist candidate in the Stretford by-election, 1940.

61. B. Pimlott, *Labour and the Left*.

62. C. Cook, 'Liberals, Labour and Local Elections', in G. Peele and C. Cook (eds), *The Politics of Reappraisal 1918–39* (London, 1975).

63. T. Griffiths, *The Lancashire Working Class*, p. 272

64. *Labour's Northern Voice*, August 1939.

Chapter 7

The Reactions of Municipal Voters in Yorkshire to the Second Labour Government, 1929–32

Sam Davies and Bob Morley

As a recent study by Neil Riddell has pointed out, Labour's travails in government between 1929 and 1931 have been for the most part dealt with by historians 'as a prelude to the events of August 1931', and at the same time with a distinctly 'high politics' approach.[1] Riddell's own study consciously eschewed these preoccupations, attempting to view the second Labour government 'in its own right' and also in the context of the wider labour movement. The purpose of this article is to add to the historical analysis of the second Labour government by evaluating the reactions of the population at large as measured by local election results in one important region of Britain. No comprehensive collection and analysis of annual local election results has previously been available to historians, so the aggregate figures have been little utilised to gauge political opinion in the interwar period.[2] The authors' own research published elsewhere aims to fill this gap, and the data utilised here is derived from this work in progress.[3]

It would be wrong of course to view the results of municipal elections as an entirely accurate or unproblematic barometer of broader party political opinion in the period. While universal suffrage had been won at the parliamentary level by 1928, the municipal franchise at this time was restricted to ratepayers and their spouses, and somewhere in the region of 25 per cent of the parliamentary electorate was thus excluded from the municipal polls.[4] The county boroughs considered in this article were also for the most part the larger and more industrial cities and towns, where working-class voters were likely to be more preponderant than in the country as a whole.[5] In addition, turnout at municipal elections averaged around the 45–55 per cent range between the wars, significantly lower than at general elections.[6] Given these reservations, however, it should be readily understood that all these factors taken together were a *constant* affecting the municipal results, and thus unlikely to distort overall *trends* in voting support. The one great merit of the county borough elections as an indicator of political opinion was that they occurred regularly every year. In the absence of opinion polls, they provide the only systematic insight available into how local electors reacted to political events over time.

This article, therefore, will analyse trends in the Labour Party's electoral support in Yorkshire, focusing on the annual municipal elections between 1929 and 1932 in 12 county boroughs in the county.[7] It is possible from this analysis to identify dramatic shifts in Labour's electoral performance between 1929 and 1932. These shifts were undoubtedly related to the momentous political events taking place nationally, and they reveal something about how people reacted at the grass roots level to the Labour government and its aftermath. The changes in political support were also mediated however by both short- and long-term socio-political differences in the localities. It was the critical tension between the local and the national that produced differential effects within Yorkshire, and these effects tell us much about the nature of Labour's grass roots support, not just within the timeframe of 1929–32 but within the whole interwar period.

An aggregate analysis of the municipal elections in the 12 Yorkshire county boroughs during the four years from 1929 to 1932 gives some idea of the overall trends during the period. Labour's performance has been calculated in Table 7.1 below in terms both of its percentage share of seats won and its share of all votes cast in the annual elections.[8]

Table 7.1 – Labour Performance in Municipal Elections in 12 Yorkshire County Boroughs, 1929–32

	1929	1930	1931	1932
Labour % of seats won	52	32	22	50
Labour % of votes cast	50	41	39	52
Turnout (%)	48	49	56	53

The trends shown in Table 7.1 can be identified as follows. In 1929, Labour did exceptionally well by interwar standards, winning just over half of all seats up for election and exactly half of all votes cast in the 12 boroughs. This strong Labour performance was achieved on a low turnout of 48 per cent, however. In 1930, by contrast, there was a serious dip in Labour's support, with the party winning only just over 40 per cent of votes cast, and winning less than a third of all seats up for election. There was also a slightly higher turnout overall but even so fewer than half of the eligible electors cast their vote. The trend against Labour was sustained in 1931 on a significantly higher turnout of 56 per cent, with the party's share of the vote falling slightly to just below 40 per cent, and its share of seats won falling as low as 22 per cent. In 1932, however, Labour made a remarkable recovery at the polls, again on a relatively good turnout of 53 per cent, restoring its share both of votes and seats won to around the 50 per cent mark, roughly the same level it had achieved in 1929. These aggregate electoral trends are clear-cut, but to gain further insight into the detail of the Yorkshire response it is now necessary to analyse each of the elections in turn to get a better understanding of how and why these trends eventuated.

1929 – 'The Intelligent Knowledge of the Electors'

County borough elections in the interwar period were held each year at the beginning of November. In 1929, therefore, they took place five months after the Labour triumph of the general election that had propelled the party into office at Westminster. Labour's success in the general election had if anything been magnified in Yorkshire: of the 29 parliamentary seats that corresponded to the 12 boroughs considered here, only five (Hull North West, Leeds North and North East, and Sheffield Eccleshall and Hallam) had not been won by Labour on 30 May 1929. The county was generally and justifiably seen as one of the heartlands of Labour support, and expectations were high that the November elections would see a repeat performance. There was also a belief on both sides that the municipal elections were to a significant extent a test of the popularity of the recently formed government. In Huddersfield, for instance, the local Labour newspaper saw them as a chance to deliver a 'vote of confidence' in the 'first trial of strength of the parties since the government came into office'.[9] The Tories had a similar outlook, and Neville Chamberlain delivered a strong message stressing the dangers of Labour 'municipalisation' and urging local parties to be 'up and doing' in the election campaign. His statement that 'every borough should regard the municipal elections as no less important than the parliamentary' was enthusiastically endorsed by the Tory *Yorkshire Herald*, which argued that 'the municipal elections in England this year are enormously important'.[10]

Surveying the situation as it stood before the elections, Labour already had overall control of four county boroughs in Yorkshire (Barnsley, Leeds, Rotherham and Sheffield) and could realistically hope to take control in another three (Bradford, Hull and Wakefield). In five others (Dewsbury, Doncaster, Halifax, Huddersfield, and York), Labour was still very much in a minority. As already noted above in Table 7.1, Labour performed extremely well in terms of votes and seats won in the 1929 municipal elections in the Yorkshire county boroughs. This was perhaps to be expected during what was still Labour's 'honeymoon' with the labour movement and the wider electorate.[11] Notwithstanding the good Labour performance in terms of votes and seats, however, Labour made on aggregate a net gain of only three seats in these boroughs. It thus failed to take control of any of its three target councils as a direct result of the elections, although in all three cases it subsequently took control after the aldermanic elections.[12] Table 7.2 below shows the results in each borough.

Analysing these figures closely, of the four boroughs situated in the Yorkshire coalfield, Labour maintained its control in Barnsley and Rotherham, but with no gains in the former and the loss of one seat in the latter. Labour made two gains in Wakefield, giving it 22 out of the 44 seats, and putting it in a position to take control after aldermanic elections had been held.[13] The result here was adjudged 'a disgrace to the Conservative Party' by local Tories, whereas the Labour election night meeting drew a huge and 'enthusiastic' crowd, and the speeches 'evoked much cheering'.[14] In Doncaster, however, Labour made no gains and still held only seven out of 36 seats, even though the party held the Parliamentary seat here. The strongly Nonconformist mining districts of Yorkshire had been strongly Liberal on the whole before 1914, and had become Labour strongholds after 1918. In this they were typical of mining areas elsewhere, described by Duncan Tanner as 'a uniquely pro-Labour bloc'.[15] There were, however, important variations in the Yorkshire mining boroughs that help to account for differences in Labour's performance. Barnsley was overwhelmingly a mining town, while Rotherham was predominantly so, although it also had substantial iron and steel works. Wakefield, however, was described as 'an isolated centre of Anglican influence in the industrial West Riding', and its miners were counter-balanced somewhat by 'a considerable portion of the middle class'.[16] Wakefield was also the administrative centre of the West Riding county council, boosting its white collar and middle-class electors.[17] Doncaster's miners were offset by the mainly skilled workers of the railway locomotive and carriage works of the London and North East Railway, which employed around 5,000 workers in the early 1920s,[18] but a quirk of the electoral system also strongly diminished Labour's chances in municipal elections here. The Doncaster parliamentary division included the adjoining mining villages of Adwick-le-Street and Bentley-with-Arksey, which between them accounted for 30 per cent of the parliamentary electorate[19], but these villages were not included in the county borough. Thus, the mining influence was much weaker than might have been expected in Doncaster's municipal elections.[20]

Table 7.2 – Labour Performance in 1929 Municipal Elections in 12 Yorkshire County Boroughs

County Borough	Labour % share of votes won	Labour % share of seats won	Turnout (%)	Labour net gains/losses	Labour position after election
Barnsley	45	44	61	0	In power
Bradford	52	57	55	–1	Took power[b]
Dewsbury	42	22	50	0	In opposition
Doncaster	45	33	49	0	In opposition
Halifax	39	33	48	0	In opposition
Huddersfield	38	0	48	–1	In opposition
Hull	55	69	46	+1	Took power[b]
Leeds[a]	96	59	13	Truce	In power
Rotherham	54	67	48	–1	In power
Sheffield	53	76	42	Reorganisation	In power
Wakefield	50	55	60	+2	Took power[b]
York	50	50	54	+3	In opposition
TOTAL	**50**	**52**	**48**	**+3**	**Hold 7 of 12 boroughs**

Notes:
[a] Electoral truce agreed between the major parties in Leeds prior to imminent ward reorganisation – only two wards were contested by Communist candidates against sitting Labour members.

[b] Labour took power after subsequent aldermanic elections.

The second major group of boroughs within the county were the textile centres, where Labour's 1929 performance was somewhat disappointing. Labour sustained a net loss of one seat in both Bradford and Huddersfield, and remained unchanged in Dewsbury and Halifax. Despite the loss in Bradford, Labour was subsequently entitled to three additional aldermen under an agreement on proportionality, and thus took control of the council.[21] Labour's relative strength here was perhaps to be expected, as Bradford was the home of the ILP and had long socialist traditions. Even so, 'a sigh of regret went round the hall' when Labour supporters gathered to hear the results in Bradford.[22] Worse was to occur in Huddersfield, though, where Labour's failure to win a single seat meant that its representation on the council fell to a miserable five out of a total of 60 councillors and aldermen. The local Labour paper adjudged it a 'grave defeat', all the more disappointing after its pre-election talk of a vote of confidence in the Labour government.[23] The results contrasted strongly with the euphoria of only a few months earlier, including a 'Victory Dance' in the town hall and a later celebration of the general election triumph adjudged 'one of the largest outdoor gatherings that has been known in a long number of years'.[24] Liberalism retained its hold on working-class allegiances far later in Huddersfield than in most other towns, with Liberals still retaining an overall majority with 33 seats on the council at this time.[25] An indication of the strength of working-class Liberalism here was the inability of Labour to forge a strong alliance with the Co-operative Party in the town.[26] Labour's weakness here can perhaps be partially explained by the fact that Huddersfield was a centre of production of the highest quality woollen cloth, with generally higher wages than in the rest of the region and relatively low unemployment between the wars. There were also many skilled engineering and chemical workers in the borough, and the relative prosperity and good housing conditions of the working class may have had some political effect.[27]

Halifax presented a similar picture, specialising in the production of high-quality worsteds, and Liberalism also remained durable here, with Labour disappointingly remaining stagnant at 17 out of 60 seats. By contrast, Dewsbury was a centre of low-quality woollen goods – the so-called 'shoddy' trade – where the textile labour force was relatively low paid, and also weakly organised in union terms. Stasis here in terms of seats held meant that Labour remained with 11 out of a total of 36 on the council. There was much frustration at Labour's performance, with one defeated Labour candidate complaining that 'it was only through working-class representatives that they were going to get emancipation from the awful housing and sanitary conditions in the borough'. An Independent victor was also heckled with the comment 'get some work going for us and spend some money for the unemployed'.[28]

In the remaining heterogeneous group of four Yorkshire county boroughs, Labour's performance was on balance reasonably impressive. Labour made net gains of three seats in York, and one in Hull, although in Leeds and Sheffield redistribution of ward boundaries masked any trends in support. York was unique amongst the Yorkshire county boroughs, being the county town and situated in the predominantly rural east of the county, but it also had a mixed industrial base. It had a surprisingly strong local Labour Party with a large membership, but it was still difficult for Labour to make much progress beyond its minority working-class support.[29] Thus, its three gains in 1929 only raised its position to 13 out of 48 seats on the council. There was nevertheless an optimistic air to Labour judgements of the results, variously described as 'a real triumph' and a 'splendid victory'.[30] In Hull, also in the East Riding, after the modest gain of one in the elections, Labour won an overall majority on the council for the first time in the succeeding aldermanic elections. This great port city, with a preponderance of dockers and fishermen amongst its working class, had not been especially strong Labour territory up to the mid–1920s, with a Lib–Lab trades council holding sway. Support for Labour had increased rapidly from 1926 onwards, however, and the party's acquisition of new aldermen was a justified reward for its previous good showing.

This only leaves the two largest cities in Yorkshire. In Leeds, the major parties had agreed to an electoral truce in 1929 in the light of the imminent redistribution of ward boundaries, so most seats were uncontested, although Communists opposed Labour in two wards. Labour's share of seats won, therefore, was simply a reflection of its performance three years previously, while its share of the vote (96 per cent) was merely a demonstration of its massive victories over the two Communist candidates. The balance of power was unaffected, with Labour retaining the slender overall majority in the council that it had achieved in 1928. Leeds was the commercial centre of Yorkshire, with a varied industrial structure, a large working class, and a well organised Labour Party. Labour was if anything even stronger in Sheffield, a veritable 'stronghold' of a city based predominantly on the iron and steel and engineering industries.[31] The party had first gained control of the council in 1926 and, following the recent changes in ward boundaries, all three seats in seven new wards were up for election in 1929 as well as the regular one seat in each of the old wards. Before the elections Labour held 41 of 68 seats, and afterwards held 57 out of 89, a slight increase in its share of the seats from 60 per cent to 64 per cent. Subsequently Labour took six of the seven new aldermen, giving the party 63 out of 96 seats on the council. Overall then, Labour had registered a slight increase in its control of Sheffield, described by the Labour leader with some exaggeration as a 'magnificent result'. He attributed victory to a combination of the 'curious failing on the part of our opponents to give the public any alternative to the policy of the Labour Party', 'the wonderful band of men and women, especially the women ... who have helped the cause and done exceedingly great work' and 'the intelligent knowledge of the electors'.[32]

One factor affecting Labour's performance in the Yorkshire county boroughs in 1929 was a perennial excuse often used when the party was on the defensive. Although it was reported on polling day in Halifax that the 'morning opened with brilliant sunshine' and 'candidates were favoured with ideal autumn weather for bringing up the electors', later comments were less positive. By the time the votes were counted in Dewsbury, 'the fog was thicker than ever' and a defeated Labour candidate stated 'he would have polled a great deal better but for the weather and the fact that Friday was cleaning day', while in York also there were comments on the foggy weather. At Wakefield as well, a Labour speaker referred to 'the awkward day' contributing to lower turnout.[33] Perhaps a more significant factor affecting Labour's performance in 1929 was the fact that the party was defending the seats that it had won three years earlier in 1926. This had been the best year ever for Labour in previous county borough elections, which meant that Labour would have had to have done exceptionally well to register substantial gains in 1929.[34] In this light, Labour's performance was perhaps more of an achievement than it appeared at first glance. In retrospect, the fact that overall Labour won half of all votes cast, and more than half of all seats up for re-election, is a truer reflection of Labour's strength in Yorkshire in 1929 – but this perspective was not of course available to anyone at the time, given the paucity of contemporary analysis of local elections. On the other hand, Labour's taking power in three of the boroughs was in all cases by means of the subsequent aldermanic elections, and it was entirely fortuitous for the party that 1929 happened to be a year when a large number of aldermen had come to the end of their six-year term.

In as much as local elections can be taken as an indicator of national trends, on the whole the judgement of Yorkshire voters on the first five months of the Labour government could be described as positive. This was perhaps understandable, given that the problems of the government were still in their infancy, most notably that of unemployment. The Wall Street Crash had only occurred in October 1929, and the rise in unemployment was only just beginning to take off. There had been 1.2 million out of work when Labour took power, and the figure did not reach 1.5 million until February 1930, before soaring to over 2.5 million by the beginning of 1931.[35] Catholic dissatisfaction with Labour's perceived lack of support for Catholic schools was still nascent in November 1929, only growing to significant proportions in early 1930 and especially around the publication of Trevelyan's White Paper in April.[36] In any case, working-class Catholic voters were generally not a significant electoral factor east of the Pennines. Internal divisions within the Labour movement were also barely visible by November 1929. The trade unions were 'generally contented with the record of the government during its first months', local Labour parties expressed 'general satisfaction', and ILP criticism was confined to the Maxtonites primarily based in Scotland.[37] The ILP and local Labour parties in general in the West Yorkshire region were especially loyal to the government, partly due to the local prestige of Philip Snowden, the Labour chancellor.[38] Conversely there were also some indications that local scepticism about Labour in power was increasing.

These adverse factors for Labour focused mainly on unemployment and especially the application of the rules on eligibility for unemployment benefits. The government had appointed the Morris Committee on Unemployment Insurance in July 1929, and the draft of the Unemployment Insurance Act resulting from this had become a source of bitter dispute by November. Reflecting the strict financial orthodoxy adopted by the government as a whole, Margaret Bondfield as minister of labour was rejecting calls from the labour movement to increase the levels of benefit, reduce the waiting period for qualification for benefit, and repeal the 'not genuinely seeking work' clause which debarred many from eligibility. While she was eventually forced to concede on the last of these issues in the final Bill, discontent at a local level was evident in November. Thus, Bondfield herself released a statement timed to appear on election day distancing herself from the 'not genuinely seeking work' clause. As the local press in Huddersfield reported, 'Miss Bondfield ... has no power to allow or disallow unemployment benefit – the decision lies with the statutory authorities and not with the minister. Actually the weekly average of claims disallowed on the ground of not actually seeking work has fallen steadily since the present government took office'. One of the particular grievances of opponents of the clause was that it especially disbarred married women claimants, and on the same day a meeting of the Huddersfield and District Employment Committee expressed concern at the treatment of married women in the district. 'It was stated that married women who had paid contributions over a long period were deterred from receiving unemployment pay ... it appeared that the Court of Referees had been acting on the opinion ... that married women should be provided for at home ... the position seemed to be that when a woman left her work to get married she had to re-establish herself in industry before she was eligible for benefit'.[39] In the textile districts, where women's paid work outside the home was especially important, this issue was plainly of great significance to working-class voters.[40]

Another issue of significance in the Yorkshire textile district was the rumbling dispute within the wool industry which soured the atmosphere in the 1929 elections. Employers had proposed an 8.3 per cent cut in wages, which the National Union of Textile Workers voted in a ballot by four to one to resist. Negotiations between the two sides had broken down ten days before the municipal elections, leading eventually to a lockout in 1930. While this did not materialise as a major party political point in 1929, there was no doubt some local discontent with the government's studied neutrality over the dispute, confirmed later by Margaret Bondfield's public pronouncement that she would not 'express any views upon the merits of the dispute'.[41] Labour had yet to reap the whirlwind fully on this and other issues, but there were pointers to the problems that lay ahead. In Huddersfield, attempts by the local party to improve its organisation in hitherto weak wards revealed a surprising degree of apathy; a ward meeting in July 1929 drew an audience of only five, prompting the scheduling of public meetings 'with a view to stimulating some interest in the ward'.[42] These forebodings were only a prelude however of what was to come in the new decade.

1930 – 'Performance Has Fallen So Far Short of Promise'

When the 1930 local elections were held, the Labour government had been in power for almost 18 months, and its problems were growing. Of greatest significance was the rise in unemployment to over 2.2 million. Criticism within the party of government handling of this issue had grown, with the Mosley Memorandum having raised much debate during the year and the ILP national conference in April 1930 articulating much discontent.[43] Despite this, widespread dissatisfaction with the government was still not commonly recognised within the wider labour movement, and local Labour parties went into the elections with guarded optimism. The results showed a disastrous slump in Labour support however. In the Yorkshire county boroughs, Labour lost overall control of Barnsley, Hull, Leeds and Wakefield, while in Bradford it remained the largest party but tied with its combined opponents. The party only held on to power in Rotherham and Sheffield. In Hull and Leeds, ward reorganisation made it impossible to calculate net losses to Labour, but even without these Labour made a net loss of 16 seats in the other ten boroughs. Just as striking was the collapse in Labour's overall share of the vote in 1930, down from 50 per cent in 1929 to 41 per cent, and its share of seats won, down even more catastrophically from 52 per cent to 32 per cent. All this was achieved on a marginally higher turnout figure of 49 per cent. The detailed figures for each borough are shown below in Table 7.3.

Table 7.3 – Labour Performance in 1930 Municipal Elections in 12 Yorkshire County Boroughs

County Borough	Labour % share of votes won	Labour % share of seats won	Turnout (%)	Labour net gains/losses	Labour position after election
Barnsley	42	33	71	–3	Lost power
Bradford	44	38	53	0	Tied
Dewsbury	44	22	56	–2	In opposition
Doncaster	36	11	49	–1	In opposition
Halifax	45	27	49	0	In opposition
Huddersfield	28	0	47	–2	In opposition
Hull	44	35	44	Reorganisation	Lost power
Leeds	40	35	49	Reorganisation	Lost power
Rotherham	44	56	51	0	In power
Sheffield	41	38	44	–6	In power
Wakefield	44	45	62	–1	Lost power
York	38	17	58	–1	In opposition
TOTAL	41	32	49	–16	Hold 2 of 12 boroughs, plus 1 tied

Looking in detail at the mining boroughs first, there was no change in the overall position of the parties in Rotherham and Labour retained control of the council. This apparent success was tempered by the fact that four of the five sitting Labour councillors due for re-election were returned unopposed, and unsurprisingly it was reported that 'public interest generally has not been manifest to any great extent during the municipal election campaign'.[44] In Doncaster, Labour lost one seat overall, with the results being seen as 'decidedly anti-Socialist', but again it was reported that 'very little interest was taken in the elections at Doncaster'.[45] Labour also lost one seat overall in Wakefield, and combined with earlier by-election losses this meant that Labour lost the control of the council that they had won the previous year. The local Labour MP G.H. Sherwood, speaking at the post-election meeting, stated 'he was disappointed at the results of the elections, but he was not disheartened', and went on to claim that 'Labour had really had a great victory against the odds' and also that 'the working class had let the working class down that day'. The Conservative leader in the council, on the other hand, proclaimed that 'the political pendulum was swinging' and that 'the votes on the Socialist side had fallen off in a most extraordinary manner', going on to argue that 'municipal elections were some small indication of what was going to happen in a General Election'.[46] Labour's biggest disappointment in the coal boroughs was in Barnsley, where three seats were lost along with control of the council.

Turning to the textile boroughs, the defeat suffered by the wool textile workers in June 1930 after the ten-week lockout was still fresh in voters' minds when they went to the polls. It was suggested in the Bradford Labour newspaper that this was a factor in the 'depressing' municipal results in November, as well as the shock parliamentary by-election defeat in Shipley in the same month.[47] In the Bradford municipal elections, however, Labour managed to escape with no change in its overall position on the council. It was still the largest single party, but it had already lost overall control due to the addition of a new ward that had elected three non-Labour councillors. Labour did lose one seat in the November elections, but the party was compensated by a freak gain in a usually anti-Labour ward after adopting a candidate with no obvious Labour convictions but who brought strong personal support with him.[48] In Halifax, too, Labour sustained no overall losses, but the party still remained a long way off an overall majority, and the elections were seen generally as a triumph for Liberalism. One victorious Liberal candidate made the rather extravagant claim for his party's progressive credentials that 'it was not long since the last Chartist had died, so there was no wonder Liberalism had conquered', while another claimed that 'whatever the Liberal position in Halifax on national affairs, it was extraordinarily strong in municipal matters'. A beaten Tory candidate, however, complained that 'the men and women of the Conservative and Liberal party objected to turn out in bad weather, but the Socialists never did. We are lazy beggars', and added sourly that 'they had too many Corporation housing estates in the ward, and the people were as "red" as the brick of which the houses were built'.[49]

In Dewsbury, Labour lost two seats, compounding its already weak position on the council, but a similar loss of two in Huddersfield reduced Labour strength to a puny three out of 60 seats. As in the previous year, Labour failed to win a single contest in Huddersfield. The verdict of the local press was damning: 'It is easy to attach too much importance to the municipal elections as indicating the trend in national politics, but the Labour slump which was so striking a feature of Saturday's polls is obviously significant. It represents, indirectly perhaps, but none the less clearly, the dissatisfaction of the country with the achievements of the present Government and its disappointment that performance has fallen so far short of promise ... If the Government are wise they will ... get more drive into their programme (especially as regards unemployment)'.[50] James Hudson, the local Labour MP had previously defended the record of the government to his local party, especially over its treatment of the unemployed and its handling of the wool textile dispute, but he refused to go along with the criticism voiced at the ILP conference and 'expressed his determination to remain a loyal member of and support the policy of the Labour Party'.[51]

Elsewhere in Yorkshire the picture was if anything even bleaker. Following the ward reorganisation in Leeds, all the seats were up for election, and Labour's previous majority of four was transformed into a majority of 22 for the Tories after the aldermanic positions had been settled. The Conservative *Yorkshire Post* reported gleefully that 'seldom in the history of municipal elections in Leeds have there been such jubilant and wildly enthusiastic scenes as were witnessed at the Leeds and County Conservative Club on Saturday night, when the results of the election were made known'.[52] In Hull as well, ward reorganisation and extension of the borough meant that all the seats were up for election in the new wards, and a comparison in terms of net losses was not possible. The final effect of the elections, however, was that Labour's narrow majority was replaced by a majority of ten for the Independents. Labour members greeted the results with a mixture of 'studied silence' and 'chagrin', and it was reported that 'it is idle to deny that the Group is disappointed at the results'.[53]

In Sheffield, Labour suffered a net loss of six seats, although it still maintained its overall control. The Labour leader described this as a 'setback', and argued that 'of course, the general unemployment difficulties had some bearing' on the result. Finally, in York, Labour lost one seat, the results being judged as 'a decided setback' and a 'severe rebuff'.[54] Ten days later the local Labour MP F.G. Burgess was forced to defend the record of the government, stating 'he was not apologising – rather he was proud of what the Labour government had been able to do', rejecting calls by supporters 'to do something drastic in the direction of Socialism', and asking 'whether it was not the best policy to get as much accomplished as possible before they were outvoted'.[55] His prospective Conservative opponent replied soon after, pointing out the verdict of the York voters in the recent municipal elections. The Tory candidate charged Labour with 'over 2,000,000 unemployed, practically doubled since they came into office. What have they done to stop that? Nothing!' He continued that 'the present Government has done worse than even its bitterest critics expected them to do. How much worse they must have done in the eyes of those who put their faith in them and voted for them at the last election?'[56] On the evidence of the municipal elections, it was difficult to demur from this view.

1931 – 'When the Hour was Darkest'

In 1931, local electors went to the polls just over two months after the resignation of the government in late August and the split in the party precipitated by the decision of Ramsay MacDonald and his followers to enter the National government. The municipal elections took place a mere six days after the subsequent general election which had seen Labour decimated across the country. Unemployment was even higher than in the previous year at 2.6 million, but it appears that it was the Labour government that voters blamed for this, rather than the new coalition. The direct consequence of the financial crisis that had precipitated the split in Labour's ranks was the harsher treatment of the unemployed, but even here the coalition largely escaped blame. The Anomalies Regulations, which restricted eligibility for benefit and especially disadvantaged married women and seasonal workers, were implemented by the National government, but were only a confirmation of the intentions of the Labour government in the Unemployment Insurance Bill of July. Across the board, reductions in benefit and increases in contributions, which were the direct responsibility of the coalition, only began to come into operation after parliament had been dissolved prior to the general election. Perhaps most important of all, the new means test for transitional payments of benefit only came in force on 12 November, after all the elections had taken place.[57] Mirroring the situation in 1929, Labour's electoral demise nationally was magnified in Yorkshire in the 1931 general election: the National coalition very nearly achieved a clean sweep in the 29 Yorkshire constituencies corresponding to the county boroughs, with only Leeds South East being won by Labour. Labour could hardly have gone into the local elections in less propitious circumstances.

Unsurprisingly, the party sustained a net loss of 34 seats in the 12 Yorkshire boroughs. In all but two of the boroughs, there was a net loss, most notably including eight seats in one of its main strongholds, Sheffield, and an even more disastrous 12 in Bradford. Labour was thus in a minority in Bradford compared to its combined opponents and conceded power. Labour did, however, manage to retain its control of Sheffield and Rotherham, albeit with a narrow majority of two in Sheffield, and in both cases sustained primarily by the sizeable group of aldermen they had acquired in 1929. The only borough to defy the trend was Barnsley, where Labour made two gains. Overall the turnout was considerably higher than in the previous two years at 56 per cent. Interestingly, however, in terms of the percentage of votes won, Labour's share of 39 per cent was only marginally lower than the 41 per cent of the previous year, whereas in terms of seats won Labour's share fell from 32 per cent to 22 per cent. This bears some resemblance to Labour's performance in the general election of 1931, in which its loss of seats far outweighed its loss of votes.[58] This anomaly can be explained for the parliamentary elections primarily by the fact that Labour was opposed in most seats by a single National coalition candidate in 1931, as opposed to numerous three-way contests with Liberals and Tories in 1929 which split the anti-Labour vote and gave Labour a much better chance of victory.[59] In the municipal elections, however, three-way contests were a rarity throughout the period 1929–32, with Labour's opponents having formed formal alliances as 'Independents' or 'Citizens' (as in Barnsley, Dewsbury or Hull) or informal pacts between Conservatives and Liberals. Only in Leeds was this not the case, where usually around a quarter of all contests were three-way contests involving the main parties. The full details of the 1931 results for each borough are shown below in Table 7.4.

Table 7.4 – Labour Performance in 1931 Municipal Elections in 12 Yorkshire County Boroughs

County Borough	Labour % share of votes won	Labour % share of seats won	Turnout (%)	Labour net gains/losses	Labour position after election
Barnsley	46	56	77	+2	In opposition
Bradford	35	0	63	−12	Lost power
Dewsbury	40	33	63	−2	In opposition
Doncaster	29	11	55	0	In opposition
Halifax	30	20	45	−1	In opposition
Huddersfield	29	0	50	−2	In opposition
Hull	41	24	50	−3	In opposition
Leeds	43	37	47	−1	In opposition
Rotherham	46	44	60	−2	In power
Sheffield	38	29	59	−8	In power
Wakefield	43	10	69	−3	In opposition
York	41	8	60	−2	In opposition
TOTAL	39	22	56	−34	Hold 2 of 12 boroughs

Amongst the mining boroughs in 1931, Wakefield saw Labour's worst performance, with only one unopposed Labour candidate being returned to the council. Labour speakers lamented that 'the general election had had its repercussion on the municipal elections', but also affirmed that they were 'out but not down'.[60] In Doncaster as well, the only Labour candidate returned was unopposed, and similar sentiments were expressed by a defeated Labour candidate who stated 'there was yet another day. The circumstances this time had been too strong for them'.[61] In Rotherham, two seats were lost, but three others under attack were retained and Labour control of the council was preserved. Councillor G.C. Ball, secretary of Rotherham Labour Party, managed to put a positive gloss on this and at the same time turn attention away from the national context of the elections by stating that 'it is certainly a vote of confidence in the policy pursued by the Labour Party in the last three years'.[62] Indeed it is significant that Labour's share of the vote here was slightly up on the previous year, as it was also in Barnsley. The local paper commented that 'Barnsley did not follow the county's example generally', with Labour making two gains.[63] Labour in fact came very close to regaining control here, now having 17 seats on the council compared to the 19 of the Independents. As the authors have stated elsewhere, 'it would appear that the Labour government's policy failures while still in power, especially over unemployment, were more crucial in Barnsley than the 1931 split in the party and collapse of the government'.[64]

In the textile boroughs, there were no bright spots to relieve the gloom for Labour. In Huddersfield, 'Labour's complete defeat' saw its last two sitting councillors beaten, leaving the party with a single alderman on the council.[65] The Labour newspaper here placed the blame firmly on the defecting leaders, stating that 'the treachery of Snowden and MacDonald had a profound effect upon many of our own people'.[66] No doubt, the women's section of the Huddersfield party now bitterly resented its investment in September 1929 of 2s 6d on a framed photo of Ramsay Macdonald to hang in the Labour rooms.[67] In Dewsbury, Labour also lost two seats, while in Halifax another seat was lost. One Labour speaker put the blame on the events that had taken place in parliament, describing their effects luridly as 'a wave of terrorism unknown in the political history of the country', while another believed that 'out of the apparently impossible position into which they had got they would have to fight their way clear ... Those who could fight when the hour was darkest were the people who were most worth while'. A Tory councillor meanwhile affirmed that 'he had worked like a nigger for the ward for three years, and the ratepayers had stood by him like a man', thus compounding his casual racism with unthinking sexism.[68] Worst of all for Labour was Bradford, where the party failed to win a single seat in 22 contests, and sustained a net loss of 12 seats overall. Foster Sunderland, president of Bradford Labour Party, described it as 'a cold bath for Labour', while a Tory called it a 'magnificent victory', and a Liberal stated that his party's candidates had got in 'on a wave of discontent against the Socialists'.[69] It would appear that the Labour Party really did reap the whirlwind here of events in Westminster, confirming the view of one study of the area that 'local attitudes towards Snowden and the Labour government became more critical from the end of 1930'.[70]

Elsewhere Labour was 'swept clean out of York', with only a solitary councillor being returned unopposed to the council.[71] In Sheffield, eight seats were lost, prompting the observation by the Labour leader that 'the panic and fear unfortunately created during the General Election, whilst considerably toned down during the last few days, was still in evidence in this election'.[72] Labour did not do quite as badly in Hull, however, the party losing only three seats overall, with a defeated candidate stating that 'the aftermath of the General Election was a factor in the result'.[73] In Leeds as well, the results were less traumatic for Labour, and it was reported that 'feeling at the Socialist headquarters ... was one of satisfaction that Socialism had not suffered a more serious reverse. After local experience at the Parliamentary election, a net loss of only one seat in the municipal elections was received almost with feelings of relief'.[74] There was one factor uncommented on at the time which helps to explain this relative success in Leeds and Hull however. In Leeds, those seats contested in 1931 had been won in the previous year when every seat on the council had been decided after ward redistribution. Thus, Labour was defending its position of 1930; a poor year when it had already been driven back to its bedrock of support, and consequently the party had little to lose. Similarly, in Hull, all the seats in the newly created wards had been contested in 1930. This contrasted with the other boroughs where the party was faced with the much harder task of defending its position of 1928, a relatively good year for Labour. Nevertheless, the Labour leader in Leeds still recognised that it had been a dark day for the party, arguing that 'socialists in Leeds had much work to do in educating the people'.[75]

1932 – 'A Sense of Great Jubilation'

One year later, the 1932 municipal elections took place with Labour firmly in opposition while the crisis of unemployment continued to dominate the political and social climate. Far from unemployment abating under the National government, it was now higher again at 2.7 million. Moreover, people's bitterness over the treatment of the unemployed had become focused on the means test and its application by local Public Assistance Committees (PACs). Unrest had grown throughout the year, especially targeted against those PACs (usually non-Labour) which enforced the test most rigorously, culminating in major riots in Birkenhead in September. At the same time, the National government was threatening with legal action those PACs (most often, but not exclusively Labour) which were applying the regulations laxly, including Barnsley and Rotherham in Yorkshire. Local Labour parties throughout the region focused much of their effort in 1932 on campaigning over the means test. In Bradford, for instance, the Labour newspaper mounted a sustained attack on the 'Mean Means Test', and a major conference was held over the issue there in May 1932. In Huddersfield, the municipal election manifesto placed great emphasis on a long and detailed separate section on 'underemployment', calling for the reversal of the 'introduction of Poor Law Tests … into the administration of Unemployment Insurance', and in the meantime 'a more humane method of administering the "means test"'.[76] Outside the Labour Party as well, the Communist-dominated National Unemployed Workers' Movement (NUWM) campaigned extensively over the issue at a local level throughout 1932, and ran candidates in the municipal elections in Bradford, Dewsbury and Leeds. In the run up to the municipal elections, the national hunger march organised by the NUWM was converging on London, and in the last few days from 27 October clashes between the marchers and police occurred daily in the capital. On the very day of the elections there were riots outside parliament and a heckler inside interrupted Ramsay MacDonald with cries of 'Down with the Means Test!' and 'Release Wal Hannington' (the NUWM leader who had recently been arrested).[77]

This was the backdrop to the municipal elections, in which Labour faced the difficult task of defending the relatively strong position it had won in the successful year of 1929. If the party was unable to reverse the downward trend of the previous two years, then it stood to lose many seats in 1932. One early encouragement for the party though had come in April when Arthur Greenwood recaptured Wakefield in the only parliamentary by-election to be held in the Yorkshire county boroughs in 1932. This favourable portent was confirmed in the November elections, when Labour made a remarkably strong comeback. In the 12 Yorkshire county boroughs, the party made a net gain overall of 12 seats, on a relatively high turnout of 53 per cent. It won 52 per cent of all the votes cast, and 50 per cent of all the seats up for re-election, both figures very similar to those of 1929. In terms of winning overall control, this performance yielded less positive results. One gain in Barnsley put Labour dead level with its opponents on the council, but it failed to take control in any of the other boroughs, even its six gains in Leeds still leaving it well short of a majority. Against the trend overall, Labour also lost one of its strongholds, two losses in Sheffield giving the Progressives overall control. The full details of the 1932 results are shown below in Table 7.5.

Table 7.5 – Labour Performance in 1932 Municipal Elections in 12 Yorkshire County Boroughs

County Borough	Labour % share of votes won	Labour % share of seats won	Turnout (%)	Labour net gains/losses	Labour position after election
Barnsley	53	56	75	+1	Tied
Bradford	48	50	54	–1	In opposition
Dewsbury	24	0	52	0	In opposition
Doncaster	45	44	58	+1	In opposition
Halifax	42	47	53	+2	In opposition
Huddersfield	35	0	45	0	In opposition
Hull	57	71	47	+3	In opposition
Leeds	53	58	44	+6	In opposition
Rotherham	60	78	64	+1	In power
Sheffield	59	63	56	–2	Lost power
Wakefield	50	64	67	+1	In opposition
York	50	42	57	0	In opposition
TOTAL	52	50	53	+12	Hold 1 of 12 boroughs, plus 1 tied

Labour performed well in all four of the Yorkshire mining county boroughs, making a net gain in each of them. Labour's share of the vote also went up very considerably in all four boroughs. In every one of them as well, all sides agreed that the means test had been the key issue in the election. In Wakefield, a Tory lamented that 'unemployment and the Means Test had had a great deal to do with the adverse result'. In Rotherham, it was reported that 'both sides agree that the Means Test has been the deciding factor in the election, and the Labour Party are particularly jubilant about what they regard as a "triumphant vindication" of their policy of refusing to administer the Means Test'. In Doncaster, a Labour candidate charged that 'the Doncaster Public Assistance Committee was recognised as one of the harshest in the country. The treatment meted out to the people who had to come before them had been of the meanest', while another described the means test as "damnable"' and 'a most abominable thing'. A Liberal replied that 'the administration of the Means Test by the Doncaster Public Assistance Committee had been more humane than in any other borough within a hundred miles of Doncaster. The measure was an inhuman one in some instances, and ought to be amended ... but ... all the Public Assistance Committee could do was to administer the measure'. In Barnsley, Independents complained about the 'bogey' of the means test costing them control – it had been 'thrust upon them, and they had enforced it with 'the utmost latitude'.[78]

The textile towns were again less fertile territory for Labour, the only progress being made in Halifax where two seats were gained and Labour's share of the vote rose from 30 to 42 per cent. It was reported that 'there was a sense of great jubilation at the ILP rooms'. A Labour speaker argued that they were 'now going forward with full support to attack ... that miserable Means Test ... they were going to fight until the Means Test was a thing of the past ... it was no earthly use any man in politics today believing he could bludgeon the unfortunate unemployed into their hovels in order that industrial prosperity would once more reign – (applause)'. A Conservative stated that 'the misrepresentation of the Means Test had done more harm to their party than anything else' while another agreed that it 'had been a deciding factor'. A Liberal echoed them that 'the Means Test was the cause of his small majority', but another Liberal stated 'my ward contains several large new housing estates and they are called by some people red houses that shelter red voters. I feel sure it is the new housing estates which have let us down'.[79]

In Dewsbury, there was no change in the elections, but Labour had already lost two councillors by defection, one to sit as Independent Labour and the other to represent the ILP (which had disaffiliated from the Labour Party earlier in the year). Labour's share of the vote also fell here quite considerably from 40 to 24 per cent, in part due to the fact that the Labour vote was split in a number of wards between official Labour and ILP, Independent Labour and NUWM or 'Workers' candidates. As the local press reported, 'the acute divisions which have taken place in the ranks of the Labour Party at Dewsbury had their effect upon the municipal elections'. Here again the main issue was clear, an Independent claiming 'I know the Means Test is a thorn in your sides but we have to carry the job out and we do it as fairly as we can, and give our people the best possible terms'. A defeated Labour candidate was indignant at the voters' verdict, the local press reporting that he stated 'last year the municipal elections followed the scare general election. After the National government's treatment he thought the workers would have given Labour more support, but evidently the workers in this district hadn't had sufficient kicks and buffets from the National government. But he didn't take Dewsbury as a criterion ...'[80] In Bradford, meanwhile, despite increasing its share of the vote from 35 to 48 per cent, Labour lost one seat, and was to lose a further two aldermen at the subsequent aldermanic elections. In Huddersfield, Labour's continued weakness was apparent, the party yet again failing to win a single seat and seeing its share of the vote increase only slightly from 29 to 35 per cent.

On the surface, Labour's best performance in the region was in Leeds, where Labour's share of the vote went up from 43 to 53 per cent, and a net gain of six seats was made. It must be noted again, however, that due to the 1930 ward reorganisation, the sitting candidates up for election in Leeds in 1932 had all been elected in Labour's poor year of 1930, so it was rather easier for the party to make gains here than in most other boroughs where the strong position of 1929 had to be defended. The same point again applied partially to the situation in Hull, where Labour made three gains and its share of the vote increased sharply from 41 to 57 per cent. Here it was reported that 'Labour claimed that their victories were a vindication of their opposition to a policy of economy which, they stated, had increased unemployment. The means test also had had a considerable influence.'[81] In York, there was no change despite a ten per cent improvement in Labour's share of the vote, but in Sheffield despite a massive increase from 38 to 59 per cent the party lost two seats at the election. Both these losses were partially explained by the intervention of Communist Party candidates splitting the vote for the left, but combined with the earlier defection of one councillor to the ILP and the subsequent loss of five Labour aldermen in the aldermanic elections, the party lost control of the council.[82] Again, it was reported that 'the administration of the Means Test provided the principal source of contention in numerous areas'.[83] Ironically, here though Labour suffered because it had been in power and therefore had had to administer the means test itself, but it had been nowhere near as prominent as the Labour PAC in neighbouring Rotherham in refusing to apply the regulations fully. The loss of Sheffield was a bitter blow (although control was to be restored in the following year) but here as in other boroughs it was the vagaries of the municipal electoral system as much as anything that cost Labour dear, and which masked the underlying strong trend towards the party. Yet again it should be emphasised though that such identification of the underlying trends was not available at the time given the lack of any systematic or comprehensive analysis of municipal election results.

Conclusions

A number of conclusions can be drawn briefly from this analysis of municipal elections in the Yorkshire county boroughs between 1929 and 1932. As far as reactions to the second Labour government are concerned, perhaps most significant is the fact that Labour support fell away so badly in November 1930, well before the split in the party and the 'treachery of the leaders'. The defection of the trio of MacDonald, Snowden and Thomas in the summer of 1931 has been one of the most potent myths the Labour Party has lived by, for generations invoked to sustain a variety of ideas as to what sort of party it should be.[84] What is clear from the evidence here, however, is that the blame for the disaster of the 1931 general election cannot be placed entirely on the shoulders of the 'traitors'. The performance of the Labour government was already by November 1930 causing a severe collapse in Labour support, so that whether or not the party was eventually to be split the prospects for the subsequent general election did not look good. The primary cause of Labour's declining support from 1930 were the issues of unemployment and the treatment of the unemployed, and perhaps the most important aspect of the 1931 debacle was that Labour's timid and conventional approach to economic policy lay at the heart of its problems. While it was Snowden as chancellor who directly implemented the policies of fiscal orthodoxy that signally failed to treat the problem of unemployment, it was the government as a whole and the wider party that to a great extent went along with these policies. The perceived performance of the Labour government itself was the primary cause of the party's local misfortunes from 1930 onwards rather than the later party split.

Allied to this point, the predominance of unemployment as an electoral issue in this period is also sustained by the evidence here. While unemployment was the key issue in 1930 and 1931 leading to the collapse of Labour support, in 1932 the means test became the overriding factor in explaining how Labour could so strongly regain its support in only twelve months. The presence of NUWM candidates in a number of the Yorkshire boroughs in 1932 also highlights the importance of the issue.[85] Although the NUWM itself won little electoral support, its campaigning over the means test brought the issue to the fore, and consequently Labour in opposition was able to win many voters over. Only in Sheffield did it prove to be unhelpful for the party, where Labour control of the PAC worked against its popularity, while conversely the Labour-controlled PAC in Rotherham gathered support by its open defiance of the means test.

A further implication of the evidence in this analysis is the remarkable volatility of Labour's electoral support during these four years. The contrast between Labour's performance in the 1929 and 1931 general elections needs no further comment, but at the municipal level the sharp fall in Labour's support between 1929 and 1930 and equally the sharp rise between 1931 and 1932 suggests that the party's core support was by no means as solid as perhaps it became after 1945. It could be countered that these were unusual times of economic and political crisis when such electoral volatility was more likely, but even so the rapid fluctuations in support for Labour indicates that political loyalties were far from rock-hard for many voters at this time.

Also significant was how much Labour performance varied within Yorkshire. In general terms, the Pennine textile towns for instance were far less supportive of Labour than the mining towns, but even within these categories there were significant differences. Thus the surviving strength of Liberalism in Halifax and especially Huddersfield, even after Liberalism's near disappearance nationally by 1931, is surprising and warrants further and more detailed analysis. Labour's strength was also consistently stronger in the mining boroughs of Rotherham and Barnsley than in Wakefield and Doncaster, to the extent that Barnsley could even go against the general trend of Labour decline in 1930. While the varying proportion of miners within the population of each borough may partially explain this variation, there were also deeper issues of socio-political traditions which again require further investigation. If Labour's support was not solid at this point, nor was it uniform even in economically and socially similar boroughs.

Finally, it should be pointed out that the complexities and anomalies of the municipal electoral system played an important part in distorting or masking the real trends in political support displayed in these elections. The three-year cycle of municipal elections created confusion, so that net gains or losses and changes in control of councils could appear to belie the underlying trend, such as in 1932 when Labour was defending its strong position of three years previously. Yet, it was the net gains or losses and the changes of political control which were the main criteria by which contemporaries judged the political popularity of parties, as no deeper analysis of the results was available to them. Moreover, unlike today, the aldermanic system (not to be abolished until 1972) introduced a complex element into the whole electoral process which could produce distortions in terms of control of councils, such as in Bradford (to Labour's advantage) in 1929 or Sheffield (to its detriment) in 1932. Only by taking these kinds of anomalies into account can a realistic estimation of municipal electoral support be constructed for this period. Such estimation, however, as this article has tried to demonstrate, can add a lot to our understanding of interwar politics.

Notes

1. N. Riddell, *Labour in Crisis: The Second Labour Government 1929–31* (Manchester, 1999), pp. 4–6; earlier major studies include R. Skidelsky, *Politicians and the Slump: The Labour Government of 1929–31* (London, 1967); A. Thorpe, *The British General Election of 1931* (Oxford, 1991); P. Williamson, *National Crisis and National Government: British Politics, the Economy and Empire, 1926–32* (Cambridge, 1992).

2. Earlier exceptions to this rule include E.C. Rhodes, 'Voting at Municipal Elections', *Political Quarterly*, 9, 2 (1938); C. Cook, *The Age of Alignment: Electoral Politics in Britain, 1922–29* (London, 1975), chapter three.

3. S. Davies and B. Morley, *County Borough Elections in England and Wales, 1919–1938: A Comparative Analysis* (8 volumes, Aldershot, 1999 onwards).

4. *Registrar General's Statistical Review of England and Wales, 1946–50*, pp. 172–3; on the municipal franchise, see B. Keith–Lucas, *The English Local Government Franchise: A Short History* (Oxford, 1952), pp. 73–76. There is no conclusive evidence as to how differences in the franchise might have skewed politically the results of the municipal elections, although on balance it is likely that Labour may have been slightly disadvantaged; see S. Davies, *Liverpool Labour: Social and Political Influences on the Development of the Labour Party in Liverpool, 1900–1939* (Keele, 1996), pp. 119–30.

5. There were a small number of exceptions to this, such as Canterbury or Chester, which had acquired County Borough status by virtue of their historical past. See S. Davies and B. Morley, *County Borough Elections, Vol. 1*, p. 677 and p. 687.

6. S. Davies and B. Morley, *County Borough Elections, Vol. 2*, p. 656.

7. There were in total thirteen county boroughs in Yorkshire, but Middlesbrough has been excluded from this analysis on the grounds that it properly belonged in the North East region. See H. Pelling, *Social Geography of British Elections, 1885–1910* (Aldershot, 1994), pp. 3–4, on definitions of regions.

8. It is important to note that 'seats won' as defined here include both contested and uncontested seats. This is arguably one of the best ways of measuring electoral performance in municipal elections in the interwar period. Alternative measures are all handicapped by the fact that a significant proportion of seats were uncontested during the period, although that proportion varied over time and from one borough to another. Thus, calculations of the percentage of *votes* won by Labour can sometimes yield a distorted picture of real electoral success. Labour was sometimes given walkovers in its strongest wards, and therefore the many votes it might have polled there could not be cast. On the other hand, Labour sometimes conceded wards where it was weak, and therefore the many votes that might have been cast for its opponents could not be recorded. By contrast these problems were much less significant at the parliamentary level: fewer than ten per cent of seats were usually uncontested at general elections, as opposed to more than 25 per cent of municipal

seats. On this, see S. Davies and B. Morley, *County Borough Elections, Vol. 2,* pp. 643–45 and p. 658.

9. *Huddersfield Citizen,* October 1929.

10. *Yorkshire Herald,* 7 October 1929.

11. See N. Riddell, *Labour in Crisis,* pp. 53–55 and pp. 139–40.

12. In this period there was one alderman for every three councillors in all county boroughs, so they comprised a quarter of the total seats on each council. Usually half the aldermen were elected in one year for a term of six years, followed by the other half three years later, and so on. They were elected by the councillors, so a party which had a majority of the councillors at the time could if it wished take all of the aldermanic seats up for election and thus boost its overall position. Alternatively, in some cases there were agreements made between parties to apportion alderman proportional to their strength in terms of councillors. The aldermanic system was finally abolished in 1972. For further details, see S. Davies, *Liverpool Labour,* pp. 110–19; S Davies and B. Morley, *County Borough Elections, Vol. 2,* p. 676.

13. *Manchester Guardian,* 2 November 1929.

14. *Wakefield Express,* 2 November 1929.

15. D. Tanner, 'The Labour Party and Electoral Politics in the Coalfields', in A. Campbell, N. Fishman and D. Howell (eds), *Miners, Unions and Politics, 1910–47* (Aldershot, 1996), p. 62.

16. H. Pelling, *Social Geography,* pp. 305–6.

17. J. Reynolds and K. Laybourn, *Labour Heartland: A History of the Labour Party in West Yorkshire during the Inter War Years, 1918–39* (Bradford, 1987), p. 6 and p. 8.

18. P. Abercrombie and T.H. Johnson, *The Doncaster Regional Planning Schemes: The Report Prepared for the Joint Committee* (London, 1922), p. 16

19. *Doncaster Gazette,* 28 October 1921.

20. By Tanner's definitions, only Barnsley of those considered here was a true 'mining' borough (i.e. with 30 per cent or more of male workforce being miners), Rotherham would just squeeze in to the 'semi–mining' category (20–30 per cent), while Wakefield and Doncaster were just below this level, although Doncaster as a *parliamentary constituency* would qualify as 'semi–mining'; see D. Tanner, 'The Labour Party and Electoral Politics in the Coalfields', pp. 64–71.

21. *Bradford Telegraph and Argus,* 2 November 1929.

22. *Ibid.*

23. *Huddersfield Citizen,* November 1929.

24. Minutes of the Huddersfield Labour Party, 11 June 1929, 29 April 1930 (LSE).

25. *Yorkshire Post,* 2 November 1929.

26. K. Laybourn, 'Introduction' to *Huddersfield Labour Party Records, c.1890–1951* (Wakefield, 1984), p. 9.

27. D. Howell, *British Workers and the Independent Labour Party 1888–1906* (Manchester, 1983), pp. 185–89; D. Tanner, *Political Change and the Labour Party 1900–1918* (Cambridge, 1990), pp. 261–65; J. Reynolds and K. Laybourn, *Labour Heartland,* pp. 8–12.

28. *Dewsbury Daily News,* 2 November 1929.

29. N. Riddell, *Labour in Crisis,* p. 249.

30. *Yorkshire Herald,* 2 November 1929.

31. See A. Thorpe, 'The Consolidation of a Labour Stronghold 1926–1951', in C. Bindfield et al (eds), *The History of the City of Sheffield 1843–1993* (Sheffield, 1993), pp. 85–118.

32. *Sheffield Daily Independent*, 2 November 1929.

33. *Halifax Courier and Guardian*, 1 November 1929; *Dewsbury Daily News*, 2 November 1929; *Yorkshire Herald*, 2 November 1929; *Wakefield Express*, 2 November 1929.

34. S. Davies and B. Morley, *County Borough Elections, Vol. 2*, p. 656.

35. N. Riddell, *Labour in Crisis*, p. 238.

36. *Ibid.*, pp. 110–14.

37. *Ibid.*, p. 53, p. 100, pp. 116–17 and pp. 160–61.

38. J. Reynolds and K Laybourn, *Labour Heartland*, pp. 83–94.

39. *Huddersfield Daily Examiner*, 2 November 1929.

40. In 1931 women made up 38 per cent of the total workforce in Bradford, 37 per cent in Halifax, 35 per cent in Huddersfield and 34 per cent in Dewsbury; by contrast, the corresponding figures for the mining towns were 19 per cent in Rotherham, 23 per cent in Barnsley, 24 per cent in Doncaster and 27 per cent in Wakefield; see *1931 Census*, Industry Tables.

41. *Huddersfield Citizen*, November 1929; N. Riddell, *Labour in Crisis*, p. 78.

42. Minutes of the Huddersfield Labour Party Executive Committee, 9 and 23 July 1929.

43. J. Reynolds and K. Laybourn, *Labour Heartland*, pp. 83–92.

44. *Rotherham Advertiser*, 1 November 1930.

45. *Yorkshire Evening Post*, 3 November 1930; *Sheffield Daily Independent*, 3 November 1930.

46. *Wakefield Express*, 8 November 1930.

47. *Bradford Pioneer*, 14 November 1930.

48. See S. Davies and B. Morley, *County Borough Elections, Vol. 2*, p. 19.

49. *Halifax Daily Courier and Guardian*, 3 November 1930.

50. *Huddersfield Daily Examiner*, 3 November 1930.

51. Huddersfield Labour Party AGM, 29 April 1930.

52. *Yorkshire Post*, 3 November 1930.

53. *Hull Daily Mail*, 3 November 1930.

54. *Yorkshire Herald*, 3 November 1930.

55. *Yorkshire Evening Press*, 11 November 1930.

56. *Yorkshire Herald*, 21 November 1930.

57. N. Branson and M. Heinemann, *Britain in the 1930s* (St. Albans, 1973), pp. 30–34.

58. Labour won 288 seats in 1929 with 37 per cent of the vote, but only 52 seats in 1931 with 31 per cent of the vote.

59. 24 of the 29 Yorkshire county borough constituencies saw three–way contests involving the three main parties in 1929, but only two in 1931.

60. *Wakefield Express*, 7 November 1931.

61. *Doncaster Gazette*, 6 November 1931.

62. *Sheffield Daily Independent*, 3 November 1931.

63. *Barnsley Chronicle*, 7 November 1931).

64. S. Davies and B. Morley, *County Borough Elections, Vol. 1*, p. 11.

65. *Huddersfield Daily Examiner*, 3 November 1931.

66. *Huddersfield Citizen*, December 1931.

67. Minutes of the Huddersfield Labour Party Women's Section, 4 September 1929.

68. *Halifax Daily Courier and Guardian*, 3 November 1931.

69. *Bradford Telegraph and Argus*, 3 November 1931.

70. J. Reynolds and K. Laybourn, *Labour Heartland*, p. 92.

71. *Yorkshire Herald*, 3 November 1931.

72. *Sheffield Daily Telegraph*, 3 November 1931.

73. *Hull Daily Mail*, 3 November 1931.

74. *Yorkshire Post*, 3 November 1931.

75 *Ibid.*

76. J. Reynolds and K. Laybourn, *Labour Heartland*, pp. 112–15; Minutes of the Huddersfield Labour Party General Committee, 24 May 1932.

77 N. Branson and M. Heinemann, *Britain in the 1930s*, pp. 36–40; *Sheffield Daily Independent*, 2 November 1932.

78 *Wakefield Express*, 5 November 1932; *Sheffield Daily Independent*, 2 November 1932; *Doncaster Gazette*, 27 October, 3 November 1932; *Barnsley Chronicle* 5 November 1932.

79. *Halifax Daily Courier and Guardian*, 2 November 1932.

80. *Dewsbury Daily News*, 5 November 1932.

81. *Manchester Guardian*, 2 November 1932.

82. A. Thorpe, 'The Consolidation of a Labour Stronghold', p. 97.

83. *Sheffield Daily Independent*, 2 November 1932.

84. For an interesting discussion of how the myth of betrayal of 1931 has been used over time, see J. Lawrence, 'Labour – The Myths it has Lived by', in D. Tanner, P. Thane and N. Tiratsoo (eds), *Labour's First Century* (Cambridge, 2000), pp. 351–54.

85. The NUWM stood five candidates in both Bradford and Dewsbury, and one in Leeds. Their best performance was in Dewsbury, where two of their candidates (standing rather ambiguously as 'Workers' candidates, although nominated by the NUWM) won 24 and 20 per cent of the poll respectively. Apart from one in Bradford with 11 per cent, all the others won less than five per cent of the votes cast.

Chapter 8

The Political Dividend: Co-operative Parties in the Midlands, 1917–39

Nicole Robertson

The new movement of Consumers' Co-operation, launched in Rochdale in 1844, stated that 'the objects and plans for this society are to form arrangements for the pecuniary benefit and the improvement of the social and domestic condition of its members'.[1] One of the principles upon which the Pioneers' Society was based was political neutrality. G.D.H. Cole has emphasised that 'political neutrality' originally meant abstention from 'faction fights' between the rival groups which were appealing for working-class support. As conditions changed, however, the term 'political neutrality' was used in a wider sense, and came to be understood as neutrality between the Liberal and Tory parties, and their competition for control of the government.[2] At the Co-operative Congress of 1917, however, this principle was abandoned when the motion calling for *direct* representation of the co-operative movement in parliament 'as the only way of effectively voicing its demands and safeguarding its interests' was passed by a majority of 1,979 to 201.[3] The passing of this resolution marked the co-operative movement's formal entrance to the political scene. In 1918, ten Co-operative candidates stood in a general election for the first time. The only one to be elected was A.E. Waterson, as MP for Kettering.[4]

Despite the fact that the first Co-op MP was from the Midlands, little has been written about co-operative politics in this area of the country. Local studies that have been published about Co-operation within the Midlands tend to be introspectively written by co-operators themselves – often to celebrate the 'progress' and 'achievement' of Co-operation – or discuss developments in a single town or city, and so do not compare trends between different counties.[5] Older work published specifically on the co-operative movement in politics, notably T. Carbery's *Consumers in Politics* (1969) and Sidney Pollard's 'The Foundation of the Co-operative Party' in Briggs and Saville, *Essays in Labour History 1886–1923* (1971), provide insights at a national level rather than explore developments within selected localities. More recently, there have been some unpublished local studies of the Co-operative Party in the North West and South West.[6]

An assessment of the role and influence of co-operative politics within the Midlands during the interwar years also provides an interesting case study, as this was one of the 'co-operative deserts' into which the co-operative movement expanded during this period. Between 1918 and 1939, the Midland Section witnessed one of the most marked expansions in co-operative society membership and co-operative trading in Britain.[7]

The Co-op's direct involvement in politics, together with the nature of the political alliances it formed, caused controversy within the movement in 1917, and this remained the case during the interwar period. Even in 1937, the issue of co-operators in politics still suffered a degree of ridicule, and the Co-operative Party was criticised by some as being:

> a sham ... [because] the Movement has never really taken politics seriously. The trading side of the Movement is only too anxious to say 'We will give you some money but do not let anybody know you are related to us'.[8]

In studying the co-operative movement in the Midlands, this chapter focuses on the Birmingham, Kettering and Nottingham parties, assessing the impact and influence of co-operative politics by discussing five issues. The first is whether the co-operative societies felt that political action was necessary, and how enthusiastically they responded to the decision to establish a political wing of the movement. Did the local retail co-operative societies actively support the local parties? The second issue concerns the ways in which the local parties evolved. How successfully did the local co-operative parties mobilise support in the three constituencies? What propaganda and educational schemes were organised, and were these aimed at any particular groups? Consideration will also be given to the part the various co-operative parties played in local labour movement politics, especially the fundamental relationship between the local co-operative parties and the Labour parties. Did the co-operative parties exercise influence on constituency Labour parties; for example, in the selection for council seats as well as parliamentary seats? Were there distinctive Co-op activists in the local Labour parties? The Co-operative Party's political programme forms the fourth issue for analysis. In particular, was it able to successfully function as a consumer pressure group representing and defending working-class interests? Did the co-op parties have a distinctive role in local politics, pressing co-operative values and engaging with local issues? When considering the impact of the Co-op in local politics, it is important not to see the co-operative parties as simply electoral machines, but also to explore their role in working-class life and communities. This discussion will conclude by considering the social activities of the parties and the extent to which they made co-operative politics accessible.

Establishing a Political Wing

In May 1917, the Co-operative Congress resolved that 'the time has arrived when co-operators should secure direct representation in parliament and on all local administrative bodies'. Five months later, at an emergency conference, the Central Co-operative Parliamentary Representation Committee was created. This was a sub-committee of the Joint Parliamentary Committee. Such arrangements, however, proved to be unsatisfactory, and so, in 1918, the National Co-operative Representation Committee was established as a separate department of the Co-operative Union. By 1919, this body had become the Co-operative Party. This direct representation of the co-operative movement in parliament, however, caused controversy amongst co-operators and was opposed by those who believed that the progress of the co-operative movement as a whole would be 'barred' if it entered politics because this would inevitably cause severe problems. Their fears were expressed thus:

> Societies will have conflicts in the election of committees, of their delegates to Congress and conferences, there will be withdrawals of members, there will be infinite troubles which we cannot see in advance.[9]

In addition to causing controversy among co-operators during this period, this action has since been the focus of debate among historians. Cole stated that the co-operative movement was brought into politics because its wartime experience had produced 'a feeling of acute grievance and a disbelief that co-operation could ever look for fair treatment from governments unless it took matters actively into its own hands'.[10] Similarly, accounts of the co-operative movement's decision to enter politics by J. Bailey, A. Bonner and T. Carbery all stress the central role played by the Great War.[11] Sidney Pollard, however, challenges this 'traditional' explanation and argues that such developments were due to 'a major ideological conversion rather than a series of *ad hoc* complaints'. More recently, Tony Adams has re-examined this evidence for a pre-war growth in support of direct political representation of the co-operative movement and, as a result, highlights the 'traditional' argument emphasising the important role the war played upon the decision for political action.[12]

What light does the action and experience of the Birmingham, Kettering and Nottingham societies throw on this early period of the Co-op Party? It appears that the wartime experiences of the Midlands societies played an important role in promoting their direct involvement in political activity. As in other parts of the country, the Excess Profits Duty (incorporated into the 1915 budget in order to tax profits above a pre-war standard)[13] roused deep resentment among members of the Kettering and Birmingham societies, as it meant that the dividend was taxed as 'profits', despite an increasing 'divi' representing price increases, rather than profit increases. This perceived injustice caused outrage and resulted in the move for direct political action to be taken by the movement. *The Kettering Co-operative Magazine* declared the Excess Profits Tax to be 'irregular, unfair, unjust, unprincipled, and most illogical', and it encouraged the desire that the co-operative movement should 'take political action and bring pressure to bear upon the government and political parties within the state'.[14] Similarly, at a quarterly meeting of the Birmingham Society, this tax was criticised as an act of 'grave injustice' that had been brought about by the non-participation of the movement in both national and local affairs. Consequently, this society pledged to support 'certain proposals which will be brought before the Co-operative Congress for the direct representation of co-operators in parliament and on local administrative bodies'.[15]

Likewise, the discrimination against co-operative societies arising from governmental intervention in food distribution provoked a similar reaction. Co-operators had been calling for greater food control since the start of the war, and many societies established their own schemes to ensure fair distribution of scarce goods among their members at 'normal' prices. There was widespread concern that certain individuals with vested interests were making unduly large profits by raising the prices of essential commodities. In December 1916, 166 societies sent delegates to a national conference that called for urgent government intervention to halt the rise in food prices. However, when the government eventually introduced rationing and price control during the latter part of the war, co-operative societies in particular were often penalised. Supplies of foodstuffs were controlled or influenced by private traders, and the quotas allotted to co-operative societies were often below their requirements and unfair compared with those given to the private trading concerns.[16] It was this action which provoked the Nottingham Society to declare to its members that:

> the Food Control Boards are dominated by private traders, and they steadily and unjustly seek to undermine our cause by the most infamous distribution. 'Tis monstrous that co-operators are not duly represented upon these boards ... Well may we seek direct parliamentary representation, and make ourselves felt where the laws are enacted.[17]

It is important to highlight that the decision to embark upon political activity did not only result from immediate grievances over specific measures, but also from the implications that these experiences held for the future. It was felt that political action in the future would ensure that co-operators would 'receive a bigger measure of recognition at the hands of the legislature than has been their lot in the past'.[18] This was of paramount importance given that even the prime minister, Lloyd George, declined to see a co-operative deputation (representing between three and four million co-operators) which wished to lay certain grievances before him, for over two months. There is a piece of co-operative folklore to the effect that on one occasion he actually opted to meet the Jockey Club instead.[19] As stated by a report by the Birmingham Co-operative Society, co-operators had been 'forced by the pressure of vested interests inside government circles to take political action to conserve what had already been gained *and secure initiative in future advance*'.[20] The Great War, and more specifically the recruitment of prominent businessmen into Lloyd George's coalition government, had highlighted the extent to which it was possible for politics to interfere with co-operative business practice, and in doing so pushed the issue of parliamentary representation to the fore. As in the words of Bonner, co-operators were increasingly convinced of the need for political representation because 'political neutrality in these circumstances might bring the same fate as the pacifism of sheep among wolves'.[21]

Although all three Midlands societies were aware of the benefits that direct political representation could bring to the movement, the nature and initial success of political activity varied among the different regions. In the aftermath of the National Emergency Conference (NEC), the special meeting held by the Kettering Society to discuss direct parliamentary representation for co-operators was accompanied by the decision to make arrangements to work closely with local Labour parties during the next general election. In so doing, they successfully returned the first Co-operative candidate (A.E. Waterson) to parliament during the 1918 general election.[22] The co-operative societies in Birmingham also responded quickly to the emergency conference decision to enter politics. The Birmingham and District Co-operative Representation Council was established by January 1918, and Co-operative candidates were organised to contest both the King's Norton and Sparkbrook divisions during the 1918 general election.[23] Although neither candidate was successful, this cannot be attributed to any lack of enthusiasm or poor organisation of the Representation Council. Rather, it was incredibly difficult for a Co-operative candidate to:

> wage a successful fight in a Conservative stronghold when a policy of thoroughness in regard to opponents was being advocated by the political leaders of the day, and willingly accepted by a large body of the electorate still imbued with a war-fever psychology.[24]

In Nottingham, unlike Kettering and Birmingham, no Co-operative endorsed candidates stood for election in December 1918. However, a Labour and Co-operative candidate successfully entered Nottingham City Council for Bridge ward at a by-election in February 1919. This campaign highlights how different elements of the local co-operative society supported the candidate. For example, nomination bills and announcements regarding the election were displayed in the Co-op retail shops, and the directors of the society granted the use of the manager's motor car on the election day.[25]

Mobilising Support

After creating the initial framework for co-operative political representation, support for co-operative politics needed to be further developed at the local level. Referring to this task, Arthur Henderson declared that 'you will never be successful in this new venture until the rank-and-file of the co-operative movement are not only co-operatively conscious, but politically conscious'.[26] The Mid-Northants Co-operative Council in Kettering was acutely aware of the necessity for new political schemes to be combined with propaganda and educational work in order to mobilise support, and there is much evidence to substantiate its claim that a 'keen political spirit is manifest, and very vigorous organisations are in existence'.[27] For example, from 1919, *The Kettering Co-operative Magazine* included a column publicising the Council's work, and there was also a regular feature called 'Peeps into Parliament' which provided an insight into the activities and experiences of those co-operators who were 'in the House'. It also organised meetings in all areas of the district (including the surrounding villages) on a regular basis, allowing local co-operative political activists to speak about various aspects of Co-operative Party policy. To attract large crowds, rallies and demonstrations were organised, and prominent MPs invited to speak. Arthur Henderson attended one of these events in 1927, and spoke critically of the Conservative government – in particular its Trades Disputes Bill – ending his speech with the hope that 'when the next election comes you will make no mistake in the Kettering Division'.[28] The Co-operative Council was able to successfully mobilise political support and Labour–Co-operative candidates dominated the county council throughout the interwar period, and were returned in the general elections of 1918, 1922, 1923 and 1929. Although unsuccessful during the general election of 1931, the Kettering party suffered 'in common with so many others [i.e. organisations associated with the Labour Party] in the country', and despite another Conservative victory in 1935, this was only by a small margin.[29] Co-operators were therefore hopeful of gaining a victory in the next general election.

The Birmingham Co-operative Party was also very proactive. It was aware that 'it is only by having a clear conception of the co-operative point of view of local and national affairs that we shall make sure and substantial progress'.[30] It consequently established extensive propaganda and educational schemes. In addition to holding regular public meetings and conferences where the party's stance on various issues was discussed, it organised annual demonstrations at which prominent politicians were invited to speak (for example, A.V. Alexander in 1927). At these meetings, the importance of work already accomplished was stressed, and some of the proposed schemes for the immediate future were outlined. However, by the 1930s, the party acknowledged that the 'tendency of the public to take less interest in public meetings is becoming more pronounced'.[31] It therefore sought other means of reaching its audience. In 1930, it recommended the publication of a monthly newspaper, and by 1934 concluded that 'the views of the parliamentary candidate and the municipal representatives, as well as our general commentary upon current political events, finds an audience that otherwise would not be reached'.[32] In 1931, it used the opportunity provided by the Birmingham Society's Jubilee celebration to place Co-operative Party literature 'in the hands of many who rarely attend ordinary meetings', and distributed 70,000 copies of a special leaflet published for the occasion.[33] In some divisions, such as the Deritend division, special monthly 'speakers classes' were introduced during the 1930s. The purpose of such classes was to enable councillors and workers to take part in debates and discussion on various topics. Classes were held on issues such as whether the Labour government should abandon the policy of free trade, and whether the capitalist system offers greater advantages than any other political system.[34]

Despite these efforts to mobilise support, the Birmingham party did not achieve success in any of the general elections during this period, and municipal elections often ended in disappointment. Its annual report for 1928 emphasised that a 'review of political events indicates the measures of our *preparedness* rather than the record of definite *achievements*', and it appealed to members to take their politics more seriously.[35] What must be highlighted is that this lack of success does not necessarily reflect a lack of effort to mobilise support, but reflects how local circumstances affected the relative collective power and identity of the workers, making it difficult to put ideas into effect. From the late 1860s until after the Second World War, Joseph Chamberlain (along with his sons, Austen and Neville) dominated Birmingham politics. For much of the interwar period, 'Labour could produce no equally persuasive alternative to the Unionist appeal'.[36] Asa Briggs also draws attention to this, commenting that 'while there were marked political ups and downs in England as a whole, Birmingham remained a stronghold of Unionism down to 1938'.[37] Labour politics were also hampered by the movement's internal disputes. Most notably, in December 1923, the Ten Acres and Stirchley Society (in south west Birmingham) passed an amendment opposing further payment of political grants from the disposable surpluses of the society. It withdrew its affiliation from the Birmingham and District Co-operative Party, and did not renew it until 1934.[38] The struggles within the Birmingham Borough Labour Party during the 1920s and 1930s also damaged labour politics, resulting in the desertion and expulsion of a number of prominent figures.[39]

In Nottingham, although it was acknowledged in 1918 that 'it is [the Nottingham Co-operative Society's] duty to become effectively organised both for Parliamentary representation and upon all local governing bodies',[40] the co-operative political machinery and the mobilisation of support developed at a slower pace than in Kettering and Birmingham. During the 1922 general election campaign, A.H. Jones (the Labour and Co-operative candidate for the east division) stated that there was no Labour or Co-operative machinery in the constituency, and that it had to be prepared in a fortnight. Similarly, in 1929, Mrs Barton (the Labour and Co-operative candidate for the central division) remarked that 'a year ago the Co-operative and Labour Party had poor organisation in only three of the five wards of the ... [central] division'.[41]

Despite the differences in rates of development and relative successes of these co-operative parties, there are similarities in the groups of people targeted by their propaganda in an attempt to develop co-operative political consciousness. In both Nottingham and Kettering, efforts were made to increase the involvement and interests of young people in co-operative politics. The Labour and Co-operative parties in Nottingham established a Young Co-operators and Labour club in 1929, where activities included music, dances, and lectures given by local Labour and Co-operative political activists. Likewise, the Mid-Northants Co-operative Council organised Young People's rallies to raise awareness of co-operative politics within this group.

In Birmingham, there was a marked effort by the Co-operative Party to mobilise the support of female co-operators. In 1918, Mrs Taylor (one of the national organisers) visited Birmingham for three weeks to encourage newly enfranchised women to support Co-operative candidates. From 1926, the Birmingham party introduced 'women's conferences' at which speeches were given on topics such as 'women and politics', and it also made appeals for members of the Women's Guild to join a local branch of the party.[42] The Nottingham party was similarly interested in mobilising this group. The Labour and Co-operative electoral newspaper, *The Nottingham Forward*, included a section entitled 'Mainly for Women', comprising articles emphasising what the

Co-operative Party had done for women and how, from its inception, it had joined the Labour Party's campaign demanding full rights of citizenship for women.

The Women's Guild developed a very politically sensitive membership. At the 1926 Guild congress, it 'agreed to the inclusion of support of the Co-operative Party in the aims and objects of the Guild' and, by 1930, over 300 branches were formally affiliated.[43] The chairmen of the 1935 Co-operative Party conference stated that the Women's Guilds were the party's most stimulating partner in the movement, and actually admitted it 'had invariably been in advance of the Co-operative Party in the matters of co-operative policies'.[44] Reports of the activities of the women's guilds in Nottingham and Kettering support this statement. In Nottingham, A.H. Jones praised the Nottingham Guildswomen for their help in his election campaign, stating that they had 'freely placed their services at the disposal of the party' during his election campaign. In Kettering, S.F. Perry (former MP for the area) declared that:

> one of the most effective parts of the organisation is the women's sections, with branches at Kettering, Rothwell and Weston Favell ... these women render most useful service in every effort that is made in the interests of the party.[45]

Co-operative and Labour Relations

An important feature of co-operative politics within the Midlands was the impact relations with the local Labour parties had on its organisation and structure. Yet accounts of the British party system rarely discuss Co-operative–Labour relations in any detail. For example, Ivor Bulmer-Thomas only briefly mentions that the two national parties drew up working arrangements regarding candidates and elections.[46] Published works specifically concerning this relationship, most prominently *Co-operative–Labour Relations, 1900–62* (1962) by G. Rhodes, tend to provide only an account at a national level rather than exploring this relationship within localities.

The 'Scheme for Co-operative Parliamentary Representation' adopted at the NEC of 1917 stated that affiliation with any political party 'is beyond our present scope, but the necessity and desirability of friendly relations with such of the party organisations as will best promote our objects is fully recognised'. Arthur Henderson reiterated this desire for a close working relationship and, in 1917, even said that 'he would be prepared that the Labour Party as now known should cease, if by doing so they could combine the whole of the democracy into a great people's party'.[47]

The form that relations with the Labour Party should take was the cause of much controversy and debate at the National Co-operative Congresses, and the tensions generated are reflected among the political organisations of the co-operative societies in Nottingham, Kettering and Birmingham. In these constituencies, the support for an alliance with the Labour Party – and the nature of the relationship that developed between the two parties – varied considerably. Although the Nottingham Co-operative Society affiliated to the local Labour Party, there were reservations among co-operators concerning the implications of this relationship. Anxiety existed about the financial implications of this alliance. Co-operators feared that the affiliation fee paid to the Nottingham Central Labour Party would be 'increased until the members became so dissatisfied that they declined to trade or leave their savings with the society'.[48] Concerns also centred upon the danger this alliance might pose to the unity and strength of the society in the future since its position had been built up by 'good members of all shades of religion and social thought'.[49]

A comparison with Kettering emphasises how much the support for Co-operative–Labour relations could vary between localities. The Kettering Co-operative Society thought that the scheme outlined for the political representation of co-operators 'did not go far enough', and so it authorised the district committee to meet delegates of trade unions and Labour associations to 'draft negotiations with a view to joint activity, believing such action will result in the common benefit of the worker'.[50] In 1919, relations were formalised by the establishment of the Mid-Northants Co-operative and Labour Council. The meetings this council held during the early 1920s are described as 'being eminently successful from the standpoint of numbers and enthusiasm', and emphasis is given to the 'cordial and loyal assistance rendered by the allied organisations'.[51]

Similarly, in Birmingham, a general desire for close relations with the Labour Party existed. In 1920, the Birmingham Co-operative Party was asked by the Rotton Park ward Labour Party to help with the municipal election, to which it replied that it would 'render all the help possible'. As the Co-operative Party developed and devised new political schemes and propaganda, it emphasised that the 'trade union branches, ILP and the Labour Party were heartily joining in'.[52]

An assessment of the agreements reached between the two parties concerning candidate selection and electoral activity provides a means of investigating the part played by the Co-op in local labour movement politics. During the 1918 general election in Kettering, the local Labour Party supported the electoral campaign of the Co-operative candidate (A.E. Waterson), and co-operators reciprocated this arrangement in the neighbouring constituencies where Labour was seeking representation. A key factor in the resulting victory of Waterson appears to be the vigorous and extensive electoral campaign of the co-operators and local Labour Party compared to that of their Liberal coalition opponent.[53] This electoral victory is even more impressive considering that the results nationally were disappointing for the labour movement. The Tory and Liberal voters tended to unite behind the coalition 'coupon' candidates. As the 'coupon' represented a symbol of fidelity to the national interest, these candidates were very hard to beat in the public election at the end of the Great War.[54]

It seems that the affiliations and experience of Waterson himself made a successful working relationship between the different facets of the labour movement possible. He was the former secretary of the Midland District Council of the National Union of Railwaymen, and had been chairman of the Derby Labour Party. *The Co-operative News* reported how 'nearly every trade union with a branch in the district, and nearly every co-operative society and democratic organisation, is represented in the signature to the nomination papers handed in on behalf of Waterson'.[55]

There are numerous examples of co-operative activists who were also active in the local Labour parties, and this appears to be a common feature. Examples are evident in Nottingham, where W.J. Allen and F. Goody – who stood as Labour candidates at the council elections for the Robin Hood ward and Market ward respectively – were prominent members of Nottingham Co-operative Society. In Birmingham, E. Reynolds (candidate for the Acocks Green ward at the municipal election of 1930) and G.A. Charles (candidate for the Yardley ward at the municipal election of 1933) were both co-operators and also members of the Labour Party.

The co-operative parties were keen to ensure that they influenced the constituency Labour parties in the selection of candidates for both municipal and general elections. In Nottingham, for example, an agreement was reached whereby:

> all candidates put forward by the [Nottingham Co-operative] society for public positions under the auspices of the Labour Party shall be duly nominated and selected by a properly convened meeting of the members of this society, and shall, along with any other Labour candidate running under Labour Party auspices, and after having received the endorsement of the Director of the Society, have the right to use the titles, stores or other property of this society, subject of such candidate being a fully paid-up shareholder of a Co-operative body in the city.[56]

This Co-operative Party firmly defended such a position, and this was evident when the St Ann's Ward Labour Association appealed to the Co-operative Society for financial assistance for the Board of Guardians election. It was declined, and its policy was reiterated that 'we only support candidates directly nominated by us'.[57]

The influence the local co-operative parties exercised over the local Labour parties, however, must not be exaggerated. As events in Birmingham between 1923 and 1925 highlight, there were instances where the local Labour Party tried to confine the electoral activities of the co-operative organisation. The Birmingham and District Co-operative Party had reached an agreement with the Birmingham Borough Labour Party to establish a Joint Advisory Committee which would 'correlate and co-ordinate the forces and activities of the Labour and Co-operative movements in respect to representation in parliament and on all local administrative bodies'.[58] Through this body, they conferred in the selection of candidates, and the organisation of both parties was utilised during the electoral campaign. In 1923, however, the Birmingham Central Labour Party repudiated the existing agreement in favour of expanding its own organisation; endeavours to obtain a settlement before the general election failed, thereby hampering the Co-operative campaign of 1923. As the dispute continued, the preparation for the municipal election in 1924 was affected, and the results were disappointing. In the Deritend division, the approval of the Co-operative candidate – Fred Longden – 'was only forthcoming from the Labour Party at the last moment, and we ... [the Co-operative Party] ... have every cause to think that if some permanent arrangement can be carried out in regard to this constituency, success will be ours'.[59] An agreement to 'correlate and co-ordinate their forces and activities' was eventually reached in March 1925.

Such an agreement (the Cheltenham Agreement) formalising the relationship between the Co-operative Party and the Labour Party was not passed by the national parties until 1927. This made provisions for a joint sub-committee to be established, and ruled that local co-operative parties were to be eligible for affiliation to the divisional Labour parties, but stated explicitly that this was not intended to interfere with existing arrangements where such an agreement had already been established.[60]

The reports given to the Co-operative Congress during the 1930s by the party portray an image where this agreement with the Labour Party was still in reasonable working order, often emphasising the possibility of strengthening it further. Yet, there appears to have been a discrepancy between this image and the reality of what was happening in the localities.[61] Friction was caused by the Labour Party's assumption that the Cheltenham Agreement was only a temporary measure pending affiliation, and its desire for the Co-operative Party to surrender its finances and autonomy to Labour's policy and organisation.[62] This was a cause of concern for co-operators, and one which is visible in Birmingham. By 1932, the Birmingham Co-operative Party was forced to develop tighter procedures over its candidates. It devised a scheme whereby the names of the prospective candidates had to be to put forward to the Co-operative Party Executive Council for approval before they could be placed on Labour Party nomination lists. The Co-op's funding for a candidate's electoral expenses (the 'political grant') would be withheld if a candidate was nominated without seeking this approval. Not only was this done to maintain closer control over their political agenda, but also so that the Co-operative Party's financial position could be guarded. This was a measure to prevent both the Labour Party forcing it to foot the bill for 'no hope' elections and, further, to prohibit Labour parties nominating a candidate who would then join the Co-operative Party and attempt to claim the political grant.[63] Despite these careful measures, the Co-operative Party was frequently required to help the Birmingham Borough Labour Party out of severe financial difficulties over the 1930s.

Relations between the two parties in Central Nottingham also weakened during this period. The Co-operative and Labour Party Joint Committee met less frequently after 1935 and, in 1937, it was announced that 'the general feeling of the Political Council was that the Co-operative Party should discontinue the joint arrangement'.[64]

Although the political alliance between the two parties continued in Kettering, there was some anxiety when the Kettering Labour Party (which had ceased activity soon after the formation of the Mid-Northants Co-operative and Labour Council) was reformed in 1936. This was a period when the National Co-operative Authority feared that the Labour Party was trying to 'hamper and confine' co-operative activities in politics.[65] Yet, in Kettering, a separate local Labour Party was reformed precisely because it felt that the co-operative movement had confined *its* activities. Thus, there were concerns that 'individual Labour membership had dropped away or had become absorbed into the co-operative movement' leading to a 'desire for the expression of political opinion through a distinctly labour channel'.[66] It was emphasised, however, that this organisation would not be in opposition to existing organisations, such as the trades council or the co-operative movement. However, by November of the same year, the two parties were 'proceeding with the same cordial relationship that [had] hitherto operated in the division', and together they made further increases in their control of the local council. In the town's first borough elections of 1939, the local paper commented that the strength of the political parties in Kettering could be clearly seen in the number of candidates that had been put forward for election: Co-operative–Labour had 16, compared with the Conservative's ten, and the seven put forward by the Liberal Party.[67]

Political Programme

What was the nature of the national Co-operative Party's policies, and how was its political programme developed and presented in the various constituencies? Defending co-operative trading concerns was of paramount importance to the Co-operative Party. At the 1917 emergency conference, the first point on the newly established programme of Co-operative policy was 'to safeguard effectively interests of voluntary co-operation, and to resist any legislative or administrative inequality which would hamper its progress'.[68] However, the party also developed a programme incorporating a wide range of working-class concerns, and engaged with local issues.

The standard of working-class housing, and the amount of rent workers had to pay, was a prominent issue throughout the interwar period, with Co-operative candidates campaigning for 'better houses' at reasonable rents. In Kettering, houses for the working classes at an economic rent were still in urgent need in the late 1930s. The Co-operative candidates urged that 'it is one of the duties of a local authority to see that its people are well housed, and we should do all in our power to press the building of more houses by the Authority TO LET'.[69]

The way in which co-operators presented their polices in the constituencies, and how these fitted in with co-operative principles, is illustrated by the campaign of T.H. Hackett (president of the Ten Acres and Stirchley Co-operative Society) in the Northfield district of Birmingham. He declared that 'Co-operators believe in a new world order wherein everyone will have liberty, freedom and an opportunity to enjoy a larger and fuller life, without any fear of want or hardships such as the present system'. He stood specifically for more nursery schools, municipal houses, better education for children, and a fairer rating system.[70]

The Co-operative Party was also heavily involved in the Aid for Spain campaign during the country's civil war. When the Voluntary Industrial Aid scheme was launched (where workers gave voluntary overtime to make goods that were needed in Spain), Barnes (chairman of the Co-operative Party) secured a place on the committee, and by doing so, ensured that Co-operators were at the forefront. The Co-operative Party's prominent role in this campaign was reflected at a local level. For example, in Birmingham, the Co-operative Party records that it was 'deeply conscious of the importance of the struggle in Spain, we have given much attention both to the political and to the humanitarian aspects'. They sent several resolutions of protest to the prime minister, distributed leaflets, and gave 'whole-hearted assistance' in the arrangement of many public meetings. They also gave generous contributions to the Milk for Spain Fund, the Basque Children's Fund, and to the International Brigade Fund. The Nottingham Co-operative Society Political Council was also very active in this respect, undertaking 'its biggest and most urgent task: to collect £500 for an ambulance for Spain'.[71]

T.W. Mercer (a key figure in the national co-operative movement) expressed his concern that the Co-operative Party lacked a philosophical basis, and had no distinct programme, adding that 'many co-operators unconsciously confuse the aims of the co-operative movement in politics with those of the political Labour Party'.[72] Certainly, the programme incorporating demands for a more equal education system, adequate housing provision for the people, and improved maternity care was very similar to the manifesto issued by the Labour Party. However, as Cole emphasises, 'the two parties stood in the main not for rival or conflicting policies but for much the same policy with differences of emphasis corresponding to the broad differences of their foundations'.[73]

The Co-operative Party was not politically emasculated, acting merely as an appendage of the Labour Party. Rather, the leaders of the Co-operative Party emphasised that this party represented a distinct economic interest in parliament which had previously been neglected: that of the consumer. An article in *The Co-operative News* highlighted that:

> no party except the Co-operative Party is able to speak with authority on behalf of all consumers, although it is the consumer who is most affected by legislation and taxation. Today, national politics turn on the price of bread, and the question of supply is of primary importance. Capitalists and landlords, manufacturers and trade unionists, all have their spokesmen in the House, and surely it is necessary that consumers also should have their chosen representatives.[74]

This important aspect of the Co-operative Party's work has often been overlooked in literature focusing upon the co-operative movement,[75] whilst notable writers on pressure groups (for example, J.D Stewart and R.T. McKenzie)[76] barely mention the co-operative movement in their work.

Of great importance to the Co-operative Party was to campaign to give statutory effect to practices in the interest of the consumer that were already in use by the movement. For example, selling tea by its net weight was a long-standing practice in co-operative stores. In 1922, against a strong attempt by the trade to maintain the practice of gross weight packing of tea, co-operative pressure helped to ensure that the Sale of Tea Act was passed. This required all traders to pack tea by net weight, and thus 'the consumer has not, therefore, any longer to pay the price of tea for paper and lead foil, and is saving in that respect approximately £4,000,000 per annum'.[77]

The Co-operative Party also campaigned for greater protection of the consumer by calling for improvements to the hygiene and safety of foodstuffs which were put into practice by the trading side of the movement. For example, in

1923, the Co-operative Party successfully campaigned to alter the pasteurisation regulations of milk. It was feared that 'a half-inch cube of milk might contain anything when received – from eight thousand to three million germs'.[78] Also in this year, the Nottingham Society opened a dairy, proudly boasting that 'the hygienic standard set up and maintained ever since has been one of the main causes of the Society's capture of the bulk of the city's milk trade'.[79]

At a local level, a key aspect of the political programme of the Co-operative candidates throughout this period was their commitment to the consumer. In the Sparbrook division of Birmingham, F. Spires' election address in the 1918 general election stated that, if he were elected, his efforts would be directed towards ensuring the consumer was charged lower prices for food, milk, coal and clothing. Similarly, in 1930, standing in the municipal election for Central Nottingham, A. E. Waterson's campaign slogan and promise was to 'hold up the flag of the consumers'. *The Co-operative News* reported how 'Mr Waterson stands four-square for the straight principles of free trade and fair play for the consumer'. His electoral address emphasised co-operative values, and drew attention to the difference between the 'Co-operative Way' of providing the consumer with value for the money they spend, and the capitalist system where:

> there are too many middlemen living on the backs of the people. The greater differences between the prices of commodities at the source of production and the price the consumer pays demands not merely serious examination, but legislation.[80]

A further aspect of Co-operative Party policy was to reflect the wider movement's desire to establish and maintain cordial relations with the trade unions. Before the Great War, the co-operative movement recognised the trade union rates of wages and conditions of employment, and the 48-hour week was established in a large number of co-operative societies. In 1918, the United Advisory Council of Trade Unionists and Co-operators issued a statement of objects they hoped to be furthered and attained. This statement encouraged trade unionists to become members, and take an interest in the progress and development of the society. The electoral programmes of Co-operative candidates often reflected this concern for the worker. In the 1918 general election, the basis of A.E. Waterson's political programme was 'More Leisure, More Treasure, and More Pleasure for the Workers'.

Tensions between trade unions and co-operators did arise particularly in the North West area in 1925, when the National Union of Distributive and Allied Workers' (the union for Co-operative shop workers) demands for wage increases led to a bitter struggle, exposing 'some of the inherent contradictions of the co-operative project very clearly'.[81] Yet, the local co-operative societies were keen to be regarded as pioneering improvements in working conditions. The Nottingham Co-operative Society emphasised how co-operative businesses led the way in raising wages, reducing hours, and improving working conditions. The 'local pages' of the monthly co-operative magazine (*The Wheatsheaf*) reported how the society's directors were 'in active sympathy with trade unions', and had already conformed to the demand of the Bakers' Union for the abolition of night work.

They always granted 'the best possible conditions to [their] fellow-members whom [they] employ, and, as a rule, somewhat above the terms granted by [their] competitors – the private capitalists'. This desire to be recognised as very progressive in employee relations was reiterated in the Labour and Co-operative Party's newspaper, *The Nottingham Forward.* Here an article was published stating how the co-operatives 'pay better wages', and 'observe better conditions' than their competitors. In the next municipal elections they asked the electors to turn down both Liberals and Tories because 'the Anti-Labour block stand to defend the right to live by exploitation, whilst [co-operators] stand for the right to build a state based on co-operative principles'.[82]

In Birmingham, the Co-operative Party specifically placed emphasis on achieving 'the stimulation of a political consciousness among the employees, and a realisation by them that their interests and welfare are intimately correlated with the political power possessed by the Movement'.[83] In an effort to achieve this, from 1932 it began holding annual meetings for the employees of the Birmingham Society, and in 1938 exhibited in the co-operative stores posters 'bearing appropriate political matter destined to impress upon the minds of the employees the value and necessity of the Co-operative Party'.[84]

Co-operative Politics and Soirées

An assessment of how the co-operative parties functioned within Birmingham, Kettering and Nottingham must also investigate the extent to which their activities went beyond the immediate political sphere, and the impact this had on co-operative politics. After the war, leaders of the Labour Party encouraged local parties to 'mix politics with the social life of the people'.[85] The importance of providing recreational facilities and social functions was also recognised by the co-operative parties from an early stage. In Nottingham, provisions were made in 1917 to tie the informal discussion of topical issues that were of great concern to co-operators into a broader social context. A co-operative cafe was opened where 'the sterner sex c[ould] smoke and discuss "excess profits", "income tax", and "smaller dividends"'.[86] Similarly, from its inception, the Birmingham Co-operative Party was aware of the benefits co-operative politics could derive from social events. During its early years, garden parties were organised to bring together members of the various societies, and provide an opportunity for the members of the party and supporters of the movement to get to know each other.[87]

In both these constituencies, the Co-operative Party continued to hold events which successfully combined discussion of co-operative politics with a programme of entertainment throughout the interwar period. In Nottingham, as part of the political propaganda work for the prospective Labour–Co-operative candidate for Central Nottingham (Mrs Barton), and the Labour candidate for West Nottingham (Arthur Hayday), their speeches were alternated with the community singing of labour songs. In 1931, the promotion of the candidature of A.E. Waterson (the Labour–Co-operative candidate for the Nottingham central division) included a combined reception, whist drive and dance to which five hundred people were invited.[88] The fluctuating attendance levels at the Birmingham Co-operative Party's annual demonstration can be used to highlight the potential benefits that could be gained by the introduction of entertainment alongside politics. By 1930, there were concerns about the poor level of attendance at these meetings. Subsequently, the party decided to modify procedures for the next demonstration by incorporating musical items. In 1931, it was reported that the 'incorporation of musical items into programme was fully justified by the results: a large and enthusiastic gathering showing unmistakable appreciation of the musical programme'. At the annual demonstrations between 1932 and 1934, music by the Birmingham co-operative choir and orchestra was blended with politics, and successfully secured large audiences. When, in 1935 – due to the wishes of the National Committee – the musical programme was abandoned, the Birmingham party concluded that this was 'no doubt responsible for the decrease in the size of the audience'.[89]

However, it is in Kettering that the most striking example of how social activities could be used to make co-operative politics very accessible and popular is found, and this seems to go some way in accounting for the remarkable success of co-operative politics in this division. By 1924, the party had realised that 'allotments and outdoor games are the strongest attraction to the majority of citizens, to such an extent that it is quite impossible for outdoor meetings to surpass them in rivalry'.[90] Therefore, the party embarked upon several new ventures. In 1925, the Mid-Northants Co-operative and Labour Council held their first flower, fruit and vegetable show, which became an annual event. In 1926, the Co-operative and Labour Institute (in which the headquarters of the Co-operative and Labour Council was based) was opened in the town centre. This provided a 'home for the party', where members could meet for recreational, educational and social purposes. The opening was described as a 'red-letter day' in the history of co-operative politics, because as well as adding prestige, the Institute provided a place where 'workers and supporters could meet and mould their forces into a great united body' within a social environment.[91] In addition to mobilising support within Kettering itself, social activities were used as an important means of mobilising political support in the surrounding villages. The Mid-Northants constituency was fairly widely scattered, being composed of four urban districts and 86 villages. Thus, the Co-operative and Labour Council devised a system in the villages involving 'sub-agents' and 'key-men', whereby these figures helped to 'keep in touch with residents by means of concerts and socials'.[92]

By the end of the interwar period, the affiliated membership of the Co-operative Party stood at 5,340,000. The co-operative societies in Birmingham, Kettering and Nottingham had affiliated to the party, and political organisations had been established (with varying degrees of electoral success) in all three constituencies. Yet, as Alfred Barnes (MP and chairman of the Co-operative Party) himself admitted, this vast official affiliated membership were not all active supporters of the party: 'they are not 5,340,000 conscious co-operative politicians and voters'.[93] The social activities and events organised by the local co-operative parties were certainly important aspects of their work, and they did attract support.

However, to get some perspective of the importance co-operators placed on co-operative politics, the activities of the local parties must be placed within the context of the other facets of the movement. An examination is needed of what it meant to be a member of the local co-operative society, what if offered, and how it fitted into the daily lives of people living in these three constituencies.

As Craigen argues, the Co-operative Party's role could, and indeed should, have been greater, but 'Co-operators were less in the business of politics than in the business of business'.[94] Indeed, the main activity of co-operation remained its commercial enterprises, and retaining its position as one of the largest retail operations in the country. This is reflected in the records of local societies, where emphasis is continually placed upon increasing trade quotas, acquiring bigger premises and establishing new business ventures, such as bakeries, dairies and laundries. The Co-op was based upon a commitment to sell good quality goods at fair prices, and this ethos attracted customers. The 'divi' was also a very attractive part of co-operation, and regular purchases from the Co-op ensured an automatic accumulation of dividends which were paid quarterly or twice a year. This was one of the simplest and easiest ways to purchase items that required high expenditure; for example, clothing and furniture. Loyalty to the Co-op meant that the 'divi would mount up to draw on in times of need', or made it easier to buy necessities, pay bills, or even finance a holiday. In this way, co-operation became 'a general provider for its members' needs'.[95] Local societies also developed other schemes, enabling members to acquire savings; for example, the Nottingham Society advertised their 'stamp club' as the most convenient way of saving small sums. During the interwar years, the granting of credit was widely practised. Most noticeably, during the year of the General Strike, co-operative societies gave a total of £596,912 credit to its members, some of which it never got back.[96]

The 'divi' was certainly a valued part of co-operation, as Paul Johnson argues.[97] Yet, other aspects of co-operation also attracted membership; the activities organised by the local co-operative societies were of great importance in the lives of the members. Since the turn of the century, holidays were an important part of working-class life, and seem almost 'to have become a social obligation'.[98] The co-operative societies in Birmingham, Kettering and Nottingham all organised annual holidays for their members which were very popular. For example, in 1927, the Nottingham Educational Society organised a trip to Denmark. Although this was 'the most co-operative country on earth', it was proposed not to spend 'an undue amount of time visiting co-operative enterprises'. Rather, the organisers emphasised that this trip should also be a holiday in the ordinary way, and plans were made to visit the Opera House, open air festivals and Hillerod (the summer residence of the Danish Royal family).[99] The Birmingham Women's Guild organised their annual holiday over the August Bank Holiday, so that members' husbands would be able to join them (in theory making this more enjoyable).[100] Day trips were also an important part of co-operative culture. The Kettering society established an 'outing fund' which members paid into throughout the year, and this enabled them to enjoy day trips and charabanc tours throughout the summer months. In both Kettering and Birmingham, the recreational aspect of co-operation occupied a prominent position within community life. The sports and leisure clubs of both the societies were very popular. This supports Mike Savage's belief that the interwar years were marked by the development of the Co-op as a lively and flourishing presence in the social life of working-class neighbourhoods.[101]

Co-operation prided itself on being an organisation that was a general provider for all its members' needs from childhood through to old age. It is important to appreciate the significant role it played in the welfare of its members. The Education Committees of the local societies annually awarded scholarships and bursaries to assist members' children to continue their education at secondary schools (thereby following the example of the Rochdale Pioneers, who attached great importance to education), as it not only provided a greater opportunity for 'getting on', but also 'meant a fuller life for the individual, spreading the principles of human betterment and providing food for the mind'.[102] The societies also cared for their members in times of financial difficulty and sickness. In 1916, the Midlands Section of the Co-operative Union established a Convalescent Fund (to assist co-operators in need of rest and 'change of air', by providing accommodation in approved convalescent homes and assisting with expenses) and an Emergency Fund (provided by the society for the relief of members in distress from sickness, unemployment or other causes). A further aspect of its impact in the community was the development of a co-operative housing scheme. Indeed, the establishment of a generation of homeowners has been described by one local historian as the co-operative movement's 'finest contribution to life'.[103] In the period before the welfare state, the 'Co-operative Good Samaritan', with its commitment to providing 'the easiest, sanest, and promptest method of self-help ... just at the time when most needed', was of considerable use to its members.[104] Thus, although the Co-operative Party was of central importance to its activists, to the vast majority of those belonging to the Co-operative Society, the movement's other activities had a greater and more immediate impact upon their daily lives.

Conclusion

The co-operative societies in Birmingham, Kettering and Nottingham were all affiliated to the national Co-operative Party. Yet the way these political organisations developed, the part they played in local labour movement politics, and how they performed in municipal and general elections varied, in some respects considerably. The co-operative political organisations in Kettering and Birmingham were more proactive than their counterparts in Nottingham in developing their party machinery and mobilising support. The parties used traditional methods of political propaganda and 'educational schemes' to increase support, but were also aware that there were considerable benefits to be gained by engaging in wider social-political activities. The social activities and recreational facilities provided by the local co-operative parties were an essential method of mobilising support. Certainly, defending the trading concerns of the movement was a key aspect of the Co-operative Party's policy, yet it also developed a distinct role in politics defending and protecting the interests of the working-class consumer.

An examination of the relationships that developed between the local parties is especially important, as although a formal agreement governing these relations was made by the national Co-operative and Labour Parties in 1927, this was not intended to interfere with the relationships that had already been established within the constituencies. Indeed, both the Kettering and Birmingham parties commented that the development of a successful working relationship between the Co-operative and Labour Parties in their constituencies had helped to pave the way for a national agreement. The effective working relationship with the Labour Party was a decisive factor in explaining the electoral success of co-operative politics in Kettering. The co-operative parties in these constituencies exercised influence on the local Labour parties in the selection of candidates for council as well as parliamentary seats, and prominent supporters of co-operative political action usually had experience in local labour movement politics. Co-operative activists were often important figures in the local Labour Party and trade unions. However, it is quite possible that in a few places, such as Birmingham in 1923–25, the relationship between the two parties stunted potential Co-operative Party electoral progress, as the higher profile Labour Party overshadowed the nascent Co-operative Party.

Notes

1. 'Original Rules of the Rochdale Pioneers, 1844', J Bailey, *The British Co-operative Movement* (London, 1960), pp. 19–20.

2. G.D.H. Cole, *A Century of Co-operation* (Manchester, 1944), pp. 78–79.

3. *Co-operative Congress Report*, 1917, p. 549 and p. 567.

4. The Mid-Northants parliamentary division comprised 92 parishes, several villages, the urban districts of Desborough and Rothwell, and the town of Kettering. Kettering was the 'electoral power-station' of the constituency and, therefore, the division was often referred to as the Kettering Division.

5. F.W. Leeman, *Co-operation in Nottingham* (Nottingham, c.1960); T. Smith, *Seventy Years of Services: The Story of Birmingham Co-operative Society 1881–1951* (Birmingham, 1951); *'Progress' One Hundred Years Forward 1866–1966: A Centenary Report of the Achievements of the Kettering Industrial Co-operative Society* (Kettering, 1966).

6. Notably, J. Southern, The Co-operative Movement in the North West of England 1919–39: Images and Realities, University of Lancaster PhD (1996); and M. Hilson, Working-Class Politics in Plymouth 1890–1920, University of Exeter PhD (1998).

7. A. Bonner, *British Co-operation* (Manchester, 1961), p. 161. J.B. Jefferies, *Retail Trading in Britain 1850–1950* (Cambridge, 1954), p. 55.

8. *Co-operative Congress Report*, 1937, p. 491.

9. *Co-operative Congress Report*, 1917, pp. 552–53.

10. G.D.H. Cole, *A Century of Co-operation*, p. 269.

11. T.F. Carbery, *Consumers in Politics* (Manchester, 1969).

12. S. Pollard, 'The Foundation of the Co-operative Party', in A. Briggs and J. Saville (eds), *Essays in Labour History 1886–1923* (London, 1971), pp. 185–210. T. Adams, 'The

Formation of the Co-operative Party Re-considered', *International Review of Social History*, 32, 1 (1987), pp. 48–68. See also S. Pollard, 'The Co-operative Party – Reflections on a Re-consideration', *International Review of Social History*, 32, 2 (1987), pp. 168–73; and T. Adams, 'Co-operators and Politics – A Rejoinder', *International Review of Social History*, 32, 2 (1987), pp. 174–79.

13. See M. Daunton, *Just Taxes* (Cambridge, 2002), p. 41.

14. *The Kettering Co-operative Magazine*, November 1916, p. 106; *The Kettering Co-operative Magazine: The Jubilee Number*, 1916, pp. 80–82.

15. Birmingham *Wheatsheaf*, June 1917. (*The Wheatsheaf* was a national 'monthly co-operative record and magazine', but each magazine also contained 'local pages' issued by the local Co-operative Society giving details of their activities.)

16. A.V. Alexander, *The Business Value of Political Action to the Co-operative Movement* (Manchester, 1928), p. 3.

17. Nottingham *Wheatsheaf*, March 1917.

18. *The Co-operative News*, 27 October 1917, p. 1025.

19. T.F. Carbery, *Consumers*, p. 21. Bonar Law, however, maintained that 'the statement that the Prime Minister refused to receive the deputation was untrue' and stated that this incident had been caused by miscommunication, stressing that 'it was impossible that any Prime Minister could ever have received so large a number of deputations from labour organisations of all kinds as had been received by the present occupant of the office'. *The Co-operative News*, 27 October 1917, p. 1025.

20. Birmingham *Wheatsheaf*, December 1918 [my italics].

21. A. Bonner, *British Co-operation*, p. 142. One such example of a businessman – and man of 'push and go' – invited into the Coalition Government is Eric Geddes. See K. Grieves, *Sir Eric Geddes: Business and Government in War and Peace* (London, 1989).

22. *The Co-operative News*, 17 November 1917, p. 1082 and p. 1090.

23. T. Hackett and F. Spires respectively.

24. T. Smith, *History of the Birmingham Co-operative Society Limited 1881–1931* (Birmingham, 1931), p. 197.

25. *Greater Nottingham Co-operative Society Directors' Quarterly Meetings*, 27 January 1919, and Nottingham *Wheatsheaf*, March 1919.

26. *The Co-operative News*, 17 November 1917, p. 1084.

27. *The Kettering Co-operative Magazine*, May 1928, p. 38.

28. *Kettering Leader and Guardian*, 24 June 1927, p. 12.

29. In 1931, the Conservative candidates won by a majority of 8,716, whereas in 1935, the Conservative majority was reduced to 1,843. As in the words of Sadler, the unsuccessful Co-op–Lab candidate for Kettering, 'we have not taken the fortress, but we had made gaps in the ramparts ... Next time we shall be able to knock the Conservatives right off their pedestal'. *Kettering Leader and Guardian*, 22 November 1935, p. 6.

30. *Birmingham and District Co-operative Party Annual Report*, 1918.

31. *Birmingham and District Co-operative Party Annual Report*, 1934.

32. *Ibid.*

33. *Birmingham and District Co-operative Party Annual Report*, 1931.

34. Minutes of the Labour Party/Co-operative Party Joint Organisation Committee, Deritend Division, 16 April 1931.

35. *Birmingham and District Co-operative Party Annual Report*, 1925. [My italics]

36. In 1931, Labour lost all six of the seats that it had won on the city council in 1929, and saw its representation slump from 36 seats to just 20 on a 120-seat council. Though there was a slight recovery in 1934, increasing Labour's representation to 39 seats on a 136-seat council, this was short-lived and, in 1939, Labour was reduced to 21 seats. In such a situation, hopes for a growth in co-operative representation on the council were unrealistic, and its influence was undermined by the steady electoral decline of the Borough Labour Party. D. Rolf, 'Birmingham Labour and the Background of the 1945 General Election', in A. Wright and R. Shackleton (eds), *Worlds of Labour: Essays in Birmingham Labour History* (Birmingham, 1983), pp. 127–55.

37. A. Briggs, *History of Birmingham, Volume 2: Borough and City 1865–1938* (London, 1952), p. 320.

38. *Birmingham and District Co-operative Party Annual Report* (1923 and 1934). Also, R. McKibbin, *The Evolution of the Labour Party, 1910–24* (Oxford, 1974), pp. 188–9.

39. R.P. Hastings, 'The Birmingham Labour Movement, 1918–45' *Midland History*, 5, (1979–80), pp. 78–92. D. Howell, *MacDonald's Party: Labour Identities and Crisis, 1922–31* (Oxford, 2002), p. 321.

40. *Nottingham Co-operative Society Quarterly Report*, 15 April 1918.

41. *The Co-operative News*, 8 July 1922, p. 4 and 13 April 1929, p. 2.

42. See *Birmingham and District Co-operative Party Annual Reports*. See also G.J. Barnsby, *Socialism in Birmingham and the Black Country 1850–1939* (Wolverhampton, 1998), p. 467.

43. It was not until 1938 that the issue of pacifism breached this alliance, and the addendum stipulating that the Guild would support the party 'providing that party policy was not inconsistent with declared Guild policy' was added. G. Scott, 'Women's Autonomy and Divorce Law Reform', in S. Yeo (ed.), *New Views of Co-operation* (London, 1988), pp. 128–53.

44. *Manchester Guardian*, 22 April 1935; J. Gaffin and D. Thoms, *Caring and Sharing: The Centenary History* (Manchester, 1993), p. 88.

45. *The Co-operative News*, 1 July 1922, p. 1 and 20 April 1929, p. 2.

46. I. Bulmer-Thomas, *The Growth of the British Party System, Vol. 1, 1640–1923* (London, 1965) pp. 244–45, and *Vol. 2, 1924–65*, pp. 32–33.

47. C. Wrigley, *Arthur Henderson* (Cardiff, 1990), p. 142; *The Times*, 19 October 1917.

48. Nottingham *Wheatsheaf*, May 1920.

49. Nottingham *Wheatsheaf*, February 1921. This bears similarities to the TUC and politics in the 1890s when great hostility to the notion of 'independent labour politics' was present among the older generation.

50. *Co-operative Congress Report*, 1918, 'Midland Section', p. 393.

51. *The Kettering Co-operative Magazine*, November 1920, p. 101 and May 1920, p. 70.

52. Minutes of the Birmingham and District Co-operative Representation Council, 21 July 1920; *Birmingham and District Co-operative Party Annual Report*, 1919.

53. See *Kettering Leader and Guardian*, 13 December 1918 and 31 January 1919.

54. Although there were 57 Labour MPs, compared with 42 in 1910, considering the vastly increased number of candidates, this election was one where it 'had polled its minimum vote'. A. Henderson at Widnes, 8 January 1920, C. Wrigley, *Arthur Henderson*, p. 127.

55. *The Co-operative News*, 28 April 1933. See also *Kettering Leader and Guardian*, 13 December 1918.

56. Nottingham *Wheatsheaf*, August 1919.

57. Greater Nottingham Co-operative Society Directors' Quarterly Meetings, 23 April 1928.

58. *Birmingham and District Co-operative Party Agreement with the Labour Party*, 1921.

59. *Birmingham and District Co-operative Party Annual Report*, 1924.

60. *Co-operative Congress Report*, 1927, pp. 95–96.

61. *Co-operative Congress Report*, 'Co-operative Party's Report', 1933, 1936 and 1937. This growing discrepancy between image and reality, whereby official publications downplayed the degree of contention aroused in the localities, appears to have been a feature of the co-operative movement during 1930s that was not only limited to politics. See J. Southern, 'Co-operation in the North West of England, 1919–39: Stronghold or Stagnation', *North West Labour History*, 19, (1994/95), pp. 97–114.

62. See G. Rhodes, *Co-operative–Labour Relations, 1900–62* (Loughborough, 1962), pp. 38–59.

63. Minutes of the Council and Executive Committee of the Birmingham and District Co-operative Party, 1931; C. Shelly, *Birmingham Co-operative Party in the 1930s: Co-operative and Labour Movement Politics*, Unpublished MA Dissertation, University of Warwick (1987), pp. 36–37.

64. Minutes of the Nottingham Co-operative and Labour Party Central Division.

65. G. Rhodes, *Co-operative–Labour Relations*, p. 53.

66. *Kettering Leader and Guardian*, 21 February 1936, p. 1.

67. *Kettering Leader and Guardian*, 28 October 1938, p. 6.

68. *National Emergency Conference Report* (Manchester, 1917), p. 7.

69. *Birmingham and District Co-operative Party Handbook* (1925). J. Sadler and W. Sumpter, *Kettering Borough Council Election*, pamphlet, 1938.

70. Birmingham and District Co-operative Party 'Commonwealth' newssheets, *Northfield Commonwealth*, October 1935.

71. J. Fyrth, *The Signal Was Spain: The Aid Spain movement in Britain 1936–39* (London, 1986), pp. 256–57 and p. 271. *Birmingham and District Co-operative Party Annual Report*, 1938. Nottingham *Wheatsheaf*, September 1938.

72. T.W. Mercer 'Co-operative Politics and Co-operative Progress' in the *People's Year Book* (Manchester, 1921).

73. G.D.H. Cole, *A Century of Co-operation*, p. 318.

74. *The Co-operative News*, 14 July 1928, p. 2.

75. Although Thomas Carbery's work on the Co-operative Party does contain a chapter entitled 'The Party and Consumer Affairs', this mainly discusses developments during the 1950s and 1960s.

76. J.D. Stewart, *British Pressure Groups* (Oxford, 1958); R.T. McKenzie, 'Parties, Pressure Groups and the British Political Process', *The Political Quarterly*, 29, 1 (1958), pp. 5–16.

77. A.V. Alexander, *The Business Value*, p. 7.

78. *The Co-operative News*, 10 November 1923, p. 13.

79. F.W. Leeman, *Co-operation in Nottingham*, p. 60.

80. *The Co-operative News*, 7 December 1918, p. 786 and 24 May 1930, front page.

81. Difficulty arose in trying to reconcile the interests of workers as both producers and consumers. See P. Gurney, *Co-operative Culture and the Politics of Consumption in England, 1870–1930* (Manchester, 1996), pp. 226–28.

82. Nottingham *Wheatsheaf*, August 1919; *The Nottingham Forward*, September 1928.

83. *Birmingham and District Co-operative Party Annual Report*, 1934.

84. *Birmingham and District Co-operative Party Annual Report*, 1938.

85. C. Howard, 'Expectations Born to Death: Local Labour Party Expansion in the 1920s' in J. Winter (ed.), *The Working Class in Modern British History: Essays in Honour of Henry Pelling* (Cambridge, 1983), pp. 65–81.

86. Nottingham *Wheatsheaf*, April 1917.

87. *Birmingham and District Co-operative Party Annual Reports*, 1918 and 1919.

88. P. Wyncoll, *The Nottingham Labour Movement, 1880–1939* (London, 1985), p. 229; Minutes of the Nottingham Co-operative and Labour Party Central Division, 9 December 1930.

89. *Birmingham and District Co-operative Party Annual Reports*, 1930–35.

90. *The Kettering Co-operative Magazine*, August 1924.

91. *Kettering Leader and Guardian*, 30 July 1926, p. 13.

92. *The Co-operative News*, 20 April 1929, p. 2.

93. *Co-operative Congress Report*, 1938, p. 571.

94. J. Craigen, 'The Co-operative Party: Out of Labour's Shadow', in B. Lancaster and P. Maguire (eds), *Towards the Co-operative Commonwealth* (Manchester, 1996), pp. 95–99.

95. *Co-operative Congress Report*, 1922, p. 4 and Birmingham *Wheatsheaf*, August 1922.

96. See C. Wrigley, 'The Co-operative Movement', *Mitteilungsblatt des Instituts für soziale Bewegungen*, 27 (2002), pp. 103–16.

97. P. Johnson, *Saving and Spending* (Oxford, 1985).

98. J.K. Walton, *Lancashire: A Social History, 1558–1939* (Manchester, 1987), pp. 294–99.

99. Nottingham *Wheatsheaf*, January 1927.

100. Birmingham *Wheatsheaf*, March 1933.

101. M. Savage, *The Dynamics of Working-Class Politics: The Labour Movement in Preston, 1880–1940* (Cambridge, 1987), p. 101 and pp. 129–31.

102. Birmingham *Wheatsheaf*, March 1933. By winter 1939, the Society had organised 'study groups' which met during the winter to study contemporary social and political problems.

103. T. Ireson, *Old Kettering – A View of the 1930s* (Irthlingborough, 1988), p. 83.

104. Nottingham *Wheatsheaf*, January 1919.

Chapter 9

Gender, Civic Culture and Politics in South Wales: Explaining Labour Municipal Policy, 1918–39

Duncan Tanner

This chapter challenges some of the most prominent interpretations of women's influence within the Labour Party after 1918.[1] It does this by looking at the pattern of change in Labour policy across South Wales, and suggesting that the findings of this case study have a broader application. In developing an alternative explanation of how gender permeated and influenced Labour politics, the chapter stresses both the importance of a nationalising discourse and also the need to demonstrate how this discourse was disseminated, received and reinterpreted by Labour parties. To understand this process, the chapter focuses on the importance of a local institutional and civic culture in constructing Labour perceptions and determining the parameters of what was desirable policy, drawing its data largely from three contrasting constituencies – Newport, Swansea and Pontypridd – but with reference to some other parts of both Wales and Britain. Developing this analysis means delving further into the gendered institutional cultures of the Labour Party – a culture which was not ostensibly favourable to the discussion of 'women's issues' – than is usual. The chapter is thus a study of central–local institutional relations within politics, of the role – but also the *limitations* – of discourse and societal culture as ways of explaining political change. Its main contribution in this respect is to demonstrate how the world of formal institutional politics interceded to refashion gendered ideas, extending debates over the role of culture, discourse and gender in explanations of political change.[2] It also builds on excellent and innovative work being done on women in Welsh life, medicine and health,[3] and adds to a small but growing literature on the relationship between Welsh and British politics, which questions Welsh 'exceptionalism'.[4]

The seminal studies of Labour's attitude to women and their policy interests have rightly received considerable praise and attention – but rather less critical scrutiny. Pamela Graves focuses in the main on national politics. She sees the 1920s as a period of internal disagreement between feminists and the Labour Party and the 1930s as a time of defeat and retreat for Labour's feminist supporters. During the depression, women party members 'waived their gender claims in favour of party unity and the struggle against the forces of class oppression'. The party's attitude to birth control, family allowances and abortion are seen as evidence for this retreat. If Graves is more than a little censorious of Labour women, others are gradually chipping away at the impression which this work has created. Hannam and Hunt, looking at the period up to 1920, draw illuminating attention to some undeveloped features of socialist women's political values, and rightly highlight the need to examine later developments more carefully. Thane and Howell question the extent to which Labour marginalised 'women's issues', but through challenging explorations rather than full studies. Both demonstrate that Labour developed an alternative discourse, in which women were not men's rivals with competing concerns but fellow citizens, workers and comrades – with a shared party agenda.[5] I have argued elsewhere that Labour's attitudes to women within the party need to take into account both this *institutional* culture and societal constructions of women's role. Unity (of family, state, society) was seen as a 'natural' feminine concern, with party unity being portrayed as a particular concern of Labour women. 'Unity', like 'loyalty', 'practicality' and 'socialism', were words with a much deeper and fuller resonance for party activists, and arguments couched in such terms could attract considerable support.[6] To understand how women fared within the Labour Party, we need to understand their capacity to tap this internal party culture.

The way in which a (largely unstudied) party culture *restricted* women has received far more attention than the way in which it could sustain newer ideas. Certainly within the pre-war ILP, 'party' concerns were meant to transcend other 'sectional' (i.e. gender-structured) issues. However, within the ILP issues that were central to women's lives were to be addressed as part of a shared socialist commitment to ethical goals – and by men and women working together in equal relationships.[7] Many of the traditions and practices of the ILP were imported into the Labour Party after 1918. We might thus expect the party to pay some attention to women's concerns as a result of this, especially where these concerns were part of, and consistent with, the moral values of socialism. Within some sections of the party, changing conceptions of male-female collaborative relationships also introduced a new element into the equation. 'Companionate marriages' did not begin after 1945, as some seem to suggest – they were an evolving part of Labour's associational life well before this.[8] Moreover, although Labour in South Wales was a very 'masculine' party, masculinity was not static, nor subject to one definition. Like femininity, it could be constructed in varying ways and produce values which justified a (paternalistic) concern for some aspects of women's lives.

The extent to which 'progressive' cultural and ideological values permeated and influenced the internal male world of the Labour Party as a whole is open to question. Little has so far been published on the experience of women within constituency politics after 1918, let alone on gender relations.[9] This chapter makes some tentative steps towards an understanding of gendered ideas, party culture and its relevance to explanations of changing policy by looking in greater depth at the political world which mediated competing policy interests. Contrary to Graves and

Savage, it suggests that during the 1930s the party was quietly moving forward, paying more attention to the stated concerns of Labour's women members than it had done before. Although this hardly meant constructing an overtly feminist agenda, it could and did mean that some progress was made in some areas which had concerned Labour's feminists, alongside major advances in areas of social policy where Labour women were vociferous advocates of change. The main purpose of the chapter is both to explain these changes, and to develop a better understanding of how the interaction between culture, discourse and politics – at the 'national' and 'local' level – can be studied.

Women in Labour Politics: Patterns and Approaches, 1918–29

Looking at the impact of gender on party politics poses a range of challenges. To date, the most illuminating work in this area has been on the Conservatives.[10] Like Graves, David Jarvis focuses on the national party – although unlike Graves he examines the discourse produced by party propagandists, rather than unpicking policy orientations and institutional structures to unearth party opinion. Jarvis' work was an important step forward, for the language of politics says a good deal about a party's construction of gender relations. Nonetheless, this approach has limitations. The national discourse of a party set the political standard, but it did not entirely determine how local parties acted. The strategic discourse Jarvis identifies was partially ignored in favour of other options, both in Wales and elsewhere.[11] If national party officers could not determine local attitudes, they were even less influential on local policy pronouncements, especially in relation to municipal affairs. This provided a fruitful arena for differences of emphasis in the Conservative Party – as in the Labour Party – because the central party's policy statements were guidelines rather than binding strictures.[12] If we wish to understand local political attitudes to women – and the gendered nature of local politics – looking at the national party's discourse can only be one ingredient, not the whole answer.

Explanations of variations in Labour's local government policy between the wars have hardly ignored gender. On the contrary, their explanations have focused on two aspects of the local environment – the proportion of actively employed women in a constituency, and the scale of women's activism within the local Labour Party. These are used as indexes of women's local bargaining power and of fluctuations in local gender relations. For Jane Mark-Lawson, Nelson in Lancashire had better provision of nurseries and maternity hospitals because married women workers in the textile industry had greater authority within the Labour Party and influenced its policy.[13] For Mike Savage, looking at the south east of England in the conclusion of his book on Preston, policies which favoured women were more apparent in areas where there were large women's sections. In such seats, politics reflected the (social) concerns of neighbourhood Labour groups, rather than the (economic) concerns of union-centred parties. Nonetheless, Labour politics in the

1930s became more male-centred and economistic, as trade unions reasserted their influence.[14]

In some respects, it is not surprising that there are few echoes of these interpretations in the literature on interwar Wales. There were far fewer women trade union members in Wales than in Lancashire. In seats dominated by the coalminers' union, Labour activists were often unconvinced of the need to recruit individual members of either sex. As a result, there were fewer individual members – and far fewer women members – than in the south east of England. In 1933, when figures first became available, fewer than 40 per cent of the individual members of the Labour Party in Wales – a fraction over 9,000 – were women.[15] Coalfield seats with huge Labour majorities – like Llanelli, Neath, Aberdare, Abertillery, Bedwellty and Ebbw Vale – all had fewer than 200 women members, even after a decade of activity.[16] Before that, party records for coalfield seats often reveal little sign of women's activity. In 1925, ILP women claimed that the Labour Party women's sections were used only for fundraising. Their own approach was no more successful. Three years later, many ILP women's groups were themselves dormant.[17]

Yet, South Wales was much more than the coalfield, and most seats were not dominated by a single trade union or a single interest. Across the understudied coastal areas of North and South Wales, and in the rural areas of Mid- and West Wales, there were diverse seats with growing council estates or small villages and settlements – seats where one might expect women to voice the concerns of an important electoral constituency. The Swansea seats, for example, contained diverse neighbourhoods, including wards with large and growing council housing estates, and separate working-class communities which did not feel part of Swansea and sought their own facilities. Rural seats, like Brecon and Radnor, also had a real need for 'neighbourhood' services. This particular seat contained both derelict mining areas and scattered and poor rural villages, which were short of proper facilities. It was also a marginal seat, in which Labour had long recognised its need to attract supporters from outside a 'core' trade union base. Yet, in both seats, party structures failed to develop around a community based activism in which women found a powerful voice as the representatives of local consumers.

The British party leadership's emphasis on attracting and involving women members was only partially reflected at local level. In 1923, the Swansea Labour Party established an organisational system which gave every ward committee two representatives on the constituency executive, one man and one woman, with additional representation from the central women's section. On paper, the position looked good. In reality, few wards had an active women's section or sent women representatives to constituency meetings. Even in 1933, the party had only 500 women members, spread over the two Swansea constituencies.[18] There was little social activity and few active ward committees. In 1926, the central women's section had to ask to be consulted when women speakers were booked for public meetings.[19] Power was vested in the (union-dominated) central party. 'Neighbourhood' party groups were not really involved in constructing policy. Indeed, establishing a central Labour club, funding the party agent and trying to establish and run a local Labour newspaper occupied far more time than policy interests of any kind. The municipal agenda was determined by Labour councillors, many of whom were senior figures who had been elected before 1914. Ward organisations were comparatively weak, and kept under by the party officials. However, the party itself was subservient to the council Labour group, despite attempts to reform party structures in 1928. Even a councillor who admitted he had 'endeavoured to do the best he could for his own family, so far as council jobs were concerned' was not removed from his position.[20] In Brecon and Radnor, although a formal party 'structure' existed, the active elements consisted of the candidate – who financed the constituency and its campaigns – and a few friends. Efforts to set up and operate a network of organisations (repeatedly) floundered. The party had no social basis in 'neighbourhood' communities. Women members were the least politically confident members of a party whose organisation had to be constructed with outside help and paid assistance.[21]

Despite this, Wales was not entirely detached from national emphases. The Newport Labour Party had more than a thousand individual members by the early 1920s, the largest element being women. The Caerphilly and Llandaff and Barry seats had substantial women's sections by the 1930s. There were indeed some similarities between the position outlined by Savage and the position in Newport. Like Preston, Newport was not a 'classic' Labour seat. The town had a Conservative MP until 1929, and a Conservative council throughout the 1930s. Like Savage's Preston, Newport was internally divided into a series of distinct residential 'neighbourhoods'. By the mid-1920s, the Newport Labour Party had a strong organisational base within these communities. Many of its members – about three-quarters of the individual membership in 1924 – were women, and the women's sections were 'one of the chief driving forces of the party'.[22] Growth continued thereafter. Nor was this a paper membership. Women's sections met regularly and played a major organising role in neighbourhood-based Labour Party's regular social activities. By 1925, practically all ward committees had organised a series of socials and dances, along with outings for children.[23] In 1928, more than 3,200 children were taken on the party's annual children's day-trip – which had to be spread over three days. Some of this activity was supported by neighbourhood-based Labour halls and clubs, a series of which were set up in the 1920s, and by a central Labour Hall.[24]

The women's sections were also quite powerful. By 1928, donations from the women's sections, individual membership fees and social activities were the main source of the party's funds. Trade union affiliation fees made up less than a quarter of its income.[25] By 1934, the position had altered a little, because the party's wealthy candidate made a substantial annual donation towards running expenses. Nonetheless, of an income totalling more than £1,000 per annum, around £800 came from members and their activities.[26] Women also had a visible and influential political role. In 1926, for example, the six women who represented ward committees and the women's sections on the constituency executive exercised considerable influence, as most executive committee meetings were attended by just twelve people. By 1928, the women's sections were making their own monthly reports to the constituency executive.[27] The Newport party also sent two delegates to every national Labour Party conference, consciously selecting one man and one woman. In 1927, the party mandated those representatives to support an increase in the number of women on the National Executive Committee (NEC). In 1928, they were to support the introduction of family allowances, the raising of the school leaving age, and other policies advanced by the local women's sections.[28] Detailed neighbourhood concerns were also put to the constituency party's general committee, resulting in loud condemnation of Labour councillors for compromising on the quality of municipal housing in 1926. Throughout 1930, the party discussed playing field provision and broken sewers in some parts of Newport, and paid considerable attention to the quality of wood stains and linoleum used in council houses.[29] These were not peripheral concerns, although some (male) Labour figures and female activists indicated their dissatisfaction with such emphases. They showed the party gave real attention to ensuring that public services were about comfort and serviceability.

If Savage's model of what prompted and determined a 'feminised' politics is correct, we would expect to find the most progressive policies in Newport, the least progressive in those areas where union hierarchies excluded women. If Graves is correct about the marginalisation of women in the 1930s, we would expect to see ever more pronounced concern with material issues in Wales during the depression, as women's specific concerns were submerged by a primary focus on economic affairs and foreign policy. Perhaps surprisingly, this was not the case. As the following section shows, Newport was far from being the more progressive authority on specific feminist demands. On issues like birth control, Labour parties in the coalfield seats, which had very few women members, pursued the most progressive policies. Nor were policies pursued by the Labour Party less consistent with the interests of Labour women in the 1930s than in the 1920s; the exact reverse was the case in many seats. Existing approaches thus do little to explain the pattern of policy on the ground. We need to go deeper to do this; to enter the political world of Labour politics; to see the process through local eyes.

Women, Politics and Policy, 1929–39

In the 1920s, feminists were demanding that free birth control advice should be given to married women through the municipal maternity and child welfare clinics. When the Labour government decreed that it was acceptable for local authorities to issue birth control advice in 1931, Newport's maternity and child welfare committee – whose deputy-chair was the wife of Labour's election agent – still declined to act. The vehement opposition of Newport's medical officer of health was one significant factor. Newport's substantial Catholic population, and the fact that it was a marginal seat, were also no doubt influential.[30] Despite the fact that the borough employed a woman doctor, and that the deputy medical officer of health was a woman, even maternity care was taken less seriously than in other seats. The council evidently expected its medical officer of health to focus on his other roles (he was paid less for his work with the maternity committee than for acting as police surgeon or as superintendent of the isolation hospital).[31] By 1932, 'very few' children in Newport attended the infant welfare centres, and inspection of midwifes was 'very much in arrear', as the officer responsible for this had 'practically no experience of midwifery practice'. By contrast, Labour parties in mining areas had supported maternity care through trade union schemes for many years. Some also supported attempts to provide birth control advice, even before this received party sanction in 1931. The first ever hospital birth control clinic was established in the mining town of Abertillery in 1925, following pressure from the local miners' agent.[32] By 1939, there were 14 local authority birth control clinics in Wales, eleven of which were established or agreed by Labour controlled councils. Most of these were in mining-dominated areas, and were operated by the Labour-controlled Glamorgan County Council.[33] In boroughs like Swansea, birth control advice was given – albeit covertly – by local doctors.

Nor did the pattern of Labour politics alter in the 1930s in the way that existing studies might suggest. True, there are echoes of the shift towards economic issues and employment generation which apparently featured elsewhere. In Newport, Labour councillors opposed policies designed to reduce the number of municipal workers. The party formed action committees with local trade union leaders – particularly from the Transport and General Workers' Union (TGWU) – to protect jobs. The women's sections here was less visible than in the past, and their leaders did not assume such a prominent position within the constituency machine.[34] Swansea Labour Party developed a more expansive programme of employment creating activity. The Labour controlled Swansea council successfully obtained over a million pounds in central government grants, which it used to build a civic centre, a power station, and to undertake drainage works.[35] It also tried to attract new industry and to protect the unemployed from the more humiliating aspects of the means test, whilst also examining the level of council house rents in order to keep costs down.[36] Nonetheless, in neither seat was this at the expense of broader concerns. In Swansea, neighbourhood-focussed activities *increased* – quite substantially – in the 1930s. The Swansea party did not turn its back on issues which were strongly supported by its women's sections; it gave them greater attention. Although the Newport Labour Party proposed ward based clinics to improve maternity and child welfare provision,[37] in Swansea both the party and the Labour-led Swansea health committee took this further. With the women's section and ward groups pushing for action, the health committee provided new antenatal sessions at existing clinics, supported the employment of additional female staff and obstetric experts, and proposed the opening of temporary clinics in community meeting places – whilst also proclaiming (in good socialist terms) that state funding and municipal provision of a proper service were essential.[38] The provision of additional nursery schools was initially rejected because of the financial crisis. However, the proposals re-emerged in 1932 and eventually, in 1936, the council opened its first nursery school. Better central provision of hospital facilities was also the party's main priority in the 1937 municipal election.[39] In coalfield constituencies, the plight of the mining industry attracted considerable attention – but women were hardly immune from the impact of economic decline. On the contrary, they were the first to feel its impact. Nonetheless, even here health, maternal mortality and other issues were far from absent from the policy agenda.

There was no major shift in the power of women's sections in the 1930s which could explain why these policies were so visible. True, overall membership across Wales increased from around 9,000 in 1933 to a peak of 12,000 in 1937. By 1934–35, Newport had one of the largest women's section in Britain and the fourth largest individual membership in the country, Caerphilly and Llandaff and Barry had a large membership, and Pontypool, Pontypridd, Neath and other seats saw persistent increases. There was even significant expansion (from a low base) in Swansea. Labour women were also more vocal and confident. Swansea's women's sections proclaimed their right to participate as equals in party activities. In 1933–34, the central women's section questioned areas traditionally assumed to be a male preserve – such as the organisation of party finance – and complained that women were insufficiently involved in the chairing of propaganda meetings.[40] Nor was this unusual. Women's sections in some mining seats also became more active. In Pontypridd, for example, the local Labour Party passed a series of resolutions which originated in its women's sections, including calls for the feeding of necessitous children and the introduction of a Peace Day in schools. More significantly, it received and closely considered proposals from the women's section for the relocation or development of new industries in the area, again traditionally a 'male' concern.[41]

Yet, despite occasionally optimistic reports of younger women attending party meetings in greater numbers, even growing women's sections (as in Caerphilly) were quite fragile.[42] Reports made to Labour officials in London were generally depressing. Inexperienced new women members felt daunted by a very male world, with meetings in public houses and constitutional and other arrangements with which they were unfamiliar.[43] The Welsh women's organiser, Elizabeth Andrews (like other women organisers in South Wales), recognised the value of women's social and other activities, especially in developing a new organisation. However, she expressed an activist's irritation at those who were unwilling to move beyond social events. She criticised the prevalent and 'silly ideas about the work of women's sections', and tried to ease women's sections away from 'just' having 'a cup of tea and a jolly evening'. She knew that men were unlikely to take women seriously unless they performed a full 'party' role – and that men would even then find ways of asserting their dominance.[44]

Whilst she underestimated the positive importance of non-political work for the party's public image, she was right to think that men would not give up power lightly. As women's sections sought a role in ward affairs, some men became 'terrified' by the perceived consequences.[45] They often reacted to new initiatives from women with demonstrations of authority. In Pontypridd, the women's sections' nominations for committees were rejected; the party's constitutional rulebook was used to justify this stance.[46] In Swansea, too, the constituency executive exercised its authority when the women's section sent a resolution directly to its national party conference without permission: 'all resolutions from women's sections in future should same be contrary to policy of the Association, must be submitted to the parent body [sic]'. There were a series of slights and small attempts to marginalise women who were seeking to play a larger part in party politics.[47]

Many male party members would accept lectures on birth control (it was difficult for socialists to reject discussion of ideas sanctioned by a Labour government). Prioritising birth control was another matter. In 1933, for example, the Lliswerry Ward Labour Party in Newport proposed the establishment of a birth control clinic. Fearing that a meeting addressed by a representative of the Birth Control Association would lead to a resolution in favour of municipally-funded birth control advice, Newport's constituency executive declined to hold the lecture. A general committee meeting overturned this decision by a substantial majority and a meeting was subsequently organised (testimony to the level of support for women within the party, augmented by the feeling that the executive had acted high-handedly). However, the executive insisted that no resolution which associated the party with support for birth control could be passed. The authority of party regulations (the national conference decision of 1925, reasserted in a letter obtained from the NEC) was used to suppress rebellion.[48] In Pontypridd, a resolution suggesting that the council take over and run the independent birth control clinic came to the Labour Party via the council's health committee. It was delayed and defeated – although the party membership objected to the way this was done and eventually overturned its decision.[49] In Monmouthshire – where four clinics received financial support from the county council – a proposal to create a fifth in the large urban centre of Pontypool was rejected.[50]

Nor is it possible to argue that policy altered because of a new national discourse, reflected and sanctioned at local level by respected authorities. Contraceptive use was growing, in South Wales as in Britain as a whole, but it was not something that was easily discussed by couples, let alone by political parties. Medical officers of health – by no means a uniform group – held varying views, but those who accepted the need for contraceptive advice kept tactfully silent. Birth control features only obliquely in the minutes of maternity and child welfare committees (like party records, a source neglected by social historians) even in areas where birth control advice was being given. By contrast, opponents proclaimed their opposition and their concern for the race and its survival. Monmouthshire's medical officer of health noted his 'bounden duty' to improve 'the health and efficiency of the race'. Glamorgan's was concerned that falling birth rates would mean that the 'quality and quantity' of the population would become a concern.[51] Traditional cultural values were also strongly entrenched within the council. Swansea's health committee declared that all senior midwives employed under the maternity act 'shall be unmarried'.[52] The maternity and child welfare committees, generally dominated by women, were not immune to such ideas. Even councils whose clinics gave birth control advice insisted that when employing midwives, 'no full-time post should be offered to a married woman', and that any unmarried midwife shall 'cease to hold her appointment in the event of subsequent marriage'.[53] Some Labour women themselves challenged the need for nursery schools when there was no tradition of married women working, arguing that 'the women comrades thought it would tend to give mothers more time to gossip'.[54] Changing cultural values did not restructure the public discourse or justify a new approach. We are left with a paradoxical situation, in which Labour parties in very traditional, male-centred areas adopted more progressive policies so far as women were concerned than parties with large women's sections.

Explaining Change: National and Local Politics

If existing explanations of changes in policy cannot account for the circumstances evident in Wales, how then can they be explained? Political choice is one possibility. The South Wales coalfield contained an unusually innovative and radical labour movement, as works focussing on the South Wales miners and their attitudes to industrial, economic and foreign policy have demonstrated.[55] Recently, scholars have added to this analysis, seeing in Labour's local support for better health provision an attempt to construct a 'proletarian public sphere founded on alternative values to the bourgeoisie'.[56] It is more difficult to demonstrate that this radicalism embraced attitudes to women. The mining union was indeed grateful for the support given by Labour women during the General Strike. Perhaps, as a result, the national miners' federation supported a motion in favour of *discussing* birth control at the 1926 Labour Party conference. However, once the party had made the decision not to consider it as a political issue, the miners followed the party line.[57] If decisions were taken which resulted in policies favourable to women being adopted, we need to see inside the male political world in order to appreciate how the decision-making process worked and why these decisions were made. However, it is equally important to study the policies adopted within Wales as part of a broader concern within a Britain-wide policy process. For although parties (and the miners) could stretch and challenge 'national' political remits, Wales did not have its own separate laws, nor its own separate party organisations. It could not separate itself *entirely* from policy agendas developed by the government, or from policy responses created by the British Labour leadership. Moreover, both within and outside the coalfield, the radicalism which the miners sponsored was being challenged by 1939, with new regional organisations playing a growing role in advocating the 'British' line.[58]

The context within which Welsh Labour parties operated was thus bounded by two features of British politics. The first was the policy agenda set by the National government. Local Labour parties – and Labour controlled municipal councils – could only do so much to challenge national policy. Those parties which declined to comply, like the Labour controlled Bedwellty board of guardians, were disbanded –

with the result that support to the weakest declined and suffering increased. This had a clear impact on other Welsh Labour parties. Although activists chafed against the constraints of National government policy in the 1930s, calls to reject capitalist laws, deny the means test and operate illegal relief scales were (sometimes narrowly) defeated.[59] Pragmatic Labour municipal councils felt that by working within the system they could mitigate the impact of the depression. And, indeed, there were opportunities to exploit. In Labour controlled authorities like Merthyr, only 1 per cent of applications for transitional benefits were refused – compared to nearly a third in a city like Birmingham. In Britain as a whole, 65 per cent of applicants for means tested benefits got the maximum award – in Labour controlled Glamorgan, the figure was 94 per cent. The argument for working within the system was not unattractive to women schooled in practicality. 'It is the plodders that do the work of the world', commented Elizabeth Andrews, 'not the shouters'.[60]

Moreover, national concerns and legislation offered specific opportunities to go forward in areas that Labour women valued. There were a host of enquiries into maternal and infant mortality, nationally and in South Wales, from the later 1920s to the mid-1930s. This culminated in the damning 'Report on Maternal Mortality in Wales', published in 1937. This placed such issues firmly on the political agenda. Nor could the National government's policy for maternity provision be ignored by Labour councils charged with delivering a service. The Midwifery Act of 1936 called for the establishment of a municipal midwifery service, supported by an expanded hospital service.[61] Labour councils were obliged to develop a response. The content of Welsh Labour politics was inevitably influenced by the need to structure that response and by the opportunities this afforded to improve the system (and to expand a council's authority and power). Most local Labour parties proposed national/municipal intervention as Labour's 'solution', constructing an ideological response to a non-socialist policy.

The second broader influence on local policy was the national policy agenda of the Labour Party. Although economic debates which took place *outside* the party machine have received most attention from scholars, across the 1930s the party's own policy machinery had been promoting a policy agenda which embraced not just economic reforms, but also new social and welfare policies.[62] This included close attention to maternity provision and pre-school education. Graves argues that in the 1930s Labour women claimed that maternal mortality was caused by malnutrition, an economic cause which men could understand, because this 'helped to integrate their agenda into the mainstream policy of the party'.[63] This conclusion is based on both a very partial inspection of party documents and a rather convoluted interpretation of what was happening. In policy debates, Labour women (and men) did not focus purely on malnutrition as the cause of maternal mortality – they pointed to a series of causes, poor antenatal care being one of the most frequently identified. Some of this was prompted by the National government's legislative interventions and the need for a tangible response. Policy committees produced a lengthy analysis of 'Maternity and Child Welfare', a paper on 'Health Visitors in Connection with Maternity and Child Welfare', and a twenty-page document on

'Maternal Mortality and the Maternity Service'. The party also conducted surveys of the provision of free meals and milk by local authorities, with particular attention to how the 'stigma' of free municipal support might be addressed.[64] Labour's policy documents used the language of natural justice and equality. They described equal access to health care as a matter of right, and the state as the guarantor of this fundamental human need. Health care created a sense of security. Collective health care was also part of the community (and the family's) concern for its members. As such, it was at the core of socialist sentiment.

Poor health certainly had a personal and an economic impact – and, in recognising this, and in stressing that women's health was in a state of crisis, Labour spoke a language that many women voters understood and appreciated. However, Labour women's nationwide malnutrition campaign in 1934 gave way to a much broader emphasis. When 'material' influences on maternal mortality resurfaced in Labour debates in Wales, it was in part a response to National government policy statements. In 1937, for example, circular 1515 from the Welsh board of health stressed the significance of nutrition for maternal mortality. This prompted a reconsideration of the provision of free milk and food to nursing mothers in Swansea and elsewhere. Even then, amongst local authorities in Glamorgan, improving local infant mortality rates were not explained by reference to a reduction in malnutrition. Rather, the council highlighted increased use of antenatal care, hospital provision and midwifery, together with 'the greater amount of individual attention which it is now possible for mothers to give to their babies than in the days of unrestricted child-bearing'.[65]

Nor was Labour support for the concerns of women members confined to maternity. Labour's education policy has again often been treated as 'economistic' and male-focused. Its support for an increased school leaving age is often portrayed as a device to reduce unemployment. Nursery education is seen as a marginal interest. However, nursery education was advanced very strongly nationally and in parts of South Wales – both as an adjunct of medical inspection, but also as the first step and the foundation of the national system of education. It was pushed hard by party experts even during the second Labour government, and an expansion of nursery schools (as opposed to nursery classes) became a feature of policy in the mid-1930s. If it seemed to be a lower priority at national level by 1938, the new Labour education advisory committee at least reaffirmed its commitment to equality, rejecting a Conservative proposal in favour of compulsory domestic science classes for girls.[66] Other issues were certainly more powerfully argued, in Wales and at national level, and Labour's language was hardly feminist. However, the party's concern with many aspects of women's lives was not artificial or marginal. Labour's welfare agenda was much more than a shallow response to rival ideas from the National government or a mask for 'economism'. It was, for some, the very embodiment of socialism.

These ideas came together in *Labour's Immediate Programme*, published in 1937. The programme included attention to pensions, welfare reforms, housing developments, and a host of other policy interventions – which hardly makes it 'economistic'. Municipal action was meant to be 'practical', to demonstrate what Labour meant by socialism. On maternity services and on pensions, the Standing Joint Committee of Industrial Women's Organisations (SJC) was positively involved in the construction of policy.[67] The success of a similar programme in London had encouraged the idea that this 'practical socialism' could be successfully applied elsewhere.[68] An admittedly crude party machinery set about promoting a broadly based programme of reforms – both as a basis for political expansion and as an alternative to the left's policy of a Popular Front, which was gaining support amongst activists. In 1937, women's sections across South Wales were encouraged to promote Labour's 'Children's Charter', its views on food prices, its pension plans, and to hold discussions on the National government's new Midwives Act, in order to secure the most positive Labour response from Labour councils. In 1938, women's sections were asked to back a national 'Cost of Living' campaign. The party in London and regional officials encouraged a nationwide and co-ordinated effort – and were discouraged when issues like Spain and the United Front movement seemed to distract some Labour women from these ends.[69]

In addition, Labour's municipal welfare policies were promoted through the party machinery, which was also used to influence Labour Party council leaders. Regional Women's Advisory Committees (there were advisory committees for East Glamorgan, Llanelli and Carmarthenshire) called on Labour councils to include support for local health clinics and nursery schools in their election manifestos.[70] These bodies were used by powerful women, such as the Glamorgan county councillor Rose Davies and the Welsh women's organiser Elizabeth Andrews, to spread support for the reorientation of Labour policy. Indeed, it was individuals within the party machinery – rather than women's sections – that were influential.[71] Their political courage and commitment can hardly be overstated. In 1926, Rose Davies used one annual meeting of the East Glamorgan Federation to argue that 'The position of the unmarried mother and her child was one that should receive their special attention as women . . . there should not be two standards to be judged by (one for men and another for women)'.[72] At an autumn educational conference of the same body in 1934, Elizabeth Andrews advanced a resolution calling for antenatal clinics in all areas, arguing also that 'birth control ought to be taught to all mothers'. Both Davies and Andrews used the East Glamorgan Advisory Committee to argue the case for nursery schools.[73] Their position within the Labour Party machine – Davies was also on the executive of the SJC – and the backing of head office gave them authority, whilst the party's growing infrastructure gave them a vehicle which was far more influential than the women's sections. In 1938, for example, a sub-committee of the South Wales Regional Council of Labour – a powerful grouping which contained regional officials from all the major unions – conducted a hospital services inquiry. Chairs of public health authorities across South Wales were called to attend and to explain their failure to adapt provision in line with national Labour policy.[74]

We also need to recognise that Labour women received support from some rank-and-file (male) party activists. Indeed, women could not have challenged the decisions of party executives on issues like birth control, nor achieved the introduction of birth control clinics in some areas, without men supporting them.[75] The reasons for this are unclear, but some possibilities can be advanced. The Labour Party was not a monolith. Its values – like broader societal values – were not static. Changing conceptions of masculinity amongst the 'modern man' – stressing the role of fatherhood, or the 'masculinity' of restraint – may have been influential. Fisher's work shows that some men in South Wales were enthusiastic advocates of birth control and indeed suggested it to their wives.[76] A consciously 'modern' and 'progressive' party might be expected to contain men who were willing to challenge social orthodoxy. Labour activists frequently took pride in flouting convention and living by their own values. Whilst 'loyalty' was increasingly being promoted as a party value, some Welsh socialists recoiled at the idea of a 'slave-like acceptance' of London's line. 'Rebelliousness' was almost a positive political virtue, a badge of identity.

We also know that across Britain, many of the women pioneers who challenged orthodox societal notions of female behaviour developed their ideas within a family tradition of political activism and dissent.[77] Many of the most politically active women in South Wales were part of a socialist relationship or had radical parents. This was true of Rose Davies and Elizabeth Andrews. The secretary of the women's section in Caerphilly was the sister of Morgan Jones MP. Prominent women activists in Merthyr, Newport and Swansea were married to local Labour figures. In Newport, the chair and secretary of the women's section were sisters. It was estimated in the 1920s that 90 per cent of women members were married to male party activists.[78] Labour's associational life could and did sustain alternative views on relationships. Some English Labour women in the 1930s were part of relationships which saw mutual respect and comradeship as a part of their (shared) socialism. Women like Margaret Cole, Vera Brittain and Naomi Mitchison were not unconstrained by societal values, but they stretched them within their own lives and challenged them in published accounts of what a marriage of equals should involve.[79] Such circumstances may have softened the attitudes of some more 'progressive' Welsh men to the arguments developed by English Labour women. Certainly, Elizabeth Andrews talked of her own marriage as 'a real partnership', based on a shared interest in the 'same social and religious problems'. She wrote of her husband's 'inspiration and encouragement'. Women activists (rather than members) were also doubly part of the Labour 'family'. People who 'did the work' could gain an additional level of institutional regard: given the current state of research, we can do not more than speculate on the extent of this development.[80]

Explaining Change: Civic Culture and Local Elites

Historical revisionism can of course go too far. If a minority were shifting their views, the weight of societal and Labour opinion was not. Even in the 1980s and 1990s, Welsh Labour parties were hardly full of 'new men', and a commitment to change had to be 'extracted' by women using the political machinery to their own advantage. The British Labour Party and the National government were hardly promoting a feminist agenda, as policies in other areas indicated. Local parties were fiercely independent, and resented direction from Cardiff, let alone from London, so the impact of national (and regional) pressures should not be overstated. Non-compliance with national Labour campaigns was quite common, and not just within the South Wales coalfield. The national and regional parties lacked the machinery to create a co-ordinated approach. It was common for adjacent Labour controlled councils to take radically different lines on issues like the level of rates.[81] We certainly need to recognise national political and institutional pressures – but we also need to understand how this was taken up at local level.

A closer examination of the position in Swansea provides one further clue as to why policy shifted in the 1930s, with health care becoming a priority. Women's sections and local Labour groups initially advanced two main health policies – support for the feeding of necessitous children and increased maternity provision. They pushed council committees to provide this and campaigned for it in elections.[82] The demand for maternity beds and health clinics within the towns, villages and estates that constituted the borough of Swansea was growing. Concrete plans to expand the supply of beds and increase nursing support were in place by 1934.[83] Labour women activists were still lobbying the health committee for action on this in 1936, and ward committees continued to lobby for local provision thereafter.[84] Yet, the precise content and timing of this programme was determined not by 'neighbourhood' groups or by the party, but by the council Labour group. To understand the pace and pattern of Labour policy, we thus need to enter their world, a male world, and to determine how party ideology and civic values influenced policy orientations.

By the later 1930s, the national Labour Party's own policy experts (drawn especially from the Socialist Medical Association and the London County Council) called for *both* local provision of health centres *and* the construction of central hospitals in cities.[85] Swansea's Labour-dominated health committee approved a similarly ambitious plan, but felt that expansion should be funded nationally and be under the control of the municipality rather than by expanding voluntary provision. Maternity support should not be provided by private bodies – municipal control, like direct labour in housing, was an item of political faith.[86] In addition, the council and civic leaders and the press more generally began to focus on the building of a grand municipal hospital, rather than piecemeal improvements in local communities. The hospital became as much a symbol of civic ambition as a commitment to public health. It was likely to bring prestige, support from the press – possibly support from the wider electorate outside Labour's heartland wards. The national party may have wanted action on health, and the party may have been pushed by its women members and wards – but the decision was ultimately made by a small group of men motivated by rather different concerns.

We should not minimise the impact of such considerations. A section of the Swansea Labour group was growing apart from the party membership by the later

1930s. Indeed, five councillors were investigated in 1939 by the NEC and regional organisers because of their reluctance to break contact with social service organisations. Their duty was to the city, they argued, and not to narrow party interest.[87] Civic grandeur came to be a significant if covert influence on decision-making. Leading figures – like the borough engineer, the mayor, senior Labour councillors and the local press – felt that Swansea had a reputation and status which should be maintained. The council saw Swansea as 'the Ocean port of the West' – and as Cardiff's rival as the capital city of Wales. The council, one local dignitary reported in 1935, was 'remarkable for its energy, its foresight, its municipal pride'.[88] It had already undertaken huge development, with its university, new public housing, power station, roads, plans for the docks and the newly completed law courts and impressively designed civic centre (lit at night to display its splendour). Cardiff had 'no right to foster fictitious ideas about its primacy'. If progressive civic ideas introduced in Birmingham were described with envy, the press enthusiastically reported the visits made by delegations from other cities that were interested in Swansea's own municipal achievements.[89] Some political figures proposed flats as the 'modern' way of accommodating the people – Swansea saw itself as an urban leader, and the 'modern' had an intrinsic attraction. It was even looking to develop an airport before Cardiff.[90] Civic pride and civic competition were evidently influential.

Money could be found for such activities. When the city treasurer became worried about further municipal expenditure, the chair of the finance committee denied that those who represented the town would either act in a profligate manner or neglect their duty. The medical officer of health described maternity services as if they were a 'true economy', a fine example of careful male stewardship of the borough's health and finances. The council was not just concerned about providing jobs. Pride in Swansea and its (Welsh) people was even identified with a national renaissance – with Swansea (seen by civic leaders as a more 'Welsh' city than Cardiff) as the 'natural' leader of that renaissance. On St David's Day 1935, Swansea's director of education argued that Wales had 'discovered her soul' and was becoming a 'land of hope'. Civic identity and a Welsh identity were complimentary, not competitive.[91] When the ministry of health publicised tables of maternal mortality rates in 1936, alderman David Williams (a long-standing and revered Labour activist and chair of the health committee) described being 'rather surprised to see that Swansea was amongst the towns that was considered abnormal'.[92] This was the climate in which health provision was debated. Both the planned airport and the construction of public amenities along the seafront were deemed to have a lower priority than health. As councillor Watkins from the St Thomas ward put it, a hospital was 'more essential than an aerodrome.[93] A major new hospital, capable of providing for Swansea and of being the medical centre for West Wales, was promoted over ward health centres or maternity units, or 'economistic' policies.

In developing this case, some Labour councillors clung to a very male-centred language. They described the desire for a central hospital as the natural desire of reasonable adults to provide for themselves. They were demonstrating the self-respect and self-reliance that one would expect of men: 'A municipal hospital will deliver us from the state of being children of pity, dependent upon charity'.[94] Their language bore little of the stamp of feminism. It contained nothing about the plight of Swansea's mothers. However, it did reflect a shift in the language of national Labour politics, reinterpreted so that it was consistent with Swansea's own civic culture. From a variety of quarters, and for a variety of reasons, a change in orientation had finally taken place.

Conclusion

This chapter has described a shift in the pattern of Labour politics in parts of South Wales – but as part of a broader analysis of the way that policy changes could take place. Labour's *British* policy programme, reinforced from within the Welsh political machine, together with local pressures from within the party and a sense of civic pride, helped to structure Labour politics in Wales. The same ingredients influenced policy in apparently very different English urban environments.[95] Of course, opportunities and local emphases varied. More local studies would no doubt produce a more variegated picture. South Wales is probably not 'typical'. But the aim has not been to suggest uniformity, but to advance an approach. That approach places less emphasis on policy as a reflection of local structural configurations than does Mike Savage. It places more emphasis on culture, gendered institutions and on the political medium through which discourse is filtered than does Jon Lawrence. It does not assume that change came about solely from women's own political pressure and action, but adds to the pot a consideration of Labour values, institutional cultures and the pressures applied through the world of formal politics.[96] However, whilst the chapter reasserts the role of a changing legislative framework and of party politics, it is still argued that broader cultural values – and gendered attitudes – permeated everything that parties did. Indeed, the chapter demonstrates how and why cultural orientations were reflected (and refracted) as they passed through the institutional structures of the Labour Party, and met with and were informed by party and civic values. This is not to suggest that these other ways of explaining local politics and policies are 'wrong'. The urban structure of Swansea evidently influenced demands for local neighbourhood provision of services. The language of civic patriotism was an influential 'local' discourse. It is not 'wrong' to argue that local Labour parties rejected feminism, or to argue that there was a tradition of radicalism within Welsh coalfield politics. But these are all ingredients of a bigger story, not monocausal explanations of Labour's political orientation in the 1930s.

This depiction of politics as an interactive mix of societal and political variables, both local and national, has implications for how we perceive central–local relations and British–Welsh history. South Wales was not exempt from a British-wide process which pushed local Labour parties towards particular issues and orientations. The borders of Wales were fluid. Wales had institutions, interests, and even a culture, that made it part of Britain, even if those institutions were under strain and Welsh ideals, memories and associations could give Welsh politics a distinctive finish. Historians of Britain often neglect what happens within Wales. Historians of Wales often find little to interest them across the border. In the world before devolution, such boundaries make little sense.

Notes

1. P. Graves, *Labour Women: Women in British Working-Class Politics, 1918–39* (Cambridge, 1994); M. Savage, *The Dynamics of Working-Class Politics: The Labour Movement in Preston, 1880–1940* (Cambridge, 1987).

2. J. Lawrence, 'The Complexities of English Progressivism: Wolverhampton Politics in the Early Twentieth Century', *Midland History*, 24 (1999); J. Vernon, *Politics and the People: A Study in English Political Culture, c1815–67* (Cambridge, 1993).

3. For example, D. Beddoe, *Out of the Shadows: A History of Women in Twentieth Century Wales* (Cardiff, 2000); A.V. John (ed.), *Our Mother's Land: Chapters in Welsh Women's History, 1830–1939* (Cardiff, 1991). Much of the best work on health display is previewed in A. Borsay (ed.), *Medicine in Wales, c.1800–2000* (Cardiff, 2003); and P. Michael and C. Webster (eds), *Health and Society in Twentieth Century Wales* (forthcoming, Cardiff, 2005).

4. D. Tanner, 'The Pattern of Labour Politics, 1918–39', in D. Tanner, C. Williams and D. Hopkin (eds), *The Labour Party in Wales, 1900–2000* (Cardiff, 2000); U. Masson, '"Political Conditions in Wales are Quite Different": Party Politics and Votes for Women, 1912–15', *Women's History Review*, 9, 2 (2000). The pioneer text is K.O. Morgan, *Wales in British Politics, 1868–1922* (Cardiff, 1963).

5. J. Hannam and K. Hunt, *Socialist Women: Britain 1880s to 1920s* (London, 2002), pp. 134–65 and p. 206; P. Thane, 'The Women of the British Labour Party and Feminism, 1906–45', in H.L. Smith (ed.), *British Feminism in the Twentieth Century* (Amhurst, 1990); D. Howell, *MacDonald's Party: Labour Identities and Crisis, 1922–31*(Oxford, 2002), chapters 20–21.

6. See D. Tanner, *An Anatomy of the Labour Party, 1900–39* (Oxford, forthcoming).

7. J. Hannam, '"In the Comradeship of the Sexes Lies the Hope of Progress and Social Regeneration": Women in the West Riding ILP, c.1890–1914', in J. Rendall (ed.), *Equal or Different? Women's Politics, 1800–1914* (Oxford, 1987); L. Ugolini, '"It is Only Justice to Grant Women's Suffrage": Independent Labour Party Men and Women's Suffrage, 1893–1905', in C. Eustace et al (eds), *A Suffrage Reader* (Leicester, 2000).

8. J. Finch and P. Summerfield, 'Social Reconstruction and the Emergence of Companionate Marriage, 1945–59', in D. Clark (ed.), *Marriage, Domestic Life and Social Change* (London, 1991). For companionate marriage in a not dissimilar area, see M. Williamson, '"I'm Going to Get a Job at the Factory": Attitudes to

Women's Employment in a Mining Community, 1945–65', *Women's History Review*, 12, 3 (2003).

9. I have discussed examples of this in 'The Prospects for Social Democratic History: Or, Why People, Institutions and Ideas Matter', Rethinking Social Democracy conference, Institute of Historical Research, London, April 2004. For pioneering studies of women in constituency Labour politics between the wars, see J. Mark-Lawson, M. Savage and A. Warde, 'Gender and Local Politics: Struggles Over Welfare Policies, 1918–39', in L. Murgatroyd (ed.), *Localities, Class and Gender* (London, 1985); S. Davies, 'Class, Religion and Gender: Liverpool Labour Party and Women, 1918–39', in J. Belchem (ed.), *Popular Politics, Riot and Labour: Essays in Liverpool History, 1790–1940* (Liverpool, 1992).

10. See D. Jarvis, 'The Conservative Party and the Politics of Gender', in M. Francis and I. Zweiniger-Bargielowska (eds), *The Conservatives and British Society* (Cardiff, 1996).

11. S. Jones, 'The Political Dynamics of North East Wales, With Special Reference to the Liberal Party', University of Wales PhD (Bangor, 2003).

12. J. Ramsden, *The Age of Balfour and Baldwin, 1902–40* (London, 1978), pp. 257–59. For Labour, J.S. Rowett, 'The Labour Party in Local Government: Theory and Practice in the Interwar Years', Oxford University DPhil (1979).

13. J. Mark-Lawson et al, 'Gender and Local Politics'. See also J. Hill, *Nelson: Politics, Economy, Community* (Edinburgh, 1997), chapter six.

14. M. Savage, *The Dynamics of Working-Class Politics*, pp. 186–7 and pp. 195–200.

15. D. Tanner et al, *The Labour Party in Wales*, pp. 302–4.

16. D. Tanner, 'The Pattern of Labour Politics', p. 120 and p. 123.

17. Welsh Divisional Council ILP, Minutes of the First ILP Women's Advisory Committee, 10 November 1925; ILP *Welsh Women's Bulletin*, April 1928 (British Library of Political and Economic Science).

18. Minutes of the Swansea Labour Association Executive Committee (EC), 20 December 1922, 14 March and 23 April 1923 All constituency records are from the microfilm edition produced by Microform Limited of Wakefield unless stated otherwise. I am grateful to the British Academy for funds to purchase these and other Welsh constituency records, held in the Welsh Institute for Social and Cultural Affairs at the University of Wales Bangor.

19. *Ibid*, 26 January 1926. Similar complaints were still made in the 1930s. See, for example, the executive minutes for 6 December 1933.

20. *Ibid*, Special EC, 6 December 1928; EC, 18 April 1929. Cross-party women's groups – like the Women's Housing Council – were no more successful. See N.A. Robbins, *Homes for Heroes: Early Twentieth Century Council Housing in the County Borough of Swansea* (Swansea, 1992), pp. 74–81.

21. D. Tanner, 'The Pattern of Labour Politics', p. 126. For the formation of women's sections, see D.T. Lewis to E.T. John, 13 August 1920 (E.T. John MSS 2643, National Library of Wales).

22. Newport Labour Party, *Annual Report and Balance Sheet, 1924* (Newport Reference Library).

23. *Ibid*, 1925.

24. *Ibid*, 1928.

25. *Ibid*.

26. *Ibid*, 1934. The new candidate, Peter Freeman, was a wealthy businessman whose considerable commitment included support for a local Labour newspaper.

27. See, for an example of attendance details, Minutes of the Newport Labour Party, 16 March and 5 May 1926. See also 6 February 1928.

28. *Ibid*, 9 August 1926 and 23 September 1927; Special General Committee, 19 September 1928.

29. *Ibid*, 23 April 1926, 21 March, 4 April, 30 May, 17 October, and 14 November 1930.

30. Newport County Borough, 'Quarterly Report of the Maternity and Child Welfare Committee, 18 August 1931' (Gwent County Record Office (CRO)).

31. Newport County Borough, Health Committee Minutes, 30 January and 20 December 1932 (Gwent CRO).

32. Medical Officer of Health, 'Annual Report of the Health of the County Borough of Newport, 1932' (Gwent CRO); M. Douglas, 'Women, God and Birth Control: The First Hospital Birth Control Clinic, Abertillery 1925', *Llafur*, 6, 4 (1995).

33. K. Fisher, '"Clearing up Misconception": The Campaign to Set Up Birth Control Clinics in South Wales between the Wars', *Welsh History Review*, 19, 1 (1998), pp. 110–14.

34. D. Tanner, 'The Pattern of Labour Politics', p. 130.

35. D. Tanner, 'Swansea Labour Party: A Brief Introduction to the Microfilm Edition of Swansea Labour Party Records' (Wakefield, 2000), p. 5.

36. Swansea Labour Association, *Annual Report*, 1932 and 1934.

37. *Newport Citizen*, October 1938.

38. For the pragmatic response, see Swansea Health Committee Minutes, 4 April 1934, 4 March 1935, 6 and 27 January 1936 – and for a reluctance to accept piecemeal additions to the existing system of voluntary and local authority provision, 30 April 1934, and 1 April 1936 (West Glamorgan CRO).

39. D. Tanner, 'The Pattern of Labour Politics', p. 130. For nursery education, see Swansea County Borough Council Minutes, 18 February 1931 (West Glamorgan CRO).

40. Minutes of Swansea Labour Association, 11 October, 6 December 1933, and 6 May 1936.

41. Minutes of the Pontypridd Trades and Labour Council, 10 October 1932, 28 May and 15 October 1934.

42. For encouraging reports on Rhondda West, see E. Andrews to Miss Sutherland, 6 May 1937 (LP/WORG/37/342, Labour Party Archive). For Caerphilly, see Minutes of Caerphilly Women's Section, 28 September 1934 and 18 July 1938 (National Library of Wales).

43. E. Andrews to Mrs. Sutherland, 27 July 1937 (LP/WORG/37/339).

44. E. Andrews to Mrs. Sutherland, 23 November 1937 and 15 February 1937 (LP/WORG/37/282 and 331). The Monmouthshire ILP organiser, Minnie Pallister, was also aware of the need to encourage women, using what they knew and valued to develop

a socialist perspective. See her pamphlets, *Socialism, Equality and Happiness*, and *Socialism for Women* (undated).

45. E. Andrews to Mrs. Sutherland, 29 November 1937 (LP/WORG/37/290), referring to the position in Merthyr.

46. *Ibid*, 27 May 1937 (LP/WORG/37/423).

47. Minutes of the Swansea Labour Association, 8 May 1935.

48. Minutes of the Newport Labour Party EC, 27 March 1933 (Lliswerry), 19 June 1933; General Committee, 21 July 1933 (rescinding EC decision by 24–10); EC, 31 July and 14 August 1933 (correspondence with NEC).

49. Minutes of the Pontypridd Trades Council and Labour Party, 19 September and 10 October 1931.

50. Monmouthshire County Council, Maternity and Child Welfare Committee Minutes, 3 May 1938 (Gwent CRO).

51. Monmouthshire County Council, *Report Upon Maternity and Child Welfare for the Year 1932*; Glamorgan County Council, *Annual Report of the Medical Officer of Health, 1936*. For popular attitudes, see K. Fisher, '"She Was Quite Happy with the Arrangements I Made": Gender and Birth Control in Britain, 1925–50', *Past & Present*, 169 (2000), and her '"Clearing up Misconception"', p. 114.

52. Swansea County Borough Health Committee Minutes, 30 December 1936 (West Glamorgan CRO).

53. Glamorgan County Council, Public Health and Housing Committee, Midwives Act Special Sub-Committee, 1 and 14 December 1936 (East Glamorgan CRO).

54. Minutes of the Caerphilly Labour Party Women's Section, 30 November 1934.

55. H. Francis and D. Smith, *The Fed: A History of the South Wales Miners in the Twentieth Century* (London, 1980); H. Francis, *Miners Against Fascism: Wales and the Spanish Civil War* (London, 1984), D. Smith, *Aneurin Bevan and the World of South Wales* (Cardiff, 1993).

56. S. Thompson, 'A Proletarian Public Sphere: Working-Class Provision of Medical Services and Care in South Wales, c.1900–48', in A. Borsay (ed.), *Medicine in Wales*.

57. P. Graves, *Labour Women*, pp. 95–6.

58. D. Tanner, 'The Pattern of Labour Politics', pp. 128–34.

59. *Ibid*, pp. 129–34.

60. C Williams, 'Labour and the Challenge of Local Government, 1919–39', in D. Tanner et al, *The Labour Party Wales*, p. 157.

61. For the substantial number of investigations and the legislative context, see M. Williams, '"The Growing Toll of Motherhood": Maternal Mortality in Wales, 1918–39', in P. Michael and C. Webster (eds), *Health and Society in Wales*.

62. See R. Barker, *Education and Politics, 1900–51* (Oxford, 1972), chapter four; J. Stewart, *The Battle for Health: A Political History of the Socialist Medical Association, 1930–51* (London, 1999); E. Durbin, *New Jerusalems: The Labour Party and the Economics of Democratic Socialism* (London, 1985); T. Buchanan, *The Spanish Civil War and the British Labour Movement* (Cambridge, 1991).

63. P. Graves, *Labour Women*, p. 195.

64. See the Advisory Committee on Maternal Mortality (Middleton Papers,

JSM/MAT/1, 2 and 9, Labour Party Archive).

65. Swansea County Borough Health Committee Minutes, 29 November 1937, for consideration of the national circular. For Glamorgan, see Glamorgan County Council, Medical Officer of Health Annual Report 1936; Maternity and Child Welfare Committee Minutes, 8 March 1935 (East Glamorgan CRO).

66. Minutes of the Labour Party Advisory Committee on Education, especially 9 December 1929. See also Minutes of the Education Advisory Committee, 7 February 1938 (Labour Party Archives).

67. Minutes of the Standing Joint Committee of Industrial Women's Organisation, 14 May 1936 and 7 July 1938 (Labour Party Archive). The TUC's more conservative policies on a national health service and on family allowances were unpopular with substantial sections of the Labour Party. Labour issued a national municipal manifesto in 1938, with the emphasis on social and welfare issues. See Minutes of the National Executive Committee (NEC), 27 July 1938.

68. See D. Tanner, 'Labour and its Membership', in D. Tanner, P. Thane and N. Tiratsoo (eds), *Labour's First Century* (Cambridge, 2000), pp. 262–3. Labour captured the London County Council in 1934, and held it in 1937.

69. E. Andrews to Mrs Sutherland concerning Cardiff, Ebbw Vale and Pontypridd, 5 December, 28 July and 25 Aug. 1937 (LP/WORG/37/254, 419, 465). See also the appeal to unity, Minutes of the East Glamorgan Labour Women's Advisory Committee, 20 April 1937 (National Library of Wales).

70. E. Andrews to Mrs. Sutherland, 1 September 1937 (LP/WORG/37/223).

71. See the biographical entries by Ursula Masson in the forthcoming *Dictionary of Labour Biography*, and L. Newman, 'A Distinctive Brand of Politics: Women in the South Wales Labour Party, 1918–39', University of Glamorgan MPhil (2003). For other examples, N. Evans and D. Jones, '"To Help Forward the Great Work of Humanity": Women in the Labour Party in Wales', in D. Tanner et al, *The Labour Party in Wales*, pp. 224–26.

72. Minutes of the East Glamorgan Women's Advisory Committee, 6 March 1926.

73. *Ibid*, 21 September 1934. In Liverpool, Bessie Braddock – another machine politician in a very male-focused party – fought a similar battle, arguing for local authority provision of birth control advice and for better maternity provision. See S. Davies, *Liverpool Labour: Social and Political Influences on the Development of the Labour Party in Liverpool, 1900–39* (Keele, 1996), pp. 180–85.

74. Minutes of the South Wales Regional Council of Labour, 19 September 1938 (National Library of Wales). The South Wales Council was set up to be the voice of Labour's London head office.

75. See above, pp. 177 and 179.

76. K. Fisher, '"Teach the Miners Birth Control": The Delivery of Contraceptive Advice in South Wales, 1918–50', in P. Michael and C. Webster (eds), *Health and Society in Wales*, and 'The Delivery of Birth Control Advice in South Wales between the Wars', in J. Bornat, R. Perks, P. Thompson, J. Walmsley and R. Wilkinson (eds), *Oral History, Health and Welfare* (London, 2000). Research on France also suggests that contemporary ideas on male roles were changing, although not necessarily in ways that

can explain this process. See K.S. Childers, 'Paternity and the Politics of Citizenship in Interwar France', *Journal of Family History*, 26, 1 (2001).

77. For pride in resistance, see *Rhondda Clarion*, September 1935, and *Miners' Monthly*, March 1939. For Labour's associational culture, see preliminary ideas in D. Tanner, 'Labour and its Membership', pp. 259–63.

78. *Labour Woman*, 1 March 1930; Labour Party, *Report of the Annual Conference of the Labour Party, 1920* (London, 1920), p. 120.

79. See, for example, B. D. Vernon, *Margaret Cole, 1893–1980* (London, 1986), chapters five and six. For a fuller discussion, D. Tanner, 'Constructing the Constructors: Institutional Cultures, Associational Life and their Impact on Interwar Politics', Pacific Coast Conference on British Studies, University of California, Berkeley (April, 2004).

80. E. Andrews, *A Woman's Work is Never Done* (Ystrad Rhondda, 1956), p. 7; C. Williams, *Democratic Rhondda: Politics and Society, 1885–1951* (Cardiff, 1996), p. 211.

81. D. Tanner, 'The Pattern of Labour Politics', pp. 128–9; C. Williams, 'Labour and the Challenge of Local Government', p. 152. For women in the 1980s, author's interview with Baroness Gale, Welsh Women's Officer 1976–84 (19 May 2004) and her comments in the *Guardian*, 11 October 2003.

82. Swansea County Borough Education Committee, Schools Attendance Sub-committee Minutes, 10 October 1932 (West Glamorgan CRO).

83. Swansea County Borough, Health Committee Minutes, 4 April 1934 and 29 June 1936.

84. Deputation from Swansea Labour Association, Swansea County Borough Health Committee Minutes, 1 June 1936 (lobbying by central women's committee), and 30 December 1936 (letter from Morriston Labour council).

85. J. Stewart, *The Battle for Health*, pp. 62–64.

86. Swansea County Borough Health Committee Minutes, 1 April 1936. The party stated there 'could be no two opinion' on direct labour, as it had been 'proved conclusively' a success (Minutes of the Swansea Labour Association Special EC and Councillors Meeting, 27 September 1927). For the alternative system of nursing support, see E. Fox, 'Universal Health Care and Self-Help: Paying for District Nursing before the National Health Service', *Twentieth Century British History*, 7, 1 (1996).

87. Minutes of the South Wales Regional Council of Labour, 17 January 1939.

88. *South Wales Evening Post*, 7 and 19 January 1935 (comments of Sir Cyril Kirkpatrick and the mayor).

89. *South Wales Evening Post*, 11 January 1935 (leader), and details of comparisons and visits, 13 and 19 February 1935.

90. *Ibid*, 18 February 1935. In particular, councillor W. T. Mainwaring Hughes supported a regional airport.

91. *Ibid*, 17 January 1935.

92. *Ibid*, 5 March 1935.

93. *Ibid*, 16 October 1935.

94. *Ibid*, 21 October 1935.

95. J. Mark-Lawson et al, 'Gender and Local Politics'. For civic pride in the East Midlands, M. Dickie, 'Town Patriotism in Northampton, 1918–39: An Invented

Tradition', *Midland History*, 17 (1992).
   96. M. Williams, '"The Growing Toll of Maternity"'.

Chapter 10

Sociable Capital: London's Labour Parties, 1918–45

Daniel Weinbren

In 1914, the Labour Party held a tiny number of seats at local and county level in Greater London; in many parts of the capital, its organisation was non-existent.[1] By 1920, it had made spectacular gains across London and, by 1934, when the party in the Commons was at its interwar nadir, it dominated the metropolis, a position it maintained for well over a decade.[2] The principal reason why Labour's vote increased between 1918 and 1945 was that potential Labour voters became comfortable voting for Labour. They came to see that as the best common sense option, because Labour's activists persuaded them it was. By emphasising the norms that aid collective action for mutual benefit, activists created the social capital necessary for the party to grow. London became a more sociable capital through Labour's activists. Across the metropolis, and particularly before it attained power, the Labour Party offered distinctive local versions of socialism in different areas and new roles to women, the Irish and the Jews. Activists were able to build on widespread phenomena, notably the impact of war on people's attitude towards state intervention, the extension of the franchise and canvassing, the decline of the Liberal Party, and widespread enthusiasm for communal leisure pursuits. On attaining power, Labour swiftly implemented immediate and concrete improvements, including better pay and improved housing, and this cemented the Labour vote. In addition, the rapid growth of industry and housing estates in outer London attracted Labour voters from the rest of the country and from east and south London. Concentrated blocs of Labour voters were diffused across the capital.

Duncan Tanner has characterised interwar Labour's policies as advocating 'a national minimum standard of living' in the period up to the early 1920s, then 'trying to show the relevance of socialism to everyday life' and, in the 1930s insisting on 'practical measures for increasing employment'.[3] In much of London, Labour could not rely on strong trade unions, local traditions of communal solidarity, or the prerequisites for participation in local civil society, social interaction, residential stability and a positive view of the local environment. All these policies required advocates at local level, who could ensure that they became part of the parochial common sense. Such an aim was reflected in the Woolwich Labour Party slogan 'the Labour Party is not politics – it is life. Do you belong?'

Woolwich was a solid Labour seat yet, as one militant shop steward recalled, there was little talk of politics in the principal workplace for the local electorate, the Arsenal.[4] Labour was able to become the 'people's party' because activists were able to offer alternatives to daily insecurities which, through their familiarity, appeared to be above the party political.[5] The case of London bolsters Philips' view that the popularity of the party between the wars derived from 'an indefinite sense that it was to be trusted better than other parties'.[6]

Different Policies and Practices

There was recognition of the need for different approaches at local level, as an instruction pamphlet for activists made explicit: 'Your job is to interpret that policy in terms of its impact upon the lives of the people around you'. In Stepney, 'every night at familiar street corners you could stand and listen to them speaking at meetings, Labour men', whereas in suburbia the party adopted the methods of door-to-door sales representatives; as one agent said, 'Labour's canvassers are Labour's salesmen'.[7] The diversity of emphases within London was also indicated by the variety of slogans. The focus in Woolwich was on uniting the town behind a Labour-led campaign for jobs at the state arsenal that dominated employment in the area. The party offered an 'appeal to our fellow citizens, the electors of Britain'. In Hendon, a candidate focused on modernity, 'Vote Labour for planned progress and efficiency'; and in Brentwood, the sole Labour councillor was 'recognised as one of the moderates of the Labour Party and probably owed his success to this being well understood'.[8] Beatrice Webb characterised the Poplar Labour Party as 'essentially a working-class benefit society', and in West Ham Labour's slogan was 'Local Labour for Local Work'.[9]

Between the wars, approximately a third of Stepney's Labour dominated council were Jewish and a third Irish, even though these groups did not make up 66 per cent of the local electorate.[10] Liberals, despite their views on Home Rule, were viewed with suspicion because of their association with nonconformist views of drink and education. It was only when they stood an Irish candidate against a Labour candidate from India in Battersea in 1929 that they got the Irish vote.[11] The Conservative Party, as the *London Catholic Herald* declared in 1923, 'is the party of privilege and monopoly. It is repulsive to every Catholic of democratic instincts'.[12] Labour made a formal pact with the United Irish League, had close ties to the Irish Self-Determination League and promoted Catholics. There were 12 amongst the 43 victorious Labour Party Stepney councillors in 1919.[13] In Battersea during the interwar years, there were generally seven or eight Irish Catholics among the Labour Party councillors on a council of 55, considerable numbers in proportion to the number of Irish Catholics in the borough.

The Conservatives were also associated with the anti-alien legislation of 1905 and 1919, the wartime campaign against German Jews, the post-1917 campaign against Russian Jews, and discriminatory county council housing and education policies. Liberals gained support from Jewish voters when they put up Jewish candidates such as Miriam Moses, Ida Samuel and Nettie Adler. Labour not only supported Jewish candidates, such as Sam Tobin, Stepney's first Jewish mayor, but also had many Jewish members.[14] Jews tended to favour Jewish candidates. In 1925, two Jewish anti-socialists were returned, against the trend, in Spitalfields East and Mile End West in preference to two non-Jewish Labour Party candidates. The Labour Party won every seat in Stepney in 1934 and kept them all in 1937 except one, which was won by a Jewish Communist. At that time, there were close links between Jewish councillor Morry Davis and the leaders of Stepney's Catholic community, in particular Jack Sullivan, who nominated Davis for mayor twice, and Jerry Long, who nominated him a third time.[15] The party focused not on further Jewish immigration to London or against anti-Semitism, but on support for Zionism.[16] From 1917–39, Labour supported Jewish rights of settlement in Palestine; indeed, 'Labour Party files rarely record so consistent a pursuit of policy'.[17] Ramsay MacDonald's *A Socialist in Palestine* (1922) credited Jewishness and Labour as twinned elements of 'good socialism'. Morrison was 'passionately pro-Zionist'.[18] When Poale Zion threatened to campaign in a Whitechapel by-election against a Labour government plan to curb Jewish migration to Palestine, the Labour Party had to concede.[19]

Activists aided the social integration into their communities of Labour policies by maintaining the network of civic life. This often involved evoking ties of friendship and kinship in order to convince people of the value of voting Labour. It was activists who created the sense of a Labour tradition. They took socialist values into their homes and drew on their home lives to make socialist values. One West Ham resident, elected as a Labour councillor in 1932, would 'talk politics and about the unemployment in the area, he commanded a large group of visitors and few disagreed with him'.[20] A number of activists made sense of their own politics by reference to their families. Jack Hart's father, an orphan, was influenced by George Lansbury's kindness during a visit to the orphanage. His mother remembered having 'to go on the RO' [that is receive benefits from the Relieving Officer] and that made her 'indignant'. His older sister and her husband were active in the Labour Party. Jack was elected ward secretary aged 16, elected to the council in 1935 aged 23, and became mayor in 1950. He also noted:

> My sister's loyalty to the Labour Party has not been based on a left wing belief but in the ordinary people with whom she lived in East Ham which she has known all her life. They're the people she is happy with and understands.[21]

Other activists recalled family members in the party and how the social and kinship ties were of importance to their long-term membership of the party. A number of women activists came from backgrounds where political activity was the norm. Annie Lansbury, daughter of George Lansbury, was involved in Labour politics, as was Susannah Turnbull, whose father and brother were active in the Woolwich Labour Party. Edith Pine was the daughter of an active trade unionist and the sister-in-law of Will Crooks.[22]

Activists made the most of the possibilities of political links as well as ethnic, kinship and cultural ties. In those areas where Labour was firmly in control, notably Woolwich, activists spurned Communists, as was national party policy.

Elsewhere, in a dozen places in London in the 1920s, local parties forged links with the Communists. They shared power with them for nine years on Bethnal Green council. Battersea had five councillors with membership of both parties and returned a joint MP representing both parties. The national party was increasingly unhappy about such ties and had disbanded eight local parties by 1930. Connections continued throughout the 1930s and, in 1940, the Hampstead party was disaffiliated because of its Communist sympathies. Activists also drew on the Liberals. In 1918, Liberals formed the basis of the Greenwich Labour Party, while a Progressive Alliance was formed in Camberwell North and Lambeth Kennington in 1922. However, both the Communists and the Liberals stood against Labour as well. Moreover, the decline of the Liberals (the Liberal vote for London County Council elections was just over 40 per cent in 1913, 24 per cent in 1919 and after that it never rose above 17 per cent) reduced the number of three-cornered electoral fights which had split the non-Labour vote.

The focus on diversity was also helpful in maintaining the local vote. After McDonald formed a 'National' government in August 1931, West Ham's focus on local issues probably helped Labour to retain all its seats bar one in the October 1931 council elections.[23] A 14-year-old East Ham activist, recalling her father's reaction to formation of the 'National' government, also noted that, while he hated MacDonald, he continued to campaign for Labour:

> We had a beautiful picture of [MacDonald] in our passage. Dad's idol. My dad's idol. I came home from school, sitting there waiting for him to come in, and there was such a commotion. We'd heard him come in with his key and there was such a commotion ... There's Dad in the passage, he's got the frame round his neck... and he's standing like this: 'You bloody traitor, you bloody –' tearing the picture up into little pieces ... And afterwards he came in and Mum said: 'What's all that about, about him being a traitor and all that?' So he said to me: 'You saw what I did?' 'Yeah.' So he said, 'Well, I think he's killed the Labour Party.'

This activist went on to help with a rent strike: 'they all marched to Bow County Court. Dad was the leader. And the repairs had to be done'.[24] Labour made it possible for local activists to despise MacDonald and still campaign on a central plank of Labour's platform, housing. Similarly, in 1924 and 1925, the Labour women's conference supported the dissemination of birth control information at public clinics. The main party voted against this in 1927, but women simply carried on campaigning at a local level and gained a partial victory in 1930.

National Changes

Important though local distinctions were, several changes at national level were also of particular significance for Labour. Notable amongst these were the extension of the franchise leading to the greater involvement of women, the development of leisure time, the importance of patriotism, and the impact of the wars. London's local government electorate grew from about 15 per cent of the population to 50 per cent following legislation in 1918. However, far more people in London could vote in general elections than in local ones because those in furnished rooms and lodging houses, transient people and servants were barred from the municipal suffrage. Furthermore, business owners, 45 per cent of London's electorate and 84 per cent in the City, had additional votes. It was not until 1948 that many of these anomalies disappeared. Labour contrasted the difference between its roots within constituencies and wards with the absence of the business voters for the areas where they could vote. In Poplar, the Labour Party issued leaflets stating: 'We all live in your midst. If rates and rents are high, we suffer with you', whilst local employers were 'wealthy plutocrats' who 'would not be found dead in Poplar except for the purpose of making money'. Riva Stanton recalled that: 'you could get hold of [West Ham councillor and later MP] Tommy [Groves] at any time of the day or night. If he was out in the street he'd talk to you. If you went to his house, no matter what he was doing, he'd take you in.'[25] Party activist Dorothy Deeming, born in 1925 in Poplar, also recalled the Labour councillors; 'they weren't isolated. They lived amongst you, they worked amongst you and they came round and took your subs'.[26]

One-and-a-half-million women joined the electorate in 1928, and Labour campaigned to attract support from women. Before the Great War, it had involved women 'as canvassers and fundraisers' far more than the Conservatives, partly because it had fewer financial resources.[27] Between the wars, women became the majority of individual party members.[28] The party ran a newspaper and conferences for women, and every June there was a Women's Week with processions, such as that of 1925, which attracted 3,000 women across Greater London.[29] By 1937, almost 37 per cent of the workforce of Greater London consisted of women and the Labour Party fought for their rights. When, in 1924, the Tory-dominated London County Council (LCC) forced female employees to leave their jobs as the male unemployment rate was high, it was Labour county councillor (and later MP) Susan Lawrence who managed to save school cleaners from being scapegoated for the widespread problem of unemployment. She showed that those who were married were not necessarily supported by their husbands. On the occasion of a strike in 1928, by women workers at Rego's of Edmonton, the strikers received the support of Ramsay MacDonald and Ben Tillett, and were offered council and co-operative movement facilities. Their strike was against new machines, short-time and the transfer of the factory from Bethnal Green and, in marching through the streets singing their protests, they were taking the mores of the East End to the outer reaches of the metropolis. Pamela Graves argues that the party as a whole did not always recognise the value of women's activities. According to the male definition, fundraising, canvassing and keeping the labour community together through social events were merely supportive services not 'real' politics. Yet, they were very effective in sustaining the financial viability and evangelical spirit of the local party.

However, men, many of whom were Labour Party members through their trade union, praised the work of women raising money and canvassing. Mr F.A. Broad from Edmonton Labour Party told the 1929 Labour Party conference that 'locally, we raise and spend in the work of the Movement perhaps ten times the amount that is handled through the central organisations and the bulk of that money is raised by women'. He added that 'nine-tenths of my canvassing is done by women'.[30] Herbert Morrison argued that a model member should not be a fiery orator but have a 'mind like a card index', and that 'canvassing on the doorstep is of much greater consequence than holding forth at the street corner'.[31] Talking of the victories across London in 1934, Annie Barnes (who was returned as a local councillor at that election) noted Morrison's attitude towards women and canvassing:

> I think this victory was due to Herbert Morrison ... I remember he used to send directives to our women's section with instructions about campaigning and I put it down to his encouragement about campaigning that we worked so hard at going round visiting and making members and building up the Party.[32]

Women were involved in raising Labour's profile in other ways. For example, the North Tottenham women's section held meetings outside the Labour Exchange to protest at the injustice and indignity meted out by the Relieving Officer, and were active against blacklegs in the General Strike of 1926. In 1934, of Labour's 729 borough councillors, 20 per cent (150) were women.[33] Labour made the most of its women candidates. Leslie Hilliard, who organised Edith Summerskill's victorious 1937 by-election campaign in West Fulham, made sure that he included sepia-tinted posters of the red-haired candidate in the campaign.[34] The party also publicised the fact that the first woman on Harlington council, the capital's first woman mayor, and London's first woman JP, were all Labour.

Activists also drew on shifting trends within the wider society. As people's leisure time increased, the Labour Party was able to hold social events to attract new members and reaffirm the commitment of those already in the party. Measuring the effectiveness of such events in terms of voter turnout is difficult, but they helped to sustain morale and build funds and communities. According to a survey in the 1940s, a time when the national party was in the doldrums, the social activities of the Tottenham women's section and the Bethnal Green Labour club's sports facilities helped to maintain local interest in the party.[35] Ealing Labour Party, founded in 1927, had 3,000 members and nine council seats within a decade. It organised dances, whist drives, football, cricket, a choir and dramatics, and ran an orchestra and a Socialist Sunday School attended by 700 children with its own naming ceremonies and harvest festivals, fetes and sports days.[36] Hendon Labour Party ran two football teams, an orchestra, a dance band and a sports club. Interviews with activists carried out in the 1930s indicate the popularity of whist drives in Willesden and Lewisham.[37] Labour attracted people by linking socialism and fun. Violette Boulton recalled how she and her sister sang and danced their way round London's Labour Party socials in the 1920s.[38] Two Tottenham activists, Tom Riley and Olive Rainbird, remembered the League of Youth hut and grounds on Tottenham Marshes in the 1930s. They both spent a great deal of their time there and, as the latter recalled, 'We had a great deal of fun in those days as well as serious politicking'.[39] Grace Oakden, born 1912, remembered the Clarion youth hostel in Hoddesdon, Hertfordshire.

Leagues of Youth from all over London used to go down there at weekends, camping.
There was a big house there. We used to have wonderful times at weekends there.
Long discussions into the night. Quite a big social programme, dances. A wonderful
way of meeting people from all over London.[40]

Set in ten acres of grounds, the hostel opened in 1933 and had a library, two
pavilions for dancing, and facilities for lectures and classes as well as for various
sports. In the summer of 1934, 13,000 Labour youth camped there mainly those
from the London area. Jack Hart recalled interwar East Ham:

If you joined the Labour Party in those days you could count on a social evening every
Saturday night. Perhaps one ward would have a concert party. There'd be a social.
Children's parties two or three times a year ... If you were interested in debate and
discussion, we'd send out the agenda and there'd be a speaker and we'd ask our
members to come along and register their opinions about those things which were not
easily solved.[41]

At Bermondsey Labour Party's monthly meetings:

discussions would take place on the important political events of the day. Tired, white-
faced dockers and their wives [after displaying] a seriousness of purpose and a down-
to-earth understanding of issues ... would join in singing 'The Red Flag'.[42]

Jim Evans, whose mother was an active Conservative, recalled that on the
Roehampton estate built by the Labour-run LCC, 'at the Labour Club there were a
lot of women helpers and they used to organise games and all sorts of things. We
would then finish up by singing "The Red Flag"'.[43] Some of the events that
brought support for the party were less well orchestrated, as Louis Heren recalled
when he suggested that while Shadwell, where he was born in 1919,

was not a homogeneous community ... a great unifying force for many was politics ...
Elections were emotional occasions. The comings and goings of the candidates were
events, especially on election nights, and processions would march to the Town Hall in
Cable Street.[44]

Ensuring that members enjoyed themselves and that the Labour Party was
associated with popular entertainment, helped nurture the party and create a sense
of its rootedness in a locality. This was particularly important in the many parts of
London where there were new arrivals in the area.

Labour was also able to relate its politics to patriotism. In Lewisham in the
1930s, the two local Tory MPs had connections with Mussolini and Hitler and
Labour offered itself as the party of the nation against agents of external foes.[45]
Many within the party saw a link between electoral success and close ties with
working-class conservatism.[46] A number of those who stood for election in London
stressed their involvement in local activities and tied this to their support of
popular imperialism or patriotism. Notable amongst these were National Socialist
MPs Will Thorne (West Ham), who paraded in his uniform as Colonel of the Essex
Volunteers, and Jack Jones (Silvertown), while Woolwich East's Will Crooks

initiated the singing of the National Anthem in the Commons on the declaration of war in 1914.[47] Ramsay McDonald lost the Woolwich East seat in the 1921 by-election following Crooks' death. The anti-war Scot, promised to Aberavon at the next election, was beaten by a local Tory with a VC who, like Crooks, was born in the workhouse. The local Conservative newspaper characterised the contest as 'pacifism vs patriotism' and the result as 'a patriot succeeds a patriot'.[48] Labour only regained the seat when it stood what its own local paper called 'one who is really a Woolwich man', Harry Snell.[49] Patriotism and local links also played a part in the 1945 manifesto of Percy Daines, 'The People's Advocate', prospective MP for East Ham, London:

> You have before you a man of the PEOPLE; a tough Londoner; a Trade Unionist; Co-operative Committee-man; ex-Councillor; ex-Royal Engineer (this war). A vigorous, forthright Britisher, with an International outlook; a Family Man, son in the Royal Navy. Advocate at Party Conferences of the Soldiers' Charter. *Daines* knows the value of every shilling to a worker's home. DAINES IS ONE OF US.[50]

Field has argued that in 1945 there was 'a great deal of grass roots organisational activity [which] helped to build a sense of nation as an authentic and democratic community. [Labour] managed to monopolise the new mood'.[51] For much of London, such activity was important throughout the interwar period.

Labour's successes after both world wars are partly attributable to the greater number of opportunities that the development of the wartime state at local level opened to Labour activists. By 1920, Labour had gained control of 13 inner-London boroughs and of West Ham, Enfield, Edmonton, Hayes and Harlington. It also held seats in Yiewsley and on seven other councils. These immediate post-war results cannot be attributed to the organisational skills of the party activists as, Woolwich apart, there were no parties with individual members in London. In 1914, Stepney, Camberwell, Bethnal Green and five other inner-London boroughs had no Labour parties, and it was only in 1914 that a London Labour Party was formed.[52] Yiewsley Labour Party was only created in 1918 and, as the mayor of Limehouse noted, 1919 was the 'first time the political Labour Movement was organised'.[53] Nor can the victories be attributed to the impact of MPs. London County Council boundaries were coterminous with those of the parliamentary seats, but only four of Labour's 57 Labour MPs were returned for Greater London constituencies in 1918. Although in the 1920s and 1930s Labour's success in London was related to the national government being of a different hue, of greater significance was the rapid wartime development of the local state. The pre-Great War London County Council, while it ran some tramways, steamboats, stores and the direct labour department, did not directly control water, gas, docks or electricity. The development of local rationing schemes during the war provided administrative roles for labour activists. They became the bulwarks of the idea that the state apparatus was the most appropriate means of securing social justice and they spread this notion through their communities.

There was also a direct relationship between the development of state activity in the Second World War and the increase in the Labour vote in 1945. Again, although some activists were in reserved occupations, Labour's organisation was by no means at its peacetime peak. In the country as a whole, individual membership of the party almost halved between 1939 and 1942, dropping from 409,000 to 219,000. Conscription, evacuation and bombing made maintaining the party in London a difficult task. In 1945, Labour won a majority in the Commons, kept control of the county, and won over 56 per cent of the votes and over 75 per cent of the inner-London borough seats. These were the highest percentages it ever achieved in the entire 62 years that the boroughs existed. By comparison, the Tory percentages in 1945 at London county and London borough level were their lowest ever. They received less than 35 per cent and fewer than 23 per cent of the votes. Throughout the period 1918–45, state intervention at the level at which people lived their lives was of significance for the party and largely led to increased support.

Municipal Socialism

Housing, health and education could all be influenced by Labour as they fell within the remit of local authorities. Whether in power, as in Woolwich, or not, as in Kingston, Labour campaigned for tenants. In order to provide housing for workers who flocked to Woolwich during the Great War, the government built estates locally. The chair of the Tenants Association was local Labour activist, later MP, Jack Mills, and the vice-president was local Labour MP Will Crooks. It was the Tenants' Association that organised successful actions over rents and conditions. As the Fabians noted, 'landlordism is easier to attack than capitalism where the only large industry is government work'.[54] Once the war was over, many Arsenal workers were tied to work at the Arsenal because if they left work they would face eviction, at a time of a national housing shortage, from the accommodation built for them during the war. Others had no wish to leave their homes because as tenants with controlled rents, under the 1915 legislation they would face the prospect of an increase in rent. Owners did not wish to try to find buyers in an area with few prospects of work once the war was over. The local Labour Party solution was to campaign for security and stability through diversification of production of non-munitions at the Arsenal. This required support from parliament, not defiance of it. The approach was exemplified in the local party newspaper headline, written when there was much local squatting, 'Tenants – watch Parliament'.[55] The party gained support. There were 2,000 members in 1919, 5,500 in 1927. Despite being in power continuously between the wars in West Ham, Labour built little. However, this lack of dynamism did not adversely affect the party for there was little land on which to build; the council focused on improving the housing stock and it sought to associate its opponents with slum housing. In the 1930s, Kingston Labour Party was disbanded for trying to form links with the Communists. However, the party was revived, held street meetings and ran a campaign for the implementation of sanitary legislation and of the Rent Control Act. Some local private tenants were able to claim up to two years back rent and the rats were cleared out of their homes. The Labour Party activists responsible for these victories were treated 'like heroes', and a rally for the tenants attracted 2,000 people and raised £478.[56] In Putney, one activist cited the example of a delegation to the town hall to get bomb-damaged houses repaired: 'that sort of thing gradually built up support for the party and that's what made the difference'.[57]

There is a correlation between Labour's association with house building and an increase in its vote, as councillors in Hammersmith and Stepney recognised. 'Housing and health I think dominated the politics of the Labour Party at that time' said Naomi Wolff, while Phil Piratin thought that 'many of the voters – stirred by the tenants' struggles ... turned with disgust away from Toryism to Labour'.[58] The *Barnet Press* in 1926 linked new buildings with the rise in the Labour vote, 'with the erection of small dwellings in Mays Lane and Barnet lane, the Arkley ward has become a Labour stronghold'.[59] It was a popular perception of the relationship between the working class and the Labour Party. *The Times* noted of the 'most remarkable' Labour victory in Fulham, that there was 'a curious paradox that the development of new housing estates, for which the Labour Party cannot claim credit, seems to increase the voting strength of the Labour Party'.[60] Labour strengthened its position by being closely associated with slum clearance and new housing. The dispersal policy of the LCC may have aided the spread of support for the Labour Party. Elected at London county level in 1934 on the slogan 'A Healthy London: Up with the Houses, Down with the Slums', the LCC re-housed 20,000 people from 1934 to 1936, and by the end of the 1930s had built 190 inner-London estates and six out-county estates.[61] Labour leader Herbert Morrison wanted to keep people near to their workplaces and original homes, possibly to preserve the Labour-voting working class within the LCC boundaries. He was also constrained because there was considerable opposition from large landowners to the out-estates, Labour strongholds in London had their own building programmes, and Conservative boroughs obstructed county council plans. Labour-controlled Bermondsey built 2,700 dwellings between 1929 and 1938; Finsbury, Fulham and Woolwich all had extensive housing programmes, whereas Tory-controlled boroughs built very little. Morrison acquired 565 areas for the Green Belt around London, and largely built within the county council area. In 1936, the LCC identified part of Stoke Newington as suitable for a new estate. It sought to demolish 185 Victorian villas and replace them with housing for 1,660 dwellings. Woodberry Down was built despite local council objections to this 'planting thousands of Labour voters in the heart of a Conservative area'.[62] The move may have helped Labour to gain two seats in the South Hornsey ward of Stoke Newington in 1945, but there were other factors at work as the party gained 18 seats overall in the borough.

In Hendon, the local Tory MP referred to the LCC's Watling Estate (on which work started in 1927) as a 'Little Moscow'. There was also a letter in the local newspaper referring to Watling and the 'red tentacles of that housing octopus'.[63] In fact, the estate only returned Labour councillors and, on the occasion that the Communists did stand, they got a tiny number of votes. Such antagonism by middle-class residents of Burnt Oak and Mill Hill may well have helped those on the estate to identify with Labour.[64] In the face of antagonism from those disturbed by their arrival, new residents on LCC estates created bonds with their fellow tenants which were often expressed in political terms.[65] Others brought their values with them from inner-London.[66] A survey of Becontree tenants in 1934 found that 10.5 per cent came from Poplar and a further 21.8 per cent from Hackney, Stepney and Islington.[67] A further investigation, 29 years later, found that nearly half the residents were East Enders by origin and concluded that 'Dagenham is the East End reborn'.[68] In 1925, after the Becontree estate was built, the Labour Party swiftly won power on the new Dagenham council. In 1926, the party gained eight seats on the newly enlarged 16-seat council.[69] In 1928, representatives of Chadwell Heath Tenants' Association, dominated by the Labour Party, stood for Dagenham council and had a majority throughout the 1930s.[70] The Labour Party also made gains on the board of guardians and the county council. The significance of these results is more evident when they are placed in the context of other results within Greater London. St Helier, a new LCC estate partly in Merton and Morden, Surrey, was second to Becontree in size. Four thousand people lived there by 1936, many of them artisans from Battersea. There were a few factories in the area before the Great War, notably the sweet manufacturer, Pascalls, and there was a Labour Party presence in Merton and Morden in 1919, two Labour victories in 1921, and three Labour councillors by 1927. In 1934, after the Labour Party had been involved in a successful campaign for rent reduction, the Labour Party gained a further three seats and the county council seat of Merton South East. On the other hand, in those places where Labour's home-producing programme was seen to be a failure, it lost votes. In Islington, Labour's 1919 policy of converting houses into flats was 'at best only a qualified success' and it soon lost power.[71] Similarly, in Finsbury, delays and disputes about the Spa Green Estate (opened 1946) may have played a part in Labour losing seats on the local council.[72]

The new estates and facilities with which Labour became associated were not only for those from London. They were also for those who moved to the capital as its industrial base grew. Throughout the period there was not one dominant employer which determined the economic conditions of Londoners. The most common pattern in London was of casual employment, such as at the docks or in numerous small-scale workshops in the south and east where firms directly employed only a few people. Making clothes, shoes or furniture was still common in London because of the high cost of space and the lack of incentive to stockpile fashionable and seasonal goods. Heavy industry was not attracted because of the distance from supplies of coal and raw materials. In such circumstances, trade unionism was difficult to establish and, in 1920, the number of Londoners in unions was less than a third of that in parts of the north east of England.[73] There were large factories in London, notably in Woolwich, Enfield and Stratford, and the party was strong in those areas. The industrial base grew throughout the period. Factories opened in Wimbledon and Beddington, while Hendon had six large factories in 1911, and 65 by 1931, employing over 13,500 people. Over four-fifths of the 644 new factories opened in Britain between 1932 and 1937 were in Greater London. The changing economy of Greater London can be 'understood as a series of industrial towns: Erith, West Ham, Silvertown, Deptford to the east, Acton, Park Royal, Harlesden to the west.[74] Workers in these areas provided support for

Labour. In 1934, the *Daily Herald* reported Labour's first seat on the Middlesex County Council as being 'due to the development of Greenford [west London] which has grown from a small village into an important industrial area'.[75] The newer industries of west London attracted migrants from the depressed areas who 'brought with them well developed trade union traditions, especially the ex-miners from South Wales'.[76] People from Porth in Wales moved to Hayes in west London and, in the early 1920s, the union won agreement to a closed shop at EMI which employed 25,000.[77] In such a way, the employees of the gramophone company contributed to the success of the Labour Party in Hayes and Harlington. The Labour Party gained power there in 1915, when munitions production in the locality was at its height, and it held power for all but five years between the wars, even though some of these jobs were lost after the Great War.[78] Labour also benefited when people of Irish origin who were loyal to the party moved from inner-London to work in food processing in Willesden or at Ford in Dagenham. There was a similar pattern of movement by Jews. In 1903, 80 per cent of London Jewry lived in Stepney, Bethnal Green and Poplar. By the end of the 1920s, only 46 per cent lived in these three areas. Their move away from the East End and manual labour did not aid the Conservatives; it spread the Labour vote.[79]

Health and education were central elements of Labour's London county-wide appeal. In 1934, Labour's campaign slogans included 'For the Children's Sake' and the party drew on the first major publication of the Socialist Medical Association, founded 1930, *For a Healthy London* (1931).[80] Hospitals were modernised, outpatients' services introduced, maternity services improved, and the Finsbury Health Centre, 'one of the most successful and conspicuous achievements of the Labour controlled council', was built.[81] It featured on a Second World War Army Bureau of Current Affairs poster designed to encourage people to see it as part of the better Britain for which they were fighting. In Bermondsey, the health centre featured a solarium, clinics for ear nose, throat and eye ailments, an antenatal clinic, and a dental surgery. Falls in the local death rate and infant mortality rate were attributed to Labour's amenities. These issues were central to Labour outside the LCC. In interwar West Ham, class sizes were reduced, provision for secondary education doubled, and for higher education nearly doubled. Footwear and meals were provided, and scholarships, nursery and special needs provision improved. Six hospitals were either built or extended, and nine new clinics and two swimming pools built.

When in position to do so, many Labour Party councillors helped their supporters and voters. This could range from personal to municipal action. East Ham councillor Annie Taylor organised a boot fund and arranged free dinners for children. Stepney mayor Clem Attlee 'gave away large sums of money from his income as a lecturer so that mothers could buy shoes for their children, or tenants catch up with the rent'.[82] People gave skills as well. Jack Hart, born in East Ham in 1912, recalled the construction 'by voluntary labour, by trade union folks' of the East Ham Labour Hall, adding:

The Labour Party provided so much education in those days. Every Sunday night at the Labour Hall they had a speakers' meeting ... a public meeting open to everybody to come along and hear well-known people. [83]

Labour parties of London focused on building on electoral successes at the civic level and moulding local communities through municipal action, paying attention to leisure. West Ham's Labour council opened libraries, provided music in the parks and planted trees. In Poplar, the Labour Party frequently held mass meetings and marches which 'served as a crucial means of communication'. When Poplar council was surcharged for refusing to raise a rate, one of its responses was to call a special meeting:

no attempt was made to restrain the crowd which packed the gallery and the body of the hall [and which sang] not only 'The Red Flag' but also a popular song, 'I want some money'. [84]

Bermondsey tried to create a distinct Labour Party municipal culture through large print pamphlets, electric moving picture signs, lantern slides, lectures, posters, newspaper advertisements and articles.[85] Between 1923 and 1948, it made at least 30 films which were first shown on a projector van which toured the municipality and later in air raid shelters. The films portrayed a new community which wore cheap, modern comfortable clothing instead of buying unclean clothes from unlicensed street traders; which attended health clinics, admired the new council housing, and which proudly looked up to the Bermondsey borough flag commissioned by the Labour Party.[86] As with other interventions that the party made into popular cultural activities, it is difficult to prove a direct relationship between votes and policies, but the activists at the time clearly saw a correlation.

Activists also saw opportunities to use the municipality to further the party's fortunes. While there was broad agreement that the Labour Party should favour expenditure on social services and further municipal trading, and that its local authorities should act as a model employer, this did not prevent councils being used as channels for class or kin interests. In Hackney, the electricity profits funded a pre-election cut in rates.[87] In Stepney, electricity was supplied only to firms which employed trade unionists and it was turned off during the 1926 General Strike. Hammersmith Council ensured that those who lived in dwellings without bathrooms could use the public baths without paying.[88] Sometimes, activists were able to use the offices of the municipality to weld local campaigns into a bloc for the Labour Party. In Poplar, where over 60 per cent of the population lived and worked in the borough and there was little formal regular waged work, Labour focused on the relief of casual workers. The party raised the pay of council workers, initiated public works to aid employment, increased relief payments — which were also made to strikers and refused to prosecute those caught red-handed removing council property to burn as fuel. As a result, 29 councillors and the mayor were sent to prison.[89] Two of the gaoled Poplar councillors were elected to the Commons, the local party had thousands of members and, in 1925, the Labour Party won all 24 seats on the Poplar board of guardians. In 1934, one of the first acts of the Labour-dominated LCC was to extend relief to 11,000 people who could not claim it before and reduce the more punitive elements of poor relief.

Some party activities reflected accepted practice amongst organised labour in east London. To work in the docks, the major printing establishments or bakeries, an applicant had to approach the relevant union and be supported by somebody on the inside. In some areas, the success of the party led casual labourers to see the possibilities for material or social advance. On Labour councils, trade union members working for the council negotiated with fellow trade unionists on the council over wages and conditions. Moreover, through involvement in the Labour Party manual workers could gain status and careers that would otherwise be denied to them. The initials SBC of Stepney Borough Council were said to stand for Sisters, Brothers, Cousins, because of the many councillors' relatives who had jobs working for the council. The *National Review* attributed Labour's success to corruption, calling subsidised housing 'a great asset to the Party managers', and municipal rents 'one of the best examples of graft'. On Becontree, the Independent councillors made much of jobs and council houses being given to councillors' relatives in 1928, and the *Saturday Review* claimed that 'in Socialist areas only Socialists need apply as tenants'.[90] Labour's 1929 conference affirmed model standing orders for Labour groups on local authorities which emphasised the distinction between councillors and those who worked for the council. However, an enquiry in 1937 found that Stepney council officials who wished to engage casual labour were required to apply to the chief whip for a list of Labour Party members. There was a similar enquiry in Bermondsey.[91] Labour was accepting conventional values in that the Conservatives had long been associated with offers of material help. According to a Labour councillor, first elected in 1934 in Stepney, on the eve of poll the Tory candidate 'had carts sent round all the poorest parts of Stepney, leaving blankets and bags of coal for the people'.[92] Jack Hart, an East Ham councillor from 1935, made a similar point:

> In the late 1920s, council membership was in the hands of local tradesmen ... Half the members were in business in the town. I'm not suggesting that they all took advantage of the fact but it was the case in those days that the gentleman who happened to have the grocer's shop in the High Street might easily have the privilege of supplying the school dining rooms with their fare ... They were privileged people who took advantage of their council membership. It was often said 'He's on the council, he's going to sell his butchery to the local authority'.

In West Ham, it was the provision made for local people by the council rather than the activists who helped sustain Labour in power on the council almost continuously for 90 years from 1898. Labour had been on the council since 1891 and the school board from 1892, when a Labour MP was also returned.[93] Control of the apparatus of the four local constituency parties was in the hands of a few men and membership was never high. For almost the whole period between 1918 and 1945, the four constituency parties of West Ham claimed in their returns to the national Labour Party that each had only 180 members. This was the minimum (until 1930) permitted numbers to enable the constituencies to send delegates to conference. The most popular of the four constituency parties never had more than half the national average number of members for a constituency party.[94]

In 1931, 47 per cent of West Ham's workforce were categorised as unskilled and semi-skilled workers, and the sizeable works department provided better wages than many private local employers as it paid union rates. For a man to get a job with the council it was alleged that he had to be a member of West Ham United Football Club, the Labour Party and a freemason.[95] Between the wars, those on the council could claim free travel on corporation trams, cars to take them home after late meetings and telephones for committee chairs. In 1943, when Labour held 57 of the 64 council seats, the Labour group had ceased to meet in many areas.

> The word retired may be interpreted exactly for Labour in the borough has now grown old and sleepy ... and do, politically, nothing. Labour election is so safe that candidates have no need to qualify themselves well as was necessary in the past.[96]

This situation continued after the war, when many younger people might have become engaged in local politics. By the 1960s and 1970s there was still little discussion of policy.[97] There was also overt racism and in some areas ward meetings were rarely called.[98] By 1974, the Labour leader had been in power for 34 years. It was only after two MPs were deselected and a number of councillors left their posts and were replaced by local Asians that Labour's support rose.[99] Labour in West Ham focused on a narrowly and rigidly defined group of supporters over a long period of time. Like Labour elsewhere in the capital, it looked after its own. This meant that the party was not renewed or invigorated, but it was successful between 1918 and 1945.

The Waning of Diversity

During the course of the years 1918–45, the national party gradually lost some of its enthusiasm for locally distinctive Labour parties. Electoral success was linked to national economic and social interventions which would have an impact on Conservative as well as Labour areas, and to national strategies which placed greater emphasis on citizenship than ethnicity. Rational, organised canvassing was also preferred to rallies and demonstrations. At the beginning of the period, the party encouraged municipal socialism. In the 1920s, there were eight attempts by Labour MPs to introduce a Local Authorities Enabling Bill which would have allowed local authorities to own the means of production. Party leader MacDonald argued at the 1926 conference that the reason why 'Poplar had a different policy from Stepney and Stepney had a different policy from other boroughs' was that whilst principles were laid down centrally, it was impossible and undesirable for details to be determined at national level.[100] However, such ideas soon appeared less attractive. According to the leader of the London Labour Party, Herbert Morrison, Poplar's well-publicised battle over the equalisation of the rates of London lost the party votes in 1922 and encouraged Conservatives, who might have stayed at home, to vote.[101] Within a few years, the possibility of power at the county or national level became more likely and differences between local and national perspectives became more evident. Morrison organised a postal ballot in order to make the London Labour Party the single borough party in London.[102] By 1945, after a war had been run from Whitehall, Attlee's government had a marked enthusiasm for centralised power.

There were other problems associated with encouraging an identification between Labour and specific ethnic communities. Attlee, recalling his time as Limehouse mayor in 1919–20, noted that the Stepney party 'had a considerable contingent of Irish Catholics and a number of Jews, and some diplomacy was needed to get a harmonious working relationship'.[103] After Attlee had completed his term, the Labour Party promoted a Jew for mayor. An Irish faction supported Joseph Cahill, who was elected to the post with the support of the opposition. Cahill and his faction were expelled, the Mile End party split, and the Catholic MP, John Scurr, resigned as constituency Labour Party chair. Some of the rifts remained, for members active in the 1930s recalled that the Jews and the Catholics continued to sit in different parts of the council chamber, and that there were divisions on religious lines over birth control.[104] Moreover, the cost of healing these divisions was that many Jews were pushed towards the Communist Party.[105] Pugh's point about East London, that 'at the local level, at least, Labour is probably best understood not as one but as two or three distinct parties' can be taken further.[106] At one time, there were two distinct Labour parties in Whitechapel, a Jewish one and a Catholic one.[107] As these splits cost the party votes it increasingly appeared to be a better strategy to make electoral appeals to more generic categories of voters, notably citizens.

In 1918, Labour's candidate in Silvertown was David Davis a quiet-spoken Baptist minister whose first language was Welsh. The *Stratford Express* said of Davis 'that he makes no claim to be a great public speaker – indeed, his involved sentences spoil some of his best efforts'.[108] By contrast the National Socialist Party candidate, Jack Jones, was, according to the memories of local constituents, a 'marvellous orator, one of the finest speakers you ever heard in your life. He could have them falling about laughing and then crying'.[109] Jones spoke frequently in public and won the seat. At that time, other local MPs were also famed for their skills at public speaking, notably Will Thorne and Will Crooks. However, raucous street meetings and soapbox rallies began to be seen as counter productive. In 1945, two of Labour's London candidates who were not local men, were less enthusiastic about such antics. Labour activists in Edmonton painted a truck red and persuaded the candidate and his wife to spend the day touring the constituency. The candidate 'called it just cheering and wasting time … they didn't want to chase up to the Town Hall to vote. They thought it was enough to shout "Good Old Labour"'. John Platts-Mills had similar memories of his campaign organiser ('a real huckster') in Finsbury in 1945. 'It was all noise and cheering. [People] would be persuaded to join in the excitement of the candidate appearing. It was all utter nonsense'.[110] The *Daily Mirror* also thought it understood that people wanted Labour to provide the framework for a quiet life. As part of its 'Vote for Him' campaign, the paper put a letter on its front page:

I shall vote for him. I know what he wants … a good house with a bit of garden. He wants a job at a fair wage … he wants a good education for the children.[111]

In 1949, it was a ordinary delegate, not an MP, who at the national conference called for 'the old evangelical spirit', for the party 'to go back to the street corner where we came from, to go back to the doorstep, to the factory gate, and to express what is truly within us'.[112] This indicates that people within the party believed that success was derived from the aptness of Labour's appeal. In order to convince people that it could resolve everyday practicalities and common sense aspirations it had to be familiar.

In London, Labour's support grew as the capital industrialised and a sense of class developed. Organised activists were able to capitalise on that change in order to make people aware of the party's policies and activities. They also used the expansion of the central state into local social life as a means of developing the electoral base of the party. It was the activists' creation and mobilisation of communities, often ones based on residence, which enabled the party to promote different messages, or aspects of socialism, in different areas. Across the metropolis, Labour parties created a sense of civic identity through their housing and rating policies, and their support for local communities' nationalist aspirations. This focus on the idea that Labour succeeded when it appeared to reflect people's everyday experiences and common sense aspirations does not marginalise class or national phenomena, but recontextualises them in recognition that Labour politics were about everyday life and class consciousness developed at the practical level.

Notes

1. London is here defined as the area that was to be administered by the Greater London Council, 1965–86.

2. For fuller election results, see D. Weinbren. 'Building Communities, Constructing Identities: The Rise of the Labour Party in London', *London Journal*, 23, 1 (1998); for inner London results see J. Woollard and A. Willis, *Twentieth Century Local Election Results: Volumes 1–3* (Plymouth, 2000).

3. D. Tanner, 'The Politics of the Labour Movement, 1900–39', in C. Wrigley (ed.), *A Companion to Early Twentieth Century Britain* (Oxford, 2003), pp. 44, 47 and 52.

4. W.R. Watson, *Men and Machines: An Autobiography of an Itinerant Mechanic* (London, 1935), p. 140.

5. S. Fielding, 'The Second World War and Popular Radicalism: The Significance of the "Movement away from Party"', *History*, 80, 258 (1995), pp. 56–58.

6. G. Philips, *The Rise of the Labour Party, 1893–1931* (London, 1992), p. 66.

7. J. Dash, *Good Morning Brothers! A Militant Trade Unionist's Frank Autobiography* (London, 1969), p. 31; 'The problems facing us in suburbia', cited in S. Fielding, P. Thompson and N. Tiratsoo, *'England Arise!' The Labour Party and Popular Politics in 1940s Britain* (Manchester, 1995), pp. 180–81.

8. Leaflet of Labour candidate Edwin Unwin; *Romford Times*, 6 April 1921.

9. Diary entry of 25 August 1928, M.I.Cole (ed.), *Beatrice Webb's Diaries* (London, 1952), p. 176; A.F.G. Edwards, 'Local Government and Politics in West Ham, 1919–1939', King's College London PhD (1999), p. 145.

10. M. McDermott, 'Irish Catholics and the British Labour Movement: A Study with particular reference to London, 1918–70', unpublished MA (Kent, 1978), pp. 176–78.

11. C. Wrigley, 'Liberals and the Desire for Working-Class Representation in Battersea 1886–1922', in K.D. Brown, *Essays in Anti-Labour History* (London, 1974), pp. 126–58.

12. 'Editorial', *London Catholic Herald*, 17 November 1923.

13. *Catholic Times*, 8 September 1919.

14. G. Alderman, *London Jewry and Local Politics, 1889–1986* (London, 1989), pp. 75–77.

15. *Ibid.*, pp. 84–86 and 163–64. On Davis see G. Alderman, 'M. H. Davis: The Rise and Fall of a Communal Upstart', *Jewish Historical Studies*, 21 (1988–90).

16. P. Keleman, 'Labour Ideals and Colonial Pioneers: Wedgwood, Morrison and Zionism', *Labour History Review*, 61, 1 (1996), pp. 45–46.

17. C. Collette, '"Le soleil du socialisme commence à se lever sur le monde": The Utopian Visions of Labour Zionism, British Labour and the Labour and Socialist International in the 1930s', in C. Collette and S. Bird (eds), *Jews, Labour and the Left, 1918–48* (Aldershot, 2000), p. 78.

18. B. Donoughue and G.W. Jones, *Herbert Morrison: Portrait of a Politician* (London, 1973), p. 435.

19. P. Keleman, 'Zionism and the British Labour Party: 1927–39', *Social History*, 21, 1 (1996), pp. 71–87.

20. C. Adams, *Across Seven Seas and Thirteen Rivers* (London 1987), pp. 40 and 60.

21. Labour Oral History Project recording held in the National Sound Archive, British Library.

22. On the importance of kinship ties within the Labour Party see D. Weinbren, 'Labour's Roots and Branches: The Labour Oral History Project', *Oral History Journal*, 24, 1 (1996).

23. A.F.G. Edwards, 'Local Government', p. 145.

24. Vi Willis quoted in D. Weinbren, *Generating Socialism: Recollections of Life in the Labour Party* (Stroud, 1997), pp. 86 and 210.

25. J. Marriott, *The Culture of Labourism: The East End between the Wars* (Edinburgh, 1991), pp. 179–82.

26. Labour Oral History Project recording held in the National Sound Archive, British Library.

27. K.Y. Stenberg, 'Gender, Class and London Labour Politics 1870–1914', unpublished PhD (Minnesota, 1993) p. ii.

28. P. Thane, 'Women in the British Labour Party and the Construction of State Welfare, 1906–39' in S. Koven and S. Michel (eds) *Mothers of a New World: Maternalist Politics and the Origins of Welfare States* (London, 1993) p. 345.

29. M. Francis, 'Labour and Gender', in D. Tanner, P. Thane and N. Tiratsoo (eds), *Labour's First Century* (Cambridge, 2000), pp. 203–4.

30. P. Graves, *Labour Women: Women in British Working-Class Politics, 1918–39* (Cambridge, 1994), pp. 126, 163–67.

31. *Woolwich Pioneer*, 1 April 1921; J.A. Gillespie, 'Economic and Political Change in the East End of London during the 1920s', Cambridge University PhD (1984), p. 397.

32. A. Barnes in conversation with K. Harding and C. Gibbs, *Tough Annie: From Suffragette to Stepney Councillor* (London, 1980), p. 40.

33. *Labour Women*, December 1934.

34. Leslie Hilliard, recording in the Imperial War Museum.

35. S. Fielding et al, *England Arise*, p. 182. See also I. Murray, 'The Advance of Labour and the Suburban Working Class: A Study of Tottenham, 1918–1929', University of Westminster MA (1993), p. 62.

36. B. Humphries, *The Roots of Labour in a West London Suburb – Ealing in the 1930s*, unpublished history of the Ealing Labour Party (London, 1993), p. 4.

37. D. Weinbren, *The Hendon Labour Party, 1924–92* (Wakefield, 1998); *The New Survey of London Life and Labour, Volume 9: Life and Leisure* (London, 1935) pp. 391, 399–400 and 405.

38. Quoted in S. Alexander, 'Men's Fears and Women's Work: Responses to Unemployment in London between the Wars', *Gender and History*, 12, 2 (2000), p. 419.

39. Olive Rainbird and Tom Riley, quoted in D. Weinbren, *Generating Socialism*, p. 42.

40. Labour Oral History Project recording held in the National Sound Archive, British Library.

41. *Ibid.*

42. J. Mitford, *Hons and Rebels* (London, 1960), p. 145.

43. Quoted in A. Rubinstein, A. Andrews and P. Schweitzer, *Just Like the Country: Memories of London Families who settled the New Cottage Estates, 1919–39* (London, 1991), pp. 79–80.

44. L. Heren, *Growing Up Poor in London* (London, 1973), pp. 12–13.

45. T. Jeffry, 'The Suburban Nation: Politics and Class in Lewisham', in G. Stedman Jones and D. Feldman (eds), *Metropolis London: Histories and Representations since 1800* (London, 1989), pp. 194–207.

46. M. Pugh, 'The Rise of Labour and the Political Culture of Conservatism, 1890–1945', *History*, 87, 288 (2002), pp. 513–37.

47. G. Haw, *The Life of Will Crooks, MP: From Workhouse to Westminster* (London, 1917), p. 318.

48. *Woolwich Herald*, 11 February 1921.

49. *Woolwich Pioneer*, 2 September 1921.

50. S. Fielding et al, *England Arise*, p. 62.

51. G. Field, 'Social Patriotism and the British Working Class: Appearance and Disappearance of a Tradition', *International Labor and Working Class History*, 42 (1992), pp. 23–32.

52. P. Thompson, *Socialists, Liberals and Labour: The Struggle for London 1885–1914* (London, 1967), p. 240.

53. C.R. Attlee, *As it Happened* (London, 1954), p. 54.

54. D. Englander, *Landlord and Tenant in Urban Britain, 1838–1918* (London, 1983), pp. 238–39.

55. *Woolwich Pioneer*, 11 June 1920.

56. Stanley Bell quoted in D. Weinbren, *Generating Socialism*, p. 3; and Eric Voysey recording at the Imperial War Museum.

57. Alf Barton quoted in H. Jenkins, *Rank and File* (London, 1980).

58. P. Piratin, *Our Flag Stays Red* (London, 1948), pp. 46–47. Naomi Wolff quoted in D. Weinbren, *Generating Socialism*, p. 210.

59. *Barnet Press*, 3 April 1926.

60. *The Times*, 3 November 1934.

61. J.A. Yelling, *Slums and Redevelopment: Policy and Practice in England 1918–45, with particular reference to London* (London, 1992).

62. S. Parker, 'From the Slums to the Suburbs: Labour Party Policy, the LCC and the Woodberry Down Estate, Stoke Newington, 1934–1961', *London Journal*, 24, 2 (1999), pp. 51–69.

63. *Hendon and Finchley Times*, 11 November 1927.

64. A.A. Jackson, *Semi-Detached London: Suburban Development, Life and Transport 1900–39* (London, 1973), p. 305.

65. R. Durant, *Watling: A Survey of Social Life on a New Housing Estate* (London, 1939), p. 22. See also E. Sewell Harris and P.N. Molloy, *The Watling Community Association* (London, 1951), pp. 21–24.

66. A. Olechnowicz, 'Becontree Dagenham: An Analysis of an LCC Estate between the Wars', University of Oxford D.Phil (1991), p. 315.

67. T. Young, *Becontree and Dagenham: A Report made for the Pilgrim Trust* (London, 1934), p. 315.

68. P. Willmott, *The Evolution of a Community: A Study of Dagenham after Forty Years* (London, 1963), pp. 18–19 and 109. The class structure is also discussed in R. Home, '*A Township Complete in Itself': A Planning History of the Becontree/Dagenham Estate* (University of East London and London Borough of Barking & Dagenham Library Services, 1997), pp. 39–44.

69. *Daily Herald*, 29 March 1926.

70. A. Olechnowicz, 'Becontree', p. 265.

71. T. Hinchcliffe, '"This Rather Foolish Piece of Panic Administration": The Government's Flat Conversion Programme in London 1919', *London Journal*, 19, 2 (1994), pp. 168–82.

72. N. Bullock, ''Fragments of a Post-War Utopia: Housing in Finsbury, 1945–51', *Urban Studies*, 26 (1989), p. 52.

73. S. Webb and B. Webb, *The History of Trade Unionism* (London, 1920), pp. 423–27.

74. S. Alexander, 'Men's Fears', p. 407.

75. *Daily Herald*, 6 March 1934.

76. J. Zeitlin, 'The Emergence of the Shop Steward Organisation and Job Control in the British Car Industry: A Review Essay', *History Workshop Journal*, 10 (1980), p. 126.

77. D. Lyddon, '"Trade Union Traditions": The Oxford Welsh and the 1934 Pressed Steel Strike', *Llafur*, 6, 1 (1993), pp. 106–14.

78. M. Glucksmann, *Women Assemble: Women Workers and the 'New Industries' in Inter-War Britain* (London, 1990), pp. 112–15.

79. G. Alderman, *London Jewry*, p. 61.

80. J. Stewart, '"For a Healthy London": The Socialist Medical Association and the London County Council in the 1930s', _Medical History_, 41, 4 (1997).

81. B. Barker, _Labour in London: A Study in Municipal Achievement_ (London, 1946).

82. Vi Willis quoted in D. Weinbren, _Generating Socialism_, p. 218; P. Addison, _The Road to 1945_ (London, 1975), p. 272.

83.Labour Oral History Project recording held in the National Sound Archive, British Library.

84. N. Branson, _Poplarism, 1919–25: George Lansbury and the Councillors' Revolt_ (London, 1979), pp. 167 and 179.

85. E. Lebas, '"When Every Street Became a Cinema": The Film Work of Bermondsey Borough Council Public Health Department, 1923–53', _History Workshop Journal_, 39 (1995).

86. F. Brockway, _Bermondsey Story_ (London, 1949).

87. J. Gillespie, 'Municipalism, Monopoly and Management: The Demise of "Socialism in One County", 1918–33' in A. Saint (ed.), _Politics and the People of London: The LCC 1889–1965_ (London, 1989), p. 113.

88. Naomi Wolff quoted in D. Weinbren, _Generating Socialism_, p. 218.

89. N. Branson, _Poplarism_, p. 15.

90. A. Olechnowicz, _Working-Class Housing in England between the Wars: The Becontree Estate_ (Oxford, 1997), pp. 111–12.

91. J.S. Rowett, 'The Labour Party and Local Government: Theory and Practice in the Inter-War years', Oxford University D.Phil (1979), pp. 260–61.

92. A. Barnes et al, _Tough Annie_, pp. 32–33.

93. P. Thompson, _Socialists_, pp. 101 and 133.

94. A.F.G. Edwards, 'Local Government', pp. 34, 75 and 258–59.

95. Quoted in J. White, _London in the Twentieth Century: A City and its People_ (London, 2001), p. 377.

96. E. Doreen Idle, _War over West Ham: A Study of Community Adjustment_ (London, 1943), pp. 32 and 60.

97. P. Chamberlyn, 'The Politics of Participation: An Enquiry into Four London Boroughs, 1968–74', _London Journal_, 4, 1 (1978).

98. Newham Monitoring Project/Campaign Against Racism and Fascism, _Forging a Black Community: Asian and Afro-Caribbean Struggles in Newham_ (London, 1991), pp. 5–6 and 31–32.

99. P. McCormick, _Enemies of Democracy_ (London, 1979); P. McCormick, 'Prentice and the Newham North-East Constituency: The Making of Historical Myths', _Political Studies_, 29, 1 (1981), pp. 80–85; H. Wainwright, _Labour: A Tale of Two Parties_ (London, 1987) pp. 17–23.

100. Cited in J.S. Rowett, 'The Labour Party', pp. 84–89, 165, 213 and 304.

101. M. Clapson, 'Localism', pp. 132–313.

102. J. Mason 'Partnership Denied: The London Labour Party on the LCC and the Decline of London Government, 1940–65' in A. Saint (ed.), _Politics_, pp. 253–54.

103. C.R. Attlee, _As it Happened_, p. 48.

104. L. Gold and Helena Roberts, quoted in E. Smith, 'East End Jews in Politics, 1918–39: A Study in Class and Ethnicity', University of Leicester PhD (1990), pp. 91–93.

105. G. Alderman, *London Jewry*, p. 97.

106. M. Pugh, 'The Rise of Labour', pp. 529 and 537.

107. M. McDermott, 'Irish Catholics', pp. 165–67.

108. M. Davies, 'From Collier to Custom House: The Life of David John Davis', unpublished manuscript (2003), pp. 38–41 and 52.

109. Quoted in J. Marriott, *The Culture of Labourism*, pp. 179–82.

110. A.V. Mitchell, *Election '45: Reflections on the Revolution in Britain* (London 1995), pp. 59 and 78

111. *Daily Mirror*, 25 June 1945.

112. Labour Party, *Report of the Annual Conference of the Labour Party, 1949*, quoted in S. Fielding, 'Labourism in the 1940s', *Twentieth Century British History*, 3, 2 (1992), pp. 145–51.

Chapter 11

'One of the Most Backward Areas of the Country': The Labour Party's Grass Roots in South West England, 1918–45

Andrew Thorpe

In Britain as a whole, the period between 1918 and 1945 saw the Labour Party move from being the third party in the state to a position of majority government. Most regions of Britain saw a similarly impressive improvement in the party's electoral fortunes. Yet the four counties to the south and west of Bristol, although seeing some progress, remained, in the language much used by Labour organisers of the time, 'backward'.[1] In Cornwall, Devon, Dorset and Somerset, Labour's profile did increase in this period, but from an extremely low base and to a far lesser extent than in most other regions. Only two of the region's 27 constituencies *ever* elected a Labour MP before 1945: Frome, in Somerset, in 1923 and 1929, and Plymouth Drake in 1929. This meant that the 189 parliamentary contests at the seven interwar general elections yielded only three Labour victories. It was only in its national *annus mirabilis* of 1945, indeed, that Labour in the South West even managed to displace the Liberals from second place in terms of votes won. But even then, only six of the 27 constituencies elected Labour MPs: all three in Plymouth, two in Somerset (Frome and Taunton), and one in Cornwall (Penryn and Falmouth). Perhaps because of this relative lack of success, historians have been slow to study the region.[2] Yet, attention to it might tell us much, not just about Labour in the South West, but also about the development of the party more generally. Therefore, this chapter seeks to offer a reappraisal of Labour in the South West in this period. It will focus on the extent of Labour's weakness, explain the reasons for it, and identify the effects that this weakness had on the outlook of the party and its activists down to, and arguably beyond, 1945.

The South Western Context

In order to understand the nature of Labour politics in the South West, it is necessary first to appreciate the very difficult conditions in which the region's Labourites had to operate in the period. The first obstacle was the social and economic nature of much of the region. Although we should avoid excessive determinism, Labour tended, in this period, to fare better in areas with a high level of industrial workers, and worse in areas where there were significant numbers of agricultural workers and middle-class people. In the South West, both of these latter groups loomed large. In 1931, agriculture was the occupation of more than 30 per cent of the male workforce in eight of the 27 constituencies; in a further seven, it represented between 20 and 30 per cent.[3] Only in the five borough seats (three in Plymouth, plus Exeter and Bath) and in largely urbanised Torquay was the figure lower than ten per cent. In South Molton, the figure was 50.4 per cent; only three constituencies exceeded this figure in the whole of the United Kingdom.[4] Similarly unlikely to pay much heed to Labour appeals were the traditionally 'Radical' fishermen of the St Ives division of Cornwall,[5] who made up 13.6 per cent of occupied males there. Conversely, industrial workers tended to be less numerous than in other parts of Britain. There was coalmining in the Frome division of Somerset, where 17.5 per cent of the male working population in 1931 were miners; tin mining and china clay in Cornwall, and quarrying in South Dorset. The footwear industry was a significant employer in the Frome constituency. But in most cases, these industries were too small, in terms of employment, to offer any chance of Labour winning the seat. Tiverton town, for example, was well known as a textile centre. But even had the workers there been inclined to Labour politics – a big assumption indeed, given the resilience of paternalism in the textile works – then the number of workers would have been dwarfed in a constituency which stretched many miles beyond the town to the Channel coast at Dawlish.[6] (In fact only 2.1 per cent of the constituency's male workers in 1931 were employed in the textile industry.) Even the major cities posed problems. Plymouth and, to a lesser extent, Exeter had connexions with the armed forces that tended to inhibit the development of Labour politics, or at least the success of Labour at the polls. If military personnel are taken as middle class then it is noteworthy that Plymouth (39.3 per cent) and Exeter (32.1 per cent) were both much more middle class in occupational composition in 1931 than what might be seen as comparable cities, such as York (27.3), Oxford (26.1), or Norwich (25.1). Exeter, like these others, was a county town and service centre for a largely agricultural hinterland; unlike them, however, it did not develop a particularly important industrial base.[7] Meanwhile, the phenomenon of an ageing population, already discernible as a result of retirees migrating to the area, was an inhibiting factor for Labour in some of the more urbanised coastal areas, like Weston (in Somerset) and Torquay.[8] Some social changes did offer greater potential, such as the very rapid development and urbanisation of East Dorset around Poole.[9] But, on the whole, the South West was not an area that seemed to offer Labour great hope in socio-economic terms.

Second, there was geography. Due to the low density of population in much of the South West, most of its constituencies were very large in area and had relatively poor communications. The unwary observer might assume that seats with the names of small market towns were compact constituencies, most of whose voters lived in or close to those towns. But they would be wrong to do so. The Bridgwater constituency in Somerset, for example, was huge, covering the whole of the northern coast of Somerset and its hinterland. It seems unlikely that it could have been won at the 1938 by-election by the Independent Progressive candidate,

Vernon Bartlett, had he not been generously subsidised by Sir Richard Acland (Liberal) and Sir Stafford Cripps (Labour), and lent an election agent and a car by the latter.[10] The constituency to the west of Bridgwater, Barnstaple, covered the whole of the north Devon coast and some way inland. South Molton, named after a small market town between mid and north Devon, in fact stretched from Crediton, close to the outskirts of Exeter, in the South, to Great Torrington in the north, a distance of about 30 miles. Similarly, Tavistock, named after the stannary town which formed its main urban centre, was actually a vast expanse which stretched from the outskirts of Plymouth to cover much of Dartmoor, a fact which placed great strain on candidates and organisers who had to try to hold meetings 'in the most remote villages'.[11] Even in Frome, ostensibly one of the more compact constituencies, it was 14 miles from Frome in the south east to Keynsham in the north west, and 16 miles from north east to south west. Given that the constituency was significantly contoured, and that main road and rail routes to and from Bristol therefore largely by-passed it, transport was an obstacle to members trying to attend Divisional Labour Party (DLP) meetings from outlying towns and villages.[12] These difficulties were especially pronounced at elections, where a lack of polling stations could involve people 'having to walk many miles' in order to cast a vote.[13] It was hard to set up new Labour groups in the scattered villages of these constituencies. Rivalry between different centres within a constituency could also lead to problems. Further problems could be created if those willing to act as DLP officials lived at the wrong end of the constituency. Of course, it was the same for all parties, but Labour tended to depend more than its rivals on constituency-level meetings on a regular basis, and the difficulty of holding these, or at least of getting decent attendances, was an obstacle. Fare pooling by delegates could alleviate some of the worst effects, where it was adopted.[14] By and large, however, Labour's rivals were more likely to be able to afford the means of overcoming such obstacles, like paid agents and generous travel expenses (including, certainly by the 1930s, a car allowance), than Labour was itself; and at election times, Labour's rivals had far more cars with which to transport supporters to the polls.[15] The Liberals and Conservatives had also developed networks of groups and clubs in many parts of the region, creating an associational culture that Labour could not hope to rival outside the main urban centres. It would have taken a massive effort by Labour, with a significant national input, to have overcome some of the worst obstacles posed by geography; and there was never the will, or the means, to mount an effort on such a scale.

These economic, social and geographical factors hindered the development of trade unionism. The onset of agricultural depression from 1920 onwards, combined with the heavy levels of indebtedness of many newly owner-occupying farmers, meant that there was little toleration of the National Union of Agricultural Workers (NUAW). Its membership in this region was low, and there was far less farming trade unionism here than in, say, Norfolk, where a different kind and scale of agriculture did offer some shelter for the union.[16] The railways, of course, had a presence across most of the region, and members of the National Union of Railwaymen (NUR), in particular, were often key figures in local Labour politics. In some smaller communities, they might be practically the only trade unionists present.[17] There were also localised centres of union strength, reflecting the prominence of particular industries: both the Somerset Miners' Association (SMA, affiliated to the Miners' Federation of Great Britain) and the National Union of Boot and Shoe Operatives (NUBSO) had a significant presence in the Frome constituency, for example. But even in conditions of full employment in 1944, the SMA had a total of only 2,600 members.[18] Workers' Union membership was high among china clay workers around St Austell in the Penryn and Falmouth constituency during the post-Great War boom; but as recession set in, early in the 1920s, it fell by 90 per cent.[19] The development of general unions like the Transport and General Workers' Union (TGWU) in the interwar period probably helped Labour by unionising at least some of the workers in the newer light industries in the region. But, in the South West as a whole, trade unionism was relatively weak. It is also worth bearing in mind that, as Claire Griffiths has shown, even when unions were relatively vibrant, this did not necessarily feed through into support for Labour.[20]

Of course, it would not do to be overly deterministic. In recent years, scholarship on the rise of Labour has moved away from socio-economic determinism and towards a new emphasis on language and agency. But the South West provides a good example of why we should not see the determinist/agency debate in 'either-or' terms. Here, what might be called the 'objective context' limited Labour's potential to find languages that could be used to mobilize support. For example, one of the party's keenest areas of propaganda, at least until the advent of the second Labour government in 1929, was to attack unemployment, making great play of the slogan of 'Work or Maintenance'. Given that it was difficult to advocate concrete solutions to joblessness, however, Labour tended to focus on the 'maintenance' part of the slogan. But the unemployment insurance scheme, which was the basis of such 'maintenance', did not cover agricultural workers before 1936, and so Labour's attacks fell largely on deaf ears. Meanwhile, Labour's advance was blocked by two further factors. The first of these was a patriotic and imperialist Conservatism, which, in the aftermath of the bloodiest war in Britain's history, and, given the region's extensive military and, still more, naval connexions, was a formidable obstacle. Second, Labour was also blocked by the continuing resilience and, for many, relevance of the language of Liberalism used by a Liberal Party which, although wounded by the party's problems of the period since 1910, remained in reasonable organisational fettle.[21] The splits of 1886 and 1916–23 were both overcome, to a very large extent, in the South West, at least in the more rural areas; as late as 1929, all the five seats in Cornwall went Liberal, and the county became something of a refuge for prominent members of the party who had lost, or were about to lose, their seats elsewhere. It might be thought that this would leave a radical legacy to which Labour could adhere, but a key problem was that the Liberalism of the South West tended to be somewhat Gladstonian in outlook, emphasising religious nonconformity, retrenchment, and self-reliance: the Cornish Liberal revival of 1929 might be at least as attributable to the controversy over the Revised Prayer Book as to the radical plans of Lloyd George's *Yellow Book*.[22] Although South Western Liberalism did ultimately succumb to a third split, in 1931–32, it still retained sufficient residual strength to hinder Labour very considerably indeed in much of the region. And, of course, agency was not the preserve of Labourites. Their political enemies were assiduous in countering any Labour appeal with alternative models and activities. As Nick Mansfield has shown, after 1918 'gentry, clergy and farmers' provided in many rural areas a 'dynamic leadership' which 'skilfully exploited the possibilities offered by new village institutions – ploughing matches, Women's Institutes, village halls and those connected with the commemoration of the war – to reinforce paternalism and discourage radical political action'.[23]

Labour's Electoral Weakness

All of these factors combined to ensure that Labour's electoral position remained very weak in most parts of the region throughout – and in many cases beyond – the interwar period. Nationally, the pattern of party competition in the pre-1914 period has been seen as one in which the Liberals were beginning to be challenged by Labour. In the South West, however, this was not the case. There was no sign at all of an imminent rise of Labour. There was not a single Labour candidate at any parliamentary election in the four counties prior to 1918. What weakening of the Liberal position there was can better be explained as part of the usual vicissitudes of two-party electoral politics.[24] Insofar as any trend was discernible, it was a drift towards the Conservatives rather than the start of any kind of lurch to the left.

The interwar period did not see any enormous swing to Labour, either. The 1918 election saw the Liberals divided, and it was this division that seemed to offer Labour its political opportunity. But in the South West, the party was able to run candidates in fewer than half the seats, and they fared badly. Although generalisation is difficult for much of the 1920s, given the varying numbers of candidates that were run by the three parties, it is clear that Labour remained in third place. At the 1929 general election – the one genuinely three-party contest of the interwar period – the Conservatives and Labour ran candidates in all 27 seats, the Liberals in all but one. Only two Independents complicated matters (although one of these did, admittedly, win at Exeter). The results confirmed Labour's third-party status in the region, despite the fact that it won at national level. It took a shade under 20 per cent of the votes cast, whereas the Conservatives took over 44 per cent and the Liberals almost 34 per cent. The two Labour victories (Plymouth Drake and Frome) were very small beer beside 16 Conservatives and eight Liberals. Labour's share of the vote in the different counties was also weak: 18.7 per cent in Devon, 17.9 per cent in Cornwall, and only 17 per cent in Dorset. Only in Somerset (24.6 per cent) did it come close to dislodging the Liberals (25.9 per cent) from second place.

The 1930s saw no great surge in Labour support. Liberal support did fall away, due to the continuing atrophy of the party in many areas, and to the 'National' coalition against Labour, especially in 1931. But it is perhaps significant that as late as 1935, when Labour was, at national level, the only conceivable alternative to the National government, Labour was still unable to outpoll the

Liberals in the South West, despite running more candidates. It was only in 1945 that Labour was able to move into second place in the region; but, even then, it was still well behind the Conservatives, and its share of the total poll (33.5 per cent) was a shade lower than that achieved by the Liberals as recently as 1929, while the number of seats won (six) was fewer than the Liberals had managed then (eight).

Table 11.1 – Share of Vote and Seats Won at General Elections in the South West, 1918–45

General Election	Conservative and allies*		Liberal		Labour		Other	
	% votes	MPs	% votes	MPs	% votes	MPs	% votes	MPs
1918	58.5	23	25.9	4	15.3	0	0.3	0
1922	50.9	21	32.5	5	13.8	0	2.8	1
1923	47.5	8	40.4	18	12.1	1	---	0
1924	52.8	25	32.9	1	14.3	0	---	1
1929	44.3	16	33.8	8	19.8	2	2.0	1
1931	63.4	25	20.0	2	15.6	0	1.0	0
1935	55.9	25	22.3	2	21.5	0	0.3	0
1945	44.7	18	18.8	2	33.5	6	3.1	1

* Includes Coalition Liberals 1918, National Liberals 1922, Liberal Nationals 1931–45.

The Nature of Labour Parties in the South West

Under the 1918 Labour party constitution, divisional Labour parties comprised, essentially, two elements: affiliated organisations (chiefly trade union branches) and individual members. DLPs in the South West were often weak in both respects in this period. This helps to explain the nature of Labour politics in the region.

Nationally, at any rate between 1920 and 1940, unions experienced many problems. But in the South West, these were often particularly acute. Even when unions could operate, their officials were often busy enough with union affairs to preclude their involvement in Labour politics. However, there were exceptions. The main urban centres did see greater union involvement. The NUR played a significant role, not least at Exeter, where it had a substantial membership and where it sponsored the Labour candidate at the 1945 general election.[25] In Plymouth, union money substantially funded the three divisional parties as well as the central (city) party.[26] Meanwhile, in Frome, various unions played important roles. Fred Swift, the secretary of the SMA, was president of the DLP from its inception in 1918 until 1938.[27] The NUBSO sponsored Fred Gould as candidate in the late 1920s and early 1930s, paying 75 per cent of his election expenses and helping fund the agent, although belt-tightening after his 1931 defeat meant that it had to remove its support from the DLP thereafter.[28] Subsequently, the TGWU sponsored W.J. Farthing, the candidate adopted in 1943 after 'Kim' Mackay's defection to Common Wealth (see below).[29]

Overall, however, union input was quite weak. There were not sufficient members of any union, in most constituencies, to make unions very interested in local Labour politics there. The prejudices of most national-level union leaders and executive committee members would not, in any case, have helped matters. And, where assistance was forthcoming to 'the West Country', then Bristol would be the first – and often last – place to spring to mind. Thus it was exceptional for candidates to receive official union sponsorship, and, indeed, became more so after the early 1920s. At a time when their memberships had been inflated by the wartime and post-war booms, unions were in expansive mode; but this soon ended following the breaking of the boom in 1920 and the subsequent defeats of the miners and engineers in the lockouts of 1921 and 1922 (see Table 11.2).

Table 11.2 – Trade Unions Sponsoring Labour Prospective Parliamentary Candidates in the South West, 1920–45

Amalgamated Society of Engineers/ Amalgamated Engineering Union	Yeovil 1920–22; Weston-super-Mare 1921; Camborne 1922; Plymouth Drake 1922
Miners' Federation of Great Britain	Frome 1920–23
National Amalgamated Furnishing Trades Association	Bath 1920
National Union of Agricultural Workers	Taunton 1920; Penryn and Falmouth 1921–22
National Union of Boot and Shoe Operatives	Wells 1922; Frome 1926–32
National Union of Railwaymen	Camborne 1921; Exeter 1945
Ship Constructors' and Shipwrights' Association	Exeter 1921; Plymouth Drake 1924
Transport and General Workers' Union	Frome 1943–45
Workers' Union	Penryn and Falmouth 1920

For the most part, then, sponsorship was short-lived and spasmodic, and, after 1924, very rare indeed: only ten of the 27 constituencies ever enjoyed it, and in all but one case (Frome) on a very short-term basis. At the 1935 election, candidates in none of the 27 seats enjoyed union sponsorship.

This lack of a strong trade union base naturally created problems for the Labour Party in the South West. It clearly went against the prevailing ideal, which envisaged a party buttressed at every level by the money and solidarity of the trade union movement. But this offered an opportunity as well as a threat, because the 'strong union' model was not always all that it might have been: it was by no means unknown, for example, for DLPs in safe seats that had a strong union base, like Barnsley in Yorkshire, to be largely inert and discouraging of wider participation in the party. This was hardly the way towards the kind of broad, inclusive party that generations of Labour leaders (at all levels) claimed to want, and which many saw as a prerequisite of a socialist Britain.

In theory at least, therefore, the relative lack of strong trade unionism in most of the South West opened up the possibility of the development of a different kind of Labour politics from that which prevailed in many other parts of Britain. By and large, though the potential was limited and not really exploited. In many parts of the South West, it was very difficult indeed to develop individual membership.[30] *How* difficult can be seen in Table 11.3. This shows how many of the region's 27 constituencies were severely handicapped in terms of recruiting individual members. Two indicators are used here, primarily. First, there were a number of constituencies where there was either no DLP in existence, or where, even though it had a secretary and, occasionally, claimed to have adopted a candidate, a DLP did not pay affiliation fees to the national party, calling into question whether it had any real existence at that point at all. Second, there are the published membership figures. From 1929 onwards, the Labour Party's *Annual Conference Report* published detailed figures for membership of each DLP in the previous year: that is, the 1929 *Report* contained the final figures for 1928, and so on. It is worth noting that constituencies had to affiliate a minimum of 240 members, although on occasions very weak parties were able to negotiate a lower figure because they simply could not afford to buy 240 membership cards from headquarters (such parties are also noted in the Table). This means that the figures at the lower end tend to be very inaccurate – a party with only 100 members would usually be forced to declare itself as having 240 in order to maintain its national party affiliation. By and large, we can take it that a party with a declared individual membership of 240 was struggling.

Although it is frustrating that we do not have full figures for the 1920s, a number of points can be made about these figures. The first is that, after a rather slow start, there were signs of real progress in the 1920s. To some extent, this would have offset the problems that came to DLPs with the downturn in trade union membership and, in particular, the virtual collapse of agricultural trade unionism in that decade. The party's aggressive stance in the later 1920s, and its determination to contest as many seats as possible at the 1929 election, undoubtedly helped it further to develop until about 1930, when the disappointments of the second Labour government began to lead to a falling off of membership. Although the heightened emotions of the 1931 crisis and general election probably helped to sustain membership at that point, the 1930s proved to be a depressing decade. Membership fell in many of the South West constituencies and, in some cases, parties that had begun promisingly in the 1920s fell virtually into desuetude. The Second World War posed a severe challenge to all the DLPs in the region, and the fact that all but seven of the 27 were either totally inactive, or at the minimum membership level, between 1941 and 1943 told its own story. Finally, however, there was a strong recovery as the end of the war approached, to the extent that only one constituency (North Cornwall) was without a functioning DLP by 1946, and all the others had memberships in excess of the 240 minimum, in some cases spectacularly so.

Table 11.3 – Weak Divisional Labour Parties in the South West, 1919–46

Year	Divisional Labour parties...			
	Not affiliating at all	Affiliating fewer than 240 members	Affiliating 240 members	Total (out of 27)
1919	10	N/a	N/a	10
1920	10	N/a	N/a	10
1921	7	N/a	N/a	7
1922	8	N/a	N/a	8
1923	3	N/a	N/a	3
1924	3	N/a	N/a	3
1925	4	N/a	N/a	4
1926	2	N/a	N/a	2
1927	4	N/a	N/a	4
1928	3	7	0	10
1929	1	7	1	9
1930	0	0	4	4
1931	1	0	8	9
1932	1	0	12	13
1933	0	0	12	12
1934	1	0	11	12
1935	1	1	9	11
1936	0	1	10	11
1937	0	1	9	10
1938	0	1	12	13
1939	1	1	12	14
1940	2	3	14	19
1941	5	1	14	20
1942	5	0	15	20
1943	5	2	13	20
1944	3	0	12	15
1945	2	0	1	3
1946	1	0	0	1

The extent of the uphill struggle that faced DLPs can be seen with reference to one of the four counties, Cornwall.[31] Here, there were five constituencies. In Bodmin, in the south east of the county, there was no DLP until 1924, when a secretary, C.F. Turner of Liskeard, was found. The party soon set to work, and indeed adopted a prospective candidate, Paul Reed, in 1925. Reed was an active candidate, but the fact that he lived in Liverpool, where he worked in the University Settlement, must have made it difficult for him to make his presence felt. At the 1931 election, it was decided that no candidate should be run, and the Liberal, Isaac Foot, was returned unopposed. The DLP then had no candidate until 1935, when H.E.J. Falconer was adopted shortly before the general election of that year; he lost his deposit. A candidate was briefly adopted in 1937, but he soon left, and there was no candidate between 1938 and 1945, when Councillor J.H. Pitts was chosen, again close to an election, and again faring badly at the polls. At no point prior to 1945 did the party's membership exceed 420, and for all but three years of that time it was below 300.

Northern Cornwall also offered poor prospects. It remained Liberal throughout the period under discussion, and its radicalism made for few opportunities for Labour. In the whole period, indeed, there were only Labour candidates at two elections, in 1929 and 1931, and both lost their deposits by a humiliating margin. There were hints of something better: it was, for example, one of the few DLPs in the region to send a delegate to every party conference between 1928 and 1934. Thereafter, however, the party fell into increasing problems, and although it adopted a candidate (D.N.C. Wakley of Plymouth) in 1936, it made no membership returns to the national party from 1940 onwards. A key problem here, of course, was that the Liberal MP from 1939 was the pro-Labour radical, T.L. Horabin, who eventually defected to Labour in 1948.[32] With the departure of the longstanding DLP secretary, J.H. Brown of Delabole, in 1945, the DLP appears to have ceased to have had any meaningful life at all.

St Ives, covering the far south western tip of the county, was another very weak DLP in the period as a whole, despite the symbolic importance of the fact, occasionally stressed by Labour speakers, that it included Land's End.[33] It had begun brightly enough, as early as 1920. Its membership was recorded as 408 in 1928, 425 in 1929, and 380 in 1930. However, the party's failure to contest the 1931 election appears to have been a heavy blow to what remained of morale, and it struggled from then right through to the end of the Second World War. In only one year, 1933, did it even manage to affiliate on the 'minimum' 240 membership. The following year, it did not affiliate; the year after that, it did so on the basis of 40 members of its women's section, presumably the only active part of the organisation that remained. No candidate was adopted at any point between then and 1945, however, leaving the 1935 general election and the 1937 by-election uncontested. There was some limited and patchy recovery of membership down to 1940, but the war again essentially terminated all but the most local-level activities until 1944, when some recovery did culminate in the running of a candidate at the 1945 election, but he was unable to unseat the Liberal National chief whip, N.A. Beechman.

But weak DLPs were not confined to what might be thought of as 'hopeless' seats. Camborne, as seen above, had a significant mining population, and almost went Labour in 1918 when G. Nicholls took 48 per cent of the votes cast in a straight fight with the Liberal, Francis Acland. But no candidate came as close again up to and including 1945. Defeats in 1922 and 1924, and the fact that no candidate was run in 1923, all served to demoralise Labourites. In the space of ten years between 1918 and 1927, the party adopted no fewer than six candidates. The party failed to pay affiliation fees to the national party in five of the six years between 1924 and 1929, and again in 1940–42; otherwise its individual membership never exceeded 240 prior to 1946, when it rose to a very unimpressive 259. Here, of course, matters were not helped by the events that culminated in the disaffiliation of the Independent Labour Party from Labour in 1932: Kay Spurrell, the adopted candidate, was refused Labour endorsement at the 1931 election, and stood (although being heavily defeated) against the Labour candidate in 1935.

Thus, the only consistently vibrant DLP in Cornwall before 1945 was at Penryn and Falmouth. This was the main mining constituency in the county, with 13.9 per cent of male workers occupied in that industry in 1931. It included four reasonably sized towns – Falmouth, Penryn, St Austell, and the county town, Truro – which made for relatively easy organisation. It was well organised, and membership boomed from 1926 onwards, judging by the high affiliation fees that were being paid to the national party from that date. Individual membership had its vicissitudes, but reached 1,518 in 1930 and – after falling to 740 in 1933 – peaked again at 1,356 in 1936. Even during the Second World War, it did not fall below 518 (in 1941), and it was once again well above 1,000 by the time of the 1945 general election. Successive candidates, most notably the scholar A.L. Rowse (candidate from 1930 to 1942), built up the Labour vote gradually at successive elections, and even 1931 did not see too heavy a falling away of support. The seat fell to Labour in 1945.

Indeed, the example of Penryn and Falmouth showed that there was the potential, in the right circumstances, for Labour to develop strong constituency parties. For the lack of strong trade unionism in much of the South West might have meant an inevitable deviation from the prescribed model, but it did not necessarily mean that DLPs had to be weak. Indeed, the very absence of strong trade unionism offered Labour an alternative way forward – that is, through high levels of individual membership.

One person who understood this very well was R.W.G. 'Kim' Mackay, the prospective candidate for Frome between 1934 and 1942. Frome had been a Labour seat in the 1929–31 parliament, but the MP, Fred Gould, had been swept away in the National landslide at the 1931 election. When NUBSO decided that they could no longer afford to sponsor his candidature, Frome found it necessary to seek another candidate who could offer some financial support. Mackay was an Australian lawyer, who came with the recommendation of Sir Stafford Cripps, MP for the adjoining constituency of Bristol East.[34] Although part of his attraction was that he was prepared to sink some of his own money into the party,[35] Mackay was not a typical carpetbagger. He was an excellent organiser, and developed a highly sophisticated system of canvassing for membership.[36] This system showed spectacular results. Membership rose from 518 in 1934 to 1,979 in 1936 and 2,111 in 1937, and even in 1940 it remained over 1,000. By 1938, the DLP was overseeing the work of 46 active local Labour parties, and had 22 organisations (mainly trade union branches) affiliated to it.[37] Mackay only lost narrowly in 1935, when a Liberal intervention almost certainly cost him victory, and in 1945 the seat was won again for Labour, although not by Mackay, who had departed in 1942 to fight as an Independent in the wartime by-election in Llandaff and Barry. For so doing, he was expelled from the Labour Party for breaching the wartime electoral truce. He subsequently became national organiser of Common Wealth, before returning to Labour and sitting as Labour MP for Hull North West (1945–50), and Reading North (1950–51).[38]

Frome was exceptional in many ways, but five other DLPs did manage to acquire an individual membership of over 1,000 at some point during the period before 1945, as can be seen in Table 11.4. These figures alone suggest that the South West was not quite the Labour desert that contemporaries, and most historians, have suggested. Furthermore, there was some spectacular expansion at the very end of the war, around the 1945 general election, and in the immediate post-war period. Between 1944 and 1946, Exeter rose from 384 to 1,053, Plymouth Devonport from 427 to 2,212, Taunton from 350 to 2,902, and Wells from 326 to 2,536. By 1946, no fewer than 13 of the 27 DLPs in the region had at least 1,000 individual members and, of these, four (Devonport, Taunton, Wells and Yeovil) had over 2,000. Most remarkably of all, perhaps, South Molton, a hopeless seat which as late as 1944 had had neither a secretary nor any members, had 869 members in 1945 and 1,000 a year later. Likewise, Tiverton, which had never affiliated more than 240 members since 1931, was claiming 930 members in 1945 and 1,011 a year later; while Totnes, whose pre-war and wartime membership levels had been scarcely more impressive, fared even better, with 1,224 members in 1945 and 1,505 in 1946. Meanwhile, East Dorset, which included the rapidly growing town of Poole, quadrupled its membership to 1,270 between 1943 and 1946.

Table 11.4 – DLPs with Individual Membership over 1,000, 1928–46

Cornwall, Penryn and Falmouth	1936, 1945–46
Exeter	1934–36, 1946
Plymouth, Devonport	1930–40, 1945–46
Plymouth, Drake	1928–29, 1935, 1946
Plymouth, Sutton	1934–37
Devon, South Molton	1946
Devon, Tiverton	1946
Devon, Totnes	1946
Dorset, East	1945–46
Bath	1945–46
Somerset, Frome	1930, 1936–40, 1945–46
Somerset, Taunton	1945–46
Somerset, Wells	1945–46
Somerset, Yeovil	1945–46

But, in reality, individual membership by itself could not have been the basis of successful DLPs, as defined by the national party. Even in the South West, trade union affiliations remained a key aim of most Labour activists. At the national level, any model which seemed to ignore trade unionism was usually regarded as naïve at best, and mendacious at worst. Strong DLPs were what the party claimed to want, but there were few in the party who could believe that DLPs could be really strong without a firm union underpinning. This meant, though, that many of the DLPs in this region could never be regarded as other than 'backward' by the party's powers-that-be.

Labour Outlooks in the South West

What, if any, were the chief common characteristics of Labour grass roots politics in South West England in this period? First, the party in the South West was not particularly left wing; moderation tended to be the dominant trend. South Western DLPs were not, at least before the popular front agitation of the later 1930s, much affected by left wing campaigns; nor were they notably critical of Labour's efforts in government in 1924 and 1929–31. Fred Gould might have been 'caught up in ideas of "Workers' Control" in industry' while secretary of the small NUBSO branch in Midsomer Norton during the Great War, but he showed no signs of radical leanings as Labour candidate and MP in the 1920s, and indeed became parliamentary private secretary to W.R. Smith, a junior minister at the Board of Trade, in 1930, at just the point when left wingers were beginning to attack the second Labour government's failings.[39]

There were a number of reasons for Labour's moderation. In part, they derived from the party's weakness. It was, for example, very difficult to argue that the party would fare better than it was doing by taking a more radical stance. Instead, Labour appeared to be best off trying to compete with the Liberals and Conservatives for centre-ground votes. A context in which many of the workers were believed to be in fear of victimisation, and where unionisation was low, seemed to confirm such a strategy. Thus, for most Labourites, the only chance of success was to couch the party's appeal in moderate terms. Such calculations would only have reinforced the continuing pull of nonconformity – especially, but by no means exclusively, in Cornwall – in the same direction.[40] The strong Co-operative influence in Plymouth and some other parts of the South West also tended to push Labour's politics towards moderation, though not necessarily blandness.[41] Conversely, the far-left was very weak indeed. Early in 1926, there appears to have been a Communist Party factory cell in Plymouth, which claimed fifteen members and a circulation of over 200 for its paper.[42] But this seems unlikely to have survived the party's loss of membership later in the decade and, other than this, it would appear that the far left had no presence to speak of in the region before the later 1930s.[43] There was some far-right activity in the 1930s. In Plymouth, an active branch of Sir Oswald Mosley's British Union of Fascists (BUF) claimed up to a thousand members, and tried to capitalise on rural discontent in nearby Cornwall through a body called the British Union of Farmers, launched at Bodmin in early 1934.[44] The BUF's fortunes appear to have dipped along with those of the national organisation after June 1934, but as late as 1939 at least one young woman fascist was making open air public speeches in prominent locations in Exeter.[45] But the native far-right threat was not such as to lead to the wholesale radicalisation of Labour in the region.

Second, the weakness of the party in most of the region meant that considerable national-level assistance would have been needed if the party were to have made more impact there. But such assistance was not particularly forthcoming, at least for large parts of the period, and while the reasons for this were often understood by the region's Labour activists, it could breed a combination of helplessness in some areas and criticism of the national party in others. The region was not left totally to its own devices. In 1920, the national party machine was reorganised, and a new regional structure was created.[46] Under this scheme, Great Britain was divided into nine areas. Area 6 (later 'F'), 'South-Western', comprised the four counties under discussion in this article, plus Wiltshire and Bristol. Like all the other areas, it had a district (later regional) organiser and a woman organiser. Their job was to work under the direction of party headquarters to advise DLPs, develop organisation where it existed and to establish it where it did not, to assist in the training of agents, and 'generally to co-operate in the organisation work of the Party as required by the Head Office'.[47] The first regional organisers were J.H. Edwards and Annie Townley. In 1924, Edwards was replaced by the Smethwick DLP agent, Clem Jones, who remained in the post until 1951.[48] Townley remained in the post of woman organiser until she retired in 1943, to be replaced by Florence Caruth of Huddersfield.[49] In short, there was considerable continuity at regional level.

But it was a lot to expect two organisers to cover so many constituencies spread over such a wide geographical area, especially given that the party was so weak.[50] The party conference reports of the early 1920s made frequent references to the 'difficult circumstances'[51] that faced Edwards, Townley and Jones in their 'arduous work' in what was variously described as 'one of the most difficult areas of the country'[52] or 'one of the most backward areas of the country'.[53] As has been seen, there was at least some progress to show in these early years; and the work of the two organisers remained a keystone of the party's construction in the region. Inevitably, though, Jones and Townley faced huge difficulties. One of these was the almost total lack of any other full-time party officials in the region. Relatively few DLPs nationally could afford a full-time agent before 1945, but the South West had an unusually low number. In the whole of the period up to 1945, only 12 of the 27 DLPs (plus Plymouth Borough Labour Party) ever had a full-time agent; and only Frome (1920–24, 1930–35, 1939) and Penryn and Falmouth (1921–22, 1925–30) had one for any significant stretch of time. There were a number of appointments in the years immediately after the Great War: four DLPs had agents in 1920, and six (plus Plymouth borough) in 1921 and 1922. Union difficulties played the largest part here, as with candidate sponsorship. For most of the period after 1922, there were never more than two paid agents among the whole of the region's DLPs: and, between 1935 and 1945, there were none at all except for a brief period in Frome in the later 1930s. It is important not to go too far, of course: some DLP secretaries managed long and, in some cases, distinguished periods in office, and thus provided safe pairs of hands with which the regional organisers could deal. J. Oxnam of Redruth was secretary of Camborne DLP from 1923 to 1935; J.H. Bennetts of Truro was the Penryn and Falmouth secretary from 1931 until the constituency's disappearance at the hands of the Boundary Commissioners in 1949; F.C. Reeves of Parkstone was secretary of East Dorset (later Poole) from 1925 until the early 1950s (latterly on a full-time basis). In other places, however, continuity was a good deal less marked. Honiton (Devon) DLP managed to get through nine secretaries in 14 years between 1933 and 1947. If, for whatever reason, the part-time secretary could not attend properly to party work, then the result was almost invariably a degree of stagnation, even inertia, on the part of the divisional party, as was the case in Plymouth Sutton during the Second World War, when the secretary found himself working very long shifts at the Royal William naval victualling yard.[54] It is worth adding, in parentheses, that few of these people ever attained national status within the party: one exception was George Brinham of the Amalgamated Society of Woodworkers, who was secretary of the Torquay party for most of the period between 1937 and 1946, and who later served on the National Executive Committee (NEC) and as chairman of the party in 1960.[55]

This is not to argue that the South West was entirely by-passed by the national party. Major national propaganda campaigns almost always included meetings there. In 1922, a series of regional conferences included rallies at Plymouth and Bristol.[56] The party's nationwide campaign against the 1927 Trade Disputes and Trade Unions Bill had its South West Regional Committee. Plymouth, Bristol, Exeter and, to a lesser extent, Taunton, Truro and Dorchester all hosted conferences connected with national campaigns on matters like election preparations in 1929, 'Victory for Socialism' in 1934, and peace aims and reconstruction during the Second World War. These meetings, attended predominantly by Labourites from the local area, enabled the party in the South West to keep touch with the party at national level.[57] Furthermore, special summer-time agricultural campaigns were geared explicitly to spreading the Labour word in regions like the South West. As Griffiths has shown, these campaigns began a little haltingly, but were pretty much an annual event during the period from 1933 onwards, and did bring succour to the often beleaguered Labourites of this, and other, regions.[58] (Doubtless, they also served to give Labourites from other areas a cheap holiday in the countryside or at the seaside.)

Nonetheless, at least some of this might have looked like going through the motions, and any special assistance was often tempered by a sense that at least some of Labour's national strategists saw little point in throwing good money after bad in the pursuit of votes in such a 'backward' area. In the 1920s, the South West was quite well covered by the campaigns. But during the 1930s it was far less so, as national-level strategists began to give up on it; and although the extensive 1938 campaign did cover a number of South West seats, it was significant that, when cost cutting led to the slashing of the 1939 programme, not a single South West seat remained in the campaign.[59] The party was also less and less concerned to provide the help of propagandists from the centre: such assistance was forthcoming in the 1920s, but far less so from later in that decade, and although the party's two remaining national propagandists did occasionally visit the South West in the 1930s, such visits cannot have been much more than brief excursions with minimal long-term impact.[60]

The perception that the party nationally was doing little to help the 'backward' regions like the South West did not go unremarked. The 1926 party conference passed a resolution calling on the NEC to do more to assist the DLPs in such areas. The delegate from Monmouth – a large and sparsely populated constituency, like many in the South West – demanded that the assistance should be real rather than token, and pointed out that many industrial constituencies paid only the minimum affiliation fee of 30s (£1.50), while 'Bath and Bridgwater were paying £2 10s [£2.50] each'.[61] But although the resolution was passed by the conference, the adverse effects on party funding of the 1927 Trade Disputes Act meant that little material assistance ensued. Thereafter, regular motions at the party conference for greater assistance were met, with equal regularity, by arguments along the lines that 'there would be no difficulty in accepting the resolution were the necessary finance available'.[62]

The establishment of some kind of organisation at the regional level might have helped to overcome some of these problems. However, the regional organisers were very much the appointees of party headquarters in London, and the regions existed for the national party's administrative convenience, rather than as forums for the discussion of common problems. Indeed, the Conservatives, Liberals, Communists and ILP all had more meaningful regional-level bodies than Labour between the wars. True, there were county federations of DLPs in all four counties for much of the period, although Somerset was by some way the strongest and most active, whereas that in Dorset was probably little more than an extension of the strongest of the four DLPs, East Dorset, whose secretary (Reeves) acted in the same capacity for it.[63] Other than in Somerset, indeed, it seems likely that the county federations were more of a pooling of weakness, with minimal headquarters assistance, than anything else.

But Labour was slow to move towards more regional-level bodies. The first such body (excluding the London Labour Party), was the South Wales Regional Council of Labour (RCL), formed in 1937. At first, its main purpose was to counter Communist influences in the South Wales coalfield,[64] but the wider benefits soon became apparent, and so further RCLs were established, first in the North West, and then during the Second World War in the North, in Yorkshire, and in the East and West Midlands. However, the process then stalled as the end of the war approached, and an NEC statement of intent to establish such a body in the South West ran up against the brick wall of finance and a modicum of indifference.[65] In the meantime, the increase in the number of Labour Party regions from nine to eleven, partly the result of the needs of the new regional councils, actually had the effect of *increasing* the size of the South West region by adding to it the Gloucestershire constituencies outside Bristol (which had been a part of the old Midlands region). This only served to increase the burdens on the regional organisers. It was only in 1948 that the South West RCL was finally established, with its headquarters in Exeter.[66]

One way in which the national party might have helped its affiliates in the region would have been to bring the party conference to it. This was by no means out of the question, given that the conference travelled widely in this period, that the 1916 conference had been held at Bristol, and that parts of the South West were tourist destinations with plenty of hotel accommodation for conference delegates. The NEC itself recognised the extent to which holding the party conference in a

particular place could benefit Labour in the surrounding area.[67] However, when
Plymouth Devonport DLP formally invited the NEC to hold the conference in the
city in 1927, it was rebuffed, partly due to some doubts about the availability of
suitable halls and accommodation, but also because, as the party secretary Arthur
Henderson put it, the 1926 conference had been held in Margate (Kent), and 'it
would be very unfair to ask people who came from the far North to go a second
time so far South as Plymouth'.[68] The fact that Plymouth delegates, having
travelled over 250 miles to Margate in 1926, then had to travel more than 300
miles to Blackpool the following year, does not appear to have entered
Henderson's calculations; and, needless to say, the conference did not go to
Plymouth after its northern interlude in the following, or any subsequent, year. It
was only in 1937 that the conference first went to Bournemouth, which was at least
close to Dorset, though not particularly easy of access from much of the rest of the
region.

**Table 11.5 – South West DLP Delegates to Labour Party Annual Conferences,
1920–47**

Year	Location of conference	South West DLPs sending delegates (max = 27)
1920	Scarborough	4
1921	Brighton	2
1922	Edinburgh	1
1923	London	6
1924	London	9
1925	Liverpool	10
1926	Margate	10
1927	Blackpool	10
1928	Birmingham	11
1929	Brighton	14
1930	Llandudno	17
1931	Scarborough	10
1932	Leicester	5
1933	Hastings	5
1934	Southport	8
1935	Brighton	11
1936	Edinburgh	6
1937	Bournemouth	8
1938	*No conference held*	*No conference held*
1939	Southport	9
1940	Bournemouth	6
1941	London	2
1942	London	7
1943	London	13
1944	London	13
1945	Blackpool	15
1946	Bournemouth	23
1947	Margate	23

One result of this, of course, was to discourage DLPs which, in many cases, were already in financial difficulties, from sending delegates to conference; and this tended to marginalise the region still further in the counsels of the party. As Table 11.5 shows, it was almost invariably a minority of South Western DLPs, and sometimes a very small minority indeed, that sent a delegate to the conference. Geography played a part, as can be seen by the sparse attendances at Edinburgh in 1922 and 1936, although the fact that 17 delegates travelled to North Wales in 1930 warns against excessive geographical determinism. So too did the overall mood of the party: the high attendances of the optimistic periods like the late 1920s and the latter part of the Second World War, or during election years like 1931 or 1935, can be contrasted with the flatter periods like 1932–34, or the early part of the war. More delegates attended when Labour was in government, as in 1924, 1929 and 1930. Some DLPs failed to send delegates simply because they were so weak. North Dorset, for example, sent one for the first time ever in 1939, and did not do so again in this period. It was not until 1946 that the first ever delegate from Tiverton DLP attended; and he was Sir Richard Acland, the former Liberal MP and Common Wealth leader, who happened to live in the constituency. He now wished to become a Labour MP and was, in effect, using the DLP as a flag of convenience to allow him to display himself to the wider party. Wells – by no means the weakest party in the region – only sent delegates in 1923, 1932, 1946 and 1947.

But the failure to integrate the party in the South West more closely with the national party was not all the fault of party headquarters, for a third feature of the Labour Party in the region during this period was a degree of parochialism, or what might less patronisingly be termed local patriotism. This could work both for and against the interests of DLPs. On the one hand, it could help to foster an identity, and a sense of common purpose. But on the other, it could serve to divide divisional parties within themselves, in large constituencies which had little historic logic, or where two or more relatively major centres within the constituency were rivals for primacy.

The Labour Party in the South West was not only set apart from its counterparts in stronger areas by its physical and mental distance from the national party, however. Another difference was that, in much of the South West, there was little success, or prospect of it, in local government elections. In its stronger areas, Labour had found such polls a crucial crucible of its progress in the Edwardian period; after the Great War, it made considerable inroads; and, by the mid-1920s, it was starting to win power in many parts of the country. Where it did so, however, it tended to find that office constrained it from the easy sloganeering of opposition, and pushed many – though not all – Labourites into more moderate positions. Although at times Labour local authorities resisted this effect, by and large it was one of the key factors in shifting Labour from one style of politics to another. In the South West, however, Labour's local election prospects were, in many cases, bleak. In Devon, the party scarcely figured at county council elections before 1945.[69] Even in places where the concept was not unfamiliar in local government polls, however, Labour had huge obstacles to overcome. In the county borough of Bath, for example, its support was confined mainly to two or three wards, and the Conservatives, in tacit alliance with the Liberals, controlled the council.[70] The largest city authority in the region, Plymouth, did not go Labour until November 1945, while the other county borough, Exeter, remained beyond the party's grasp.[71] If these large urban authorities remained unwinnable before the end of the Second World War, then it is no wonder that the urban and rural districts, and still more the county councils, afforded Labour so little success.

It is in this context – of poor immediate prospects, residual Liberal strength, and the fact that Labour's weakness in local elections and government meant that there was no 'administration' effect or Conservative–Liberal alliances at local-level – that the support evinced in the South West for broader left alliances in the later 1930s should be seen. The idea of a popular front – an electoral and/or political alliance against the National government, to include Labour, the Liberals, Communists and others – was a non-starter at national level. However, some Labourites in the South West held out hopes for some kind of broader co-operation from the mid-1930s onwards, and this belief had some important advocates.[72] After all, the broad, expansionist optimism of the 1920s had now given way to a combination of 'heads-down' graft in the few seats that seemed to offer any prospect of success, combined with a degree of pessimism, shading into resignation and even hopelessness, elsewhere. The November 1935 general election, in which Labour's results in the South of England outside London were dismal in the extreme, merely compounded the fact. Furthermore, Liberalism in the South West, although by now clearly in decline, was still clinging stubbornly to life, and appeared likely to remain strong enough to block independent Labour challenges to the Conservatives for some years to come. The absence, also, of a strong Communist Party in the South West paradoxically helped popular front politics: first, because there were no powerful local memories of the Communists' denunciations of Labour during the 'class against class' period (1928–34); and, second, because the idea that broader alliances would lead to a Communist takeover of the Labour Party at local-level could be dismissed with derision. Meanwhile, increasing numbers of Labourites in the region were affected from 1936 onwards by the popular front literature of the Communist influenced Left Book Club. The politics of broader alliances also had some notable advocates in the region, not least Rowse, the candidate for Penryn and Falmouth, who favoured the idea in a much publicised speech at the Liberal Summer School in 1934.[73] This pressure for a broader front culminated in the Bridgwater by-election of 17 November 1938, when the withdrawal of the Labour and Liberal candidates allowed the journalist and broadcaster Vernon Bartlett to win the seat from the Conservatives as an 'Independent Progressive' candidate.[74] The ripples of this result were to be felt for some time: it undoubtedly helped speed up the controversy at national level that culminated in the expulsion of Sir Stafford Cripps (himself the MP for nearby Bristol East) from the party in January 1939, while also affecting a number of DLPs in the South West.[75] Ultimately, however, the outbreak of war, and the significant improvement in Labour's fortunes that it eventually brought, left South West Labour once again at the margins, and closed off this potential route of advance: if the best way forward in the South West was progressive unity, the 1945 general election proved that no such compromises were needed at national level, with the result that Labour in the South West was left once again to fight a frontal campaign, when some kind of deal with the Liberals might have helped it get better results at the local level.

Conclusion

In a sense, of course, it did not matter. This region was not significant enough in terms of the number of parliamentary seats it represented to make much of a difference to Labour's fortunes one way or the other. It is therefore easy to see why it has been neglected in accounts of the party's development. But it will not do to leave it there. Labour may well have been doomed to fail in the vast rural tracts of South Molton and North Dorset. But its failure even in the *cities* of the South West was more disturbing. To some extent, of course, this was cause and effect of the party's weakness in the wider region. But the extension of this weakness into the urban local government arena did have some profound implications. One, noted above, was that the party's activists did not begin to face the dilemmas of being in power at local level, which caused a tension between the politics of protest with which Labourites were comfortable, and the politics of responsibility which were often burdensome. Second, if one accepts the view that, so far as working-class people were concerned, Labour-controlled authorities offered better opportunities and life chances at local-level during the interwar period, then one is forced to conclude that Labour's electoral failure materially impoverished the lives of ordinary people in places like Plymouth and Exeter, and meant that they gained fewer benefits from local government than did people in, say, Sheffield after 1926 or the London County Council area from 1934 onwards. A third point is more speculative, and difficult to prove empirically. However, it may well be that the weakness of Labour in this region – the realisation that the party might *never* win many of the seats, and in particular would never gain control of local government – was a factor in the thinking of the post-war Labour government, in its tendency towards centralisation and the reduction of the powers of local authorities. Fourth, the failure to have more impact here did dent Labour's aspirations to be seen as rivalling the Conservatives as a 'national' party in this period. Had Labour been able to win even half a dozen of the seats in the South West on a regular basis between the wars, it would have been able to make a much stronger claim to 'national' status. As it was, the Conservatives could portray it, all too easily, as sectional – the party of organised labour, representing narrow trade union interests in particular geographical areas, rather than all the people in the country as a whole. It is perhaps noteworthy that one factor in Labour's victories in 1997 and 2001 was its ability, given the collapse of city Conservatism from the 1960s onwards, and the Conservatives' increasingly shattering defeats in Scotland and Wales from the 1980s onwards, to portray its opponents in this 'sectional' light.

Finally, if Labour's organisers and managers had realised to a greater extent the virtues of some of the Labour parties in this area, rather than merely seeing them as 'backward' offenders against the 'one-size-fits-all' model that so many of them clung to, then they might have been able to develop a type of Labour politics that would have been both richer in its cultural and political variety, as well as more robust in resistance to the assaults on their preferred model in the period from the 1960s onwards. The South West was never going to dominate the Labour Party's thinking, but the fact that it was so easily dismissed for much of the time quite possibly did the party nationally more harm than good.

Notes

1. Labour Party, *Report of the Annual Conference of the Labour Party* [hereafter *LPAR*], *1924* (London, 1924), p. 7.

2. Though see D. Hearl, A. Lee, M. Rush and J. Stanyer, 'Politics and Government in the Far South West', in M. Havinden, J. Queniart and J. Stanyer (eds), *Centre and Periphery: A Comparative Study of Brittany and Cornwall and Devon* (Exeter, 1991), pp. 203–13; G. Tregidga, *The Liberal Party in South-West Britain since 1918: Political Decline, Dormancy and Rebirth* (Exeter, 2000); M. Dawson, 'Liberalism in Devon and Cornwall, 1910–31', *Historical Journal*, 38 (1995), pp. 425–37.

3. Statistics in this paragraph are from the author's calculations, based on the 1931 *Census*.

4. Leominster (Herefordshire), Holland with Boston (Lincolnshire) and South West Norfolk.

5. H. Pelling, *Social Geography of British Elections, 1885–1910* (London, 1967), p. 164.

6. Tiverton Divisional Liberal Association, informal meeting, 18 February 1938 (4996G/A2, Devon Record Office).

7. W.G. Hoskins, *Two Thousand Years in Exeter* (London, 1960), pp. 130–1.

8. N.J. Morgan and A. Pritchard, *Power and Politics at the Seaside: The Development of Devon's Resorts in the Twentieth Century* (Exeter, 1999), p. 79; H. Pelling, *Social Geography of British Elections*, p. 174.

9. J. H. Bettey, *Dorset* (Newton Abbot, 1974), pp. 142, 144–46.

10. V. Bartlett, *I Know What I Liked* (London, 1974), pp. 121–25.

11. *The Times*, 16 October 1931.

12. See A. Thorpe, *Frome Divisional Labour Party, 1918–49/North Somerset Constituency Labour Party, 1949–83: A Brief Introduction to the Microfilm Edition* (Wakefield, 1998), p. 2; R. Atthill, *The Somerset and Dorset Railway* (Newton Abbot, 1967), pp. 38, 89, 93, 95, 165–72.

13. Frome DLP Management Committee, 21 December 1918 and 18 January 1919 (A/AAW 24, Somerset Record Office); General Committee 18 October 1929 (A/AAW 26).

14. Frome DLP Annual Meeting, 29 April 1922 (A/AAW 25). Whereas DLPs typically met at least monthly, Conservative Associations met less frequently: see, for example, Camborne Conservative Association [CA] minute book 1919–34 (DDX 387) Cornwall Record Office); North Cornwall CA minute book 1926–31 (DDX 381/3); West Dorset CA minute book 1919–41 (D399/3/1, Dorset Record Office).

15. For the reminiscences of one Labour candidate, see R. Ollard (ed.), *The Diaries of A.L. Rowse* (London, 2003), p. 378, entry for 18 September 1966.

16. C.V.G. Griffiths, 'Labour and the Countryside: Rural Strands in the British Labour Movement, 1900–39', University of Oxford DPhil (1996), pp. 81–2.

17. D. Howell, *Respectable Radicals: Studies in the Politics of Railway Trade Unionism* (Aldershot, 1999), p. 21; J.H. Porter, 'Devon and the General Strike, 1926', *International Review of Social History*, 23 (1978), pp. 333–56, esp. 333, 336–41.

18. A. Marsh and V. Ryan, *Historical Dictionary of Trade Unions, Vol. 2* (Aldershot, 1984), p. 247.

19. R. Hyman, *The Workers' Union* (Oxford, 1971), p. 152.

20. C.V G. Griffiths, 'Labour and the Countryside', pp. 143–4.

21. P. Payton, *The Making of Modern Cornwall: Historical Experience and the Persistence of 'Difference'* (Redruth, n.d. [1992]), pp. 139–63, esp. pp. 140–1, 156–9.

22. G. Tregidga, *The Liberal Party in South-West Britain*, pp. 46–7.

23. N. Mansfield, *English Farmworkers and Local Patriotism, 1900–30* (Aldershot, 2001), p. 205.

24. H. Pelling, *Social Geography of British Elections*, p. 173.

25. *LPAR, 1945*, p. 53.

26. Plymouth Central Labour Party, financial statement for the year ending 31 December 1938 (Middleton papers, MID 62/5, Ruskin College, Oxford).

27. Frome DLP, First Annual Conference, 17 April 1918 (A/AAW 24); Annual General Meeting, 22 January 1938 (A/AAW 28). For a brief account of Swift's career, see J.M. Bellamy and J. Saville (eds), *Dictionary of Labour Biography, Volume II* (London, 1974), pp. 361–4.

28. Frome DLP, Adoption Conference, 10 October 1931 (A/AAW 27); Executive Committee, 31 December 1931, 26 January 1933 (A/AAW 27).

29. *LPAR, 1943*, p. 105.

30. All membership figures are taken, unless otherwise stated, from the *LPARs*.

31. Information for this paragraph, and the four that follow, is taken from the *LPARs*.

32. G. Tregidga, *The Liberal Party in South-West Britain*, p. 118.

33. *LPAR, 1926*, p. 3.

34. Frome DLP, Executive Committee 20 July 1933 (A/AAW 27). Cripps spoke at his adoption meeting while Mackay was away in Australia: see *ibid.*, special general committee 28 October 1933.

35. Frome DLP, Executive Committee 20 September 1933 (A/AAW 27).

36. Frome DLP, Executive Committee 16 January 1936 (A/AAW 27).

37. Frome DLP, Annual General Meeting, 22 January 1938 (A/AAW 28).

38. For Mackay, see K. Gildart, D. Howell and N. Kirk (eds), *Dictionary of Labour Biography, Volume XI* (Basingstoke, 2003), pp. 186–95.

39. A. Fox, *A History of the National Union of Boot and Shoe Operatives* (Oxford, 1958), p. 400; M. Stenton and S. Lees, *Who's Who of British Members of Parliament, Volume III: 1919–45* (Hassocks, 1979), p. 131.

40. See M. Kinnear, *The British Voter: An Atlas and Survey* (London, 1968), pp. 125–29, for details of nonconformist strength in the area. See also G. Davie and D. Hearl, 'Religion and Politics in Cornwall and Devon', in M. Havinden et al, *Centre and Periphery*, pp. 214–23.

41. See, for example, M. Hilson, 'Consumers and Politics: The Co-operative Movement in Plymouth, 1890–1920', *Labour History Review*, 67, 1 (2002), pp. 7–27.

42. 'Report of the Factory Cell Department to the Org. Bureau of the Communist International', 26 January 1926 (495/25/300, fo. 3, Russian Centre [RC], Moscow).

43. Anonymous document, 'Party membership', n.d. [but c. February 1939] (495/100/1040, fos. 1–3, RC).

44. J. Stevenson and C. Cook, *Britain in the Depression: Society and Politics, 1929–39* (London, 1994), p. 236; G. H. Tregidga, 'The Liberal Party in Cornwall, 1918–39', University of Exeter MPhil (1991), p. 199.

45. Private information. For fascism in Dorset, see Robert Saunders Papers (MS119, Sheffield University Library).

46. For this, see R. McKibbin, *The Evolution of the Labour Party, 1910–24* (Oxford, 1974), pp. 163–78; *LPAR, 1920*, pp. 17–18.

47. *LPAR, 1920*, p. 18.

48. *LPAR, 1951*, p. 14.

49. *LPAR, 1943*, p. 28.

50. R. McKibbin, *The Evolution of the Labour Party*, p. 176.

51. *LPAR, 1922*, p. 51.

52. *LPAR, 1923*, p. 46.

53. *LPAR, 1924*, p. 7.

54. See F. Lyndon to Lucy Middleton, 13 October 1939 (Middleton papers, MID 62/61–3); C. Townsend to Middleton, 17 January 1940 (MID 63/20); Townsend to Middleton, 20 April 1942 (MID 67/38); Florence Caruth to Middleton, 1 March 1944 (MID 72/67).

55. But he came to a tragic end: see A. Horsfall, 'Battling for Wolfenden', in B. Cant and S. Hemmings (eds), *Radical Records: Thirty Years of Lesbian and Gay History, 1957–87* (London, 1988), p. 21.

56. *LPAR, 1923*, p. 47.

57. See, e.g., *LPAR, 1929*, p. 10, *LPAR, 1934*, p. 49, *LPAR, 1940*, pp. 24–5.

58. C.V.G. Griffiths, 'Labour and the Countryside', esp. pp. 89–126.

59. *Ibid.*, pp. 96, 102, 105, 353–7.

60. For the propagandists, see *LPAR, 1922*, p. 54; *LPAR, 1924*, p. 9; *LPAR, 1928*, p. 5.

61. *LPAR, 1926*, pp. 250–1.

62. *LPAR, 1935*, p. 219.

63. *LPARs, passim*.

64. C. Prothero, *Recount* (Ormskirk, 1982), p. 54.

65. *LPAR, 1944*, p. 14; *LPAR, 1945*, p. 7.

66. *LPAR, 1950*, p. 18. It moved to Bristol in March 1952: See *LPAR, 1952*, p. 19.

67. *LPAR, 1927*, p. 55.

68. *LPAR, 1927*, p. 204.

69. J. Stanyer, *A History of Devon County Council, 1889–1989* (Exeter, 1989), pp. 27, 104.

70. S. Davies and B. Morley, *County Borough Elections in England and Wales, 1919–38: A Comparative Analysis: Volume 1, Barnsley–Bournemouth* (Aldershot, 1999), pp. 103, 105–7, 115.

71. R.A.J. Walling, *The Story of Plymouth* (London, 1950), p. 287; C. Gill, *Plymouth: A New History, Volume II: 1603 to the Present* (Newton Abbot, 1979), pp. 215–6.

72. See G.D.H. and M.I. Cole, *The Condition of Britain* (London, 1937), pp. 411–24, 443–51.

73. M. Freeden, *Liberalism Divided: A Study in British Political Thought, 1914–39* (Oxford, 1986), pp. 341–3.

74. See G. Tregidga, *The Liberal Party in South-West Britain*, pp. 87–96.

75. Frome DLP Executive Committee, 21 April 1939, for Timsbury local Labour Party protesting against the NEC's action (A/AAW 28). See also Taunton DLP General Committee, 11 February 1939 (DD/TLP/1/1, SRO).

Chapter 12

The Formation of Party Milieux: Branch Life in the British Labour Party and the German Social Democratic Party in the Interwar Period

Stefan Berger

On the surface of things, there can be no real comparison between branch life in the German Social Democratic Party (SPD) and the British Labour Party in the interwar period. Local parties in Britain and Germany seemed to start from very different preconditions after the Great War. With a few local exceptions, the Labour Party did not have individual membership before 1918. Local parties were federations of trade unions and socialist organisations, such as the ILP.[1] The SPD, by contrast, was the biggest socialist party in the world before 1914 with about one million individual members. After it emerged from the repression of the Anti-Socialist Law in 1890 it built up an elaborate network of organisations which went far beyond the party and incorporated leisure-time organisations, consumer co-operatives, children's clubs and burial associations. If your parents were Social Democrats, you were born into a Social Democratic milieu that cared for you from cradle to grave.[2] Social Democratic officials often saw the war as a mere interruption to the ongoing organisational effort to bring more and more workers into the orbit of the SPD. Such a spirit is reflected, for example, in this extract from a letter of a Social Democratic official to party members in the trenches: 'Our organisation is a powerful political edifice that the war could not destroy and we hope that after the war has ended we will redevelop the party to its old glory ... All letters that we get from members in the field show the spirit of ardent devotion and love for the organisation.'[3] In some respects then, the SPD expected to pick things up where they were left in 1914.

But this was not to be. The Social Democratic milieu was badly affected by the split of the SPD in 1917. Local parties were torn apart, and individuals had to decide whether they wanted to join the anti-war USPD or the pro-war MSPD. From 1917 onwards, most locations in Germany had (at least) two socialist parties competing for working-class support. They often shared the same traditions, commemorated the same historical events, celebrated the same festivals, sang the same songs and made use of the same symbols, and there is considerable evidence that many rank-and-file socialists were deeply unhappy about the split. Not for

nothing was the most popular slogan in the early days of the revolution of 1918
one which called on the working-class parties to unite and lead the revolution.
With the establishment of the Council of People's Representatives in 1918, this did
indeed happen, but soon differences over the question of how far to take the
revolution broke the tentative realignment of USPD and MSPD. Under the
conditions of a bloody civil war lasting from 1919 right through to 1923, socialists
fought against socialists in many areas of Germany. This created bitter memories
and lasting antagonisms. After the USPD had failed to resolve its many internal
contradictions,[4] the Communist and the Social Democratic milieux found it
difficult to put the years of civil war behind them and follow appeals for working-
class unity. Although feelings of mutual hostility were not the same everywhere
(much depended on local conditions during 1919 to 1923)[5], and although
Communists and Social Democrats continued to be members in the same cultural
and leisure organisations and the same trade unions until 1928, the rift, which had
opened up in the early years of the Weimar Republic, was stark and difficult to
bridge. Different attitudes to the parliamentary republic and liberal democracy, as
well as the effective Sovietisation of the KPD from the mid-1920s onwards,
prevented any rapprochement. The particularly high turnover of KPD members
meant that many of the organic personal links to an older Social Democratic milieu
were cut in the 1920s. By the early 1930s, the Communist and Social Democratic
milieux in Germany shared much less common ground than the MSPD and USPD
had done in 1918.

In Britain, of course, the war had much less of an impact on Labour Party
organisation. Although the differences between the pro- and anti-war camps within
the party were equally substantial, the party retained unity. A number of factors
were crucial: first, the absence of individual membership meant that pro- and anti-
war socialists continued to belong, by and large, to different associations, the
broadly anti-war socialist societies and the broadly pro-war trade unions. Party
leaders such as Arthur Henderson, who could mediate between the two camps and
were trusted by both sides, played a major role in retaining unity. Last, but not
least, the Labour Party milieu was less dogmatic and sectarian and more willing to
regard itself as a broad church which allowed considerable differences of opinion.
Not only did the war mark less of a watershed for the Labour Party than for the
SPD, it was equally significant that Britain did not experience a revolution at the
end of that war. True, there was much talk about revolution, as well as action in the
form of strikes and industrial conflict in some 'red' strongholds such as Clydeside
and pockets of the South Wales and Scottish coalfields, but no bloody civil war
tore the labour movement apart. Lacking the strong radical tradition of the SPD
before 1914, and without the experiences of a wartime split and revolution, the
Communist Party of Great Britain (CPGB) remained a small side-shoot of the
labour movement. More importantly for the Labour milieu in the interwar period,
many Labour activists continued to see Communists as part and parcel of the wider
movement.

In the second half of the 1920s, the Labour leadership did clamp down hard
on any fraternisation with Communists and disaffiliated a number of local parties
on account of alleged Communist infiltration. After 1928, the 'class against class'

policy of the CPGB brought denunciations of non-Communist Labour leaders which could sour relations for a long time to come, but on the whole many local activists were far more willing to ignore party political labels than was the case in Germany. In interwar Britain, Labour Party and Communist members remained part of the same labour movement milieu in Britain. This was simply not the case for SPD–KPD relations in the Weimar Republic. Memory played a major role in explaining this. In Germany, both Social Democrats and Communists laid claim to a long and distinguished history ranging back to the first socialist organisations of the 1860s and further back to the revolutionaries of 1848. Specific questions about the interpretation of that legacy and about the betrayal of it by one or the other working-class milieu characterised the struggle between Communists and Social Democrats in the 1920s. As far as the Labour Party was concerned, its history as a mass membership party only started in 1918. Hence, there was no contested history and conflicts over memory remained rare. We certainly find Labour supporters in the interwar period celebrating the traditions of Chartism, and there are fond memories of the smaller socialist parties and associations of the late nineteenth century. Socialists did construct a usable past for their contemporary struggles, but these constructions were, on the whole, far less divisive than in Germany, where the labour movement milieu was weighed down by history to a far greater extent than was the case in Britain.

Given the longer and more successful history of the SPD, the greater impact of war and revolution in Germany, the emergence of a stronger and more conflictual Communist milieu, and the importance of memory to the labour movement overall, it would seem reasonable to assume that Social Democratic and Labour Party branch life in the interwar period moved on entirely different trajectories. Yet, as we shall see below, this was not the case. For a start, a number of socio-economic factors which encouraged the setting up of strong and vibrant party branches tended to be similar in both countries. Both parties had their strongholds in the urban industrial centres, as they received most support from their core clientele: urban, skilled industrial workers. Traditions of radical working-class politics in both countries were often shaped by the nature of the industrialisation process and the diverse experiences of work. Furthermore, forms of industrial conflict and the existence of alternative working-class communities (such as, for example, mining communities) impacted significantly on the development of party milieux in both countries. Yet, as recent labour history has rightly emphasised, social and economic factors alone cannot explain the strength or weakness of labour movements. The agency of the labour activists and the languages they spoke need to be studied closely to understand how they attempted to construct the social and economic world around them and how they made use of and interpreted this world in order to build stronger parties.[6] The emphasis on agency also draws out the importance of personalities in the different localities. Where labour activists played a pivotal role in the organisation for several decades, this could have an important impact on the character and success of local party organisations. Where by contrast such personal continuity was lacking, it often had a detrimental effect on branch life.

In what follows, I would like to discuss the character of SPD and Labour Party branch life in the interwar period. Beginning with a brief summary of the strength of the Social Democratic milieu in Germany, I will ask how successful the Labour Party was in emulating this success story after 1918. In particular, I would like to focus on the development of a party milieu oriented labour movement culture in both parties. The final part of this article will then seek to illuminate reasons why the Labour Party's attempt to build a party milieu ultimately remained far behind the milieu orientation of the SPD.

German Social Democracy as a Model for Labour Party Branch Life

In the 1890s and early 1900s, local SPD branch life was extremely varied, and it was not until 1905 that some streamlining was introduced from the centre. Strong local parties were sub-divided into districts and even further into sub-districts which sometimes mirrored city quarters. Districts and sub-districts had their own executives which together formed the executive of the constituency party. Sometimes one Social Democrat was even responsible for specific streets or blocks of flats.[7] Appointed by general assembly of the local party, these local activists were crucial as mediators between the party and the wider working-class milieu. They communicated the party's aims and ambitions to the wider working-class electorate and, at the same time, they could bring the concerns and problems of the workers in the neighbourhoods to the party. Where the SPD managed to install itself within working-class communities, it was not the least due to the tireless efforts of these local activists. At best then, local party branches were neighbourhood-based organisations which became meaningful to the everyday lives and struggles of workers.

This was, of course, not the same everywhere. Many branches looked much less impressive. Branch life was often dominated by a few activists who shared all the functions between them and struggled to connect to a wider working-class milieu. Membership assemblies were not well attended.[8] Complaints surfaced at the 1924 party conference that the organisational work at local level was often shouldered by very few people.[9] The new electoral law and the greater possibilities of the SPD to influence municipal politics after 1918 meant that this problem was exacerbated in the Weimar Republic. Hence, the SPD appointed even more full-time paid officials to make sure that all the necessary work could be carried out. Double mandates were more frequent than before 1914.[10] Egon Wertheimer's assessment that about 75 per cent of SPD members were active in local organisations therefore seems inflated.[11] This was perhaps the case in some of the strongholds of the party, but certainly not everywhere. And, of course, even in the SPD's most formidable strongholds only a minority of workers were ever organised by the party. Take, for example, the 'Red Vienna' of Saxony, Freital near Chemnitz, where, despite near-total dominance of the SPD over local politics, 90 per cent of the workers in the town remained unorganised by the SPD.[12]

But the image of the SPD at home and abroad was that of a mean organisational machine, and it was this image of a 'model party' that Social

Democratic leaders emphasised time and again.[13] There were certainly many Labour Party members who saw the SPD precisely as an organisational model. As Tom Fox put it in his 1914 presidential address to the Labour Party conference, the prime cause for the Labour Party's failure lay in the 'deplorable inefficiency of our methods of organisation ... Our German brethren have learned their lesson better and are using their experience to better purpose in spite of the greater political handicap they have to bear.'[14] The London Labour Party (LLP) after 1918 is the best example of how the SPD was held up to improve local party organisation and branch life within the Labour Party.[15] But the drive for better organisation was not restricted to the capital. Everywhere local parties attempted to expand the full-time agent system. *Labour Organiser* stressed time and time again that it was the aim of Labour to create 'a skeleton party in every constituency [and to weld] these parties into intelligent units'.[16] The importance of vibrant branch life to the Labour Party was underlined by Arthur Henderson: 'One important feature of the constitution is that it makes the local groups the units of organisation rather than the national societies and thus establishes a more direct relationship with the individual electors in every constituency.'[17] In May 1922, the national agent noted with some satisfaction how rapidly local Labour branches had been set up after 1918.[18] By 1924, only three constituencies in Britain had no ward parties, and G.D.H Cole has recorded the number of 3,000 local parties in the interwar period.[19]

The 1920 reorganisation of the Labour Party was of crucial importance for this organisational drive.[20] In particular, the appointment of regional and women organisers for the nine new areas had an often invigorating impact on party organisation. Divisional Labour parties, aided by the regional organisers, sought to appoint full-time or at least part-time secretaries who doubled up as election agents wherever possible. Furthermore, they sought to develop the kind of labour movement milieu that provided such an important interface between party comrades and the wider working-class communities in Germany. However, the reorganisation of the Labour Party was not a straightforward success story. Many of the new divisional Labour parties had few individual members and were heavily dependent on local trades councils or socialist groups. Trade union officials dominated the constituencies in many areas, particularly, of course, where strong trade unions already existed such as in mining areas. Even in London, the financial muscle of the unions was of major importance, despite Herbert Morrison's attempts to bring the local parties to the forefront of the organisation.[21] Considerable amount of apathy characterised many working-class constituencies. It was often impossible to establish ward parties.[22] In many Liverpool wards, for example, the ward secretary was a general without any troops; Labour Party branch life was practically non-existent.[23] Ward meetings in Doncaster and elsewhere in local Labour parties were not well attended.[24] Double and triple mandates were necessary to fulfil all the necessary functions. The problem was exacerbated by the fact that Labour was a much poorer party than the SPD. Hence, it could not employ as many paid officials. In some respects, the setting up of an efficient constituency organisation did remain an illusory goal.[25]

Yet, the number of well-organised local Labour parties increased steadily throughout the interwar period. In many branches, the implementation of ward steward systems increased ward activities considerably. Labour's remarkable electoral successes in Sheffield were built on vibrant local parties.[26] Ward secretaries and (paid) local agents organised propaganda meetings, social functions, fund-raising events, public demonstrations and electioneering campaigns. Herbert Rogers, agent for Bristol in the early 1930s, compiled lists of streets indicating sympathisers and opponents of the Labour Party for all wards. They, of course, proved very useful at election time and in membership drives.[27] In Edinburgh and Bristol, and perhaps most famously in London, machine-building became the biggest item on the agenda of local Labour parties.[28] Individual membership campaigns were popular throughout the interwar period. 'Labour weeks' were held in many constituency Labour parties to win over new members.[29] Individual membership went up from nil in 1918 to an impressive 447,000 in 1937,[30] although Labour membership statistics have, of course, always been very unreliable. Woolwich and Bermondsey in London became working-class areas closely associated with the Labour Party just as, say, the Hammerbrook area in Hamburg became associated with the SPD. A number of local Labour parties were successful in transforming themselves into neighbour-based parties which tapped into the everyday experiences of workers in a particular locality. For Preston, Michael Savage has argued for the 1920s: 'the character of Labour politics at the local level changed considerably ... it changed from a party based on certain trade unions to one based on neighbourhood organisations.'[31]

Party Milieux and Intra-Party Democracy

Ordinary party members tended to be overwhelmingly loyal to their leaders in both the SPD and the Labour Party. In the case of the SPD, many local reports on elections of executives echoed this one from Berlin-Lichterfelde: 'The whole executive was re-elected by acclamation. This is a happy sign for the good co-operation between executive and officials and for the confidence that the executive enjoys.'[32] For Baden, it has been shown that the rank-and-file in local assemblies tended to support the regional party leadership.[33] As Otto Buchwitz, a Social Democrat official before the Great War, remarked in his memoirs: 'The masses of workers felt traditionally bound to the SPD or they were personally bound to local and district leaders, of whose personal integrity they were convinced.'[34] The same could be said about the British Labour Party. David Clark, for example, has argued that the 'rule' of Chuter Ede over the interwar South Shields Labour Party was based on a 'relationship with the local party [that] was almost akin to that of a paternalistic master to trusty retainers'.[35] A considerable amount of hero-worshipping went on in both parties. Ramsay MacDonald was celebrated in the Labour Party as an almost cultic figure in similar ways to 'King Ebert' or the 'Red Czar of Prussia', Otto Braun, in the SPD.

The emphasis on loyalty and strong leadership in both parties meant that discipline came to be regarded as a high virtue. Factionalism had acquired a bad name in the SPD well before 1914. Party conferences organised by a party minority against policies represented by the party majority came to be seen as heresy. During the Weimar Republic, the SPD absorbed little democratic theory and retained its autocratic potential. Anti-pluralistic tendencies could be found in the determination to avoid intra-party conflicts, in the assumption of an essential identity of interests between the leadership and the rank-and-file, and in the endless efforts to homogenise various interests within the party.[36] As you might expect from a party which had successfully avoided a split in the Great War, party theorists such as G.D.H. Cole and Harold Laski, but also administrators writing in the pages of the *Labour Organiser*, stressed the importance of avoiding autocratic practices and keeping intra-party discussion and democracy alive. A greater willingness to tolerate dissent was, however, subtly matched by the belief that party discipline was essential. As George Hodgkinson remarked in his memoirs of a life in the Coventry Labour Party: 'It was always a guiding principle that the party is bigger than any individual in it, and loyalties held firm ...To go 'agin the group' is one of the deadly sins ... [A] voluntary discipline [is established,] the absence of which can endanger the very existence of the [council] group and the party.'[37]

But overall, conflicts and differences of opinion were more readily accepted in the Labour Party than in the SPD. This was nowhere more visible than in the greater diversity of the party press in Britain. The press was widely regarded as major means of intra-party communication within both the Labour Party and the SPD. The German Social Democrats owned 179 printing works by 1927. In the mid-1920s, 169 SPD papers had a total circulation of 1,090,000 copies. The SPD's provincial press was of very different strength in different regions of Germany. Its strongholds tended to be also the party's electoral strongholds.[38] It preached to the converted as it was bought and read largely by SPD members. But most striking about the SPD's press empire was its amazing uniformity. The widespread use of a few Social Democratic press services had a large part to play in this state of affairs, but more important was the effective streamlining of the press by dominant party opinion in those area organisations which controlled the newspapers in their regions.

In Britain, a remarkable number of provincial Labour journals flourished in the interwar period.[39] Will Henderson, the press secretary of the party, gave expression to his belief that the local weekly papers were far more important to increase Labour's influence in the localities than a national Labour daily.[40] But attempts to found more Labour weeklies in the localities often failed after a few months or years. Finance often proved to be an insurmountable object. The *Woolwich Pioneer*, for example, was founded in 1899–1901. It played a crucial role in building up the party in Woolwich and making it the dominant political force there, but in 1922 it still had to cease publication due to lack of advertising (most of the local shop owners and trades people were not Labour sympathisers) and a lack of subscriptions. Throughout it had only been possible to maintain the *Pioneer* through the donations of a wealthy benefactor of the Labour Party, Joseph Fels. A Labour press service, along the lines of the SPD press services, could not be maintained by the Labour Party for financial reasons. Lacking centralisation of effort and lacking finance were therefore major reasons for the relative failure of regional Labour papers. But the local Labour press still served as an important channel of communication between the rank-and-file of both parties. It advertised the activities of the local labour movement, and reported on its progress, successes and perceived problems. It therefore maintained the very party milieux that both parties strove to build and maintain in the interwar period.

Party Milieux and Labour Movement Culture

In Hamburg, the Social Democratic milieu was at heart a broad cultural movement which aimed to educate the Hamburg working class.[41] The Leipzig party held speakers' classes to turn comrades into 'orators' who would be important tools in the educational work to be carried out among the workers.[42] In 1929, about 2,500 Social Democratic workers' libraries existed in Germany with about one-and-a-half million books.[43] The notion of the labour movement as an educational movement was also strong within the Labour Party, which carried on an older educational tradition of the socialist societies. Thus, many local Labour parties organised public lectures, study circles and lending libraries. In 1928, the LLP compiled a panel of 47 speakers for local educational work. It also bought two vans from the Clarion movement, which it lent out to local parties in order to increase the amount of educational activity.[44] Some parties appointed educational officers to plan and co-ordinate the various educational and cultural activities.[45] Speakers' classes were held to educate the future educators.[46] A number of parties also promoted the appointment of literature secretaries.[47]

Education was a particular concern of the parties' youth work. Youth sections had been popular in many local SPD parties well before 1914. They organised a wide variety of social activities and, in the bigger cities, they sometimes acquired their own youth centres. In Frankfurt on Main, for example, their activities comprised visits to museums, reading and discussion evenings, rambling, handicraft workshops, and social events.[48] The *Kinderfreundebewegung* formed an institutional framework for the six-to-fourteen-year olds. It organised 'children's republics' and local groups provided ample opportunities for play and early experience of a 'socialist way of life'.[49] In the Labour Party, we also encounter numerous supporters of the idea to promote the setting up of young people's sections. W.A. Peacock, for example, argued in the pages of the *Labour Magazine* that such youth organisations would be 'training centres for the movement of tomorrow'.[50] By 1929, 300 youth branches had been set up locally.[51] They mainly organised the sons and daughters of Labour Party members up to the age of 18: activities included educational classes and meetings, socials, rambles and other forms of 'rational recreation', visits to theatres and museums, discussion clubs and the publication of local youth papers.[52]

Socialist Sunday Schools (SSS) were active on behalf of the Labour Party as well.[53] By the mid-1920s, the SSS ran about 120 schools across Britain which catered for approximately 6,000 children. Their idea was to create a socialist atmosphere which would be a counterweight to the children's 'capitalist education'. They sought to develop the feeling of 'socialist fellowship' within the children, and their activities often included drama classes, Morris dancing, singing, nature studies, rambles into the countryside, Esperanto and the participation in political campaigns, especially where they concerned children.[54] Another socialist youth organisation with strong connections to local Labour parties was the Woodcraft Folk, set up in 1925. It was co-educational, non-religious, non-military, and it tried to combine naturalism with the teaching of socialism. It had an active membership of about 3,000 in the mid-1930s.[55]

Labour Party and SPD milieus were not only strengthened by youth associations, but also by very impressive women's sections, which often were the hub of social life in the branches. Special committees to win women members were set up, as were women-only reading and discussion clubs and women-only evenings. Women's sections in both parties organised special women's classes, lectures, conferences, socials and excursions. They also organised demonstrations on political issues which concerned women, and they published their own separate journals. By the end of the 1920s, the Berlin women's sections of the SPD had almost 20,000 members; Hamburg was lagging not far behind with almost 18,000. In Berlin alone, 428 women officials had the task of organising activities for women in 1930.[56]

Within the Labour Party, a National Women's Organiser, Marion Phillips, was appointed in 1918. Sixty-two advisory councils were set up to enable representatives of women's sections to meet and keep in touch. Nine district organisers tried to encourage the growth of the women's sections locally. Labour women had their own paper, the *Labour Woman*, as the SPD women had their paper, *Die Gleichheit* (but local SPD women also often had additional papers; in Berlin alone there were two, the *Frauenstimme* and the *Frauenwelt*). By 1932, 1,705 women's sections had been formed in Britain. In 1926, the Labour Party recorded a quarter of a million individual women members.[57] By comparison, the SPD in the same year mustered 165,000 women members.[58] In the London area alone, 70 women's sections were active by the mid-1920s.[59]

The importance of women to the party milieux of both Labour Party and SPD is beyond doubt. And yet, women's sections in both parties encountered considerable difficulties with male prejudices. In Preston, for example, the local Labour Party after 1918 actively attempted to prevent the organisation of women in a party which did not address women's issues in its political campaigns.[60] Women's sections tended to be more prominent in constituencies which were occupationally and socially diverse. But even there, the relations to male dominated local parties were often strained. In 1932, the Acting Chief Women's Officer, Barbara Ayrton Gould, spoke of a difficult relationship between many local parties and their women's sections.[61] Contrary to all programmatic statements of the SPD in the 1920s, the position of women in the party was still a subordinate one and the policy making organs of the party at all levels remained dominated by men.[62]

If women were at best reluctantly tolerated in key party posts, they could play a more central role in the various leisure-time activities organised by the labour movement culture. Drama, music and sports associations played a particularly important role within local branch life. Closely associated with the SPD was the People's Theatre Movement, which had an overall membership of 600,000 in the

1920s.[63] Drama could equally be found within local Labour parties. The Gateshead Dramatic Club, for example, staged 'The Pitman's Pay', a play by the miner Thomas Wilson dating from 1826 celebrating the communal aspects of everyday life in a mining community.[64] In 1924–25, the LLP Dramatic Federation was established on the basis of constituency dramatic activity: 17 constituency Labour parties had established drama societies in London.[65] After 1918, the Arts League of Service established as a travelling company which could be hired by local Labour parties and labour movement organisations more generally. Leeds Industrial Theatre consciously referred to the German Social Democrats' ancillary organisations as a model.[66] The People's Theatre Movement was founded in Birmingham in 1924 and, in Newcastle-upon-Tyne, a similar movement had been in existence since 1911.

Choirs and musical societies were popular within local Social Democratic associations well before the Great War.[67] Their social life was often at least as important as the singing. They developed their own tradition of song fixed in the publication of songbooks. Choirs became an integral part of Social Democratic festivities. They performed regularly at May Day, Revolution Day and Day of the Republic festivities.[68] Similarly, Labour choirs flourished in local Labour parties in the 1920s.[69] LLP Choral Union had 15 choirs with 500 members in 1925, and the party organised musical festivals and choir contests throughout the 1920s.[70]

Workers' sports and athletics clubs could be found in every local SPD organisation. They catered for almost every sport, with cycling, acrobatics, gymnastics, athletics and football coming top of the list. By the end of the 1920s they owned 249 gymnasia, 1,265 sports and playing fields, 100 swimming pools, 48 boat houses, two ski jumps, four regional residential homes and one cycle factory.[71] Local sports associations could also be found within many local Labour parties.[72] After 1930, they organised under the umbrella of the British Workers' Sports Association (BWSA). The declared aim of the BWSA was to organise national competitions in several different sports. The first National Workers' Sports Day was held at Crystal Palace on 30 June 1931. The LLP established a LLP Sports Association in July 1928. It established a football league, held Labour Sports Meetings and catered for cricket, tennis, darts, billiards and swimming.[73]

In their strongholds, the local party milieux of SPD and Labour Party often centred on Labour Clubs (*Gewerkschafts-/Parteihäuser*). Both institutions usually had a bar and a hall for large public meetings as well as offices for officials. Sometimes they also incorporated a library and accommodation for invited guests or visitors. They worked as educational and cultural centres for the branch life of both parties.[74] In the Rhondda Valley, Labour clubs were places of learning and discussion which had their own libraries and organised discussion clubs and educational classes.[75] The clubs were crucial in preparing annual Labour festivals, such as May Day, when local parties would often publish May Day journals with articles describing the central demands of the labour movement. Participants wore a red flower or a red handkerchief, poems were read and songs were sung. Labour festivities were important for generating feelings of community among the party faithful. They confirmed the widespread belief among Labour Party and SPD activists that socialism was a new faith which should inform their whole way of life. Both parties developed a specific club language and a symbolical politics centred on banners, songs, poems and annual festivities. Socialism became a performative act to be expressed through a multitude of images which all confirmed the spirit of communitarianism in the labour movement. The activities of the local labour movement culture in Frankfurt on Main, for example, reflected a longing for a 'new society' and a 'new man' which was also one of the major themes in the plays by Ernst Toller, popular with labour movement theatres in both Britain and Germany in the interwar period.[76] Hence the members of the party milieux in Britain and Germany felt most at home among other party members and tended to laugh, socialise, practise sport, make music and discuss politics within the confines of the labour movement.[77] The organisers of the Nuneaton League of Youth in the 1920s, Harry and Kitty Grey, emphasised the fact that members have kept in touch all the time: 'we have always mixed with socialists, all our life.'[78]

Why was the party milieu in the Labour Party less developed than in the SPD?

Both parties tried to provide an entire life-world for their members, and both produced a rich community culture based on feelings of solidarity and common aims and beliefs. But qualitatively the German labour movement organised many more socialists. The size and scope of its labour movement culture dwarfed that of the Labour Party. Hundreds of thousands of members in the German case compared with thousands in the British. Why was German Social Democracy so much more successful than the British Labour Party in creating a distinct party milieu? Was it, as Ross McKibbin has suggested, the case that the German working class was more politicised than its British counterpart? Were British workers more integrated into their national culture?[79] I think not. It is important not to mix up working class and labour movement culture. Many workers inside the parties were equally politicised, but the vast majority of workers in both countries, of course, remained outside the remit of party organisations. Oral history research on the German working class has revealed a wealth of information about working-class culture, and much of it was entirely unrelated to formal politics.[80] The Social Democratic labour movement culture in Germany was much bigger than its British equivalent, but different levels of politicisation are not sufficient for explaining this difference. One has to look instead, first, to organisational differences between the two parties, in particular different degrees of regionalisation and different financial preconditions. And, even more importantly, one has to take account of chronology. Let me explicate this at somewhat greater length.

In the interwar period, the Labour Party was the most centralised of all the political parties in Britain. The party leadership was, for the most part, actively hostile towards any meaningful regionalisation of the party, as it feared disintegration and loss of overall control. The introduction of regional organisers was meant to strengthen the hand of the centre rather than lead to any effective regionalisation. That was very different for the SPD, where, well before 1914, the most effective centralisation took place at regional party level. Regional parties were powerful enough in terms of their financial muscle and administrative capabilities to help out local parties and initiate local party activities in targeted areas. That never was the case in Britain. Local parties here did not receive the support they would have needed to make their efforts to become mean organisational machines work. Money in the SPD could be distributed more equally through the regions, whereas the difference between rich and poor constituency Labour parties remained a decisive one, despite an attempt by the national agent to propagate a scheme whereby more well-to-do Labour parties were to 'adopt' less fortunate parties and attempt to help them out.[81] And, of course, the lack of financial muscle of the Labour Party had also much to do with the fact that it set the membership fee at a trifling 1s per annum for male members and 6d for female members. Thus, individual membership could not become an important financial resource in the way that it was for the SPD. Despite the fact that by the late 1930s individual membership numbered in the hundreds of thousands, Labour remained heavily dependent on the financial muscle of the trade unions.

Party finance and organisation could have made a difference, but the different strength of the party milieux in Britain and Germany had also much to do with timing. The Social Democratic labour movement culture emerged in Germany before the turn of the century, at a time when commercialised mass culture was not yet strongly developed.[82] The absence of the latter facilitated the formation of the former. When commercialised forms of mass leisure, such as the cinema, spectator sports and excessive alcohol consumption in pubs and bars, entered the frame, Social Democrats steadfastly denounced their consumerism and 'mere entertainment' value. The labour movement culture, by contrast, was depicted as part and parcel of the efforts of Social Democracy to educate their fellow workers and make them into more civilised human beings.

By the time the Labour Party attempted to follow in the footsteps of the SPD and build its own party milieu, British workers were already firmly in the grip of commercialised forms of mass leisure which developed earlier in Britain than in Germany. In some cases, the labour movement could build on the attempts of workingmen's clubs, labour churches and socialist societies to form a socialist counter-culture which can be traced back to the 1880s and 1890s.[83] Their efforts were characterised by the same civilising mission and educational ambition that marked out the Social Democratic cultural milieu. And it could produce the same gulf between ordinary workers and the party milieu. After all, the values and norms of the labour movement seemed often at odds with the marked individualism, the idea of self-help, the nationalism and the defensive class-consciousness of a large section of the British working class.[84] The isolation of the British Labour milieu was arguably all the more marked because commercialisation of mass leisure had been effective for longer in Britain than in Germany.

But timing also played an important role in another respect. The SPD developed its party milieu under conditions set by an Imperial German state which was deeply mistrustful of Social Democracy and sought to hinder and repress the SPD wherever possible. Such enforced isolation produced sentiments of self-isolation in which an inward-looking labour movement culture could flourish.

After 1918, the situation was quite different. The SPD was now a party of government on the national, regional and local level to an extent that had been unthinkable before the war. As far as local politics were concerned, one can see a direct correlation between the increased opportunities to shape municipal policies and the weakening of the concentration on labour movement culture. Thus, for example, the SPD stopped developing its own educational institutions and instead began to co-operate closely with the municipal *Volkshochschulen*, which provided education for a wider working-class public.[85] In the same spirit, many of the Social Democratic workers' libraries were dissolved after 1918 and taken over by city public libraries.[86] Similarly, where the Labour Party came to develop municipal policies in the interwar period, such as in Bermondsey in the 1920s and Coventry in the 1930s, Labour tended to concentrate on extending municipal social and recreational amenities rather than developing their own separate Labour milieu. In both countries, therefore, influence over local politics weakened the party milieu, whereas exclusion from such influence strengthened it. In Britain, the rise of a Labour milieu coincided with greater influence over local politics, and the latter therefore undermined attempts to build a party milieu. In Germany, by contrast, the party milieu had already been built up by the time the SPD gained a significant influence over local politics.

The SPD's isolation before 1914 was far more pronounced than the isolation of the Labour Party either before or after 1918. Nineteenth-century civil society in Germany was far more fractured and pillarised than its British counterpart.[87] This continued into the interwar period, although it became less pronounced during the Weimar Republic. Yet, the SPD, more so than the British Labour Party, found it difficult to shed its utopian and communitarian ethic which had underpinned the Social Democratic milieu to a considerable extent. In fact, the continuing strong milieu orientation of the Weimar SPD produced considerable difficulties for the party's attempts to build coalitions. Bridges across the ideological divides, which had been so prominent in Imperial Germany, were hard to build in the 1920s.

A good example is provided by the relationship of the SPD to organised religion. Catholic priests and Protestant ministers had been in the forefront of the anti-socialist struggle in Imperial Germany. The SPD, in turn, identified strongly with the secular Jacobinism of the nineteenth century and saw religion as a private matter. In the Weimar Republic Social Democrats and Christians attempted a tentative rapprochement. It was, for example, no longer frowned upon if a Social Democrat was active in a church.[88] Election leaflets of the SPD routinely included an appeal to working-class Christians. They often made the argument that the ideals of the labour movement were not dissimilar to Christian ideals. Johannes Kleinspehn, a local SPD activist from Nordhausen in Saxony, argued that the 'proletarian babe' from Bethlehem mattered for modern day socialists.[89] The Social Democratic minister of culture in Prussia in 1918, Konrad Haenisch, stressed the need for tolerance in all religious affairs and tended to avoid all confrontation with the churches.[90] Some of the most hostile anti-religious institutions, such as the free thinkers, who attempted to ally themselves closely to the SPD, never managed to commit the party to endorse free thinking and condemn religious beliefs.[91] Few Social Democrats, it seemed, had radically broken with organised religion.[92]

Of course, all of this was a far cry from the much greater influence of religion on branch life in the Labour Party. In Britain, there was a strong tradition of political religious dissent reaching back to Elizabethan England. Liberalism – from which socialism in both countries descended – was more associated with religion in Britain than in Germany and, consequently, the formative influence of Christianity on many British labour leaders was much bigger.[93] In Britain, the churches were on the whole more sensitive to the social problems of the working class. In 1923, a memorial signed by over 400 ordained members of the Church of England and the Episcopal Church of Scotland pledged the memorialists to actively support the efforts of the Labour Party. The Reverend Gordon Lang was not alone in his belief 'that the ideas of the modern Labour Movement are ideals which are inherent in the religion professed by all churches'.[94] Religion was undoubtedly a strong influence on local Labour Party cultures and politics.[95] Many Labour leaders started their careers as preachers in local chapels. Frank Hodges, Fred Jowett and Ben Tillett were all famous examples. The Labour press in Britain carried many positive articles about religion and showed a considerable interest in Christianity.[96] Labour Party ideology had strong Christian roots, and Labour activists often were very interested in church/chapel affairs.[97]

But the differences to German Social Democracy can easily be overstated. After all, in many places the relation between church/chapel and the local labour movement was quite tense. Many churches/chapels had close ties to either the Conservative or the Liberal Party. In Bradford, nonconformist ministers largely ignored social issues and remained wedded to the Liberal Party.[98] The Labour Party was routinely attacked for its alleged 'atheism', however much its representatives protested their innocence. In Liverpool, up to 1923, the Catholics tended to support the Irish Nationalists while the Conservatives dominated the Protestant vote.[99] Socialists like G.B. Shaw or Robert Blatchford, and working-class newspapers such as *Reynolds' News*, had a strong tradition of being hostile to organised religion. Overall, the stronger religious discourse of Labour did by no means signal an unproblematic relationship to the churches.

Conclusion

Branch life in the Labour Party and the SPD was, then, not as dissimilar as one would have perhaps expected, given the very different starting points of both parties in the interwar period. The SPD was an influential model for the Labour Party, especially where the latter attempted to build up a party milieu. Where such a party milieu could become part and parcel of wider community aspirations and relate to the everyday concerns of the voters, as was the case in SPD and Labour Party strongholds such as Leipzig, Hamburg, Berlin, Coventry, the Rhondda and Bermondsey, it helped considerably in establishing a strong electoral hegemony over a particular locality. But, equally, the party milieu could also become deeply problematic. Its inward-looking nature could turn party branches into communities of the faithful who might have regarded themselves as the avant-garde but were regarded by many in the wider community as cranks and outsiders. Strong solidaristic links within the parties could go hand in hand with an inability to reach out and relate to voters outside of the party.

The greater milieu orientation of German society, the more severe exclusion of Social Democracy from the state and from bourgeois civil society, and the deeper roots of the SPD in nineteenth century history, as well as its more effective regionalisation and its greater financial prowess, allowed the German Social Democrats to forge stronger links with working-class milieux. Ironically, though, such greater success in building a party milieu produced at the same time much greater difficulties for the SPD when it attempted to break free of this working-class milieu and move towards a 'catch all' party in the 1920s. It was only towards the end of the Weimar Republic that some of the younger SPD leaders began to problematise the strong emphasis on the party milieu. Alexander Schifrin and Carlo Mierendorff, for example, voiced their concerns that it ultimately had a depoliticising effect on the SPD as it made Social Democrats focus almost exclusively on the world to be found inside the Social Democratic subculture.[100] They did not have to engage with the outside world and with the political choices and compromises that had to be made. Hence, party milieux were often counterproductive when it came to pragmatic policy making. After all, it needed more than mean organisational machines and solidaristic communities of the faithful to bring working-class parties into power. Here the less milieu-oriented Labour Party was in a stronger position than the SPD.

Notes

1. The best overall assessment of the regional development of the Labour Party before 1918 remains D. Tanner, *Political Change and the Labour Party, 1900–18* (Cambridge, 1990). The rich vein of regional and local evidence for the development of the ILP before 1906 is also analysed in D. Howell, *British Workers and the Independent Labour Party, 1888–1906* (Manchester, 1983).

2. The most detailed description of the organisational empire of the German labour movement before 1917 is provided by D. Fricke, *Handbuch zur Geschichte der deutschen Arbeiterbewegung, 1869–1917*, two volumes (Berlin, 1987); for a brief survey in English see S. Berger, *Social Democracy and the Working Class in Nineteenth and Twentieth Century Germany* (Harlow, 2000).

3. Letter from Hermann Kahmann to Social Democrats at the front, 8 January 1915 (St. 10/228, nos. 67–70, Stiftung Archiv Der Parteien und Massenorganisationen der DDR im Bundesarchiv (SAPMO).

4. D.W. Morgan, *The Socialist Left and German Revolution: A History of the German Independent Socialist Democratic Party, 1917–22* (London, 1975).

5. K. Mallmann, 'Milieu, Radikalismus und lokale Gesellschaft: Zur Sozialgeschichte des Kommunismus in der Weimarer Republik', in *Geschichte und Gesellschaft*, 21 (1995), pp. 5–31.

6. A. Croll, 'The Impact of Postmodernism on Modern British Social History', in S. Berger (ed.), *Labour and Social History in Great Britain: Historiographical Reviews and Agendas* (Essen, 2002), pp. 137–52.

7. A good description of the thriving sub-organisations of the SPD is provided by M. Nolan, *Social Democracy and Society: Working-Class Radicalism in Düsseldorf, 1890–1920* (Cambridge, 1981).

8. R. Paetau, *Konfrontation oder Kooperation: Arbeiterbewegung und bürgerliche Gesellschaft im ländlichen Schleswig-Holstein und in der Industriestadt Kiel, 1900–25* (Berlin, 1985), p. 76. See also A. von Saldern, *Vom Einwohner zum Bürger* (Berlin, 1973), p. 126.

9. Protokoll des SPD Parteitags 1924, p. 143.

10. G.A. Ritter, 'Kontinuität und Umformung des deutschen Parteiensystems', in G.A. Ritter, *Arbeiterbewegung, Parteien und Parlamentarismus: Aufsaetze zur deutschen Sozial- und Verfassungsgeschichte des 19. und 20. Jahrhunderts* (Göttingen, 1976), pp. 139–41.

11. E. Wertheimer, *Portrait of the Labour Party* (London, 1930, second edition), pp. 230 ff.

12. F. Walter, T. Dürr and K. Schmidtke, *Die SPD in Sachsen und Thüringen zwischen Hochburg und Diaspora: Untersuchungen auf lokaler Ebene vom Kaiserreich bis zur Gegenwart* (Bonn, 1993), p. 55 f.

13. P. Nettl, 'The German Social Democratic Party, 1890–1914 as a Political Model', *Past and Present*, 30 (1965), pp. 65–95.

14. *Report of the Annual Conference of the Labour Party, 1914* (London, 1914), p. 91. For more examples, see S. Berger, *The British Labour Party and the German Social Democrats, c. 1900–31: A Comparison* (Oxford, 1994).

15. On the London Labour Party, see Dan Weinbren's article in this collection. Also, S. Berger, 'Herbert Morrison's London Labour Party in the Inter-War Years and the SPD: Problems of Transferring German Socialist Practices to Britain', in *Europa: European Review of History*, 12 (2005), forthcoming.

16. *Labour Organiser*, June 1930, p. 97.

17. A. Henderson, 'Labour Looks Ahead', *Daily Herald*, 12 January 1918, p. 5.

18. E. Wake, 'The Principles of Party Organisation', *Labour Organiser*, May 1922, p. 5.

19. G.D.H. Cole, *A History of the Labour Party from 1914* (London, 1948), p. 140.

20. R. McKibbin, *The Evolution of the Labour Party, 1910–24* (Oxford, 1974).

21. H. Morrison, *Labour Party Organisation in London* (London, 1930), pp. 11–13.

22. *Labour Organiser*, April–May 1923, p. 5.

23. R. Baxter, 'The Liverpool Labour Party, 1918–63', University of Oxford DPhil. (1969), p. 223.

24. K. Teanby, '"Not Equal to the Demand": Major Concerns of the Doncaster Divisional Labour Party, 1918–39', University of Sheffield MPhil. (1983), pp. 24–34. This was also a frequent issue among the local Labour Party annual reports collected in the Labour Party Archive.

25. C. Howard, 'Expectations Born to Death: Local Labour Party Expansion in the 1920s', J. Winter (ed.), *The Working Class in Modern British History: Essays in Honour of Henry Pelling* (Cambridge, 1983), pp. 65–81. For a 'backward' region in terms of Labour Party organisation see also Andrew Thorpe's contribution to this volume.

26. *Annual Report Presented by the GMC to the Individual Members of the Westminster Labour Party* (Westminster, 1925); J.S. Rowett, 'Sheffield under Labour Control', *Society for the Study of Labour History Bulletin*, 39 (1979), p. 12.

27. Interview with Herbert Rogers, 30 March 1990.

28. J. Holford, *Reshaping Labour: Organisation, Work and Politics – Edinburgh in the Great War and After* (London, 1988), p. 179; *A Brief History of Bristol South East Constituency Labour Party* (Bristol, 1979), p. 7.

29. *Report on Membership Organisation*, edited by the Southampton Labour Party (Southampton, 1936), p. 1.

30. H. Pelling, *A Short History of the Labour Party* (London, 1986, eighth edition), p. 194.

31. M. Savage, *The Dynamics of Working-Class Politics: The Labour Movement in Preston, 1880–1940* (Cambridge, 1987), p. 194.

32. Report about the district conference in Lichterfelde, *Vorwärts*, 10 July 1925.

33. P. Brandt and R. Rürup, *Volksbewegung und demokratische Neuordnung in Baden 1918–19: Zur Vorgeschichte und Geschichte der Revolution* (Sigmaringen, 1991), p. 55.

34. O. Buchwitz, *50 Jahre Funktionär der deutschen Arbeiterbewegung* (Düsseldorf, 1949), p. 107.

35. D. Clark, 'South Shields Labour Party', in M. Callcott and R. Challinor (eds), *Working-Class Politics in North East England* (Newcastle upon Tyne, 1983), p. 101.

36. D. Klenke, *Die SPD-Linke in der Weimarer Republik: Eine Untersuchung zu den regionalen organisatorischen Grundlagen und zur politischen Praxis und Theoriebildung des linken Flügels der SPD in den Jahren 1922 bis 1932*, 2 vols (Münster, 1983), pp. 510–88.

37. G. Hodgkinson, *Sent to Coventry* (London, 1970), pp. 104 and 127. See also G.W. Jones, *Borough Politics: A Study of the Wolverhampton Town Council, 1888–1964* (London, 1969), pp. 163–70.

38. K. Koszyk, *Die Presse der deutschen Sozialdemokratie: Eine Bibliographie* (Hanover, 1966).

39. Lists of local Labour papers and journals were regularly published in the columns of the *Labour Organiser*.

40. W. Henderson, 'The Press and Labour', *Labour Organiser*, April 1922, p. 7.

41. J. Schult, *Die Hamburger Arbeiterbewegung als Kulturfaktor* (Hamburg, 1955).

42. R. Lipinski (ed.), *Arbeiterführer für Leipzig und Umgebung: Nachschlagewerk* (Leipzig, 1909), p. 70.

43. *Jahrbuch der SPD* (1929), p. 208 f. See generally on the workers' libraries and their functions: D. Langewiesche and K. Schönhoven, 'Arbeiterbibliotheken und Arbeiterlektüre im Wilhelminischen Deutschland', *Archiv für Sozialgeschichte*, 16 (1976), pp. 135–204.

44. *Annual Report of the Executive Committee of the London Labour Party* (1924–25), p. 6; *ibid* (1928–29), p. 7.

45. For a report on Sheffield, see the *Labour Organiser*, September 1925, p. 9 f.

46. W. Howard, 'How to Run a Speakers' Class', *Labour Organiser*, April 1925, p. 10 f.

47. Organisational Sub-Committee Minutes, 23 March 1932 (Labour Party Archive).

48. *Arbeiterjugendbewegung in Frankfurt, 1904–45: Material zu einer verschütteten Kulturgeschichte* (Lahn, 1978).

49. K. Löwenstein, 'Die Aufgaben der Kinderfreundebewegung', *Sozialistische Monatshefte*, 35 (1929), pp. 1,116–20.

50. W.A. Peacock, 'Labour and the Coming Nation', *Labour Magazine*, 5 (1926–7), p. 307.

51. *Labour Organiser*, December 1929, p. 235 f. See also P. Williams, 'Give Young Britain its Chance', *Labour Magazine*, 10 (1931–2), p. 509, citing the continental youth organisations of Social Democratic parties as an inspiration and model.

52. See the League of Youth bulletins published in the *Labour Organiser* from May 1930 onwards.

53. Middleton papers, JSM/SU, p. 8 (Labour Party Archive).

54. F. Reid, 'Socialist Sunday Schools in Britain, 1892–1939', *International Review of Social History*, 14 (1966), pp. 18–47.

55. J. Springhall, *Youth, Empire and Society* (London, 1977), p. 116 f.

56. R.E. Pore, 'The German Social Democratic Women's Movement, 1919–33', University of Morganstown PhD (1977); *Jahresbericht des Bezirksverbands der SPD Berlin* (1930), p. 102.

57. M. Phillips, 'Organising the Women Electors', *Labour Organiser*, May 1922, p. 12 and October 1922, p. 22. Also, *Labour Magazine*, 5 (1926–27), p. 266, and Organisation Sub-Committee Minutes, 1932: therein paper on women's organisation, p. 3 (Labour Party Archive).

58. H. A. Winkler, *Der Schein der Normalität: Arbeiter und Arbeiterbewegung in der Weimarer Republik, 1924–30* (Berlin, 1985), p. 350.

59. *Annual Report of the Executive Committee of the London Labour Party* (1926–27), p. 6; for the many activities of the lively women's section in the Stockport Labour Party see, Minutes of the meeting of the women's section of the Stockport Labour Party, 13 Jan. 1925 to 3 May 1927, in Stockport Labour Party files, D.G. Clark (ed.), *Origins and Development of the Labour Party* (Microfilm, Wakefield, 1980).

60. M. Savage, *The Dynamics of Working-Class Politics*, pp. 167–9.

61. Organisation Sub-Committee Minutes, 1932: Letter from Barbara Ayrton Gould to Miss Taverner, 8 March 1932 (Labour Party Archive). On the difficulties of combining feminist and socialist beliefs in the women's sections of the Labour Party, see the contribution of J. Hannam and K. Hunt to this volume and, idem, *Socialist Women: Britain, 1880s to 1920s* (London, 2000).

62. K. Hagemann, *Frauenalltag und Männerpolitik: Alltagsleben und gesellschaftliches Handeln von Arbeiterfrauen in der Weimarer Republik* (Bonn, 1990), pp. 630–8.

63. W.L. Guttsman, *Workers' Culture in Weimar Germany: Between Tradition and Commitment* (New York, 1990), p. 212.

64. J. Boughton, 'Working-Class Politics in Birmingham and Sheffield, 1918–31', University of Warwick PhD (1985), pp. 300–3; H.G. Klaus, *The Literature of Labour: Two Hundred Years of Working-Class Writing* (Brighton, 1985), pp. 62–88.

65. *Annual Report of the Executive Committee of the London Labour Party* (1924–5), p. 14.

66. J. Amott, 'Factories and Footlights: Leeds Industrial Theatre', *Labour Magazine*, 1 (1922–23), pp. 489–91.

67. D. Dowe, 'The Workingmen's Choral Movement in Germany Before the First World War', *Journal of Contemporary History*, 13 (1978), pp. 269–96. For the Weimar Republic, see D. Klenke, P. Lilje and F. Walter, *Arbeitersänger und Volksbühnen in der Weimarer Republik* (Bonn, 1992).

68. *Vorwärts und nicht vergessen: Arbeiterkultur in Hamburg um 1930* (Hamburg, 1982), pp. 207–20.

69. S.G. Jones, 'The British Labour Movement and Working-Class Leisure, 1918–39, University of Manchester PhD (1983), p. 276 f.; I. Watson, 'Alan Bush and Left Music in the 1930s', *Das Argument*, special vol. 29 (1978), pp. 80–89.

70. *Annual Report of the Executive Committee of the London Labour Party* (1925–26), p. 18; *ibid* (1926–27), p. 22, *ibid* (1930–31), p. 7. See also S.A. Court, 'Music and the People: A Message to the Labour Movement', *Labour Magazine*, 2 (1923–24).

71. H. Überhorst, *Frisch, Frei, Stark und Treu: Die Arbeitersportbewegung in Deutschland, 1893–1933* (Düsseldorf, 1973).

72. G.H. Elvin, general secretary of the BWSA, in the pages of the *Labour Organiser*, November 1930, p. 212.

73. *Annual Report of the Executive Committee of the London Labour Party*, from 1927–28 onwards.

74. P. Thompson, 'London Working-Class Politics and the Formation of the London Labour Party, 1885–1914', University of Oxford DPhil (1963), p. 438. For a good local example from Halle in Germany, see W. Piechocki, *Der Volkspark als Kultur- und Bildungsstätte der halleschen Arbeiter* (Halle, 1968).

75. C. Williams, *Democratic Rhondda: Politics and Society, 1885–1951* (Cardiff, 1996).

76. R. Stübling, *Kultur und Massen: Das Kulturkartell der modernen Arbeiterbewegung in Frankfurt am Main, 1925–33* (Offenbach, 1983), pp. 35–42; T. Thomas, 'The WTM: Memoirs and Documents', *History Workshop Journal*, 4 (1977), p. 105.

77. For the SPD see P. Lösche (ed.), *Solidargemeinschaft und Milieu: Sozialistische Kultur- und Freizeitorganisationen in der Weimarer Republik*, 4 vols (Bonn, 1990–93); for the Labour Party, see the evidence in D. Weinbren, *Generating Socialism: Recollections of Life in the Labour Party* (Stroud, 1997). Also, J. Seabrook, *What Went Wrong? Working People and the Ideals of the Labour Movement* (London, 1978).

78. Interview with Harry and Kitty Grey, Nuneaton, 30 April 1990.

79. R. McKibbin, 'Why was there no Marxism in Britain?', *English Historical Review*, 99 (1984), p. 234.

80. A. Lüdtke, *Eigen-Sinn: Fabrikalltag, Arbeitererfahrungen und Politik vom Kaiserreich bis in den Faschismus* (Hamburg, 1993).

81. *Report of the Annual Conference of the Labour Party, 1924* (London, 1924), p. 181 f.; F. Brockway, *Bermondsey Story* (London, 1949), p. 139.

82. L. Abrams, *Workers' Culture in Imperial Germany: Leisure and Recreation in the Rhineland and Westphalia* (London, 1992), has argued that commercialised forms of mass leisure only took off in the first decade of the twentieth century.

83. S. Yeo, 'A New Life: The Religion of Socialism in Britain, 1883–96', *History Workshop Journal* 4 (1977), pp. 5–56.

84. G. Stedman Jones, *Languages of Class: Studies in English Working-Class History, 1832–1982* (Cambridge, 1983), pp. 235–38; R. McKibbin, *The Ideologies of Class: Social Relations in Britain, 1880–1950* (Oxford, 1990), chapters two and three; S. Meacham, *A Life Apart: The English Working Class, 1890–1914* (Cambridge, 1977), p. 200 f.; R. Hoggart, *The Uses of Literacy* (London, 1957), p. 279 f.

85. D. Langewiesche, 'Freizeit und Massenbildung: Zur Ideologie und Praxis der Volksbildung in der Weimarer Republik', in G. Huck (ed.), *Sozialgeschichte der Freizeit* (Wuppertal, 1980), pp. 223–48.

86. A. von Saldern, 'Arbeiterkulturbewegung in Deutschland in der Zwischenkriegszeit', in F. Boll (ed.), *Arbeiterkulturen zwischen Alltag und Politik* (Munich, 1986), p. 46.

87. F. Trentmann, *Paradoxes of Civil Society: New Perspectives on Modern German and British History* (Oxford, 2000).

88. J. Siemann, 'Die sozialdemokratischen Arbeiterführer in der Zeit der Weimarer Republik', University of Göttingen PhD (1955), p. 50 f.

89. F. Walter et al, *Die SPD iin Sachsen und Thüringen*, p. 244.

90. K. Haenisch, *Neue Bahnen der Kulturpolitik: Aus der Regierungspraxis der deutschen Republik* (Berlin, 1921), p. 116 ff.

91. J. Kaiser, *Arbeiterbewegung und organisierte Religionskritik: Proletarische Freidenkerverbände im Kaiserreich und in der Weimarer Republik* (Stuttgart, 1981).

92. H.A. Winkler, *Der Schein der Normalität*, p. 158; G. Beyer, 'Die Probleme zwischen Katholizismus und Sozialismus', *Sozialistische Monatshefte*, 35 (1929), p. 289 f.

93. H. McLeod, 'Religion in the British and German Labour Movements, c. 1890–1914: A Comparison', *Society for the Study of Labour History Bulletin*, 55 (1986), pp. 25–35.

94. Revd. G. Lang, 'Labour's Challenge to the Churches', *Labour Organiser*, 1922–23, p. 539 f.

95. D. Tanner, 'Ideological Debate in the Labour Party Before the First World War', E.F. Biagini and A. Reid (eds), *Currents of Radicalism: Popular Radicalism, Organised Labour and Party Politics in Britain, 1850–1914* (Cambridge, 1991), p. 289 f.

96. T. Ichikawa, 'The Daily Citizen 1912–15: A Study of the First Labour Daily Newspaper in Britain', University of Wales MA thesis (1985), pp. 68–71.

97. S. Mayor, *The Churches and the Labour Movement* (London, 1967).

98. J.A. Jowitt, 'Late Victorian and Edwardian Bradford', in R.K.S. Taylor and J.A. Jowitt (eds), *Bradford, 1890–1914: The Cradle of the ILP* (Bradford, 1980), p. 14.

99. R. Baxter, 'Liverpool Labour Party', pp. 16–28.

100. P. Lösche and F. Walter, 'Auf dem Weg zur Volkspartei? Die Weimarer Sozialdemokratie', *Archiv für Sozialgeschichte*, 29 (1989), pp. 751–36.

Index